The Russian Language in
the Twentieth Century

The Russian Language in the Twentieth Century

BERNARD COMRIE
GERALD STONE
MARIA POLINSKY

Second Edition, Revised and Expanded, of
The Russian Language Since the Revolution
by Bernard Comrie *and* Gerald Stone

CLARENDON PRESS · OXFORD
1996

Oxford University Press, Walton Street, Oxford OX2 6DP

Oxford   New York
Athens   Auckland   Bangkok   Bombay
Calcutta   Cape Town   Dar es Salaam   Delhi
Florence   Hong Kong   Istanbul   Karachi
Kuala Lumpur   Madras   Madrid   Melbourne
Mexico City   Nairobi   Paris   Singapore
Taipei   Tokyo   Toronto
and associated companies in
Berlin Ibadan

Oxford is a trade mark of Oxford University Press

Published in the United States
by Oxford University Press Inc., New York

First edition published 1978
© Oxford University Press
Second edition published 1996
New material © Bernard Comrie, Gerald Stone,
and Maria Polinsky

British Library Cataloguing in Publication Data
Data available

Library of Congress Cataloging in Publication Data
Data available

ISBN 0-19-824066-X

10 9 8 7 6 5 4 3 2 1

Typeset by Regent Typesetting, London
Printed in Great Britain
on acid-free paper by
Biddles Ltd., Guildford & King's Lynn

Preface

The first edition of this book appeared in 1978, under the title *The Russian Language since the Revolution*. The general plan of the book has remained unchanged but the authors felt the need to expand the temporal limits of the period, first, by adding data on the Russian language in the 1900–17 period, secondly, by discussing the 1970s and 1980s. This explains the change in the title of the book; the new title also reflects, if indirectly, the recent political changes in the then Soviet Union, which are probably no less significant than the 1917 Revolution.

The general plan of the book and the Introduction are the result of our joint efforts; Chapters 1, 2, 4, and 6 were written for the first edition by Bernard Comrie, Chapters 3, 5, 7, and 8 were written for that edition by Gerald Stone; all the chapters were revised and expanded by Maria Polinsky, who also wrote the Conclusion.

In the vast majority of cases we have given Russian words in the Cyrillic alphabet; in particular, we have used Cyrillic for the titles of bibliographical references, both in the body of the text and in the References. Transliterations have been made according to the International System. Readers unfamiliar with this system may at first be surprised by the transliterated form of well-known Russian writers or politicians, such as Puškin (Pushkin), Čexov (Chekhov), Solženicyn (Solzhenitsyn), Xruščev (Khrushchev), and Gorbačev (Gorbachev). The phonetic transcriptions follow the system of the International Phonetic Association.

We hope our book will be read not only by students of Russian, and we have therefore given English translations of all the examples where this could possibly be of use to the reader. Though some of the literary works cited in this book are available in established English translations, we have tried to present our own literal—not necessarily literary—translations of cited Russian examples. Word-stress is not shown except where it is, or might be thought to be, relevant to the argument. Dates preceding 1 (14) February 1918 are given in the Old Style, and from then on, in the New Style. Where works have appeared in several editions, we have tried to use the latest edition (excluding photographic reprints); but if the differences between editions are significant, reference is made to the relevant edition.

We wish to record our thanks, for bibliographical advice, to D. Andrews, Ju. A. Bel´čikov, R. Channon, N. I. Formanovskaja, A. Israeli, S. Pratt, T. Seifrid, V. P. Trofimenko, and A. Žolkovskij.

May 1994   B.C.
                                                                    G.S.
                                                                    M.P.

Contents

Abbreviations

CSR	Contemporary Standard Russian
MAS	*(Малый академический) Словарь русского языка*
OM	Old Moscow (pronunciation)
OPb	Old St Petersburg (pronunciation)
Pb.	(St) Petersburg
RJaŠ	*Русский язык в школе*
RJaSO	Русский язык и советское общество
RJK	*Русское языкознание. Республиканский межведомственный научный сборник* (Киев)
RR	*Русская речь*
SAR	*Словарь Академии Российской*
SCRJa	*Словарь церковно-славянского и русского языка*
SPU	*«Словарь произношений и ударений»*
SRJa	*Словарь русского языка*
SSRLJa	*Словарь современного русского литературного языка*
VJa	*Вопросы языкознания*
VKR	*Вопросы культуры речи*
*	The asterisk is used to indicate ungrammatical sentences

List of Phonetic Symbols Used

(see p. 54)

VOWELS

1	a	as in сад
2	ã	nasalized a, as in French *fiancé*
3	e	as in лето
4	ẽ	nasalized 3, as in French *fin*
5	eⁱ	vowel between 3 and 7, but lower than 8 (see p. 54)
6	eɨ	vowel between 3 and 9, but lower than 10 (see pp. 54–5)
7	i	as in кит
8	iᵉ	vowel between 3 and 7, as in весна (see p. 54)
9	ɨ	high central vowel, as in сын
10	ɨᵉ	vowel between 3 and 9, as in жена (see pp. 54–5)
11	ı	lowered and retracted 7, as in пестрота (see p. 54)
12	ɨ	lowered 6, as in выше
13	o	as in сон
14	ǫ	raised 13 (see pp. 66)
15	õ	nasalized 13, as in French *bon*
16	œ	front rounded vowel, as in French *fleur*
17	u	as in зуб
18	y	front rounded vowel, as in French *lune*
19	ʌ	back half-open unrounded vowel, as in вода
20	ə	central vowel, as in ма́сло

CONSONANTS

21	b	as in банк
22	bʲ	palatalized 21, as in бить
23	d	as in дом
24	ᵈ	faintly pronounced 23
25	dʲ	palatalized 23, as in дядя
26	f	as in фон

27	fʲ	palatalized 26, as in фильм
28	g	as in город
29	gʲ	advanced (palatalized) 28, as in гибкий
30	ɦ	'voiced h', as in бухгалтер (see p. 38)
31	j	as in мой, я ([ja])
32	k	as in кот
33	kʲ	advanced (palatalized) 32, as in кит
34	l	as in лапа
35	lʲ	palatalized 34, as in липа
36	m	as in мышь
37	mʲ	palatalized 36, as in мило
38	n	as in наш
39	nʲ	palatalized 38, as in нет
40	p	as in палка
41	pʲ	palatalized 40, as in петь
42	r	as in рот
43	rʲ	palatalized 42, as in редко
44	s	as in сам
45	sʲ	palatalized 44, as in сесть
46	ʃ	as in шаг
47	ʃʲ	palatalized 46, occurs geminated in щи (Moscow pronunciation) (see pp. 33–5)
48	t	as in там
49	tʲ	palatalized 48, as in тётя
50	ts	affricate, as in отец
51	tsʲ	palatalized 50, does not occur in standard Russian but is attested in some Russian dialects
52	tʃʲ	affricate, as in честь
53	v	as in вы
54	vʲ	palatalized 53, as in Вера
55	x	as in холм
56	xʲ	advanced (palatalized) 55, as in хитрый
57	z	as in зонт
58	zʲ	palatalized 57, as in зима

59	ȝ	as in жар
60	ȝʲ	palatalized 59, occurs geminated in дрожжи (OM) (see p. 35)
61	ɣ	voiced 55, i. e. fricative corresponding to 28 (see pp. 36–8)
62	'	placed before stressed syllable of non-monosyllabic word

Introduction

OUR objective in this book is to trace and illustrate the main changes that have taken place in the Russian language since the beginning of the twentieth century, and particularly those between 1917 and the late 1980s, a time which can be identified as the Soviet period, by now a reasonably complete stage in the history of Russia and the former Soviet Union.

The period addressed in this book witnessed the unprecedented expansion of the standard Russian language, both stylistically and geographically. Around 1900, the range of functions of standard Russian increased, in some instances replacing Church Slavonic, in some instances with the emergence of new phenomena. Russian replaced Church Slavonic as the language of sermons (parallel to the maintenance of Church Slavonic as the language of liturgy); standard Russian emerged as the language of the courts (especially following the judicial reform of the 1860s), of political debate in the Russian Parliament (Duma), of growing business and trade, and as the language of poetry and prose read to large audiences from the stage of concert-halls and literary cabarets. Theatre, the most popular type of entertainment in Russia of the second half of the nineteenth century and at the beginning of the twentieth century, played a very important role in promoting a uniform language norm, especially in pronunciation; the role of theatre as the bearer of such a norm became clear by the mid 1800s (Panov 1990: 94). In the twentieth century, radio, cinema, and television, gradually taking over from the theatre, gave the standard language the ability to travel, unknown in earlier periods; mass media, together with compulsory mass education, became much more effective than writing alone in acquiring new speakers for the emerging standard. These new speakers of the standard, in turn, had a profound effect on the language itself: never before had it borne the fingerprints of so many diverse speakers, many of whom were, following M. V. Panov's characterization, 'new recruits to culture' (Panov 1990: 18, 22).[1]

The development of Russian in the twentieth century was and still is affected by the social and political changes and the historical events that

---

[1] See also Krysin (1965a: 117–19) and references there.

brought about these changes. The year of the October Revolution, famous in the first place for the initiation of political, economic, and social change, is also of significance in the history of the Russian language. Indeed, language change is dependent, to a considerable extent, on sociological factors, and in many respects the way in which Russian has changed in the Soviet period is due, directly or indirectly, to the changes in Russian society brought about by the Revolution. Some of the new features of present-day Russian can be attributed quite specifically to new attitudes and institutions. These features are particularly prominent in the lexicon and in speech etiquette. Many other features of course would probably have appeared even if there had been no October Revolution. These latter changes are often related to language-internal factors and represent a logical continuation of the tendencies that were present in the language at a prior stage; changes in the phonology and inflectional morphology are probably most representative of these. However, even the pace of internal, structurally motivated changes may be affected by external factors, such as population migrations and language planning.

The recent political changes that have taken place in the Soviet Union and its successor states conclude a dramatic period in the history of the country and, probably, in the history of the world. The conclusion of this period, which spans over seven decades, offers an incredible opportunity to a linguist: to follow the changes in a language partially determined by sociological factors and to see abrupt changes evolve into continuous tendencies, coming to a logical completion with the end of the political age. The interplay of external and internal factors in language development is particularly apparent in periods of great political or social change and Russian in the twentieth century is one of the little-studied test cases in this respect.

It is our impression that the extent to which present-day Russian differs from the language of the nineteenth century has been widely ignored or underestimated, and that consequently many students of Russian mistakenly regard reading the nineteenth-century classics as an appropriate method of acquiring practical language skills. This would seem to suggest that there is a lack of information on the ways in which Russian has changed since the beginning of the twentieth century and, particularly, during the Soviet period. One of our objectives is to provide such information in a systematic way.

The choice of the time frame that will be discussed in this book motivates the use of a number of geographical names below: while describing pre-Revolutionary Russia, we will use the names that were current then, for example, St Petersburg or Nižnij Novgorod; speaking of the Soviet period, we will use names such as Leningrad and Gor´kij. Many of the Soviet names have recently become obsolete, following the renaming campaign of the late 1980s to the early 1990s. However, these new names, which often correspond to the revived pre-Revolutionary names, belong to a new period which is beyond the scope of this book.

Whatever the proportion of sociological to purely linguistic factors in the changes which have taken place, however, it is clear that the process of change has been gradual and continuous. The developments in the Russian language in the beginning of the Soviet period were comparable in abruptness to the rapid political events of 1917 and the consequent economic and social changes. It is only now, when we can look back over more than seven decades of Russian in use in Soviet society, that we can see the extent to which it has changed. The inevitable conclusion is that, while it has been gradual, the extent of change during this period has been considerable. The new period that Russia is entering with the decline of communism and development of a new society, the shape of which is still hard to predict, seems to be affecting the Russian language rapidly and dramatically again; however, this change is still ongoing and hard to evaluate, and this justifies our choice of the Soviet period as a distinct stage in the development of Modern Russian.

Throughout this book, we will use the term 'standard language' in referring to present-day Russian for what is usually called in Russian литературный язык 'literary language' (less commonly стандартный язык). It is also common, in the English-language literature, to refer to this language as Contemporary Standard Russian (CSR). While the Modern Russian period is usually reckoned from Puškin's time, Contemporary Standard Russian is used as a special term describing the standardized language whose norms started to form in the late 1800s and stabilized by the middle of the twentieth century.[2] One of the main reasons for dividing Modern Russian into two periods—roughly, the language of the nineteenth century and the language of the twentieth century—is the difference in the perception of a standard language as such. In the nineteenth century, following Nikolaj Karamzin's literary

---

[2] The latest Academy Grammar (*Русская грамматика* 1980: i. 7) defines the 'modern literary language' (современный русский литературный язык) as the language of the nineteenth and twentieth centuries ('from Puškin's time to modern times') but such an inclusive treatment of the term CSR can hardly be justified; for criticism, see, for example, Gorbačevič (1978: 41–3), Kalakuckaja (1984: 13).

reform, the standard language was oriented towards the speech of educated Russians; in the twentieth century, particularly after the orthographic reform of 1918, the standard language has been oriented towards the written form of Russian (Kalakuckaja 1984: 16–44, 56). According to Šmelev (1977: 32), various functional styles of the contemporary language are determined, in a significant manner, by the standards of the written language. This orientation explains the growing discrepancy between spoken educated Russian and codified spoken language (see below).

Our preference for the term 'standard language' is explained by the fact that the English term 'literary' is inevitably associated with literature. The Russian term литературный, meanwhile, has two meanings, namely, 'pertaining to literature' and 'standard'. The two notions can be distinguished in speaking of certain earlier periods and/or other languages. Thus русский литературный язык в эпоху Киевского государства 'the Russian literary language in the period of the Kievan state' (Gorškov 1969) does not imply the existence of a standard language at that time. Meanwhile, speaking of the modern language, it should be borne in mind that литературный язык does not refer exclusively to the language of (artistic) literature, nor indeed exclusively to the written language, since one can equally speak of разговорный вариант литературного языка 'the spoken variant of the literary language', or литературная речь 'literary speech' (Zemskaja 1981: 22–40).[3]

For the most part we have dealt with the standard language, though some account has been taken of non-standard varieties, and, in particular, of non-standard features which have either become standard or at least tended to do so. The study of non-standard Russian for its own sake does not come within the scope of this book, but standard and non-standard are not discrete categories and it is thus impossible in tracing change in the standard to ignore the overlap. The standard language itself is in any case not uniform, but its development always tends towards uniformity in certain respects. In so far as changes in the standard depend on some kind of change in attitudes as to what is correct, they are attributable to sociolinguistic causes. Similarly, decisions as to what is to be codified as standard and attempts deliberately to

---

[3] The general term for spoken language in Russian is разговорная речь, though the term разговорный язык is also used sometimes (see below). Skrebnev (1987) presents a review of terms and approaches to the spoken language, both standard and non-standard; see also below.

direct the course of development of the Russian language are sociolinguistic matters. The control, or attempted control, of language
development comes under the heading of a particular branch of sociolinguistics called 'language planning'. This has been defined as 'the
establishment of goals, policies and procedures for a language community' (Haugen 1969: 701).[4] Similar activities and their study come under
the Russian heading of культура речи,[5] языковое нормирование,
and, more recently, языковая кодификация.[6] For the most part, both
language planning and its Russian counterpart in the Soviet period are
concerned with questions of the standard language (Stone 1973: 166–9).
In general, the attempt to control the language is typical of any standard
language. The interesting question is whether this process, which, as
was just mentioned, is sociolinguistic by nature, differs depending on
the social and political structure of the society (one would assume, as in
fact is claimed by Rževskij (1951), Fessenko (1955), that standardization would be greater and more rigid in non-democratic societies).
Another question concerns the strategies of standardization; in theory,
standardization can be based either on the elimination of variants offered
by the language or on the differentiation of such variants as pertaining
to different styles.[7] This book will probably leave both questions open:
to answer them, a cross-linguistic study is needed, comparing several
standard languages developing under different socio-political circumstances. However, if the material collected in this book can bring us
closer to the solution of these questions, the authors will feel that they
have fulfilled their task.

The standard language exists in both spoken and written forms. In
literate societies educated people use varieties of the spoken standard
in certain situations. In some European speech communities (in
Switzerland, for example, and in some parts of Germany) educated
speakers use non-standard varieties in many types of situation, and the
use of the spoken standard is restricted. In such communities the distribution of standard and non-standard speech is mainly functional. The

---

[4] For various other definitions, many of which are based on Haugen's work (1959;
1966a; 1969), see Cooper (1989: 29–45).

[5] An earlier term was also культура языка, for example, used by Ščerba (1925) and
G. O. Vinokur (1929).

[6] In Graudina (1980: 3), language codification is defined as a more specialized process
than standardization; codification is concerned primarily with prescriptive rules, while
standardization includes the descriptive approach as well.

[7] For example, as is the case with forms или and иль 'or', where the second form is
clearly identified with poetic style.

use of the non-standard variant is not stigmatized and is considered socially acceptable. The Russian speech community, on the other hand, is representative of another type in which the distribution of standard and non-standard is mainly on the basis of who the speakers are rather than of what kind of situation they are in. That is to say, the distribution is mainly social rather than functional. Notably, non-standard speech is much more stigmatized in Russian society than it is in the societies mentioned above. However, non-standard speech is a multi-dimensional phenomenon in itself. With regard to Russian, it is important to distinguish between the non-standard vernacular or popular speech (commonly referred to as *prostorečie* in Russian linguistics)[8] and non-standard or sub-standard variants which are determined by the geographical origins of the speaker. These two dimensions overlap but *prostorečie* is clearly characterized by lower social prestige.

Well-educated speakers of Russian generally aspire to use the standard language in all situations. A common view is that the main difference between the educated speaker of Russian and the non-standard speaker is in the ability to control different registers, including non-standard ones: while educated speakers can easily switch registers (using non-standard forms, for instance, as a sign of solidarity among certain social groups, or for language games), the speaker of *prostorečie* is locked in one speech code (Vinokur 1984; Šmelev and Zemskaja 1988: 12).

Turning to local characteristics, there are many members of the Russian speech community whose speech has these characteristics. The Russian speech community, like Soviet society generally, has had and still has a high rate of upward social mobility. This means that there are today many speakers of Russian who aspire to use standard varieties but do so only with varying degrees of success, owing to their early linguistic socialization in non-standard (regional) varieties. Social mobility is an important factor in language change, especially where the distribution of standard and non-standard is mainly socially determined. An additional factor in the rise of local characteristics in modern Russian was the interaction between Russian speech communities and speech communities of the Soviet republics, where the ethnic language was well preserved (for example, in the Baltics, in Georgia and Armenia). In

[8] In view of the difficulty in finding an English equivalent for the words *prostorečie* and *prostorečno*, we have throughout this book retained the transliterated Russian terms. Patton (1990) is a recent discussion of *prostorečie* and related phenomena, where a number of English equivalents are proposed.

the Soviet period Russian was undoubtedly the language of social prestige and upward mobility.[9] Everywhere in the Soviet Union, Russian was taught as a second language (Lewis 1974: 2142, 2149). The Russian acquired by speakers of ethnic groups in the Soviet republics certainly influenced the variant spoken by the Russian speech community in those republics. This led to the development of the so-called ethnolects or territorial dialects (Russian территориальный диалект), the study of which is in its incipient stages in Russian linguistics (some recent findings are summarized in Lapteva 1976: 84–95; Manaenkova 1989; Mixnevič 1985; *Русский язык в национальных республиках Советского Союза* 1980).

Apart from changes in the power and prestige structures, there have been a number of other social developments contributing to linguistic change. These include: the growth of literacy (aided by the spelling reform, discussed in detail in Chapter 8), the introduction of universal education for the masses, the increasing urbanization of the population, and equality of rights for women.

At the time of the 1897 census only 21 per cent of the population of the Russian Empire (excluding children under the age of nine) was able to read.[10] The figure for both sexes (over the age of nine) in Russia itself was 27 per cent and for European Russia it was 30 per cent. But the disparity between the sexes was considerable: in European Russia only 18 per cent of women could read, as opposed to 43 per cent of men. It should not be forgotten that in many parts of the Empire the situation was far worse: in Central Asia, for example, only 10 per cent of men and 3 per cent of women could read. In Poland, on the other hand, the percentages were higher than average, and they were highest of all in the Baltic States. In Estonia (*Èstljandskaja gubernija* of Russia) they reached an astounding 95 per cent for men and 97 per cent for women. This was the only part of the Empire where more women than men were literate. However, the situation in the Baltic States was, of course, totally untypical.

The ability to read was far more widespread in the towns than in the countryside, but in 1897 only 13.4 per cent of the Empire's population

---

[9] It is symptomatic that the Soviet party élite in the ethnic-speaking republics invariably educated their children in Russian; attendance at Russian-speaking schools was incomparably higher than that at schools where education was maintained in the language of the republic—all this despite the official statements that the language of the republic was as important as Russian. (For further discussion, see Kreindler 1989; Moskovich 1989.)

[10] No question as to the ability to write was included in the 1897 census.

lived in towns. Among the *gubernii* (provinces) of European Russia, that of St Petersburg had the highest figures: 76 per cent for men and 51 per cent for women—a total of 62 per cent. The Moscow *gubernija* came next with 66 per cent for men and 31 per cent for women—a total of 49 per cent. The rates for the St Petersburg and Moscow *gubernii* were the highest because they included the two largest cities, where the figures would obviously have been higher still.

It is true that the 1897 figures show that illiteracy was already receding, though slowly, and the proportion of those able to read was higher in the group aged 9 to 49 than in the whole population over 9. But the rate at which it was receding rose with startling rapidity after the Revolution. The figures most often quoted in order to demonstrate the drop in illiteracy during the Soviet period are those for the 9 to 49 age-group of the entire population at the censuses of 1897, 1926, 1939, 1959, and 1970.[11] They provide the following picture:

Year	Total %	Men	Women
1897	28.4	40.3	16.6
1926	56.6	71.5	42.7
1939	87.4	93.5	81.6
1959	98.5	99.3	97.8
1970	99.7	99.8	99.7

In 1979, the overall literacy rate was at 99.8 per cent.

No less significant than the total figures are those showing the sudden decrease in the disparity between men and women on the one hand, and between town and country on the other. The disparity between the sexes had been virtually eliminated by 1959, but the fact that formerly there was such a marked difference leads us to assume that until recently (perhaps still) non-standard speech was more common among women than men. There are no figures to support this, but it seems to be a reasonable assumption.

The separate statistics for town and country show that whereas in 1897 only 23.8 per cent of the rural population could read, by 1959 the

[11] The 1979 and 1989 censuses omit the gender breakdown in reporting literacy, which makes comparison with the prior censuses impossible. The criterion of literacy in the 1970 and 1979 census was still (as in 1897) the ability to read (*Всесоюзная перепись . . . 1969*: 46, 62; *Вестник статистики* 1980: 51). No criterion of literacy is mentioned in the overview of the 1989 census (*Уровень образования . . . населения СССР . . .* 1990). See Liebowitz (1986) for further discussion of education and literacy data in Russian and Soviet censuses.

figure was 98.2 per cent; by 1970 it was 99.4 per cent, and by 1980 it was 99.7 per cent. At the same time there had been a rapid urbanization of the whole population: whereas by 1913 the proportion of town-dwellers had risen from 13.5 per cent (1897) to 18 per cent, by 1970 they were for the first time in a majority (56 per cent). By 1986, the urban population further increased, to 65.6 per cent (*Население СССР* . . . 1988: 38).

The rise in the standards of education throughout the population is no less striking than the rise in literacy. In 1897 0.07 per cent of the population had received (or was receiving) a higher education. Those with (or receiving) a secondary education constituted 1.03 per cent. In 1970 the figures for those aged 10 and over were: higher education 4.2 per cent, secondary education 44.1 per cent. In the 1979 census the respective figures rose again, to 6.8 per cent for those with higher education, and to 57 per cent for those with secondary education. In education, too, the disparities between the sexes and between town and country have been greatly reduced. The 1970 census showed that of those aged 10 or over 52.2 per cent of men had higher or secondary education against 45.2 per cent of women; in 1979 the figures were 68.5 and 59.7 respectively. The discrepancy between town and country, however, is still serious; in 1970 59.2 per cent of the urban population (in the over-10 age-group) had higher or secondary education, against only 33.2 per cent of the rural population.[12] In 1979 the percentage of the town population with secondary or higher education was 72.3, against 49.2 of the rural population. The gap between town and country closed for the gainfully employed part of the population: in 1987 about 90 per cent of the urban population in the over-10 age-group had higher or secondary education, and the percentage for the rural population rose to 80 (*Население СССР* . . . 1988: 187–8).

These dramatic improvements in literacy for the population as a whole have meant a corresponding increase in the number of norm-bearers (i.e. those commanding and using the standard language) at the expense of those using only non-standard varieties such as *prostorečie* and local varieties. If one considers the question purely in terms of the space scale, it is possible to say that at the beginning of the twentieth century the majority of members of the Russian speech community, being illiterate, were users of maximally localized varieties exclusively. The position by the late 1980s, on the other hand, was that only a

---

[12] The statistics on literacy and education quoted here are taken mainly from *Уровень образования* . . . (1960) and *Численность, размещение* . . .(1971).

minority used maximally localized varieties exclusively. These are the informants sought by dialectologists, and as time goes by they are more and more difficult to find. The vast majority make use of the standard written language and include in their spoken repertoires varieties which are localized to a minimal or zero degree.

But it was not just a matter of the formerly illiterate and uneducated majority acquiring standard varieties. If it had been so, the standard itself might have changed very little. In the new power structure following the Revolution of 1917, those who spoke or had spoken non-standard varieties and now rose to positions of prestige and power were able to assert the acceptability of many features of their own speech or at least to reject some features of the speech of traditional norm-bearers. In reality, however, neither was the old standard language entirely rejected, nor was a new one, based on working-class varieties, established. More than anything else, changes in the social prestige structure brought about changes in the acceptability of language registers: what had been colloquial became stylistically neutral, and what had been non-standard became colloquial standard.

The legalization of features which had formerly been stylistically un-acceptable, as well as certain other innovations, came as a shock to those who had been norm-bearers before the Revolution, and they expressed concern. In some *émigré* circles the belief is till now held that the Russian language has been somehow damaged by the Bolsheviks (Seliščev 1928; Rževskij 1951; Fessenko 1955; Granovskaja 1983: 64–7).[13]

In the seven decades of the Soviet regime that followed, the standard language was fixed and promoted, through schooling, by normative grammarians. What started out as a rapid set of changes unleashed by the political and social overhaul eventually developed into a relatively static, conservative system that was far behind developments in the spoken language.[14] The gap between the standardized language, pre-

[13] This may be seen, for example, in the journal *Русская рѣчь*, Paris, 1958–63, published (in the old orthography) by the Union for the Defence of the Purity of the Russian Word (Союзъ для защиты чистоты русскаго слова). A number of publica-tions, primarily the newspaper *Русская мысль*, Paris, take great pains in avoiding any similarities with the Soviet standard press (Golubeva-Monatkina 1994). The assumption that Russian has been damaged by the communists is crucial for a large number of dissi-dent writers, particularly Aleksandr Solženicyn, who consciously dissociate themselves from the Soviet norm and from the Westernized language as well. However, this view of CSR as contaminated by unnecessary borrowings is shared by some official Soviet writ-ers, for example, A. Jugov (1975), K. Jakovlev (1976).

[14] It seems that rapid linguistic changes in post-Gorbačev Russia, which we will just

scribed by a succession of Academy grammars (the latest published in 1980) and largely fixed by official Soviet literature, which did not tolerate slang or spoken language, became particularly clear in the latest stages of the period, with the appearance of surveys of spoken standard Russian (Zemskaja 1973; 1981; 1983; Zemskaja and Kapanadze 1978; 1987; Sirotinina 1974; Kolesov 1991). As a result, claims started appearing in the linguistic literature that changes in the standard language did not go far enough, and that Russian standardized by normative grammars is too archaic, one of the earliest such claims being Grigor´ev (1961).

However, linguistic censorship, not uncommon even in more democratic societies than the Soviet system, was not the only reason for this gap between the spoken standard language and normative grammar. Another reason was the aspiration of the majority of speakers to speak a language that can be called the average educated standard. This orientation towards educated speech as the neutral register was fully supported by the school system, by the popularity of reading and by the reading list which, owing to government control, was fairly restricted and, therefore, shared by the majority of speakers.

An essential prerequisite to a proper understanding of standard Russian within Soviet society is a knowledge of the actual usage of native speakers, in particular of educated native speakers. The traditional way of monitoring actual usage and changes in usage has been to observe the practice of writers. In dealing with earlier periods, this is usually the only way to proceed: this approach has been applied to the Russian language of the nineteenth century, for instance, and changes in the usage of writers noted (Bulaxovskij 1954; Vinogradov and Švedova 1964). It is one of the methods applied by Gorbačevič (1971) in comparing nineteenth-century usage with current usage. However, this approach has a number of drawbacks, so where possible (as in investigations of current usage) other methods should be given preference. One drawback is that in this way one can monitor the usage of only one social group, namely professional writers and journalists; as we shall see below, and in detail in the subsequent chapters, the reactions of writers and journalists to linguistic variants often differ markedly from those of other sections of the population, tending towards a more conservative assessment of the norm. Another drawback is that editors very often modify an author's text quite considerably before allowing it to be pub-

briefly discuss at the end of this book, are undoing this static system, in a manner not dissimilar from that in which linguistic changes took shape after the Revolution of 1917.

lished, so that in many cases the printed texts from which one works have been normalized, representing the editor's conception of the standard language rather than the author's actual usage; typically, one does not also have access to the author's manuscript. Finally, in this way one can monitor only the written language, and not usage in the spoken language: even dialogue in novels and drama is only an artistic reflection of the spoken language, and a printed text typically gives no indication of the author's choice of pronunciation variants.[15]

In monitoring current usage, more direct methods of analysis are available, in particular the survey methods familiar from sociology, whereby the views of a representative sample of the population under investigation are elicited. A number of sociolinguistic surveys of this kind were carried out in the Soviet Union in the 1950s and 1960s: the most comprehensive of these is that carried out by the RJaSO (Русский язык и советское общество 'Russian language and Soviet society') team of the Russian Language Institute of the Soviet Academy of Sciences, and it is to this survey that we shall principally refer, although mention will also be made of smaller surveys covering more restricted points of usage.

For practical reasons, the RJaSO team decided against conducting a large series of face-to-face interviews, but rather to rely on answers to written questionnaires: this reduces enormously the amount of time that is actually required to conduct the polling, since it is not necessary to wait for the particular variant in which one is interested to occur spontaneously in speech (and some variants, especially lexical variants, are of very low frequency), although it does bring with it certain theoretical disadvantages that will become apparent below. During the period 1959–64 questionnaires were prepared covering pronunciation, morphology (including stress), word-formation, and vocabulary; these were then distributed to informants during 1963–6 (Krysin 1974: 3). No comparable survey of syntactic usage has been done; given the general traditional orientation of Russian linguistics, it is unlikely that such a survey would appear soon. Some of the results of the processing of replies to these questionnaires are incorporated in Panov (1968), and a more detailed and specific analysis of the results of the questionnaires is Krysin (1974), with a briefer account in Krysin (1973). In only a few cases, in particular with the questionnaire on pronunciation, were

---

[15] To some extent, verse can give information on the author's choice of stress (from the metre) and pronunciation (from the rhyme); but verse does not correspond directly to anyone's ordinary usage.

informants interviewed personally, with a view to assessing whether their actual usage corresponded to their own assessment of their usage as reflected in their replies to the questionnaire (Krysin 1974: 34). Most of the questions in the questionnaires are of the following form: informants are presented with two or more variants, both of which are known to be used by speakers of the standard language, and are asked sometimes to make an assessment of them and sometimes to indicate which of them they use (Krysin 1974: 29–31). Although this is a very simple method for the compiler of a questionnaire to use, it has a number of disadvantages which must always be borne in mind when evaluating the results of this survey.

Firstly, it is essential that the informant should understand the question: in most cases this presents little difficulty with educated informants, although in certain instances, such as questions about details of pronunciation, given that very few of the informants were phoneticians, the formulation of the question so that it is comprehensible to the layman is in itself a formidable task (for discussion of how this and other difficulties were partially overcome, see Panov 1971*a*). Secondly, this technique presupposes that, when asked to do so, informants can correctly monitor their own usage, i.e. that they will indicate that variant which they actually use, rather than the variant they would like to think they use (for prestige reasons); again, in the case of pronunciation, the possibility of a simple error from a non-phonetician is highly probable. This is in fact the main disadvantage of asking informants to monitor themselves, rather than having the linguist register actual usage in one or more situations.[16] To some extent allowance can be made for this factor by including check questions, for instance by having a number of questions, distributed through the questionnaire, asking for essentially the same piece of information: the hypothesis is that informants will not be absolutely consistent in citing prestige forms that do not correspond to their own usage. Another type of check question consists in giving pseudo-variants, i.e. forms that are known not to occur; if an informant then selects such forms with any degree of frequency, that informant can be excluded as unreliable (Krysin 1974: 29–31). For the pronunciation questionnaire, an additional check was provided by actually recording some of those who replied to the questionnaire, and comparing their recorded replies with their written replies (though this is still

---

[16] This latter technique was pioneered by Labov (1966) in his investigation of New York speech, and by many Western sociolinguists influenced to varying degrees by Labov's work, but was used only to a very limited extent in the RJaSO survey.

not spontaneous speech). Although the results of this comparison (Barinova *et al.* 1971) demonstrate a high degree of correlation between reported and actual usage, there are many individual cases, particularly involving positional variants, where the discrepancies between the two are significant (ibid.: 342): error rates (difference between percentage of informants claiming to use a given pronunciation and the percentage of occurrences of that pronunciation in their actual speech) of over 80 per cent were found for ужаснётесь and бог-то, for instance, and error rates above 60 per cent are not infrequent. Finally, since the questionnaire was designed primarily to investigate the usage of speakers of the standard language, only variants that are acceptable within the standard were included, or at least only variants for which a case can be made for considering them normative. In considering the stress of the plural of фронт 'front (military)', for instance, both genitive plural фронто́в (the usual current form, and that recommended by most dictionaries) and фро́нтов (now archaic) were included in the questionnaire, whereas the variation in the nominative-accusative plural фро́нты/фронты́ was excluded because the variant фронты́ is 'clearly non-standard' (явно нелитературное) (Krysin 1974: 230); the result is that, unfortunately, we have no detailed evidence as to how widespread among educated speakers the variant фронты́ actually is. This criterion is not applied with absolute rigour, however, so that the questionnaire does include the stress variants распреде́лит, прибы́л, созда́лось, доску́, and the morphological variants бухгалтера́ 'book-keepers', жгёт 'burns', although the authors explicitly note that they do not claim that these are acceptable within the standard language, but that they only wish to ascertain the reactions of different social groups to the forms (Krysin 1974: 15–16, 232–3).

Another consequence of the fact that this questionnaire was concerned with the standard language is that questionnaires were sent out only to those people who are, or can be considered to be, speakers of the standard language. For practical purposes, this was defined to be those who (*a*) were native speakers of Russian, (*b*) had completed higher or secondary education, and (*c*) were urban residents (Krysin 1974: 17–18).[17] The inclusion of the last two factors follows from the informal

[17] In view of the restriction of this Soviet survey to educated people, and of the elicitation techniques used, it is doubtful whether any direct comparison can be made between these results and those obtained in a number of sociolinguistic surveys of the United States (Labov 1966; Eckert 1991), since the latter concentrate rather on non-standard speech, and include spontaneous speech in addition to more controlled registers. Apart from traditional dialect studies, based on the comparative and historical method, research

definition of standard Russian as the language of educated urban residents, in particular those of Moscow, and also serves explicitly to exclude as far as possible non-standard variants that owe their origin to regional dialects (which are most tenacious in the speech of the rural population, and of those who have not undergone complete secondary education). The individual questionnaires were sent out to between 12,000 and 18,000 informants satisfying these three conditions; some 20–30 per cent of the questionnaires sent out were completed and returned, of which a few were rejected on the basis of inconsistencies revealed by check questions (Krysin 1973: 38). For each questionnaire there were thus 3,000 to 4,300 informants, or an estimated 0.01–0.02 per cent of the total population of the Soviet Union satisfying the three criteria given above (Krysin 1974: 31–3). In order to ascertain what correlations exist between various social groups and attitudes to the individual variants, informants were asked a number of preliminary questions about their education, residence, age, etc. The education para-meter has been largely dealt with already—all informants had higher or complete secondary education (apart from some comparative material on the pronunciation questionnaire using informants with partial secondary education (Krysin 1974: 21))—although a further classifica-tion was made into those with and those without higher education.

Informants were classified regionally into the following groups: Moscow residents; Leningrad residents; Moscow *oblast´* (Moscow and vicinity) residents; Leningrad *oblast´* (Leningrad and vicinity) residents; North Russian urban residents; South Russian urban residents; Central Russian urban residents; native speakers of Russian resident in Ukraine; native speakers of Russian resident in the Baltic republics. The initial hypothesis was that residents of Moscow and Leningrad would show minimal influence of regional dialects, while residents of provincial towns would show more influence from the surrounding regional dialects (including South Russian for Ukraine, North-West Russian for the Baltics), and residents of the Moscow and Leningrad *oblasti* would occupy an intermediate position. In general, these predictions were borne out (cf. the summary table in Krysin (1974: 350), and the more detailed breakdown in the text), suggesting that a dialect-coloured environment tends strongly to favour the choice of that variant which is closest to the form found in the dialect. Although the questionnaire provides information not only on place of longest residence, but also

into non-standard Russian has only recently started (see Nikitina 1982; *Городское прос-торечие* 1984; Šmelev and Zemskaja 1988; Kolesov 1991; T. V. Šmeleva 1992).

on place where the informants' childhood was spent, where they were educated, and on their parents' geographical origin, it was found that the essential factors can be restricted to the place where the informants spent their childhood and to the place of longest residence.

The division of provincial speakers into North Russian, South Russian, and Central Russian in the RJaSO survey follows the division of Russian dialects into northern, southern, and central in Durnovo *et al.* (1914), since the more recent classification of the Russian dialects, based on the results of detailed dialectological surveys and embodied in Avanesov and Orlova (1965) (see also Avanesov and Gorškov 1985; Avanesov and Bromlej 1986–   ; Avanesov and Moraxovskaja 1987), was not available at the time the questionnaires were distributed. The main difference between the two dialect classifications, corresponding in large measure to the retreat of specifically southern or northern dialect features in favour of the more neutral central dialects, has been the tendency for the central dialect area to expand southwards and even more strikingly northwards (see the two maps accompanying Avanesov and Orlova 1965). Thus one feature of the development of the Russian language in the Soviet period, which is rather masked by the material of the RJaSO survey but will be alluded to in the individual chapters below, is the relative tenacity of southern dialect features. Northern dialect features have shown a much greater tendency to recede.

On the parameter of age, the informants were divided into ten-year age-groups (born 1890–9; 1900–9; 1910–19; 1920–9; 1930–9; 1940–9) for some of the questionnaires (e.g. on pronunciation), and into twenty-year age-groups (born before 1899; 1900–19; 1920–39; born after 1940) for the others (e.g. word-formation), depending on the degree of precision required (Krysin 1974: 20–1). The overall results show that age is an important correlate of choice among different variants. However, there are several exceptions, where there is either no correlation with age, or where one finds a form relatively little used by the oldest informants, relatively frequently used by the middle-aged, and relatively little used again by the youngest. To some extent, the different preferences shown by different age-groups at the present time can be mapped into a diachronic representation: the responses of the oldest informants represent the average stage of affairs when they were younger, while the responses of the youngest informants represent those forms that will become even more frequent, and ultimately predominant. However, there are dangers in making this mapping.[18] For instance, the replies to

[18] For what has become a classical counter-example to this method, see Denison (1968)

the questions on pronunciation by even the oldest informants often depart significantly from descriptions of Moscow pronunciation at the beginning of the century, in the direction of being closer to the usage of younger Muscovites. Clearly, as people grow older they will still interact with the younger generation, and are likely to adopt some features of its language.

The third factor which proved to correlate highly with choice of variants is the informant's social position (and, to a much lesser extent, the social position of the informant's parents). For this purpose, an overall classification was made into intellectuals,[19] white-collar workers (служащие), industrial workers (рабочие), and students. Of the total number of 3,000–4,000 informants, 40 per cent were intellectuals, 33 per cent students, 18 per cent white-collar workers, and 9 per cent industrial workers (Krysin 1974: 33). The expectation, borne out in the vast majority of cases by the questionnaire results, was that intellectuals would come closest to the traditional norm and workers least close (even workers who speak the standard language are likely to work together with others who do not), with white-collar workers occupying an inter-mediate position; students fall rather outside this categorization, since they are mostly distinct in age as well as in social position, and though in many respects close to the intellectuals are also particularly prone to the influence of student slang. For some purposes, a finer sub-classification of some of these groups was used: thus intellectuals and students were subdivided into philologists (филологи, i.e. specialists in language and/or literature) and non-philologists, with the subgroup of writers and journalists being further abstracted from the class of philolo-gist intellectuals. The expectation, again borne out in general, was that philologists would be even closer to the traditional norm than non-philologist intellectuals and students, and that writers and journalists would be closest of all.

In connection with professional and other social groups, we may note

---

on Sauris (N. Italy), where the correlation between age and choice of language in a multi-lingual community remains largely unchanged over a considerable period.

[19] Here and elsewhere we use 'intellectuals' to translate the terms интеллегент, интеллигенция, used in Soviet works on sociology (including sociolinguistics) of the Soviet Union, i.e. to refer to employed persons engaged in mental work. The term has thus rather wider reference than English 'intellectual' ('highbrow') usually has. In our discus-sion of twentieth-century language, we prefer not to use the term 'intelligentsia', which in English has different overtones from the Russian term, stemming largely from the use of this term with regard to nineteenth-century Russia. See Müller (1971) on the dynamics of this notion in Russian society of the nineteenth and early twentieth centuries.

that certain professions often adopt linguistic features at variance with general standard usage, particularly with regard to items that are especially frequent in the speech of the professional group concerned. Deviant stresses are particularly common: thus sailors usually say компа́с (standard: ко́мпас) 'compass', and actors хара́ктерный 'characteristic' (for характе́рный). Similar deviations are found in syntax, as in the expression на фло́те, used by sailors for standard во фло́те 'in the navy'. Further examples are given in the relevant chapters.

A number of other factors that might correlate with choice among social variants were considered by the RJaSO team, but only one of these actually figures in the presentation by Krysin (1974), namely the extent to which informants listen to the radio. The expectation seems to have been that frequent listening to the radio, i.e. for the most part to trained speakers from Moscow, would increase the degree of accommodation to the varieties used on the radio. In fact, the overall result indicated that exposure to broadcasts is not a significant factor: the table in Krysin (1974: 350) shows the radio as relevant only to pronunciation, and even then the plus sign indicating relevance is placed in parentheses. The only feature for which there was a marked correlation with exposure to radio broadcasts is the pronunciation of post-tonic non-high vowels after palatalized consonants, and here the results obtained by the RJaSO team differ considerably from those obtained by other elicitation techniques, as will be seen from the discussion in Chapter 1 on pronunciation. Listening to the radio is essentially a passive occupation—the listener is not required to interact with the radio announcer, indeed it is impossible for the listener to do so—so that on a priori grounds there is in fact little reason to suppose that exposure to broadcasts should significantly affect pronunciation.

In the presentation of results in Krysin (1974), age, territory, social position are treated as separate parameters. This means that it is impossible to ascertain detailed correlations, such as the correlation of different pronunciation variants with Muscovites of different age-groups, or the correlation of different morphological variants with different social groups from southern Russia, i.e. any correlation which includes more than one of these parameters. The presentation of such material would of course have increased the size of Krysin (1974) immensely, and detailed statistical analysis would have been impossible because of the small size of the groups involved, but this does represent one unfortunate limitation on the use to which these data can be put. The

RJaSO survey does not cover gender differences, and in general, little attention has been paid to these differences in the Russian linguistic tradition, but there is a recent work by Zemskaja *et al.* (1990).

The great advantage of the RJaSO survey is the large number of informants, from various social groups, who were covered by the investigation. Most of the other surveys on current usage have had much smaller coverage (typically, the students taught by the linguist conducting the survey or the colleagues of this linguist; see below on Zemskaja's study of spoken standard Russian). Many of these other surveys concerned pronunciation and stress (they are discussed in detail in Chapter 1). In many cases, they differ from the RJaSO questionnaire by simply asking informants how they pronounce a given word, rather than asking them to choose between a limited number of variants, so that the existence of certain widespread but non-standard forms can be ascertained. Where surveys focus on language aspects other than pronunciation, they seem to be lacking a systematic approach to data elicitation: the linguist conducting the survey behaves as a passive observer, who records random spoken data and then draws generalizations on the basis of these data. However, such surveys have the advantage of monitoring actual usage when the informant's attention is completely distracted from the fact that his or her linguistic performance is being observed.

Particularly interesting from this viewpoint are pronunciation tests where the informant is asked to read a passage, so that he or she is not aware of the particular points of pronunciation that are being tested (though the informant may, of course, modify his or her normal pronunciation, simply given the general conditions of a test recording). Several surveys of this kind, where the informant is unaware of the material tested, are discussed in Krysin (1974): on pp. 38–9, we find the discussion of Andreev's test on pronunciation of adjectives in -кий (see Chapter 1 for details); on pp. 163–4—RJaSO's test on use of masculine or feminine profession/occupation names (see Chapter 6 for details), and on p. 91—RJaSO's observation of the genitive plural of fruit names (see Chapter 3 for details).

On the basis of such surveys, it is possible to gain some idea of current educated urban usage. However, this still does not answer the question as to the precise relation between this usage and the norm. The word norm has been used many times throughout this introduction without a special explanation. Meanwhile, in Soviet linguistics, two different approaches to language norm can be distinguished. The first, more prescriptive one, is expressed, for example, in recent Academy grammars: norm is defined as 'such formation and usage of [language] forms and categories that is reproduced, with absolute consistency, in the community of standard speakers' (Švedova 1970: 4) or as a 'socially determined and consciously adhered to system of rules that represents obligatory realization of language laws' (*Русская грамматика* 1980: i. 10). These definitions insist on the rigidity of the norm and clearly associate the norm with such social policies as language planning. However, we have already seen that in Russian (Soviet) society of the twentieth century there is no great chasm between actual and standard usage; a number of Russian normative grammarians in fact acknowledge that the linguistic norm is something objective, immanent in the speech community (Ickovič 1968: 4–5).[20] This latter understanding of the norm, as an objective dynamic system with its core and periphery, seems to be a more adequate reflection of language reality than the one recommended by Academy grammars. The norm thus understood is differently perceived by different groups within a speech community and often remains impenetrable to prescriptive practice (cf. Filin 1981: 311–12).

The difference between the two conceptions of the norm, the one that is viewed as a tool of eliminating variation in favour of one and only one acceptable form, and the one that admits variation as an essential characteristic of the linguistic system, is particularly apparent from the comparison between two orthoepic dictionaries of Russian, viz. Avanesov and Ožegov (1959) and Borunova *et al.* (1983). While the former sees its task in recommending 'one, major, variant' (Avanesov and Ožegov 1959: 7), the latter views variation as a 'regularity of the standard language stemming from language evolution' (Borunova *et al.* 1983: 3). Accordingly, the latter dictionary is more lenient than its predecessor in accepting pronunciation and stress variants as permissible or at least 'additional' (дополнительные варианты).[21] The two approaches contrast, in a similar way, in the original edition of the most complete dictionary of Russian (*SSRLJa* 1948–65) and the second edition (*SSRLJa* 1991–), which differs from the first one in greater attention to the educated spoken language as well as in a more critical

---

[20] Cf., much earlier, Peškovskij's opposition of the objectivized and normative approaches to language introduced in his 1923 article «Объективная и нормативная точка зрения на язык» (Peškovskij 1959: 50–62, esp. 54). See also Švarckopf (1985) on Vinogradov's views of the norm and standard.

[21] For a detailed comparison of the two dictionaries, see Lehfeldt (1985).

view of *hapax legomena* attested in the literary works of Russian and Soviet writers (*SSRLJa* 1991– : i. 4, 8–9).

Overall, the conception of the norm as a rigid system which can be monitored through language planning, and the so-called 'dynamic' conception of the norm, represent two successive stages in Soviet linguistic tradition. The emergence of the latter conception, represented by Gorbačevič (1978), Ickovič (1968; 1982), Graudina *et al.* (1976), Graudina (1980), Borunova *et al.* (1983), and, hopefully, *SSRLJa* (1991–), is in no small part due to the results of the RJaSO survey, which was a pioneering study in revealing and acknowledging variation in the standard language, and the studies of educated spoken Russian done in the 1970s and 1980s (see below).

In the following discussion, we base ourselves primarily on those studies that maintain the dynamic conception of the norm, acknowledging, however, the other conception as a valid stage in the description of Russian. However, even within one approach, not all normative grammarians would agree, and in practice recommendations sometimes differ from one handbook to another, and are sometimes at variance with educated usage as elicited, for instance, by the RJaSO survey. Even within the dynamic approach, normative handbooks tend to lag behind changes in usage: an especially clear instance of this is the recommendation of many features of the Old Moscow pronunciation by orthoepic handbooks long after it had become a minority pronunciation among educated speakers (see Chapter 1 on pronunciation). This is partly due to the above-mentioned usual conception of the 'modern Russian literary language' (современный русский литературный язык) as the Russian language from Puškin to the present day (see n. 2); this inevitably introduces an element of archaization into the codification of the norms of the modern literary language. Indeed, if one of the social functions of the Russian language is considered to be the provision of cultural continuity between the literature of Puškin's time and the present day, then there is some merit in a relatively conservative attitude towards codification of the norm, to prevent uncontrolled change away from the language of the early nineteenth century. In practice, however, discrepancies between the recommendations of normative grammarians and educated usage are often the basis of criticisms voiced against the recommendations in question; as one example among many, we may note Gorbačevič's criticism (1971: 187–8) of the attempt by Avanesov and Ožegov (1959) to distinguish between such genitive plurals as гренадир and гренадиров 'grenadiers' semantically (collective versus individual plurality). In somewhat similar vein, Panov (1967: 299–300) considers the hardening of word-final soft labials, as in голубь 'pigeon', to be non-standard, and a pronunciation error that orthoepists must do their utmost to combat; but concedes that if in the future this pronunciation does become more widespread, then orthoepists will be forced by changed circumstances to alter their recommendations, allowing the final hard labial as a possibility, perhaps ultimately as the only possibility.

Apart from the general conservativeness of normative grammarians, however, there is another way in which some normative grammarians have attempted to draw a distinction between usage and the standard, i.e. by defining a class of cases where some variant is non-standard irrespective of how widespread it may be. Ickovič (1982) makes a distinction between the system of a language—its general principles of organization—and the structure of a language—contingent details of the organization of a language, such as the fact that the verb касаться 'touch' takes the genitive case in contemporary Russian. Ickovič argues that variants may be accepted into the standard language if they become widespread, provided they do not violate the system of the language, although there is no requirement that they should not introduce changes in the structure of the language (as with касаться + genitive, for earlier касаться до + genitive, the latter reflecting French influence, from *toucher à*, one of many examples of the influence of French on standard literary Russian of the nineteenth century).

In practice, it is not at all easy to see how the distinction between system and structure is to be drawn in all cases. For instance, one of Ickovič's examples (1968: 23–7) of a variant that would violate the system of contemporary Russian is *Вы писал 'you were writing', addressing a single person, since a general rule of Russian requires the plural of a past tense verb with subject Вы irrespective of whether one or more people is being addressed; however, from a different point of view, this is simply an accident of the structure of Russian, since some other predicates stand in the singular with Вы of singular reference (e.g. Вы старый 'you are old', with a long form adjective). The clearest examples cited by Ickovič of forms that violate the norm because they violate its system, namely Вы писал and прочитающий 'about to read' as a perfective future participle, are not really telling because they also violate current usage: neither of these forms is widespread among educated urban Russians. When applied to examples widespread in current usage, Ickovič's criterion often gives results differing from those of other normative grammarians: thus Ickovič rejects купированный 'consisting of compartments' (said of a train) on the grounds that there is no related verb купировать in this meaning,[22] and the only productive model for forming such adjectives is as past participles passive of verbs; Ožegov (1972), however, lists купированный without any qualification. Ickovič (1968: 39) introduces another criterion, namely whether or not the new form serves some function in the language, e.g. by having a meaning distinct from all existing forms. Thus he allows the acceptance of купированный into the standard if, as some linguists have claimed, its meaning differs from that of the more traditional form купейный (incidentally, in Ožegov (1972), the two words are treated as simple synonyms). Thus the role of the criterion 'corresponding to the system' is at best relative. The great danger of the introduction of criteria other than that of current educated usage is that the definition of the norm is no longer objective, but coloured at various points by the subjective feelings of the individual linguist; compare the disagreement between Ickovič and Ožegov over купированный.

In general, discussions by Russian normative grammarians concern whether or not innovatory forms should be admitted as standard, alongside the traditional standard, and perhaps ultimately replacing it; the objective criterion of correspondence to current educated usage is typically modified in favour of greater adherence to the traditional norm, either explicitly so (e.g. on the grounds of the need for continuity of tradition), or on the basis of more or less subjective additional criteria (conformity with the general organization of the language, semantic need for the new form). Sometimes, though not frequently, one finds a new form being actively encouraged by a linguist. For instance, in Švedova's discussion of new constructions with the preposition по, such as инженер по технике безопасности 'safety engineer' (1966: 40–52), there is very little discussion of the status of such constructions relative to the norm, apart from condemnation of blatant tautologies; Popova (1974: 183–4), however, considers that, since these constructions enable a semantic relation to be expressed between the nouns involved without any additional semantic specification, this construction fulfils a real need in the Russian language and should perhaps be positively encouraged ('merits . . . perhaps, gradual tactful codification').

---

[22] The verb купировать is attested with a different meaning in medical language, viz. 'to put an end to an undesirable phenomenon' (e.g. купировать сердечный приступ 'to stop a heart attack'); it also occurs, in a different type of specialized use, in such expressions as купировать собаке уши 'to clip a dog's ears' (*MAS* 1981–4).

But overall, deliberate attempts to introduce or foster innovatory forms are not characteristic of Russian language standardization in the Soviet Union.

Newer developments in standard Russian have received at least preliminary acknowledgement in the study of speech of educated urban Russians, primarily in Moscow and in Leningrad (Zemskaja 1973; 1981; Zemskaja and Kapanadze 1978; Kolesov 1991). Like the RJaSO study, the study of spoken standard Russian was based on those speakers who had Russian as their first language, who were born and grew up in an urban environment and who had secondary or higher education (Zemskaja 1987: 4; Zemskaja and Širjaev 1988: 122–30).[23] The method of study, however, differed from the RJaSO method in that there were practically no questionnaires, and the data were collected primarily through passive observation.

The study of spoken standard Russian revealed that many forms are current in the language that would not be considered standard by normative grammarians and which are not usual in literature, even in dialogue. On the other hand, it was found that very few lexical items that are identified as разговорные 'colloquial' by the dictionaries of Modern Russian do indeed occur in spoken standard Russian. According to Sirotinina (1974: 67), many of the words listed as разговорные in the Ožegov dictionary (Ožegov 1968)[24] never occurred in her sample of actual spoken Russian. Meanwhile, 'in the reference edition "2,380 Most Common Words in Spoken Russian", only 17 can be identified as разговорные from Ožegov's standpoint (парень 'guy', видно 'it seems', немножко 'a little bit', девчонка 'gal', дочка 'daughter; girl', мальчишка 'boy', пятерка 'excellent grade' or 'five-rouble bill', картошка 'potato', неделька 'week', бумажка 'paper', бабка 'old woman; grandmother', минутка 'minute', ей-богу 'truly', вовсе 'altogether', ишь [exclamation], ребятишки 'kids')' (Sirotinina 1974: 67). The variety of connotations covered by the single label разговорное has led to the suggestion that colloquial style is defined negatively, i.e.

---

[23] Judging by many examples in the descriptions of the spoken language, much of the data was elicited from philologists: the examples often include references to galley proofs, conference presentations, visits to the library, lectures. This reflects the immediate social contacts of the investigators, but this also indicates that the study was not without limitations, because linguists are more likely to participate in word play and *ad hoc* creation of new words (noted as an important feature of the spoken language; see Zemskaja 1981: 71–89; 1983: 172–214).

[24] An edition of Ožegov's dictionary that preceded the 9th edn. (Ožegov 1972).

as the style that does not occur in academic writing, formal writing, and in newspapers (Šmelev 1977: 117).

The discrepancy between the results of the surveys of spoken Russian and normative grammars resulted, if partially, from the rigidity of language planning in the Soviet Union, and from the excessive use of the formal, 'bureaucratic', style as the basis of the standard. The inadequacies of this style, promoted by the centralized media, became apparent in the 1960s–1980s; linguists reacted to these inadequacies by introducing a new distinction, between the codified standard in its written and spoken varieties (кодифицированный литературный язык or книжный литературный язык 'bookish literary language') and the non-codified spoken language (разговорный язык (*sic*) as reflected in разговорная речь) (Zemskaja 1973; 1981). Even though this distinction is relatively novel in Russian linguistics, it would be unreasonable to assume that the spoken language as a separate, largely autonomous sub-system is also new: its realizations are found, here and there, in the literature of the late nineteenth and early twentieth centuries (Panov 1990: 21), when the informal mode of speech was finding its way into the standard. Spoken Russian, accordingly, seems to have originated from the informal communication register, which gradually, in the course of this century, became more dramatically opposed to the standard, even in the spoken version of the latter. Academic censorship common in the Soviet Union notwithstanding, this development of spoken Russian from a register was probably the main reason that it remained largely unnoticed by scholars for a long time; the study of spoken Russian is still in its early stage, and a comprehensive grammar of it is still to be written.[25] Spoken Russian seems to differ from the standard primarily in the degree of variation, and the standard language of the 1980s was making the first steps towards acknowledging some of this variation.

The mention of the informal register brings up a more general question that we have not discussed and whose omission could lead to over-simplification, namely the question of different registers and styles, since it is clear that a given form may be more appropriate in one style than in another, indeed that a given form may be completely inappropriate in certain styles while perfectly normal in others. In Soviet normative handbooks lexical items and forms are often accompanied by

---

[25] Zemskaja's 1979 book, revised in 1987 (see Zemskaja 1987), is the first attempt to compile a handbook of spoken Russian; the limitations of the survey on which Zemskaja's study is based have already been mentioned.

specification of their stylistic value, implying that such items and forms are not acceptable in all styles. One such qualification, mentioned above, *prostorečno*, indicates that the given form is non-standard; the only reason for including such forms in a normative handbook, apart from the desire to warn people not to use them in the standard language, is that they may appear in literature in dialogue which aims to reproduce popular speech. Another stylistic qualification, устаревшее or устарелое 'archaic', presumably indicates that the form is no longer standard, but must still be known by the educated Russian since it will be found in classical literature. Particularly within the written language, further stylistic subdivisions are possible; see, for instance, Vinokur and Šmelev (1968); Šmelev (1977); Vinogradova (1984). The following are those styles that we have found it necessary to refer to in this book; the list is not claimed to be exhaustive for the language as a whole: artistic literature (narrative); journalistic and popular scientific; academic (i.e. the language of learned non-fiction, more rigid in Russian than in many other European languages (Lapteva 1968; Nichols 1988)); poetic; conversational (in so far as it approximates to the colloquial); official (the language of official documents, letters, etc.). Just as there have been changes in the acceptability of various forms into the standard during the Soviet period, and debates over their acceptability, so too have there been changes in stylistic value—more colloquial forms becoming accepted in artistic literature, forms from higher styles filtering down into speech—and disagreements over the stylistic values of various forms. Examples of such changes and disagreements will be found in the individual chapters. One particularly important channel for the interplay between 'higher' (e.g. artistic literature, bureaucratic) and 'lower' (e.g. colloquial) styles in the beginning and at the decline of the Soviet period was the rapid development of journalism, of the press as a mass medium. The need to reach the ordinary people led to the inclusion of many colloquialisms in this variety of the standard written language, while by the same token newspapers were for many ordinary people the first and most concentrated contact with the standard written language, leading to the adoption of features from the written language into their speech (Kostomarov 1971: 12–13; Baranov and Kazakevič 1991).

The discussion of social changes that have led to changes in the evaluation of the norm in the Soviet period may be summarized as follows. Although even before the Revolution of 1917 the Russian language was much less varied geographically and socially than many other European languages, the rigid class structure meant that even relatively slight divergence from the accepted standard could be a mark of social status; this was reinforced by the fact that education, particularly at the higher levels, was available only to the privileged classes. One of the results of the Revolution has been the 'democratization' of the Russian language. On the one hand, the rise to power of new social classes led to the adoption of some features of their speech into the standard; on the other hand, the spread of education led to the adoption of standard features into the speech of those who had previously used non-standard varieties of the language. Overall, the latter has been the more powerful factor: except perhaps for the immediate post-Revolutionary years, there has been no trend to reject the traditional standard as a whole in favour of a norm closer to the actual usage of the working class. The fact that only 9 per cent of the informants for the RJaSO survey were industrial workers probably reflects difficulty in finding speakers of standard Russian among the working class. Non-standard (hence low-prestige) forms are still mainly found among workers, whose social prestige otherwise was established as high in the official Soviet system. The closed society that characterized the Soviet period in general was reflected in the language in that the standard was codified and promoted by schooling and by the heavily censored literature; as a result, the standard language, as reflected, for instance, in the latest Academy Grammar (1980), was far behind developments in spoken standard Russian. This led to a greater gap between the spoken and written language, a gap that is probably going to close in the next decade when the democratization of Russian society has allowed more spoken and even colloquial variants into the standard language.

1 Pronunciation

A T the beginning of the twentieth century, the standard pronunciation of Russian was considered to be that of educated Muscovites (Košutić 1919: vii; Ožegov 1955: 16; Panov 1967). There was considerable interest in phonetics in the late nineteenth and early twentieth centuries, and we are fortunate in having on-the-spot descriptions of this kind of pronunciation, usually referred to as the Old Moscow (OM) pronunciation; of these, the best is usually considered to be Košutić (1919).[1] In addition, we can take advantage of the reminiscences of those who were alive at that time, and of early gramophone recordings, as well as less satisfactory sources such as rhyme in poetry. One of the main characteristics of OM is that in many respects it diverges from Russian orthography; numerous specific examples are given below, but two examples will suffice for this general introduction: the OM pronunciation of ходят 'they go' as ['xodʲut], and the OM pronunciation of тихий 'quiet' as ['tʲixəj]. Although St Petersburg was the capital of the Russian Empire, and although its pronunciation differed in several respects from that of Moscow, Muscovite pronunciation was nevertheless considered standard.[2]

In the pre-Revolutionary period, the OM pronunciation was transmitted by and large within the family, from generation to generation, so that this style of pronunciation was acquired by the younger generation with little modification, and before spelling was learnt, the idiosyncrasies of OM being able to maintain themselves. After the Revolution, this situation changed radically. The standard language, including standard pronunciation, was no longer the exclusive property of educated Muscovites, but rather of the whole nation, so that non-OM speakers started adopting the standard pronunciation, at least in part, and in turn

---

[1] A briefer account, restricted to those aspects that distinguish OM from other pronunciations, is given by D. N. Ušakov (1968). A short bibliography is given by Kuz´mina (1966: 6). Differences between OM and OPb (Old St Petersburg) and the stabilization of OM as the norm in the second half of the nineteenth century are discussed by Panov (1990: 53–4, 149–86). See also V. V. Vinogradov (1938: 477).

[2] A short bibliography of works on the Old St Petersburg pronunciation is given by Panov (1967: 295). According to Panov, some descriptions of OPb, for example, the one by Černyšev (1915), fail to differentiate between standard and non-standard pronunciation (Panov 1990: 53 and n. 41, 149–51 and n. 93).

influenced it themselves. Many people made their acquaintance with the standard language through its written form, so that there was considerable pressure against characteristic OM pronunciations that contradicted the spelling. Of course, the standard language was spread not only by the written word, but also by broadcasting (Moscow radio and television programmes were broadcast throughout the Soviet Union, in addition to local programmes), so that spelling pronunciations contrary to general principles of the standard language have been unable to make headway, such as *okan´e*, the distinction of unstressed *o* and *a*, characteristic of northern dialects.

Nevertheless, the loss of some of the idiosyncrasies of OM has meant that OM can no longer be considered the only norm, nor indeed the preferable norm, for Russian pronunciation, although the force of tradition has meant that certain OM pronunciations now used only by a minority, even in Moscow, are often not considered incorrect in current speech. OM was still promulgated as the norm by D. N. Ušakov (1935: vol. i, pp. xxxi–xxxiv), but his recommendations were already out of touch with changing reality (Shapiro 1968: 3–4). The current standard is often referred to as Contemporary Standard Russian (CSR).[3] The 'best' CSR is presumably still that of educated Muscovites (those who do not cling to OM), though it is much more widespread outside this circle than was OM, and was normally insisted on for broadcasting purposes throughout the Soviet Union. OM, or rather many of the features distinguishing OM from CSR, was still maintained, up to the late 1970s, with some degree of consistency on the stage, particularly in performances of classical plays (Il´inskaja and Sidorov 1955; Kuz´mina 1963; L. N. Kuznecova 1963). The most widely accepted description of CSR is that by Avanesov (1984).[4] One of the most recent dictionaries that recorded the current state of CSR pronunciation is Borunova *et al.* (1983), based on Avanesov and Ožegov (1959).[5]

Standardization in pronunciation is much more difficult to enforce than standardization of those aspects of language that are reflected directly in the written language. It is possible for a writer to write standard Russian while using non-standard pronunciations in his or her

[3] See also the Introduction, p. 3.

[4] This is the latest edition of a work that first appeared in 1950; differences among successive editions reflect the development of CSR. Shapiro (1968: 4–6) accuses Avanesov of being too conservative, but this seems more applicable to the earlier editions, and in general Avanesov is rather liberal in allowing pronunciation variants.

[5] See the Introduction, p. 20, for a brief discussion of differences between these dictionaries.

speech even when, for instance, reading his or her works out aloud; thus Maksim Gor´kij retained traces of the *okan´e* dialect of his native Nižnij Novgorod. Standard pronunciation is not insisted on as much as the written standard in schools. Ušakov's failure to impose OM must be considered one of the major defeats of normative grammarians of Russian.

Monitoring current pronunciation can in many cases be carried out simply by listening to the normal speech of speakers of the standard language and to recordings of broadcasts, etc. This is the method used by Avanesov, e.g. in Avanesov (1984); as a rough-and-ready method it has obvious methodological drawbacks, although the high degree of correspondence between Avanesov's observations and those derived by more detailed and rigorous techniques is a tribute to Avanesov's skill in using the more informal method. However, for some of the more elusive details of pronunciation such methods are inadequate, since one needs to work with recordings of a higher quality, such as can really only be obtained in the artificial environment of a phonetic laboratory. Moreover, when it is necessary to survey the pronunciation of a given word or set of words by a statistically significant number of speakers, specially designed questionnaires are often the only way of obtaining the required data within a reasonable period. It is the exception, rather than the rule, that someone devises a Labovian test like that described by Andreev (1963), where passers-by were asked the names of various stations, bridges, etc., in Moscow and Leningrad; their attention was concentrated on the informational side of what they were saying, and they were given no indication in advance that the centre of interest was the pronunciation of adjectives in -ский.

The tests that have been carried out under laboratory conditions fall into two main types. In the first, informants are asked to read isolated words, which are then analysed; the defect is that the informants are normally aware of the purpose of the test—it soon becomes apparent what the relevant feature of pronunciation is in a list of words—and they may adjust their pronunciation accordingly if they feel that a certain pronunciation is more correct than the one they normally use. The advantage is that the recordings of the individual words are particularly clear. Reading whole sentences or connected texts, the second type of test, can often overcome this disadvantage, particularly if the features of interest are sufficiently camouflaged amidst the rest of the text, but has the disadvantage that the forms of interest may not be pronounced sufficiently clearly in the more rapid reading style that characterizes reading of whole sentences or texts. This can partly be compensated for by putting the pronunciation feature of interest in a position that receives maximum prominence; in Russian, this usually means stressed sentence-final position (cf. the use made of this position in the survey of pronunciation of unstressed endings noted below). The general problem of the validity of reading tests in gathering data on pronunciation is discussed by Glovinskaja (1966). In addition to such tests for individual points of pronunciation, noted below, Drage (1968) gives the results of a series of tests in which 17 informants, either born or living in Moscow, were asked to read a series of short sentences; the results are classified according to speaker, speaker's regional provenance, that of speaker's parents, and speaker's age.

For the pronunciation section of the RJaSO survey, informants were sent a written questionnaire, in which they were asked, for each point, which of a number of variants they used (Barinova and Panov 1971; Barinova *et al.* 1971; Panov 1971*a*; Krysin 1974: 38–155). In addition to the drawback of any method allowing informants to control their responses, this method implies a rather optimistic view of the ability of non-phoneticians correctly to assess phonetic distinctions that are often extremely fine (e.g. between post-tonic [ə] and [ɪ] after a soft consonant, or degree of palatalization in palatalization assimilation); see the criticisms of Bondarko (1973). The RJaSO team, in the publications noted above, admit the unsatisfactory nature of some of their materials but acknowledge that this approach allowed them successfully to interview a large pool of speakers. They tried to rectify the inadequacies of their method, to some extent, by interviewing some of their informants (Barinova *et al.* 1971). Although informants were still able to control their responses, extreme discrepancies between written and oral replies were noted in many cases, although the RJaSO team concluded that overall the discrepancies were not large enough to invalidate the materials. In addition to other surveys covering specific points of pronunciation and discussed below, we should note the survey carried out by Superanskaja (1959), in which some 700 students in Moscow (not all Muscovites) were asked which pronunciation they preferred for individual words and phrases; by the time of publication, 234 responses had been classified for some points, 150 for others.

In discussing pronunciation, it is important to make clear what style of pronunciation one is dealing with, in particular the speed and degree of clarity of articulation, since certain phonetic processes tend to characterize more rapid rather than slower speech, for instance various kinds of assimilation. Following the terminology of Shapiro (1968: 8–9; see also Panov 1963), we may distinguish between an explicit code, with the minimum of assimilation, etc., and usually characterizing speech in more formal situations, and an elliptic code, with the maximum of assimilation, etc., and usually characterizing less formal situations; the former is closest to the codified standard, and the latter borders on colloquial speech. In practice there is, of course, a continuum rather than a dichotomy of codes. One feature of this distinction between explicit and elliptic codes is that when people are asked which of a number of phonetic variants they prefer, or use, they tend to over-report the more explicit variants; similarly, in reading (especially of word-lists) the percentage of explicit forms is much higher than in ordinary speech. Some of the variants discussed below are subject to the difference between explicit and elliptic codes: thus the pronunciation [ʃʃ] for щ rather than [ʃtʃ] is elliptic, as is palatalization assimilation, and the use of unstressed [ɪ] rather than [ə] in inflectional endings after a soft consonant. In surveys carried out to test people's pronunciation of these variants, in each case the more explicit variant was over-reported, irrespective of whether it corresponded to the traditional OM standard (as with [ə] in unstressed endings after a soft consonant) or conflicted with it (as with [ʃtʃ] and lack of palatalization assimilation). With most other components of the language, over-reporting from educated Russians is found only in the direction of greater adherence to the traditional standard, and while this is often found with pronunciation where the difference between explicit and elliptic codes is not involved, the relevance of this difference must always be borne in mind, as otherwise one could gain the impression that there is often an unexplained tendency to over-report innovatory forms.

One final question to be considered briefly in this introduction, and in greater detail at the end of this chapter, is the motivation for the various changes in pronunciation that distinguish CSR from OM, on the assumption that not all such changes are the result of chance. The factor that is most often advanced is the influence of spelling, given that there are many discrepancies between OM and Russian orthography, many of which have been lost in CSR; a more sceptical attitude towards the relevance of spelling pronunciations is taken by Shapiro (1968: 19). Another external factor that might be considered relevant is the influence of other forms of spoken Russian, in particular the Old Petersburg variety, and regional dialects. In addition to such external factors, there are also possible internal factors, of which morphological analogy (the tendency for a given morpheme always to have the same pronunciation) and morphological boundaries (i.e. a tendency for morphological boundaries to be marked phonetically) have been suggested. The possible relevance of these various factors will be discussed in the detailed treatment of the various individual points below, and the various strands drawn together in the conclusion to this chapter.

Pronunciation of щ and жж

(i) Pronunciation of щ

One of the most striking differences between OM and OPb is that for orthographic щ (e.g. щи 'cabbage soup'), also spelt сч (e.g. счастье 'happiness'), and зч (e.g. извозчик 'horse cab-driver'), Muscovites at the turn of the century pronounced a long palatalized fricative [ʃʲʃ], whereas in St Petersburg the norm was for a single fricative followed by an affricate [ʃʲtʃ]. In the period after the Revolution, the distinction between Moscow and St Petersburg/Leningrad pronunciations became less marked. Many linguists—mainly natives of Leningrad, e.g. Černyx, Obnorskij, Bojanus, who are criticized on this count by Panov (1967: 330)—claimed that OM [ʃʲʃ] had lost its prestige, and that the usual pronunciation of Russians, other than native Muscovites, was the Leningrad [ʃʲtʃ]. Similarly, Jones and Ward (1969: 140) say that 'by and large, at least the younger generation seems to prefer the pronunciation [ʃʲtʃ] rather than [ʃʲʃ]'. The surveys carried out in the Soviet Union in the 1960s and 1970s indicate that this view is mistaken.

An important factor in the discussion is whether the sound in question occurs across a morpheme boundary after a preposition or prefix, or not:[6] [ʃʲtʃ] is more common in the former case than in the latter, with intermediate values where the presence or absence of a morpheme boundary is unclear to a speaker (e.g. счастье 'happiness').[7] The pronunciation [ʃʲtʃ] is also more common the slower the rate of speech, and informants tend to over-report this variant (Krysin 1974: 96).

We may start with the pronunciation not across a morpheme boundary, looking first at the situation in Moscow. Barinova (1966) reports the

---

[6] The morpheme boundary between stem and suffix, e.g. in извоз-чик, seems to have no effect.

[7] Though this word is diachronically analysable as consisting of the prefix and root -част- (Fasmer 1986–7: iii. 816), this morphological division has long become obsolete, hence the spelling щастие, щастье in eighteenth- and early nineteenth-century Russian.

results of a survey which consisted of two tests: reading a word-list and reading sentences. In both tests, the overwhelming majority of participants used the long fricative [ʃʃ], particularly in reading the sentences (where greater speed was an added factor), although even in the word-list the majority for the long fricative was quite clear in each case. When the results were broken down according to age-group, it was found that the fricative pronunciation increases in frequency the younger the age-group investigated—precisely the opposite tendency from that suggested by the studies cited above. The study of the younger people's norm, carried out in the late 1980s, also showed that the long fricative pronunciation remained a more neutral, non-emphatic variant (Kalenčuk 1993: 24).

Even more interesting was the situation in Leningrad, reported by Ivanova-Luk´janova (1971): for here too, where the sound does not occur across a morpheme boundary, the overwhelming preference was for a long fricative pronunciation, and not for the OPb norm. Of 100 secondary school students (aged 15–17) interviewed, only 6 used [ʃtʃ] in борщ 'borsht, beetroot soup', while 94 used the fricative; for щи the figures were respectively 9 and 91, with similar figures for other words tested. The figures were broken down according to whether the informant's parents and/or grandparents were also from Leningrad, and from this it emerged that the affricate pronunciation is more widespread among those who are natives of Leningrad of several generations' standing (the informants themselves were all natives of the city and had lived there all their lives). Thus even in Leningrad (and later St Petersburg), [ʃʃ], corresponding to the OM standard, is the more widespread form among the younger generation; the older OPb form was maintained essentially only among natives of the city of several generations' standing (коренные петербуржцы/ленинградцы), and even then only rarely. Of course, another corollary of these findings is that the OM pronunciation was transferred to the CSR pronunciation thus becoming an overwhelming standard. Current orthoepic handbooks give preference to the long fricative pronunciation, when not across a morpheme boundary, although the OPb pronunciation is still admitted as a less widespread orthoepic variant (Avanesov 1984: 113–14; Borunova *et al.* 1983: 676).

When we turn to the position across a morpheme boundary, e.g. из чайных ложек 'out of tea-spoons', рас-считать 'to calculate', the picture is essentially the inverse of that where there is no internal morpheme boundary, although both variants [ʃʃ] and [ʃtʃ] are still found (Kalenčuk 1993: 24). Even OM, as described by Košutić (1919:

70), allowed the affricate pronunciation here, particularly in slow speech, and the tendency has been for this affricate pronunciation to become more frequent (see the statistics in Barinova (1966: 48–9) and Borunova (1966: 71)). In Leningrad (and later St Petersburg), the predominance of [ʃtʃʲ] across clear morpheme boundaries is equally marked, rather more so, as might be expected, among natives of several generations' standing, where there is a greater tendency towards [ʃtʃʲ] anyway (Ivanova-Luk´janova 1971).

The fact that [ʃtʃʲ] is the commoner variant across a morpheme boundary might be thought to indicate that the Leningrad pronunciation has here won out over the Moscow pronunciation. We would like to suggest a different explanation. Even at the turn of the century, when OM was effectively the unchallenged standard in Moscow, we know that [ʃtʃʲ] was possible across a morpheme boundary (Košutić 1919: 70). The increase in the incidence of this pronunciation is probably an internal development within Moscow pronunciation: the presence of the morphological boundary, which is in turn reflected in the spelling (not щ), is making itself felt phonetically, in that we clearly have morphologically с or з followed by ч, and the assimilation is only to [ʃtʃʲ] without the further development to [ʃʃʲ].

(ii) Pronunciation of жж

In addition to [ʃʃʲ], OM also has the voiced equivalent, long [ʒʲʒʲ].[8] This sound occurs where in spelling we have the group жж (as in жжёт 'it burns', вожжи 'reins', жужжать 'burble'), зж (as in визжишь 'you scream', брызжет 'it splashes', езжу 'I travel'), occasionally also жд (in дожди 'rains (noun, pl.)', pronounced [dʌˈʒʲʒʲi]; the nominative singular дождь is pronounced [doʃʃʲ] in OM). The sound [ʒʲʒʲ] occurs only within the morpheme; across a morpheme boundary or across a word boundary only long hard [ʒʒ] is possible, e.g. сжечь 'burn', с жаром 'with heat'.

The tendency over the twentieth century has been for this pronunciation with long palatalized [ʒʲʒʲ] to recede. In the case of дождь and other forms from the same stem, the spelling pronunciation [ʒdʲ] has prevailed, i.e. nominative singular [doʃtʲ], nominative plural [dʌˈʒdʲi]. Elsewhere, [ʒʲʒʲ] has been replaced by and large by the long hard fricative [ʒʒ]. In the survey reported in Barinova (1966: 50–1), there was in nearly all cases a majority for the hard pronunciation among younger

---

[8] In the Russian phonological tradition, this sound is represented as [ʒ´:].

speakers—the decrease in the frequency of [ʒʲʒʲ] correlating with lower age is quite spectacular. The process has been more rapid with less common words: this suggests that for those younger speakers that have [ʒʲʒʲ] at all, this pronunciation is a marked feature of the word, bolstered by hearing and using it frequently. With only two of the words tested, брызжет 'it splashes' and дрожжи 'yeast', was there a (slight) majority among younger speakers in Barinova's sample (born 1930–49) for the soft pronunciation. Avanesov (1984: 180) still recommends the soft pronunciation, which is also the pronunciation required on the stage, but admits that the hard pronunciation is admissible (допустимо)[9] and that it is replacing the soft pronunciation, which is becoming characteristic rather of OM. Younger speakers of CSR (those born in the 1950s and later) predominantly demonstrate the hard pronunciation (Kalenčuk 1993: 25), but the mass media are still promoting the soft pronunciation.

Panov (1990: 25–7) explains the decline of the soft pronunciation by system-internal factors, noting that the palatalization of [ʒ], as opposed to other palatalized consonants, is due to the lengthening of the sound; this correlation between lengthening and palatalization, otherwise rare in the Russian consonantal system and found elsewhere only in [ʃʲʃʲ], makes the feature relatively unstable. Next, as palatalization of ж occurs only within a morpheme, the frequency of the soft pronunciation is lower than, for example, of [ʃʲʃʲ], which can occur both morpheme-internally and across a boundary. The influence of the hard pronunciation, the only one possible over a morphological boundary, adds to the instability of the soft pronunciation and can explain its rapid decline.

The Pronunciation of г

In standard Russian, as in the northern and central dialects, the pronunciation of г is as a velar plosive [g]. In southern dialects of Russian and in Belarus, it is pronounced as a velar fricative, [ɣ], and in Ukraine it is pronounced as a voiced or murmured glottal fricative [ɦ]; the two fricative pronunciations are quite close and are in striking contrast to the

---

[9] The label допустимый, widely used in the orthoepic dictionary by Borunova *et al.* (1983), is assigned to those words that have several standard, correct, pronunciations, though one of the variants is considered best. It is notable that the use of this label increases in the 1970s and 1980s, which suggests that the standard language becomes more open to popular variants.

velar plosive pronunciation.[10] In standard Russian the fricative occurs through regular voice assimilation, e.g. он издох бы ['on iz'doɣ bɨ] 'he would die', in OM also by dissimilation of г in consonant clusters (see the section on consonant clusters in this chapter).

Although the pronunciation in standard Russian, whether OM or CSR, is with the plosive [g], fricative [ɣ] normatively occurs in OM in a few words that have Church Slavonic connotations: Бог 'God' ([box], with word-final devoicing), genitive singular Бога ['boɣa][11] (or ['boɦa]), господь 'Lord' and the common vocative господи, used as an interjection, благо 'blessing; grace' (the genitive plural is accordingly pronounced [blax]), and богатый 'rich', also derivatives of these, such as благодарить 'thank'. However, with the exception of Бог and Господи, the OM fricative has been replaced in CSR by the plosive. The replacement of the fricative by the plosive in Бога and in certain case forms of благо was noted already in the 1920s, by Polivanov ((1927) 1974: 181), who attributed this change to the decline in the influence of the Church and of the Church pronunciation in particular. According to Avanesov (1984: 238), the fricative pronunciation has been retained only partially, and then only in the speech of the older generation. This conclusion is borne out by the pronunciation of the Moscow students investigated by Superanskaja (1959: 160).

In these cases, the fricative pronunciation is now archaic, and is characterized as such by current dictionaries. To this general trend away from the fricative pronunciation there are a few exceptions. Even in CSR, Бог is pronounced [box],[12] although the oblique cases are now usually pronounced with the plosive [g] (Panov 1990: 28). The only domain where the fricative pronunciation is still alive and well is the interjections, which often have their own phonology, related to their expressive function. The greater tenacity of the fricative in interjections is probably connected with the 'expressive' use of the non-standard pronunciation [ɣ] noted by Reformatskij (1966), for instance in the interjection [ɣ]усь for (ну и) гусь, (хорош) гусь 'goose' used in

[10] In this respect, the usage of the Orthodox Church quite exceptionally follows the South Russian pronunciation; this is usually attributed to the influence of Ukrainian and Belorussian literary figures in seventeenth-century Moscow, such as Simeon Polockij and Epifanij Slavineckij (Uluxanov 1972: 67).

[11] This applies strictly only to the Christian God; other gods are often referred to by the same word with plosive [g] in OM and in CSR, particularly in the plural боги and invariably in the exclusively pagan feminine богиня 'goddess'.

[12] This is the only word from the list above for which the fricative pronunciation is indicated in Borunova *et al.* (1983).

disapproval or as an insult. In the interjection господи! the fricative pronunciation has proved more stable, although the plosive pronunciation is
also possible. Thus Avanesov and Ožegov (1959) identify the fricative
pronunciation as archaic in nearly all cases, but for господи!, though
recommending plosive [g], they say the fricative is permissible in
current usage. The expressive function of the non-standard pronunciation is also confirmed by the use of [ɣ] or [ɦ] in interjections, for
example, ого [oɦo] 'hey', ага [aɣa] 'sure, yeah; here you go', гоп [ɣop]
(also [ɦop] and [gop]) 'lo and behold' (Borunova *et al.* 1983: 669;
Panov 1990: 28, n. 14).

Another situation where the fricative pronunciation occurred, until
recently, is in the pronunciation of the preposition к 'to' before words in
г-, for example, к городу ['ɣgorədu] 'to the city'; in the speech of
younger representatives of CSR, born after 1950, it is being effectively
replaced by the combination [kg] (Panov 1990: 43). (See the discussion
of consonant clusters below, p. 40.)

The use of the fricative [ɦ] in standard Russian is rather different. It
is used in some interjections and onomatopoeic words, and in foreign
names (Avanesov 1984: 112, 210). In addition, it occurs in some loan-
words, mainly Western European loans, e.g. габитус 'habitus', бухгалтер [buˈɦaltjɪr] 'bookkeeper', where the [ɦ] pronunciation was more
or less *de rigueur* until the middle of the century. It was also the recommended pronunciation in another German loan-word, бюстгальтер
[bjuzˈɦaljtjɪr] 'brassiere', according to Avanesov and Ožegov (1959),
but no longer according to Borunova *et al.* (1983). In the survey carried
out by Glovinskaja (1971: 62), 38 people out of 41 pronounced [g] in
бюстгальтер, as opposed to only 10 out of 41 in бухгалтер. Panov
(1967: 333) considers бухгалтер the only word where this pronunciation is obligatory (a similar recommendation is given in Borunova *et al.*
(1983)) but he notes that this pronunciation is also on the decline (Panov
1990: 52).

Although this book is concerned mainly with the development of
standard Russian, it is worth digressing for a moment to consider the
pronunciation of г in South Russian (and similarly, Russian as spoken
in Belarus and Ukraine, whether by Russians or by Belorussians and
Ukrainians). The main point to notice is the surprising stability of the
fricative pronunciation despite the influence of the standard language.
Even in the speech of intellectuals from the South, fricative [ɣ] or [ɦ] is
often retained—indeed it is often the only southern dialect feature
retained in what is otherwise standard Russian. So tenacious is the frica-

tive pronunciation, at least in the speech of those that remain in the South, that Parikova (1966: 129–30) goes so far as to consider this one feature of a South Russian variant of the standard language. She goes on to say that 'complete command of the pronunciation of plosive г in the conditions of a South Great Russian linguistic environment is a happy exception, rather than a usual occurrence'. While continued residence is a potent factor in the retention of the fricative, it is by no means a necessary factor, since the fricative pronunciation is retained by many southerners who leave the area where the fricative is autochthonous. The whole question is discussed by Pen´kovskij (1967), who adopts a strongly normative position: southerners must be taught to use [g] correctly, the only problem is how. One of the problems he faces is that many southerners are unaware of or indifferent to the fact that their pronunciation differs from that of the standard. Pen´kovskij (p. 69) quotes the case of a Russian student from Vinnica (Ukraine) taking an examination in dialectology in Vladimir, who answered correctly that fricative [ɣ] characterizes southern dialects, then said that in her own speech she used only 'plosive [ɣ] [*sic!*] in accord with the literary norm'. In fact, she had usually used [ɣ], occasionally [g]. Moreover, it is not that southerners find physical difficulty in pronouncing the plosive sound: [g] occurs in their Russian speech in much the same situations as [ɣ] or [ɦ] in standard Russian, namely as a result of voice assimilation, in interjections and onomatopoeic words, and in loan-words. Southerners rarely carry over fricative [ɣ] to completely foreign languages: Pen´kovskij (p. 63) mentions a teacher from Mglin (Brjansk *oblast´*) whose Russian has only [ɣ], but whose English has only [g]. Many southerners who do make the attempt to adopt the standard pronunciation pronounce [g] perfectly in certain phonetic environments, but retain [ɣ] or [ɦ] (presumably unconsciously) elsewhere, especially between vowels. Clearly, the basic conclusion is that many people are not sufficiently aware of their own pronunciation to rid themselves of this regional feature, particularly in so far as the pressure to adopt plosive [g] is minimal or non-existent for most of them, especially if they remain in the South. Indeed southerners may even take a certain pride in their local [ɣ] (Kogotkova 1970: 122).

The difference between the status of *okan´e*, the most characteristic feature of northern dialects, and *ɣakan´e*, the most characteristic feature of southern dialects, is aptly summed up by B. V. Gornung (*Ответы на вопросник*. . . 1965: 212) who notes that, while *okan´e* has almost died out among speakers of the literary language, fricative г, on the other hand, shows greater stability and may even be spreading. However, among speakers of northern and central Russian and particularly speakers of the standard language, $\gamma akan'e$ is considered to be one of the most stigmatized features.

Consonant Clusters

The pronunciation of consonant groups in Russian involves a number of peculiarities, and here we are unable to go into all the details, particularly as a more detailed treatment of these problems is already available in English (Drage 1968: 355–73). We do wish, however, to draw attention briefly to some of the ways in which the pronunciation of consonant clusters differs between OM and CSR.

(i) г, к, ч before a plosive

In OM, г and к were regularly pronounced as fricatives ([ɣ] and [x] respectively) before plosives, as in тогда 'then', кто 'who', к кому 'to whom', pronounced [tʌɣ'da], [xto], [xkʌ'mu]. In the vast majority of words, this pronunciation is now archaic, and apart from the speech of the oldest Muscovites is non-standard (Avanesov 1984: 187). There are, however, a few exceptional words where the older fricative pronunciation is still required by the current standard, and is usual in practice (Drage 1968: 371), namely: the adjectives лёгкий 'light' and мягкий 'soft' and their derivatives, like легче 'lighter', смягчать 'to soften'. The plosive pronunciation here is considered non-standard. The masculine short-form adjectives лёгок and мягок are pronounced with [g], since the consonant is not before a plosive.

The pronunciation of что 'what' as [ʃto] is part of the same phenomenon—an affricate is pronounced as a fricative before the plosive [t]—and here the fricative pronunciation is the only one sanctioned by the standard language (Avanesov 1984: 186) in the nominative-accusative, although [tʃʃto] was sometimes heard and was considered correct in the pronunciation of older speakers from Leningrad.[13] Other forms of this pronoun have [tʃ], since there is no immediately following plosive, e.g. genitive чего. The derivative ничто 'nothing' allows both pronuncia-

---

[13] The loss of this feature is confirmed by the survey of 220 speakers from Leningrad and Moscow conducted in the 1970s–1980s, which revealed that the pronunciation [ʃto] had no exceptions (Verbickaja 1990: 15).

tions, [nʲiˈʃto] and [nʲiˈtʃʲto] (Avanesov 1984: 186). The group чт is pronounced as written in other words.

(ii) Pronunciation of чн

In earlier periods of the language for which we have evidence, in Moscow the group чн in non-learned words was pronounced [ʃn], and was in fact often spelt шн. This is evidenced, for example, by the children's rhyme from the early twentieth century каша-яша, from ячневая каша 'barley porridge', quoted by A. A. Reformatskij (b. 1900) (Panov 1990: 46): such rhyming was possible only given the pronunciation я[шн]евая. In the vast majority of these words this pronunciation has now been replaced by [tʃn]. Among the few words where the fricative pronunciation is still required (Borunova *et al.* 1983: 676), are конечно 'of course' (though not the etymologically related adjective конечный 'final, finite' and its derivatives), скучно 'boring', яичница 'fried eggs, omelette', пустяшный/пустячный 'immaterial', прачечная 'laundry, wash-house', скворечник 'bird-feeder', and women's patronymics in -инична, e.g. Ильинична.[14] In addition, there are some words where the older pronunciation is still permissible (Shapiro 1968: 30), hence doublets in the pronunciation of булочная 'bakery', молочник 'creamer'. In a number of words the [ʃn] pronunciation is considered obsolete, for example, коричневый 'brown', гречневый 'buckwheat'. Even for some of the words where the older pronunciation is still required by orthoepists, the younger generation, according to the results of the survey by Superanskaja (1959: 159), sometimes shows a preference for the other pronunciation. Another important indication of the decline of the pronunciation [ʃn] is the obligatory [tʃn] pronunciation in new formations, for example, съёмочный 'related to film-making' (Borunova *et al.* 1983: 676). The rise of the [tʃn] pronunciation seems to have two explanations, namely, the influence of the OPb pronunciation, where [tʃn] always dominated (Košutić 1919: 75; Panov 1967: 301), and the influence of spelling on pronunciation. Throughout this chapter, several instances are noted where pronunciation becomes closer to spelling, and this latter explanation seems more consistent with the general tendency in CSR pronunciation.

---

[14] Older speakers from Leningrad maintain [tʃn] in these words, too (see section (i)).

(iii) Loss of consonants in clusters

All styles of modern Russian have at least a tendency to drop certain consonants in consonant clusters, although OM and CSR differ in the specifics of syncopated clusters. Thus Avanesov (1984: 190) considers the pronunciation of поездка 'trip, journey' as [pʌˈjeskə] to be either OM, or colloquial, while as the current standard he recommends [pʌˈjestkə].

A few words show the reverse tendency: thus, while the current standard prescribes the pronunciation of бездна 'abyss' as [ˈbʲeznə] or [ˈbʲezᵈnə], OM had it as [ˈbʲezdnə] and this pronunciation is still retained by older speakers of CSR (Panov 1990: 32). And according to Panov (1990: 33), the absence of [tʲ] in the pronunciation of счастливый 'happy' has become lexicalized by speakers of CSR born after 1950.

In practice, several other factors intervene: for instance, consonants are more likely to be dropped in familiar words than in rare, learned words, and of course are more likely to be dropped in rapid than slow, careful speech. Further details are given by Ganiev (1966), Drage (1968: 372–3), Avanesov (1984: 187–93), Flier (1990), Kalenčuk (1993: 22–3).

(iv) Palatalization assimilation

In combinations of consonants of which the last is soft (palatalized), earlier consonants in the group were often palatalized by regressive assimilation, for example, сестра [sʲieˈstra] 'sister' (nominative) but сестре [sʲieˈsʲtʲrʲe] 'to sister' (dative). Numerous instances of such palatalization assimilation were attested, primarily for OM, by Košutić (1919: 157–8) and Grot (1899: 222, 241–3). Palatalization assimilation was not typical of OPb and of the subsequent Leningrad pronunciation norm, and Panov attributes the overall decline of this phenomenon in CSR to the spread of Leningrad pronunciation (Panov 1990: 54). This, however, is an unlikely interpretation given the general decline of the variant features of the Leningrad norm.

The rules determining whether or not assimilation may or must take place are complex, depending basically on the place and manner of articulation of the consonants involved, but also partly on morphological position, stress, and morphological parallelism (Drage 1967a: 142), also on the individual word in certain cases. Assimilation is also more likely in rapid speech, and informants tend to over-report non-assimilation. Recommendations as to the standard are given by Avanesov (1956:

170–1, 174–82; Avanesov 1984: 145–68; Panov 1967: 91–100, 324–7), though many of the generalizations are called into question by the results of the survey reported by Drage (1967*a*) and by the new observations briefly surveyed in Panov (1990: 31–44). Overall, there has been a tendency for palatalization assimilation to decrease during the present century, so that many assimilations that are normal in OM are not part of the CSR standard. Fuller details are given by Drage (1967*b*), who compares the pronunciation of his readers with descriptions of Russian pronunciation in the late nineteenth and early twentieth centuries; the data are summarized according to the consonant groups involved, some of the more striking changes being as follows (in each case, the consonant in italics is normally soft in OM, and is hard for the majority of Drage's informants): dental plosives before labials, e.g. за*т*мение 'eclipse', *Д*митрий, *т*вердый 'hard', ме*д*ведь 'bear' (but, exceptionally, the д of две 'two (feminine)' is still soft for the majority of informants, 14 out of 17); p before labials, e.g. ско*р*бь 'grief'; p before dentals, e.g. че*р*ти 'devils'; labial fricatives before velars, e.g. де*в*ки 'girls'.[15] The Academy Grammar (*Русская грамматика* 1980, i.: 44) lists a number of biconsonantal clusters, which allow soft or hard pronunciation, indicating that in all instances the absence of palatalization assimilation is consistent with the modern standard and the palatalized variant is characteristic of OM pronunciation; for example: *т*мин 'caraway seed', с*м*ена 'shift', з*м*ея 'snake', ве*т*ви 'branches' (nominative plural), на*с*ледие 'heritage', з*л*иться 'to be angry', ко*н*сервы 'canned foods'. Palatalization remains obligatory in пе*н*сия 'pension' (*Русская грамматика* 1980: i. 44).

The pronunciation of words in -изм such as социализм 'socialism', коммунизм 'communism', импрессионизм 'Impressionism', merits special attention. The OM norm required that з be palatalized before м in the prepositional case (e.g. при социализме); otherwise, both consonants remained hard. It is likely that non-standard speakers of Russian, acquiring a number of the words in -изм that penetrated the language in the beginning of this century (Seliščev 1928: 182), hypercorrectly generalized the palatalized pronunciation over the entire paradigm, which resulted in the non-standard pronunciation коммунизьм(ь) [zʲmⁱ⁽ʲ⁾], etc. The spread of this pronunciation forced normative handbooks specifically to condemn it as a serious mistake (for example, Avanesov 1984: 149); it is probably in an attempt to attain

---

[15] In combinations including л before a soft consonant, л invariably remains hard, for example, о молве 'about rumours'.

uniformity of the paradigm that palatalization assimilation was declared non-standard in the prepositional case of words in -изм as well as elsewhere in borrowings: thus, Avanesov (1984: 148–9) warns against the palatalized pronunciation of кадмий 'cadmium', о дарвинизме 'about Darwinism'. However, for a significant period in the history of the Soviet Union, the palatalized pronunciation of -изм served as a sign of solidarity among the party élite, which led to an unusual case of intertwining of politics and pronunciation. The trend was probably started by Stalin, hardly a bearer of standard Russian, of whom F. Burlackij writes: 'I fail to understand why he so stubbornly pronounced коммунизьм with a soft з . . . I am a hundred per cent sure that he did this on purpose, creating a certain standard, to be followed by all the initiated . . . One after another, all the members of his inner circle, including those with university education, leaned towards that pronunciation. This jargon was a sort of key to the room at the top, into the narrow circle of people closely knit to one another both by shared activities and also by shared cultural background' (quoted by Panov (1990: 18)).[16]

Other than when politically motivated, instances of an increase in the soft pronunciation are quite exceptional,[17] and the overall tendency in CSR is towards the elimination of palatalization assimilation. Palatalization assimilation is still the rule, without exceptions, in the pronunciation of н before ч and before щ, for example, бараба́нчик 'little drum', бараба́нщик 'drummer'. Panov (1990: 37) explains the tenacity of this palatalization by its interaction with morphophonemics: the occurrence of н before ч or щ is typically across a morphological boundary, which prevents the loss of palatalization, although he does not explain why a boundary should have this effect.

Other combinations where palatalization assimilation is still very much alive include: dental before soft dental (шесть 'six', коснись

[16] Stalin's accent, a research question in its own right, was most likely a combination of spontaneous Georgian accent and some deliberate mannerisms, possibly including the pronunciation -зьм. The soft pronunciation of з was expectably apparent in the speech of N. S. Xruščev, who was a speaker of southern Russian and Ukrainian. A popular joke of the 1960s was that Xruščev's contribution to Marxism consisted of the soft sign (марксизьм).

[17] Exceptionally, Drage (1967b: 202) reports that his informants pronounced soft ж and ш in прежде 'before' (the soft pronunciation was that of the majority of the informants, 16: 1) and здешний 'local', although ш and ж are normally said to be invariably hard in native words (Avanesov 1984: 162). There might be some interfering factors in Drage's study, because a survey of ten educated speakers of CSR, from Moscow, Leningrad, and Riga, done by one of the authors of this book, did not reveal a single instance of the soft pronunciation of these words. The overall tendency in the second half of the twentieth century has been towards hard pronunciation.

'touch');[18] labial before soft labial (*вместе* 'together'). However, in these cases, the new pronunciation without palatalization assimilation is on the rise: speakers of CSR born after 1950 pronounce вакансия 'vacancy', если 'if', о после 'about ambassador', надменный 'arrogant', о любви 'about love' without palatalization (Panov 1990: 36–8; see also Avanesov 1984: 241–2). Some authors consider palatalization assimilation in the combination dental before a soft dental more acceptable than in the combination dental before a soft labial: thus, Verbickaja (1990: 9–10, 15) indicates that in the pronunciation of степь the variants with or without palatalization assimilation are equally acceptable, while in the pronunciation of дверь the variant without assimilation is to be preferred. (The prevalence of this latter pronunciation is consistent with the OPb pronunciation.) Two other factors affecting palatalization assimilation in various types of clusters are the position of the cluster in the word and the consistency of the cluster in the paradigm. The loss of palatalization assimilation is more pronounced in word-initial clusters, cf. [svʲ]инья 'pig' and на[sʲvʲ]инячить 'to make a mess; to make a pigsty of one's location' (Kalenčuk 1993: 20). Next, those words whose paradigm includes forms with a hard consonant lose palatalization assimilation faster, cf. бо[mb]a, бо[mbʲ]e 'bomb' but бо[mʲbʲ]ежка 'bombardment' (Kalenčuk 1993: 20–1).

Overall, inconsistencies in the occurrence of palatalized and non-palatalized consonants in various combinations of two or more consonants indicate that this particular change is still incomplete.

The Reflexive Particle

In OM the reflexive particle, though written -ся or -сь, is pronounced with hard [s], with one rather strange exception: end-stressed gerunds have obligatorily soft [sʲ], e.g. боясь [bʌˈjasʲ] 'fearing', but собираясь [səbʲiˈrajəs] 'intending; gathering'. In current usage, the palatalized pronunciation of the reflexive particle is widespread, and where the particle occurs after a vowel this is by far the most prevalent pronunciation in contemporary educated usage; cf. the results reported by Superanskaja (1959: 159) from her survey of Moscow students. The older pronuncia-

---

[18] All Drage's informants had soft [sʲ] before soft labials in *свет* 'light', *смерть* 'death', *спина* 'back' (1967*b*: 200–2). According to the Academy Grammar, the soft pronunciation of [s] and [z] is obligatory before a soft dental, for example, *степь* 'steppe', *здесь* 'here' (*Русская грамматика* 1980: i. 44).

tion was retained by the majority of theatres until the 1970s. Indeed, Panov (1967: 322) notes that some actors, in trying to maintain OM here, overdo it by pronouncing forms like боясь with hard [s].

After consonants the pronunciation of the reflexive particle in current usage is more complex, and the best approach is to summarize the recommendations of Avanesov (1984: 205–8) and Borunova *et al.* (1983: 678–9), which give an indication of the general tendencies (see Table 1.1). Where the dictionaries recommend only the soft pronunciation, the hard pronunciation was still possible in OM, and was required on the stage until the early 1980s.

The tendency towards uniformly soft pronunciation becomes quite clear if we compare the recommendations by Avanesov (1972: 163–5, summarized in Comrie and Stone 1978: 37) and the recommendations summarized above (as is done in Table 1.1): wherever the earlier recommendation was for the hard or preferably hard pronunciation (e.g. in the imperative in a hard consonant, in the past tense), modern usage has eliminated this pronunciation in favour of the soft one (with the exception of third-person forms and infinitival forms in -ться).

Adjectives in -гий, -кий, -хий

Since end-stressed adjectives with a stem-final velar have -[oj] in the masculine singular nominative long form, e.g. дорогой 'dear', морской 'marine', плохой 'bad', one would expect such adjectives with stem-stress to end in -[əj], and this was, predictably, the pronunciation in Russian dialects characterized by *akan´e*, and was then maintained in the OM standard, despite the spelling in -ий, e.g. строгий 'strict', звонкий 'sonorous', тихий 'quiet'; the endings of these adjectives as well as their spelling are in fact taken from Church Slavonic. Rhymes with this pronunciation were the norm in the nineteenth century, as in the following well-known stanza from Lermontov's *Парус* (1832), where the spelling одинокой is sometimes used to ensure the correct pronunciation:

> Белеет парус одинокий
> В тумане моря голубом!..
> Что ищет он в стране далекой?
> Что кинул он в краю родном?..
>
> A single white sail
> Appears in the blue haze of the sea.

TABLE 1.1. *Pronunciation of the reflexive particle after a consonant*

Part of speech	Pronunciation recommendations of Avanesov (1972)	Pronunciation recommendations of Avanesov (1984), Borunova et al. (1983)	Examples
Participle	Soft	Soft	оставшихся
Imperative			
in a soft consonant	Soft	Soft	двиньcя, заботься
in a hard consonant	Preferably hard	Soft[a]	утешься
Past tense			
in с, з	Hard	Either	нёсся, грызся
in other consonants	Preferably hard	Soft[a]	ушибся, боялся
Present tense			
in шь	Preferably hard	Soft	видишься
in м	Either	Soft	беремся
in т	Hard	Hard[b]	несется, кладутся
Infinitive			
in чь	Preferably hard	Soft	стричься
in ть	Hard	Hard[b]	учиться

[a] Although he acknowledged the soft pronunciation, Avanesov (1984: 206) still recommended the hard pronunciation as the preferable one here.

[b] In infinitives (but not imperatives) in -ть, and in present-tense forms in -т, the final т, whether hard or soft in the non-reflexive form, combines with the reflexive particle to give -[ttsə], i.e. an affricate with a long stop component.

What does it seek in a far land?
What has it left in its native land?

Likewise, in Puškin's *Памятник*, the dative singular feminine великой 'great' rhymes with the masculine nominative дикий 'wild' (CSR pronunciation ['dʲikʲij]).

The pronunciation with final -[gʲij], -[kʲij], -[xʲij] was considered non-standard and even vulgar; in the following excerpt from Lermontov's *Сашка* (*c*. 1836) the two pronunciations, the standard голландской -[kəj] 'Dutch (of cheese)' and the non-standard варяжский -[kʲij] 'Varangian' were put together against the normal expectation, according to which a shield should be described in an elevated style and cheese, more likely, in a lower style.[19] This contradiction of styles, rendered through pronunciation variants, creates a humorous effect (Lermontov is apparently mocking romantic poetry here):

> Луна катится в зимних облаках,
> Как щит варяжский или сыр голландской.

> The moon is rolling in winter clouds
> Like a Varangian shield or a Dutch cheese.

The pronunciation with final -[gʲij], -[kʲij], -[xʲij] existed in spoken Russian for a long time, parallel to the learned pronunciation in -[əj]. By the end of the nineteenth century, the pronunciation with final -[gʲij], -[kʲij], -[xʲij] had left the domain of *prostorečie* and started being associated with OPb; thus, Košutić (1919: 83–4) notes the -[gʲij], etc., pronunciation in St Petersburg, but considers it still non-standard.

In the first edition of Avanesov's handbook on standard pronunciation, published in 1950, only the older pronunciation -[əj] was considered correct. However, by 1961 the same author (Avanesov 1961: 10) acknowledged that the spelling pronunciation, i.e. ['strogʲij], ['zvonkʲij], ['tʲixʲij], was more widespread. In this we do, incidentally, seem to be dealing unambiguously with a spelling pronunciation, since on the basis of morphological parallelism we would expect the OM pronunciation: the oblique forms of these adjectives unambiguously include [ə], for example, genitive singular masculine тихого ['tʲixəvə]. In subsequent editions (Avanesov 1972: 155; 1984: 194–7), the newer pronunciation is the one recommended for most purposes. The OM pronunciation is still recommended for the stage, and is insisted on by many theatres; otherwise, unless it is used as a deliberate archaism, the older pronunciation

---

[19] The difference in spelling, often forgone by later editions, ensured that the reader would be aware of this stylistic conflict.

is considered by Avanesov to be either high style, or non-standard (it is the usual pronunciation in dialects, without spelling influence). It is interesting to observe that, as the newer pronunciation has spread in the 'middle', neutral style, the older pronunciation has come to characterize equally deliberately elevated and non-standard speech (Avanesov 1984: 197).

When the pronunciation of these adjectives was tested by Superanskaja (1959: 159), the overwhelming majority of informants preferred the newer forms. This test suffered from the disadvantage that those asked were aware of the purpose of the enquiry, and were therefore on their guard against giving pronunciations they considered incorrect, even if these were their normal pronunciations. A rather different experiment is reported by Andreev (1963): the data here were obtained by asking passers-by of various age and social groups for the names of railway stations (e.g. Ленинградский вокзал), bridges (e.g. Кировский мост), streets (e.g. Ленинский проспект) in Moscow and Leningrad. Those asked were not told that the investigator was interested in pronunciation. Of 2,280 subjects (1,378 in Moscow, 902 in Leningrad), only 3, in Moscow, used the pronunciation in -[kəj], the three being a woman guard (сторожиха) in her late fifties, a nun (*sic*!) in her eighties, and a 'famous linguist of the older generation'. When subsequently asked specifically about the pronunciation of these adjectives, only six informants insisted that the older pronunciation was the only correct one, although five of these used the -[kʲij] pronunciation regularly in ordinary conversation; the sixth, perhaps not surprisingly, was the aforementioned linguist.

A similar change has taken place in the pronunciation of verbs in -ивать after a velar consonant, e.g. натягивать 'stretch', помахивать 'wave', помалкивать 'keep quiet'. In OM these are pronounced with hard velars: [nʌ'tʲagəvətʲ], etc.[20] Nowadays the usual pronunciation follows the spelling (Superanskaja 1959: 159).

Reduction of Post-Tonic i/ɨ

One recent tendency which is becoming apparent in the speech of those born after 1950 is the increasing reduction of [i/ɨ] in post-tonic position, except in open final syllables, as in самова́ры 'samovars', where this

---

[20] No difference is usually made in pronunciation between the unstressed verbal endings -ывать and -овать, both pronounced -[əvətʲ] (Avanesov 1984: 165).

sound is still well preserved (Avanesov 1984: 194–7; Panov 1990: 49).
As a result, a new pronunciation of unstressed adjectival endings is
emerging, which is intermediate between the OM pronunciation in -[əj]
and the -[ij] pronunciation that was standard for the most part of this
century (see the preceding section); this new pronunciation is eliminating the number of pronunciation variants in post-tonic position.

The reduction of post-tonic [i/ɨ] is affecting a number of paradigms in
CSR. One example where this reduction leads to paradigm levelling and
increasing homonymy is in the pronunciation of the masculine nominative singular and feminine oblique singular adjectives. The orthographic
difference between masculine nominative singular трудный 'difficult',
синий 'blue', and feminine oblique singular трудной, синей, is due to
spelling conventions borrowed from Church Slavonic. While older
speakers of CSR distinguish them in pronunciation (-[ɨj] versus -[əj],
-[ij] versus -[ɪj]), most younger speakers have no distinction, often with
-[əj]/-[ɨj] and -[ɪj]/-[ij] and intermediate pronunciations in free variation.
Thus, in the line by Alexander Blok:

> и нежный—нежной жал он руку
>
> and he, tender, was pressing the hand of tender her . . .

the distinction between the two adjectival forms is increasingly hard to
perceive (Panov 1990: 11, 50); a special emphatic pronunciation is
required to underscore the difference in gender and case.

From the diachronic point of view, this latest change is particularly
notable in adjectives, as it completes a historical circle: first, the [ə]
pronunciation was replaced by the [ɨ] pronunciation and now this latter
pronunciation is evolving back into [ə] again.

The reduction of [ɨ] under way involves both verbs and nouns; thus,
выжил 'survived' and выжал 'squeezed' are no longer distinguished in
the pronunciation of younger speakers of CSR since they are both pronounced with -[əl] (Panov 1990: 49; Kalenčuk 1993: 10).

Some other instances of the [ə]/[ɨ] variation will be discussed below,
in the section on unstressed a, o after soft consonants.

Pretonic жа, ша, ца, же, ше, це

Normally, immediately pretonic a after a hard consonant is pronounced
[ʌ], as in вода 'water'; after a soft consonant it is pronounced [iᵉ], e.g.
гляди 'look'. In OM, after ц, ш, and ж, which are always hard, imme-

diately pretonic a was pronounced not [ʌ] but [ɨᵉ], i.e. the retracted equivalent of [iᵉ],[21] e.g. жара 'heat', шаги 'steps', шары 'balloons', двадцати 'twenty' (oblique form).[22]

In current usage, this pronunciation is, for most words, archaic. The usual pronunciation of such words is with [ʌ], corresponding both to the spelling, and to the general rule for pronouncing unstressed a after a hard consonant, for example, ржаветь 'rust' [rʒʌ'vʲetʲ] (Superanskaja 1959: 160; Avanesov 1984: 243; Panov 1990: 44–50). Significantly, in such cases the older standard is no longer insisted on even on the stage, except as a deliberate stylistic effect in the speech of certain characters. I. P. Kozljaninova, an elocutionist at the Moscow Theatrical Institute, writes in *Современное сценическое произношение* (1967: 44) that even on the stage the older pronunciation [ɨᵉ] is now definitely considered archaic.

Although the change in pronunciation noted above has taken place for most words, there are still a few that resist. Thus Avanesov (1984: 93–4) considers the [ɨᵉ] pronunciation correct for жалеть 'pity' and related words, including к сожалению 'unfortunately', and for жакет 'ladies' jacket', жасмин 'jasmine', жавель 'liquid bleach', бешамель 'Bechamel sauce', end-stressed forms of лошадь 'horse', e.g. genitive plural лошадей, and oblique forms of the words двадцать 'twenty', тридцать 'thirty' (see also Borunova *et al.* 1983: 663).[23] The results of Superanskaja's survey (1959: 160) indicated that this was reflected in the current pronunciation, since a large number of informants (for some words, the majority) had [ɨᵉ] in such words, despite having [ʌ] usually. This illustrates an important principle of linguistic change: it is not always the case that all words containing a given sound change at precisely the same rate: often the behaviour of individual words is idiosyncratic. The figures quoted in Panov (1968: iv. 35–6) suggest that, whereas the [ɨᵉ] pronunciation is on the decrease for the majority of words, it is on the increase for some, especially those noted in this paragraph. It is worthy of note, however, that younger speakers, born after

---

[21] In Old Russian, ж, ш and ц were soft (Kiparsky 1979: 125–6).

[22] According to Avanesov (1984: 93), D. N. Ušakov (1873–1942), whose speech was consistent in representing OM norms, pronounced his own name [uʃʌ'kof]. Meanwhile, other names in OM pronunciation still had [ɨ] or [ɨᵉ], for example, Шаляпин (Avanesov 1984: 93).

[23] We may also note here that in forms of the verb целовать 'kiss' where the це- is the immediately pretonic syllable, in OM the usual pronunciation was [tsʌ]-, i.e. [tsʌ'luju] (the first person present tense form was occasionally even written цалую), for CSR [tsɨᵉ'luju] (Avanesov 1984: 95; Krysin 1974: 110–11).

1960, pronounce more words with [ʌ] than the consultants in the RJaSO survey: thus, in the pronunciation of жасми́н, [ʌ] and [ɨᵉ] vary (Panov 1990: 45), and such words as жара́ 'heat', вожака́ 'leader (genitive or accusative)', шала́ш 'hut', шабло́н 'template, stencil' are invariably pronounced with [ʌ] (Kalenčuk 1993: 10).

Though few statistics on variation of [ʌ] and [ɨᵉ] in the pronunciation of younger CSR speakers are available, it is our impression that the [ɨᵉ] pronunciation is better retained in non-initial syllables. Thus, in observing two young Moscow speakers, one born in 1976, the other in 1980, we noticed that they consistently used [ʌ] in жале́ть but had 12 [ɨᵉ] pronunciations out of 16 occurrences of к сожале́нию; in oblique forms of the -дцать numerals, too, the [ɨᵉ] pronunciation was predominant (14 instances out of 22).

The quality of the sound occurring in the words that resist the [ʌ] pronunciation, also, differs in the standard of the first and second half of this century; while older speakers retain [ɨᵉ], younger speakers often pronounce the same sound as [eⁱ], thus, сожа[eⁱ]ление 'regret'. Ironically, this brings the norm of the late twentieth century back to the OM norm, where the pretonic sound was less narrow and resembled [e] more than [i]; this pronunciation, known as *ekan´e*, is retained in the theatre (Avanesov 1984: 97), though, interestingly, it is losing ground there (Panov 1990: 48).

Loan-words with pretonic шо, жо are normally pronounced with [ʌ], for example, шофер [ʃʌˈfʲor] 'driver', жокей [ʒʌˈkʲej] 'jockey' (Avanesov 1984: 92), and the data in Kalenčuk (1993: 10) indicate that this pronunciation has become the absolute standard for younger speakers. Although Avanesov recommends not reducing o in the foreign names in шо, жо, for example, Ж[о]ре́с or Ш[о]пе́н, this recommendation is commonly violated, even by modern TV announcers.

In native Russian words, pretonic ше, же, це were invariably pronounced earlier with the [ɨᵉ] sound, for example, жена́ 'wife', шепта́ть 'whisper', цена́ 'price', танцева́ть 'dance'. In the second half of the twentieth century, the pronunciation of [ɨᵉ] started shifting towards [eⁱ]; however, this change is by no means complete (Panov 1990: 92).

Overall, the changes in the pronunciation of pretonic a, o, e after ш, ж, ц result in an increase in vocalic variants: instead of using one sound, [ɨᵉ], indiscriminately, CSR starts distinguishing between this sound (and its successors, [eⁱ]) and [ʌ]). This new pronunciation is largely determined by the spelling: while [ɨᵉ] is retained in words spelled with e or o, words that have a in spelling develop the pronunciation [ʌ]; some words in ша, жа that retain the older pronunciation will either remain in the language as lexicalized exceptions or gradually develop the pronunciation [ʌ] by analogy.

Ikan´e

In a phonological system which has *ikan´e*, only two vowels can occur in the first pretonic position after soft consonants: the unrounded [iᵉ] and the rounded [u], as shown by the pronunciation of the following infinitival forms:

любить [lʲuˈbʲitʲ] 'love' as opposed to: делить [dʲieˈlʲitʲ] 'divide' (cf. the stressed e in делит [ˈdʲelʲit])

трясти [trʲieˈsʲtʲi] 'shake' (cf. the stressed a in тряс [trʲas])

нести [nʲiesʲtʲi] 'carry' (cf. the stressed o in нёс [nʲos])

чинить [tʃʲieˈnʲitʲ] 'repair' (cf. the stressed и in чинит [ˈtʃʲinʲit])

In syllables other than the first pretonic, *ikan´e* occurs as early as the fourteenth century (Kiparsky 1979: 70); by contrast, the establishment of *ikan´e* in the first pretonic syllable is a fairly recent phenomenon, which became apparent only at the turn of this century. The rise of this type of *ikan´e* was recognized by D. N. Ušakov and Durnovo, both in their own idiolects and in the standard language (Panov 1990: 134). Their pronunciation was opposed to the pronunciation of the nineteenth century, where OM distinguished, in the pretonic syllable, three vowels: [u], [i], and the vowel intermediate between [e] and [i]. Thus, in this older pronunciation, the verb чинить differed from делить, трясти, нести in having [i] in the first syllable.

At the beginning of the twentieth century, *ikan´e* was still associated with urban *prostorečie* and was considered non-standard. However, it was clearly adhered to, even by highly educated speakers; not only D. N. Ušakov and N. N. Durnovo (see, for example, Durnovo and Ušakov 1927) but also N. S. Trubeckoj, whose consonantal system was fairly conservative, in full agreement with OM, consistently used *ikan´e* (Trubetzkoy 1934 (1987)). That *ikan´e* took its toll on pronunciation variants becomes clear from the co-occurrence of different spellings in the early normative dictionaries: thus, D. N. Ušakov (1934–40) gives снеток, сняток, сниток 'sparling' (in modern spelling, only снеток is acceptable); *SSRLJa* (1948–65) gives вязига and визига (modern визига) 'dried spinal cord of cartilagenous fish', and the second edition of this dictionary (*SSRLJa* 1991–) gives визига as standard and вязига as archaic (see also Gorbačevič 1978: 21).[24]

Avanesov (1972: 66–8) still gives as the basic variant of the standard language a form of what may be described as moderate *ikan'e*, where unstressed e and a after a soft consonant are pronounced as a sound between stressed e and и, symbolized [i^e] (immediately pretonic), or [ı] (elsewhere), while unstressed и is pronounced [i]. He notes, however, that in rapid speech e/a and и are often not distinguished, since unstressed и tends to be lowered slightly, i.e. approaches [e], while unstressed e is raised towards [i], with the possibility of them meeting in the middle. Avanesov criticizes strong *ikan'e*, i.e. the pronunciation where unstressed e/a is pronounced identical to stressed и; however, he recommends a variety of moderate *ikan'e*, especially in slow, careful speech, i.e. distinguishing пре[e^i]да́ть 'betray' and при[i^e]да́ть 'impart', ле[e^i]са́ 'forests' and ли[i^e]са́ 'fox', ча[ə]стота́ 'frequency' and чи[i^e]стота́ 'cleanliness'.[25] The acceptance of moderate *ikan'e* as the orthoepic norm (acknowledged, if somewhat vaguely, in Avanesov 1984: 95–8) also resulted in the spread of pretonic retracted [i̵^{e}] discussed in the preceding section. The growing prevalence of moderate *ikan'e* in the 1970s–1980s is demonstrated in Verbickaja (1990: 13).

The overall assessment of *ikan'e* still remains problematic, primarily because of unclear phonetic values of the sounds pronounced under *ikan'e*: it seems that the [i^e] sound characteristic of *ikan'e* proper alternates, even within one idiolect, with a more open [e^i]; accordingly, the retracted variant [i̵^{e}] can be more open as well (see also *Русская грамматика* 1980: i. 25–7). (Undoubtedly, spelling has a certain effect

[24] Note that the older form was вязига, invariably; this form is cited, for example, in *Словарь русского языка XI–XVII веков* (1975–).

[25] The overall discussion of *ikan'e* is not helped, incidentally, by some confusion in the use of the terms *ikan'e* and *ekan'e*, as noted by Thelin (1971: 68–81), who discusses the range of variants in greater detail. While it is occasionally maintained that the older standard is with *ikan'e*, now being replaced by *ekan'e* (e.g. Gvozdev 1958: 69, and other references cited by Panov 1967: 305), the discussion by Panov (1967: 301–8) and the statistical data given in Panov (1968: iv. 22–30) demonstrate that the tendency by the middle of the century was towards *ikan'e*, replacing the older pronunciation with *ekan'e*. It is worthy of note that the latest Academy Grammar (*Русская грамматика* 1980: i. 24–9) does not mention *ikan'e* or *ekan'e* in the discussion of phonetic variants.

on pronunciation, and words spelled with e in the pretonic position are more likely to be pronounced with the more open sound than those spelled with и.) The situation gets even more complicated if other pretonic syllables than first are included, because the reduction is stronger in those syllables (*Русская грамматика* 1980: i. 26–7). The problem is further complicated by the fact that *ekan´e* has been retained in emphatic, expressive pronunciation (Panov 1990: 80; Kalenčuk 1993: 7–9). If anything, it is unrealistic to expect strong *ikan´e* to establish itself as a standard pronunciation feature; as to moderate *ikan´e* and moderate *ekan´e*, these are likely to form a pronunciation continuum, where individual phonetic realizations are affected by speech register, spelling, and probably individual characteristics of the speaker.

Unstressed Endings

In general, the rules of Russian that specify the pronunciation of unstressed vowels operate irrespective of morphological or other grammatical criteria. With certain inflections, however, this regularity is not maintained, especially in the case of unstressed a and o after soft consonants, the precise nature of irregularities differing somewhat between OM and CSR. Since only inflectional endings are involved, there is clearly some interference from morphological factors, and we shall see below that the pronunciation of these endings is in fact conditioned by additional morphological criteria, especially in OM.

(i) Second conjugation verb forms in unstressed -ят, -ящий

The clearest such difference between OM and CSR concerns the pronunciation of the unstressed ending of third-person plural present verbs of the second conjugation, e.g. хо́дят 'they go'. Where this ending is stressed, as in сидя́т 'they sit', OM and CSR agree in having [sʲiˈdʲat]; хо́дят, however, is pronounced [ˈxodʲut] in OM (Košutić 1919: 93), with the first conjugation ending, whereas CSR has [ˈxodʲət]. The same applies to present participles active, e.g. сидя́щий 'sitting' with [a] in both OM and CSR, but стро́ящий 'building' with [u] in OM and [ɪ]/[ə] in CSR.

As late as the mid-1930s, D. N. Ušakov (1935–40: vol. i, p. xxxiv) admitted only the OM pronunciation of such verbal forms. But by the late 1940s, Avanesov (1947a: 5) noted that the new form [ˈxodʲət] was

more widespread, and from its first edition (1950), his *Русское
литературное произношение* calls the OM forms archaic, while the
CSR forms are recommended as the current orthoepic standard. The
older form is now used for deliberate stylistic effect, as when Ju.
Kazakov (quoted in Gorbačevič 1971: 96) has one of his characters say:
у вас там, в Москве, небось босиком не ходют 'in Moscow, where
you live, I don't suppose people go round barefoot'; the spelling ходют
indicates that the author is contrasting this with the standard pronunciation. At present, the pronunciation in -[ut] is still to be met from older
Muscovites. Elsewhere, Avanesov (1972: 159–60; 1984: 200–3) now
considers it non-standard; it occurs more often with verbs that are
themselves non-standard or colloquial, and is more likely with the
third-person plural than with the participle (which is in any case a more
literary form).

Many Russian dialects have a distribution of -[ut] and -[at]/-[ət]
which does not correspond to that of the written language, i.e. to the
difference between first and second conjugations, especially when the
endings are unstressed (Bromlej 1973). Forms like ['xodʲut] are
common in the dialects of the Moscow area, as is the inverse phenomenon, stem-stressed first conjugation forms like ['platʃət] for плачут
'they weep'. The latter forms are not infrequently to be heard from educated Muscovites (Panov 1968: iii. 142); in the RJaSO survey, 32 per
cent of informants gave the non-orthoepic pronunciation for борются
'they fight'.

(ii) Feminine accusative singular adjectives

In OM, particularly in rapid speech, the unstressed feminine accusative
singular adjective ending was often pronounced -[əju]/-[ɪju], e.g.
дóбрую ['dobrəju] 'good', си́нюю ['sʲinʲɪju] 'blue' (Košutić 1919: 100).
Avanesov (1984: 199–200) specifically warns against this pronunciation, and insists on ['dobruju], ['sʲinʲuju] in CSR. He does not mention
the possibility of the other pronunciation in OM, and considers this pronunciation to be a dialect feature among standard Russian speakers.

(iii) Unstressed a, o after soft consonants

The data for other unstressed endings, with the vowels a and o after soft
consonants, are taken for the most part from Kuz´mina (1966), who
gives the results of a reading test using 100 Moscow students aged from

18 to 27 (all born in Moscow, with parents also born in Moscow), showing how many used [ə] and how many [ɪ] in individual forms. The forms to be tested were given sentence-finally, phrase-finally (but not sentence-finally), and phrase-medially. The results of this test show that the pronunciations [ə] and [ɪ] are most consistently distinguished sentence-finally, and the discussion is based on this position; phrase-medially, there is a greater tendency for [ɪ] to be used in all cases, and more generally the incidence of [ɪ] is higher the more rapid the speech. The data obtained in this way were then compared with descriptions of OM, in particular Košutić (1919: 88, 93–6, 100, 111). The correspondences between OM and CSR are summarized in Table 1.2, which gives the majority pronunciation for each position.

TABLE 1.2. *Pronunciation of post-tonic a, e after a soft consonant and morpheme boundary*

			OM	CSR
V#	a	дыня 'melon'	⎫	⎫
		по́ля 'field (genitive sg)'	⎬ [ə]	
		кры́лья 'wings'	⎪	
		по́мня 'remembering'	⎭	⎬ [ə]
		рва́лся 'tore (reflexive)'	(hard [s])	
	e	по́ле 'field (nominative)'	[ə]	⎭
Vj	a	си́няя 'blue (feminine)'	⎫	⎫
	e	си́нее 'blue (neuter)'	⎬ [ɪ]	⎬ [ɪ]
		си́ней 'blue (feminine oblique)'	⎭	⎭
VC'	a	приоса́нясь 'dignified'	(hard [s])	⎫
		дынями 'melons (instrumental)'	[ə]	⎬ [ɪ]
	e	е́дете 'you travel'	[ɪ]	⎭
VC°a	a	го́нятся 'they chase (reflexive)'	[u]	⎫
	e	си́нему 'blue (non-feminine dative)'	⎫	⎬ [ɪ]
		си́него 'blue (non-feminine genitive)'	⎭ [ɪ]	⎭
VC°#	a	дыням 'melons (dative)'	⎫	⎫
		дыняx 'melons (prepositional)'	⎬ [ə]	⎬ [ə]
		го́нят 'they chase'	[u]	⎭
	e	мо́рем 'sea (instrumental)'	⎫	⎫
		сту́льев 'chairs (genitive)'	⎭ [ə] (nouns)	
		си́нем (non-feminine prepositional)	⎫ [ɪ] (non-	⎬ [ɪ]
		ки́нем 'we shall throw'	⎭ nouns)	⎭

Key: V = vowel, C° = hard consonant, C' = soft consonant other than [j], # = word-boundary.

In order to ascertain which particular vowel's unstressed version we are dealing with, the morphological form in question should be compared with an equivalent form with stress on the ending. Thus in дыня ['dinʲə], a nominative singular of the second declension, we have the unstressed ending -a, cf. простыня 'bed-sheet'. Usually, this corresponds to the spelling, but not invariably so; in nominative-accusative поле 'field' we have unstressed o (cf. ружьё [ruʒʲjo] 'gun'), while in prepositional singular (o) пóле we have e (cf. (o) ружьé [ruʒʲje]). (In the old orthography they are distinguished as поле and полѣ respectively.)

When the unstressed vowels a and o are not in inflectional endings, they are pronounced [ɪ] after soft consonants in both OM and CSR, e.g. случай ['slutʃʲɪj] 'chance', вынес ['vinʲɪs] 'carried out'. For a few words, e.g. зáнял '(he) occupied', зáнят 'occupied, busy', сегóдня 'today', the statistics are not systematic, but show a tendency towards the [ə] pronunciation, perhaps because of uncertainty as to where the morpheme boundary lies.

If we look at the predominant pronunciation of the endings in question, some unusual features emerge. One is that in OM, not only is the morphological information that the vowel is in an ending relevant to its pronunciation, but also the particular part of speech, in that o is pronounced [ə] before a word-final hard consonant in nouns, but [ɪ] in other parts of speech. Further, it is often claimed (e.g. Shapiro 1968: 40; Avanesov 1972: 70) that in nominative-accusative поле CSR tends towards the pronunciation [ɪ], the same as the prepositional, and different from the [ə] pronunciation of word-final unstressed -a. But the results reported by Kuz´mina contradict this. The pronunciation ['polʲə] was used by 98 of the 100 informants sentence-finally, 79 phrase-finally, and 64 phrase-medially—the highest figure for [ə] of any of the word-forms tested (Kuz´mina 1966: 16). The figures broken down according to age-group equally fail to show any overall trend towards [ɪ] here (Panov 1968: iv. 52).

With regard to morphological criteria, we may note that the relevance of such criteria has been reduced in CSR. The only morphological information relevant is whether or not the vowel is in an inflectional ending, and even this only word-finally or before a word-final hard consonant. The tendency for OM [ə] to be replaced by [ɪ] means that in CSR the general rule that unstressed a and o are pronounced [ɪ] after a soft consonant has widened its sphere of applicability to encompass many of the classes of forms that were exceptions in OM.

Although we have taken OM as our point of departure, OM is itself the result of historical development, and we have some indications of the pronunciation of these endings in the preceding period. Košutić (1919: 100) gives only the [ɪ] pronunciation for синего, синему, синем in OM, but notes that the [ə] pronunciation occurred in non-standard Moscow speech even after having been lost in the standard language. Shapiro (1968: 17–18) assumes, but unfortunately does not substantiate, an earlier form (which he identifies, rather simplistically, with OM) where post-tonic a and o are always pronounced [ə] after soft consonants, even in stems (e.g. вынес). Extrapolating from the data available, we may hypothesize that OM (as described by Košutić) and CSR are two intermediate stages on a development from consistent [ə] to consistent [ɪ] for unstressed a and o post-tonically, intermediate stages that demonstrate the complexity of this change.

In fairness, we should point out that some other investigators have failed to note the [ə]/[ɪ] distribution claimed by Kuz´mina: Thelin (1971: 104–22), using a small number of informants and spectrographic analysis; Bondarko and Verbickaja (1973), although the latter tests speakers' ability to *perceive* the distinction, rather than to produce it; Krysin (1974: 111–16), although the author notes that the RJaSO survey techniques are particularly unreliable here, and it is doubtful whether the results show anything more than a tendency to over-report the more explicit variant [ə].

Observations on the speech of younger Muscovites, done in the 1970s–1980s, confirm the overall tendency to replace [ə] by [ɪ] in unstressed endings; thus, Panov (1990: 82–3) presents the following contrasts between the pronunciation norms of the first and second half of the twentieth century (the left-hand transcription represents the older norm, the right-hand one the new norm):

медве́дем -[əm]/-[ɪm]
медве́дями -[əmʲi]/-[ɪmʲi]

Loan-Words

Loan-words in Russian, and in particular loans from Western European languages in the nineteenth century, often originated in the speech of members of the gentry and intelligentsia who were familiar with the pronunciation of the language in question, and attempted to retain something of the original pronunciation when using the word in Russian, even where this meant contradicting the normal rules of Russian pro-

nunciation. Polivanov (1974 [1931]: 211–19) noted that in the following
loan-words, the retention of the non-Russian nasalized and front-
rounded vowels was obligatory in the speech of the pre-Revolutionary
intelligentsia: [õ] in бомонд 'beau monde', лонгшез 'lawn-chair'; [ã]
in шансонетка 'frivolous song; female music-hall singer', рандеву
'rendezvous'; [œ] in бретёр 'swash-buckler', блеф 'bluff';[26] [y] in
ревю 'revue', парвеню 'upstart', and меню 'menu'; to this list may be
added портфель [port'fœj] 'briefcase', [ẽ]нтерьер 'interior decoration'
(Panov 1990: 51). In Glovinskaja's survey of the speech of the contemporary Soviet intelligentsia, of 41 informants only 17 retained the
foreign pronunciation in бомонд, 8 in ревю and парвеню, 7 in бретёр,
4 in лонгшез, шансонетка, and меню, 3 in рандеву, and 2 in блеф
(Glovinskaja 1971: 87–8). Clearly, there is a marked trend away from
the pronunciation that retains elements of the foreign pronunciation
that conflict with the usual rules of Russian pronunciation. The natural
retention of non-Russian sounds is probably typical of the intellectual
speech of the first two decades of this century; in the speech of younger
generations, such retention is indicative of language play or, in Panov's
terminology, linguistic ornamentation (1990: 52–3).

(i) Unstressed [o]

In the speech of pre-Revolutionary educated circles, many foreign
words were pronounced with retention of unstressed [o]. This particular
tendency has decreased considerably during the present century. Writing
in 1915, Černyšev (quoted in Gorbačevič 1971: 94–5) said that in
educated speech бокáл 'goblet', вокзáл 'railway station', комáнда
'command', костю́м 'suit', поэ́зия 'poetry', поэ́т 'poet' should be
pronounced with unstressed pretonic [o]. Nowadays, this pronunciation
for these words is either archaic or affected—it is used, for instance, by
actors portraying aristocratic ladies in productions of the Moscow Arts
Theatre (Gorbačevič 1971: 95). The loss of unstressed pretonic [o] is
further evidenced by the change in recommendations given by orthoepic
dictionaries. Thus Avanesov and Ožegov (1959) recommended the
pronunciation of поэт and related words with unreduced [o], allowing

---

[26] Panov (1990: 53 n. 40) quotes the following exchange between two famous Russian
philologists, B. V. Gornung (b. 1899) and A.A. Reformatskij (b. 1900): while Gornung
pronounces [blœf], following the French pronunciation, Reformatskij replies using the
English pronunciation [blʌf]. Since they belong to one generation, the difference in pronunciation reflects the speakers' personal preferences. Both pronunciations contrast with
Vladimir Majakovskij's (b. 1893) nativized бл[e]ф.

the variant with vowel reduction as a permissible variant. That this recommendation was no longer adhered to was shown by the survey reported in Glovinskaja (1971: 95): all 40 of her informants had a reduced vowel in поэт; in Borunova *et al.* (1983), the pronunciation with the unreduced vowel is already identified as optional; the same view is expressed in Verbickaja (1990: 9). The authoritative dictionaries follow this evolution, if somewhat reluctantly: thus, Avanesov and Ožegov (1959) allow only the unreduced vowel in фойе, while the absence of any remark on the unstressed vowel of портвейн should imply that the only admissible pronunciation is with the vowel reduced; Avanesov (1972: 167) lists both портвейн 'port (wine)' and фойе́ 'foyer' as words where the pronunciation with unreduced [o] is to be preferred, although the reduced vowel is permissible; Avanesov (1984: 211) indicates that the pronunciation with [ʌ] is the only norm in neutral style.[27] Glovinskaja's informant responses were, for портвейн: 1 non-reduced, 42 reduced, and for фойе: 3 non-reduced, 32 reduced (Glovinskaja 1971: 95).

One reasonably common loan-word that, until recently, retained the unreduced [o] in the unstressed position is шоссе́ '(surfaced) highway'. Here, Avanesov and Ožegov (1959) allow only the pronunciation with unreduced [o], Avanesov (1972: 167) allowed [ʃʌs'se] as a permissible variant, and Borunova *et al.* (1983) reversed the variants, giving [ʃos'se] as optional.[28]

In general, the position of the unstressed vowel plays an important role in the choice between the reduced and non-reduced pronunciation. The non-reduced pronunciation is more common if the unstressed o is followed by another vowel (боа 'boa', оазис 'oasis') or if it occurs word-finally (Verbickaja 1990: 14). Thus, the retention of unreduced [o], in post-tonic position, is recommended by orthoepic dictionaries for the following words: какао 'cocoa', радио 'radio', адажио 'adagio' (Borunova *et al.* 1983: 666). In rapid speech, however, the unstressed [o] can be replaced by [ə], for example, [ka'kaə] (какао). Orthoepic dictionaries also recommend pronouncing [o] in the word хаос 'chaos'; the other admissible stress variant is хао́с, which reinforces the

---

[27] In Borunova *et al.* (1983), the pronunciation of фойе with the unreduced [o] is already identified as optional; there is no remark on the pronunciation of the unstressed vowel in портвейн.

[28] Normally, after [ʃ] and [ʒ] stressed o (often written e) becomes [ie] (written e) when unstressed, e.g. жена 'wife' (cf. plural жёны); both pronunciations given so far for шоссе make it an exception to this rule. Note that among Glovinskaja's informants, 4 had unreduced [o], 9 had [ʌ], while 18 had [ie]/[ɨ].

retention of the unstressed [o]. The choice of the reduced or non-reduced pronunciation is also determined by the frequency of the word: as shown by Verbickaja (1990: 14) and Kalenčuk (1993: 25–6), more frequent words and more informal registers favour the reduced pronunciation: in Verbickaja's sample, the words шоссе, бордо 'bordeaux (colour)', тоннель 'tunnel', поэт 'poet' were pronounced with the non-reduced [o] in 5 per cent of cases, while вето 'veto' and досье 'dossier' had [o] in 30 per cent of cases. Accordingly, the nativization of a name makes the reduced pronunciation more likely; thus, Avanesov (1984: 212) notes that while Palmiro Togliatti's name should be preferably pronounced as Т[о]льятти,[29] the city named after him is Т[ʌ]льятти, even in the standard language.

(ii) Consonants before e

Another feature of foreign pronunciation often carried over into loan-words is the retention of a hard (non-palatalized) paired consonant before e. One might expect that this relic of foreign pronunciation would also tend to disappear with time, particularly as Russian spelling does not normally make use of the special letter э to mark the hardness of the preceding consonant in such words. And indeed, a number of words that would once have been permissible with a hard consonant are now admissible only with a soft consonant, unless deliberate affectation is intended, e.g. текст 'text', профессор 'professor'. In several words, for example, тема 'theme', музей 'museum', the retention of a non-palatalized consonant has become non-standard, hence the label 'wrong' (неправильно) in the latest orthoepic dictionary (Borunova *et al.* 1983: 576, 268).

The tendency to replace the hard consonant by its palatalized counterpart before e has not proved so strong as that against unstressed [o]. This leads to interesting results in words that have both unstressed *o* and a consonant before *e*, e.g. сонет 'sonnet'. One possible pronunciation is with unreduced [o] and hard [n]: [so'net]. Another is with reduced o and soft [nʲ]: [sʌ'nʲet]. Yet another is with reduced o but hard [n]: [sʌ'net]; this is the form recommended by Borunova *et al.* (1983). The fourth logical possibility, unreduced [o] but soft [nʲ] is a contradiction in terms, since reduction of unstressed o is far commoner than palatalization of

---

[29] In general, the retention of the unstressed [o] is recommended in the pronunciation of foreign proper names, for example, Бодлéр (Baudelaire); see also above (p. 52) on the pronunciation of Шопéн and Жорéс.

consonants before e in foreign words, so that the pronunciation [so'nʲet] is effectively excluded (Halle 1959: 73).

Table 1.3, based on the material in Glovinskaja (1971: 93–4), gives some of the results of a survey on whether Russians pronounce hard or soft consonants before e in loan-words. Three possible pronunciations are distinguished: hard, medium, and soft. From the data given by Glovinskaja, the author notes a number of statistical tendencies, in particular: (1) dental consonants are more likely to remain hard than labials, which are in turn more likely to remain hard than velars; (2) a hard consonant is more likely to be retained if it immediately precedes the stressed vowel than if it occurs earlier in the word; (3) the hard pronunciation is commoner in words of medium frequency than in words of very common or very rare occurrence. The last point is perhaps rather surprising at first sight, but not entirely unexpected: very common words naturally fall under the general rule palatalizing consonants, in so far as they come to be felt as part of the native vocabulary; words in which the consonant remains hard are marked items, and words of infrequent occurrence are unlikely to be well enough known for the average native speaker to have assimilated the irregular pronunciation. One further generalization, not mentioned by Glovinskaja, is that the hard pronunciation is less common with derived words with native suffixes than with the simple word, cf. секс and сексуальный and, even more clearly since there is no stress difference, купе and купейный.

In addition, in Table 1.3, we have added the recommendations of Avanesov and Ožegov (1959) and Borunova *et al.* (1983). In the vast majority of cases, the recommendations given in the earlier dictionary

TABLE 1.3. *Pronunciation of consonants before e in loan-words*

	Hard	Med-ium	Soft	A&O 1959	Borunova 1983
агре́ссор 'aggressor'	59	1	29	[a]Soft (not hard)	Either
атеи́ст 'atheist'	83	0	7	Hard	Hard
ателье́ 'tailor's shop'	41	0	0	Hard	Hard
бандеро́ль 'package'	37	1	3	[a]Soft (not hard)	Either
бутербро́д 'open sandwich'	37	0	4	Hard	Hard
бухга́лтер 'book-keeper'	0	0	40	Soft (not hard)	Soft (not hard)
бюстга́льтер 'brassiere'	28	0	12	Hard	Hard

TABLE 1.3. *Pronunciation of consonants before e in loan-words* (cont.)

	Hard	Med-ium	Soft	A&O 1959	Borunova 1983
*г*éтто 'ghetto'	23	21	46	Soft	No indication[b]
дека*д*éнт 'decadent'	30	0	1	[a]Soft (not hard)	Either
*д*ека*д*éнт 'decadent'	20	4	16	[a]Soft (not hard)	Either
кó*д*екс '(legal) code'	40	0	0	Hard	Hard
кó*ф*е 'coffee'[c]	0	6	31	Soft (not hard)	Soft
кó*ф*е 'coffee'[c]	6	19	71		
ку*п*é 'compartment'	37	4	0	Hard	Hard
ку*п*éйный 'having compartments' (adj.)	11	2	28	[a]Hard	Soft (hard not recommended)
медре*с*é 'madrasah'	24	0	1	Hard	Hard
медре*с*é	21	2	3	Hard	Hard
*м*едре*с*é	7	2	31	[a]Hard	Soft
*м*еню́ 'menu'	2	3	37	Soft	No indication[b]
мо*д*éль 'model'	40	0	0	Hard	Hard
пар*т*éр 'stalls'	35	0	0	Hard	Hard
резю*м*é 'résumé'	14	6	14	[a]Hard	[a]Hard
сви́*т*ер 'sweater'	37	0	2	Hard	Hard
*с*екс 'sex'	22	2	16	Not given	Hard
*с*ексуальный 'sexual'	15	1	26	Soft	Either
со*н*éт 'sonnet'	32	3	5	Hard	Hard
*т*еáтр 'theatre'	0	0	43	Soft	No indication[b]
*т*éзис 'thesis'	36	1	3	Hard	Hard
тен*д*éнция 'tendency'	40	0	0	Hard	Hard
*т*ен*д*éнция 'tendency'	39	0	1	Hard	Hard
фо*н*éтика 'phonetics'	40	0	0	Hard	Hard
фо*н*ети́ст 'phonetician'	42	0	0	Hard	Hard
шо*сс*é 'highway'	41	0	1	Hard	Hard

Key: A&O = Avanesov and Ožegov (1959); Borunova = Borunova *et al.* (1983)

[a] The pronunciation recommended does not correspond to the largest figure in Glovinskaja's study (for резюме an equal number of informants had hard and soft м; note that both dictionaries recommend hard м but soft p).

[b] Where Borunova *et al.* (1983) give no indication, the soft pronunciation is the default one.

[c] This word was tested on two different occasions, whence the two entries in the table.

agree with the most widespread usage recorded by Glovinskaja—
surprisingly so, given that Avanesov and Ožegov (1959) is based not
on informant-polling, but on intuitive and rough-and-ready methods.
Where the consonant in question is a labial (купейный, медресе,
резюме), Avanesov and Ožegov appear to tend towards a norm with
more hard consonants than the general trend of informant responses, but
in fact they are hesitant about the phonetic status of these labials (pp.
681–2), and suggest that the orthoepic pronunciation is rather half-soft
(medium). In the other examples, and in several other words noted by
Glovinskaja (1971: 91), the recommendations given by Avanesov and
Ožegov (1959) differ from majority usage in over-recommending the
soft pronunciation, i.e. in suggesting that these words are more assimilated to the native pattern than in fact they are. Clearly, in the pronunciation of loan-words with e, two possibilities are available: either the
word is nativized entirely and is pronounced with a soft consonant
before e, or the word, perceived as a loan-word, retains a hard consonant. Under the latter possibility, the hard pronunciation of consonants
before e is coming to be felt more and more an integral part of the
Russian sound system. This two-way distinction is reflected in the
recommendations given by Borunova *et al.* (1983): though they follow
many recommendations of the earlier dictionary, they, on the other
hand, clearly bring the pronunciation standards closer to actual usage, as
reflected in Glovinskaja's study.

The difference between the fate of unstressed [o] and that of hard
consonants before e gives a clear indication of the two ways in which the
Russian language has been 'democratized': in the first case, the non-
popular pronunciation has tended to be lost, while in the second case the
non-popular pronunciation has been adopted by a much wider section of
the social spectrum.

Miscellaneous

(i) Soft p between e and a hard consonant

In older stages of the language, soft [rʲ] was used in many words,
between e and a hard consonant, where CSR has hard [r]. Occasionally,
the soft pronunciation was indicated in spelling, as on the Bronze
Horseman monument to Peter the Great (Петру перьвому) in St
Petersburg. In OM of the turn of the century, this pronunciation was still

usual for certain words, at least among the older generation. Košutić (1919: 158) notes верх 'summit', церковь 'church', четверг 'Thursday', and points out that in some other words the soft pronunciation had recently been ousted by the hard, e.g. зеркало 'mirror', первый 'first', стерва (derogatory, 'witch', originally 'carrion'). Avanesov (1947*b*: 152; 1984: 142) notes that L. Tolstoj pronounced первый with soft [rʲ].

In CSR, the pronunciation is with hard [r] in all these words, although церковь is rather more complex. The main text of Avanesov (1972) does not mention this word in this connection, but the index gives it with soft [rʲ]. Professor Avanesov kindly informed us that церковь was the only word in this class where he considered soft [rʲ] preferable, although hard [r] was widespread. By the 1970s, the hard pronunciation of [r] became dominant.

(ii) Pronunciation of их, им, ими

In OM, the oblique forms of the third-person pronoun их, им, ими were pronounced with initial [ji], the only words to be so pronounced. Avanesov (1972: 92) notes this pronunciation, but considers it definitely archaic or non-standard in CSR. Drage (1968: 379–80) reports that of his 17 informants, only one used the initial [j], and then only in one of four different test sentences with these words.

(iii) Pronunciation of солнце 'sun'

In the word солнце the л is silent, in both OM and CSR. However, in OM the pronunciation of the stressed vowel is much closer than usual (symbolized [ọ]) (Trubetzkoy 1958: 56). In this pronunciation, the quality of stressed o is closer before л, so the OM pronunciation of солнце retains a trace of the 'silent л' which is pronounced in other derivatives from the same stem, e.g. солнечный 'solar'. In CSR, there is no such marked difference of quality between stressed o before л and elsewhere, and the pronunciation of солнце does not differ from that of an imaginary word сонце. Since Trubetzkoy's example has become one of the canonical examples of phonological theory, it is worth emphasizing that his argument is based on data from OM, while CSR does not provide the relevant data.[30]

---

[30] Alexis Manaster-Ramer (personal communication) finds no evidence for this pronunciation of солнце in other sources, so it may have been restricted even in OM.

(iv) Word-final palatalized labials

Many Russians do not distinguish hard and soft labials in word-final position, pronouncing кров 'roof, shelter' and кровь 'blood' alike with hard [f]. In fact, of all Russian regional dialects, only some central Russian dialects of the region around Moscow retain this distinction (Avanesov and Orlova 1965: 88). Loss of the distinction among people who are otherwise speakers of standard Russian is commoner in Leningrad (later St Petersburg) than in Moscow. Although this pronunciation, on the evidence of other dialects and Slavonic languages, may be a sign of the way Russian is developing, it is not admitted as standard at present (Avanesov 1984: 131–2). Panov (1967: 299–300) considers the hard pronunciation a serious mistake, to be combated.

(v) Word-initial и after a hard consonant

In standard pronunciation, when words beginning with и occur without pause after a word ending in a hard consonant (e.g. a preposition), the initial и is pronounced [ɨ], e.g. в Италию 'to Italy' ([vɨˈtalʲiju]), unlike Виталию 'to Vitalij (dative)' ([vʲiˈtalʲiju]), к Ире 'towards Ira' ([ˈkɨrʲɪ]), unlike Кире 'to Kira (dative)' ([ˈkʲirʲɪ]). The pronunciation, fairly common nowadays, of both members of such pairs with [i] (i.e. indiscriminately [vʲiˈtalʲiju] and [ˈkʲirʲɪ]) is not admitted as standard (Avanesov 1984: 144). Avanesov notes further that many Russians adhere to the norm where the consonant is not velar, but deviate from it where the consonant is velar: within the morpheme, [kɨ] is not, of course, a possible sequence in Russian; within OM, the same phenomenon was noted by Košutić (1919: 163).

Conclusion

As noted in the introduction to this chapter, having discussed various changes between OM and CSR, and also changes that are taking place within CSR, it is useful to try to ascertain what have been the motive forces behind these changes, in particular the relevance of spelling pronunciations, other forms of spoken Russian (dialects, OPb), morphological analogy, and morphological boundaries. In many cases, of course, we may expect more than one of these factors to interact.

The influence of morphological boundaries has been advocated in particular by Glovinskaja *et al.* (1971: 21–2), as part of the general movement towards analytism: the various morphemes are set off more clearly from one another, by giving phonetic expression to the morpheme boundary. Unfortunately, clear instances of the relevance of morphological boundaries are rare (see Bondarko 1973), the best example being the relevance of such boundaries in fostering the pronunciation [ʃˈtʃ] across a morpheme boundary; although this pronunciation was noted by Košutić, it seems to have become more frequent during the present century. The alleged role of morpheme boundaries in fostering the loss of palatalization assimilation is brought into doubt by the results of Drage's survey (1967*a*), and also by the extreme degree of over-reporting of lack of assimilation in the RJaSO survey. At best, one can perhaps say that over-reporting of lack of assimilation is more likely where there is a boundary than where there is not. The same would apply to the pronunciation of post-tonic a and o in inflectional endings after a soft consonant, where the discrepancy between the results of reading tests and the RJaSO survey suggests over-reporting in the latter; indeed, the reading tests suggest that these boundaries are tending to be less marked phonetically, as OM [ə] gives way to CSR [ɪ]. The pronunciation of word-initial и as [i] rather than [ɨ] after a hard consonant in non-standard CSR is another instance of the loss of phonetic marking of morpheme boundaries. Another piece of evidence for the loss of morpheme boundaries, also coming from spoken Russian, is the extreme degree of vowel reduction and elimination of consonant clusters, occurring over morpheme boundaries (Zemskaja 1973: 44–71, 74; Zemskaja 1987: 201–9). The tendency is becoming particularly prominent in the speech of Muscovites, especially those born in the 1960s and later. Compare the transcription of the pronunciation of one and the same date (12 October 1992) by a female Muscovite born in 1932 (L) and by a female Muscovite born in 1976 (K), both speakers of CSR.[31]

Сегодня двенадцатое октября тысяча девятьсот девяносто второго года

Today is 12 October 1992.

L: [sʲieˈvodnʲie dʲvʲieˈnatˑtsətəjə əktieˈbrʲa tisʲietʃə dʲievʲieˈtsot dʲievʲieˈnostə ftʌˈrovə ˈgodə]

K: [sʲiodnʲə dʲvʲeiˈnatˑtsətə əkteiˈbrʲa tiʃətʃə dʲvʲieˈtsot dʲiviˈnostəftərəə ˈgodə]

---

[31] The sample elicited from the younger speaker confirms, among other things, the mixing of strong *ikan'e* with the more open pronunciation of the pretonic vowel after a soft consonant.

There seems to have been little, if any, influence of regional dialects on the development from OM to CSR; indeed, OM is usually closer to regional dialects, especially the central dialects, than CSR is. In particular, there is no tendency for southern dialect forms to penetrate the standard language. On the other hand, southern dialect features, in the speech of those who do not speak consistent standard Russian, are much less susceptible to the influence of the standard than are northern dialect features, so that there is evidence from outside the standard for the greater tenacity of the southern dialects. Slightly more complex is the possible influence of OPb, since in many respects CSR seems closer to OPb than to OM. However, in each instance where CSR seems closer to OPb than to OM (e.g. pronunciation of adjectives in -кий, verbal forms like ходят), the CSR pronunciation can be explained by means of spelling pronunciation or morphological analogy, and there is no need to invoke OPb. Sometimes, the problem is rather to explain the origin of OPb, for example, with regard to the pronunciation of adjectives in -кий, where the pronunciation -[kʲij] can only be a spelling pronunciation, and is certainly not that of the regional dialects closest to Leningrad/St Petersburg. Filin (1973: 5–6) suggests that most of the characteristics of OPb are the result of earlier and more widespread spelling pronunciations there than in Moscow at the turn of the century, and this explanation fits the facts well.

The main difficulty arises in discriminating between the influence of spelling and that of morphological analogy, since in the majority of cases both of these criteria would give the same result: in the tendency not to simplify consonant clusters (which are split up by fleeting vowels in certain morphological forms, and which are present in the spelling), in the pronunciation of immediate pretonic ша, жа as [ʃa], [ʒa] (given the general rule for pronouncing immediate pretonic a after a hard consonant, and also the general rule relating the pronunciation of the same vowel stressed and unstressed in related morphological forms), in the pronunciation of ходят as ['xodʲət] (the spelling has я, not ю, and verbs of this conjugation with end-stress have -[at]). There is, however, the one clear case of a spelling pronunciation, namely the pronunciation of adjectives in -кий, etc.: this spelling contradicts morphological parallelism (the stressed ending is -[koj]), and also finds minimal support in Russian dialects, none in those of the Moscow or Leningrad/St Petersburg area. There are also some minor changes between OM and CSR that seem attributable only to spelling pronunciation (or at least, to this rather than to any of the other factors noted above): the loss of soft [rʲ] in words like церковь, the pronunciation of forms of целовать, the loss of initial [j] in их. CSR developments contrary to the spelling are extremely rare: one such development was *ikan´e*, but even this seems to be becoming less frequent, at least in modern Moscow pronunciation. Another instance where pronunciation deviates from the spelling is the hardening of final soft labials. On the other hand, it is difficult to find convincing examples of morphological analogy that are not also cases of spelling pronunciation: perhaps the non-standard pronunciation of verb forms like плачут as ['platʃʲət], using the second conjugation unstressed ending, if this is not due to the influence of regional dialects on those who otherwise speak near-standard Russian.

Overall, then, the evidence seems to point in the direction of spelling pronunciation as the main (though not the only) factor in the development from OM to CSR. It is interesting to note, moreover, that many of the unstable points in CSR correlate with inexplicitness of the orthography: the pronunciation of [e] or [o] when stressed after soft consonants (the special letter ё being rarely used outside school-books) (Es´kova 1967); the pronunciation of single or double consonants in loan-words (the orthography has double consonants in many cases where only a single consonant is pronounced) (Glovinskaja 1971: 63–9); the pronunciation of hard or soft consonants before e in loan-words (since the special letter э is rarely used in their spelling, e does not adequately indicate the pronunciation of the preceding consonant) (Glovinskaja 1971: 76–87, 93–4). Finally, the overview of Russian pronunciation in this century reveals that some changes in language may be fairly short-lived: an example of such transitory change is the pronunciation of unstressed adjectival endings in the masculine singular (from -[əj] to -[ɨj] and now gradually back to the reduced pronunciation, reminiscent of -[əj]).

2 Stress and Intonation

STRESS in Russian is free (i.e. can occur on any syllable in the word) and mobile (i.e. the position of stress can change in the inflection of a word, or between derivationally related words). The rules determining position of stress are complex (Zaliznjak 1967: 151–75; 1985: 386–7), and the stress of many individual words and word-forms is seemingly idiosyncratic. In addition, a large number of Russian words can be pronounced with or without a secondary stress (`), for example, мѐлодра-матѝчный and мелодрамати́чный 'melodramatic'. This leads to a certain amount of inconsistency even among native speakers,[1] a factor which is reinforced by the existence of different stress patterns in different regional dialects, and by the fact that stress is not marked in the orthography (except in some school-books). Thus there are variant stresses in current usage, and there have been changes in normative stress between the nineteenth century and the present day.

Since stress is not marked in Russian spelling, our main source of information about stress in earlier periods comes from verse, where the stress of individual words can be deduced from the metrical scheme. In using verse one has, of course, to remember that a poet may use an unusual stress to fit the metre, although such examples are in fact rare in nineteenth-century Russian poetry (Tobolova 1974; Voroncova 1979: *passim*), and where we find a given stress used consistently by a large number of poets at the same time, we can be reasonably sure that this stress was admissible at that period. In addition to verse, for the late eighteenth and nineteenth centuries there is also the evidence of early normative dictionaries.

For current usage we have, apart from the practice of contemporary poets, evidence from the various surveys: in addition to the RJaSO survey, reported in Krysin (1974: 223–41), these include Kolesov (1967), as well as surveys concerned with particular problems of stress, as noted below. These may be compared with the recommendations of normative dictionaries. Most often, normative dictionaries qualify all

---

[1] See Nicholson (1968: 130): 'The memory burden which the stress system places on the Russian is often forgotten, although the demonstrable gaps and inconsistencies in the stressing practice of even highly educated native speakers may be in large measure due to this burden rather than to the specific influence of dialect forms.'

but one of the variants as non-standard, less commonly one of the variants is archaic or permissible, while only occasionally is more than one
variant equally recommended. Even here a certain amount of reservation
may be expressed, as in Ožegov (1972: 14): 'only in isolated cases are
stress variants given as of equal normativity in the literary language
(in this case the preferred variant is given first . . . e.g. творо́г, -а́ (-ы́)
['cottage cheese'—CSP] and тво́рог, -а (-у)).' Apparently, some
variants are more equal than others. Besides the normative dictionaries,
a comprehensive attempt to describe Russian stress as a system is presented in Zaliznjak (1967; 1980: 9–10, 30–4, 56, 71–3, 80–3), and this
system is followed by *Русская грамматика* (1980: i. 90–5, 511–30).
A very good historical overview of changes in Russian stress from the
eighteenth to the twentieth century is given in Voroncova (1979).

As noted above, there are marked differences in stress patterns
between different Russian dialects, in particular between the northern
and southern dialect groups, with the northern or north-western dialects
tending to be more archaic, the southern dialects (and also Ukrainian and
Belorussian) more innovatory.[2] This pattern corresponds by and large to
the findings reported in Krysin (1974: 23–41), where Russians from the
northern dialect area tend to be closer to the traditional standard, and
even educated Russians from the southern dialect area (and likewise
Russians from Ukraine and Belarus) tend to be more innovatory, while
those from Moscow, Moscow *oblast´*, and Leningrad (which here goes
with Moscow, rather than the surrounding northern dialects) occupy an
intermediate position, i.e. are open to some extent to the influence of the
newer southern dialect forms.[3]

While there have been changes in the stress of individual words, such
as библиоте́ка 'library' (archaic библио́тека, still to be heard in
émigré circles), the most interesting area of study from the viewpoint of
general tendencies in the development of stress patterns is the interaction of stress variation and (inflectional and derivational) morphology.

---

[2] The special position of north-western dialects in the history of Russian is demonstrated in Zaliznjak (1985).

[3] Recent detailed dialectological work, already noted by Krysin (1974: 238) but not
taken into account in the RJaSO survey, indicates that the northern area is in fact less
homogeneous than this, with archaic stress patterns characteristic primarily of the north-
eastern dialects, and the north-western varieties of Russian, including those spoken in the
Baltics, sometimes even more innovatory than the southern dialects (cf. the preponderance
of newer stress forms in the speech of Russians living in the Baltics). One may hypothesize that the difference between southern and north-eastern informants would be even
greater than that between southern and northern informants noted by Krysin. See also
Bukrinskaja (1983), Kuznecova (1985).

Overall, changes in the stress system are likely to be affected by paradigmatic stress levelling and by the influence of productive derivational models. In stress assignment, Russian tends to avoid positioning the stress on the word-initial and word-final syllable. This tendency towards positioning the stress over word-medial syllables is sometimes characterized as the rhythmic balance tendency (Gorbačevič 1978: 64) and is explained as a means of maintaining more or less equal intervals between stressed syllables (according to some statistics, presented by Gorbačevič (1978: 64), there are, on average, three unstressed syllables separating stressed syllables).

Gorbačevič (1978: 65, 98–9) appeals to the rhythmic balance tendency in explaining the recessive shift of stress common in verbs in -ировать (see below, in this chapter): the final stress on such verbs results in an inappropriately long interval between two successive stressed syllables, for example, in the forms of analytical future (бу́дет аккомпанирова́ть), while the recessive shift of stress shortens this interval by at least two syllables (бу́дет аккомпани́ровать). Although this explanation may be challenged in this particular case (the recessive shift of stress can be effectively explained by the influence of the German stress pattern on the verbs in -*ieren*, see Ogienko (1914: 112–13)), it probably explains the progressive shift of stress from the first syllable in adjectives such as таи́нственный 'mysterious', счастли́вый 'happy',[4] обще́ственный 'social' occurring in the second half of the nineteenth century.

It is unclear how the rhythmic balance tendency can account for stress recession towards the first syllable of the word, commonly observed in both native and borrowed masculine nouns. For example, in the beginning of the twentieth century the words бо́ндарь 'cooper', то́карь 'turner', ко́жух 'leather-coat', о́бух 'butt', кре́мень 'flint', на́сморк 'head-cold', за́говор 'plot, scheme', при́говор 'verdict', ло́моть 'loaf', де́спот 'despot', су́ффикс 'suffix', скульпто́р 'sculptor' had two stress variants (Gorbačevič 1978: 70–7). In the contemporary language, то́карь, на́сморк, за́говор, де́спот, скульпто́р, су́ффикс have all lost the possibility of final stress. For бо́ндарь, the variant with ultimate stress is listed as admissible in Borunova *et al.* (1983). This dictionary also cites as permissible stress variants ломо́ть, ло́моть, обу́х, о́бух (in that order), but classifies кре́мень, ко́жух as wrong and при́говор as not recommended. The word планёр (планер) 'glider'

---

[4] For example, in Puškin's *Евгений Онегин* (1823), I. v: 'Имел он счастливый талант' 'He had a lucky gift . . .'

(from French *planeur*), cited as having only final stress in Ožegov (1972), is given in two stress variants in Borunova *et al.* (1983). Recessive stress shift is also typical of words in specialist use (Gorbačevič 1978: 79). This shows that recessive stress shift is still an ongoing process in the contemporary language, confirming the observation that sound change progresses from one group of words to others, in a wave-like manner.

It seems that the rhythmic balance tendency can be taken into account, if only partially, particularly when it accompanies other relevant factors such as paradigmatic levelling and stress levelling by analogy.

Stress Levelling in Noun Declension

In noun declension, six major types of stress are distinguished (Zaliznjak 1967: 153–91; 1980: 31), represented in Table 2.1.

In addition to these major patterns, four minor patterns are recognized which bear some similarity to one of the patterns in Table 2.1. In the description of these patterns, we will follow the system by Zaliznjak, who assigns them the same letter indices as the respective major patterns, adding the prime sign. Thus, stress pattern B' differs from pattern B above in that the instrumental singular form has stem stress; for example, рожь 'rye' (nominative/accusative sing.), ржи (dative, prepositional sing.), but рожью (instrumental sing.). Patterns D' and F' differ from patterns D and F respectively in that the accusative singular form has stem stress, for example, D': спина́ 'back', accusative sing. спи́ну; F': голова́ 'head', accusative sing. го́лову.

As is clear from the description of patterns B', D', and F', with a number of Russian nouns in the singular the stress of the nominative is changed in some oblique forms. In the plural, many nouns have a different stress in the nominative(-accusative) and in the oblique cases (see patterns E and F in Table 2.1).[5] One of the major tendencies in the recent development of noun stress patterns has been to reduce the amount of stress alternation within the singular and within the plural. Here, as with many recent and current changes in stress, there are two possible factors: firstly, the internal factor of analogy, i.e. the tendency to reduce the amount of morphophonemic alternation; secondly, the external factor of the influence of southern dialects, which have less morphophonemic

[5] Where a word has no ending, as with голо́в, genitive plural of голова́ 'head', end-stress is realized as stress on the last syllable of the word.

TABLE 2.1. *Noun declension: major stress patterns*

	A ка́рта 'map'	B очко́ 'point'	C мо́ре 'sea'	D вино́ 'wine'	E вещь 'thing'	F губа́ 'lip'
Singular	Stem-stress	End-stress	Stem-stress	End-stress	Stem-stress	End-stress
Nominative plural[a]	Stem-stress	End-stress	End-stress	Stem-stress	Stem-stress	Stem-stress
Genitive, dative, instrumental, prepositional plural[a]	Stem-stress	End-stress	End-stress	Stem-stress	End-stress	End-stress

[a] Accusative plural coincides either with nominative plural or genitive plural.

alternation than do the northern (especially north-eastern) dialects. In general, it is difficult to separate the two factors, particularly since the current situation in the southern dialects is largely the result of more widespread operation of analogical levelling. Analogical levelling itself may be due either to grammatical or to semantic factors, i. e. a word may undergo stress change due to the formal analogy with some other word, usually a common one, or due to the semantic affinity to some other words of its class (Zaliznjak 1977; Voroncova 1979: 107–15). Finally, there are always words that are perceived as more 'exotic' and less integrated into the language than others; such words, simply due to their lower frequency and less familiar character, would be more resistant to change than commonly used words. This phenomenon, first noted by Grot (1899: 328), was recently attributed to the influence of *pragmatic factors* (Zaliznjak 1977: 74–5): words viewed as rare and alien to everyday language are overtly marked as such by retaining more traditional stress and a more traditional paradigm in general. This factor is responsible for a common discrepancy between the standard language, on the one hand, and professional or non-standard varieties, on the other: the perception of certain words as 'exotic' is often different across these varieties. Because of pragmatic factors, words with marked stylistic connotations often also retain older stress and/or inflection; for example, poetic words, often viewed as exotically archaic, sometimes retain the unusual stress pattern as the only one or as a permissible variant. An example of such a word is челн 'boat (poetic)', which, according to Avanesov and Ožegov (1959) and Borunova *et al.* (1983), has both end-stress and stem-stress in the plural; the stem-stressed plural, though, has clear poetic connotations (see also Voroncova 1979: 103).

Accusative singular in -y

In the standard language there are only some two dozen nouns for which all dictionaries agree on requiring or recommending stress pattern D', i.e. with a stress-shift in the accusative singular to stem-stress (in addition to спина, given above, cf. водá 'water', accusative вóду; бородá 'beard', accusative бóроду), plus a small number of words where the stress-shift is qualified as preferable (e.g. полосá 'stripe', accusative пóлосу and permissible полосý (Borunova *et al.* 1983));[6] most of these

---

[6] Variations in recommendations become evident if we compare those given in Avanesov and Ožegov (1959) with those given in Borunova *et al.* (1983): while the former dictionary gives preference to полосý, identifying пóлосу as permissible, the latter gives пóлосу as the first variant, followed by полосý.

are, however, very common words. Many of the words that have the stem-stressed accusative denote body parts (борода, голова, нога, рука; cf. also душа, which may be viewed as an inalienable possession, too), and stem-stress in these nouns may be retained by association with other semantically related nouns (Voroncova 1979: 41).

In the nineteenth century, there were rather more words in this class, including весна 'spring', зола 'ashes', изба 'hut', нора 'burrow', овца 'sheep', роса 'dew', соха 'wooden plough' (V. V. Vinogradov *et al.* 1960: i. 200; Voroncova 1979: 35–9). An example of nineteenth-century usage here is the first line of Puškin's poem *Утопленник* (1828):

> Прибежали в избу дети . . .
>
> Children ran into the hut . . .

For all seven of these words, Avanesov and Ožegov (1959) give only the form with end-stress, except that both избу and избу are given (in that order), the latter presumably under the influence of literary tradition (Gorbačevič 1971: 73), since it does not correspond to current usage.

In addition to those words that have clearly gone over to fixed-stress in the singular, there are a few words in this class subject to variation. V. V. Vinogradov *et al.* (1960: i. 202) allow, in addition to the stresses реку 'river', цену 'price', and зиму 'winter', the forms реку, цену, and зиму, which are identified as newer forms. Avanesov and Ožegov (1959) give both реку and реку (in that order), строку and строку, косу and косу, condemn цену, and cite зиму without any comment. In Borunova *et al.* (1983), no comment is given in the citation of цену, as the only possible form. Of the informants polled in the RJaSO survey (Krysin 1974: 232), 36 per cent gave the stress реку.

Oblique plural forms

End-stress in the oblique cases with stem-stress in the nominative (-accusative) is common in the plural of a number of types of Russian nouns, in particular those of the second declension such as губа 'lip' in Table 2.1 above (plural губы, dative plural губам), but also less commonly with first-declension nouns (e.g. волк 'wolf', plural волки, dative волкам), and quite commonly with third declension nouns (e.g. часть 'part', plural части, dative частям). Over the recent history of the Russian language, there has been a tendency for such stress-shifts to be levelled out, usually in the direction of the nominative plural,[7] particularly with second-declension nouns.

In nineteenth-century usage, for instance, земля́ 'land' and вода́ 'water' had stress on the inflection (end-stress) in the oblique plural cases, whereas nowadays these forms have stem-stress. With земля, the older stress is still retained in the genitive plural земе́ль. This is true of a number of words that seem to have participated in this stress change: thus хло́поты 'troubles', dative хло́потам (D. N. Ušakov (1935–40) still gives хлопота́м) but genitive хлопо́т, and семья́ 'family', dative plural се́мьям (cf. nominative plural се́мьи), but genitive plural семе́й. In a few cases, the opposite change occurs: thus, normative dictionaries allow only деревня́м as the dative plural of дере́вня 'village', although дере́вням is frequently heard from educated Russians, especially of the older generation; the genitive plural is still дереве́нь.

Two words which are subject to variation in this respect in current usage are волна́ 'wave' and стена́ 'wall'. The attitude of normative handbooks to these two words is different, being more liberal in allow-ing both variants with волна; thus Avanesov and Ožegov (1959) give stem-stress as a permissible variant in the oblique plural cases of волна, alongside the recommended end-stress; Borunova *et al.* (1983) simply list both stress variants for волна, giving the end-stress variant first. For стена, Avanesov and Ožegov (1959) give only inflection-stressed oblique plural forms; meanwhile, Borunova *et al.* (1983) identify стена́м as an archaic form. The change in recommendations clearly reflects the completed change in the language: according to Gorbačevič (1971: 70–2), stem-stressed forms are more common with стена than with волна (in conflict with the recommendations of Avanesov and Ožegov (1959)). In the survey reported in Kolesov (1967: 100) prefer-ence was for в волна́х (162 informants, with only 56 for в во́лнах, and 1 for both), but for в сте́нах (preferred by 82 informants, with 57 for в стена́х, and 17 for both). In the RJaSO survey (Krysin 1974: 232) only 14 per cent of those replying gave в во́лнах.

While several words of the second declension have lost stress alter-nation in the plural, a few words have, exceptionally, undergone the reverse development; the most common word in this group is де́ньги 'money', dative деньга́м (archaic де́ньгам); the genitive retains the older stress, де́нег.

---

[7] With masculine nouns of the first declension, however, the reverse levelling is also common; for instance, the nominative plural волки́ is attested only as a non-standard form.

Some nouns of the third declension have undergone a similar change: thus the traditional stress of the genitive plural of ведомость 'register' (nominative plural ведомости) is ведомостей, and Avanesov and Ožegov (1959) specifically condemn the newer variant ведомостей. However, in the RJaSO survey (Krysin 1974: 232) the latter form was given by 74.8 per cent of informants; in Borunova *et al.* (1983), this form is cited as permissible. The analysis of poetic works of the early twentieth century suggests that the number of such words is even higher (Voroncova 1979: 79); the development of stem-stress in such words can be explained by formal analogy with the nominative plural, where the stress is also on the root or stem (Voroncova 1979: 79). There are also some nouns that have gone the other way, such as тень 'shadow', nominative plural тéни, genitive plural тенéй; тéней is archaic, though it is usually retained in the expression цáрство тéней 'the kingdom of shades'.

According to Nicholson (1968: 80), end-stress on the oblique plural cases is a southern dialect feature. If this is true in general, it would provide interesting evidence in deciding the relative importance of analogy and southern dialect influence, since analogy would favour stem-stress (like the nominative plural), while southern dialect influence would favour end-stress; in fact, the tendency is towards stem-stress. However, the generality of Nicholson's claim is called into question by the results of the RJaSO survey (Krysin 1974: 264), for в волнáх 'in waves' and в рекáх 'in rivers', where stem-stress is commoner with southern than with northern informants. Based on her analysis of the RJaSO survey, Voroncova (1979: 276–85) also concludes that the role of territorial factors is often obscured by other variables, such as education.

Stress and number

The shift from stress pattern F (see Table 2.1 above) to stress pattern C (for example, from a paradigm such as водá—вóды—водáм to водá—вóды—вóдам) makes the stress alternation purely a marker of number, rather than a complex marker of number and case; the spread of the nominative plural in -a of masculine nouns, noted in Chapter 3 on morphology, has the same overall effect; meanwhile, the shift from the older pattern E as in дуб 'oak' (genitive singular дýба)—дýбы—дубóв to current pattern C (дуб—дýба—дубы́—дубóв) again increases the number differentiation. Any decrease in number differentiation seems to be incidental, as in the newer variants of the paradigm ведомость—

ве́домости—ведомосте́й (newer ве́домостей, see above). In a few cases, it is possible to trace the gradual introduction of number stress differentiation. An interesting example here is фронт '(military) front'; the word had stem-stress in the singular, but, as a relatively recent development, probably at the turn of the century,[8] end-stress in the oblique plural, e.g. genitive фронто́в. Avanesov and Ožegov (1959) give the nominative plural фро́нты, but the form фронты́, completing the pattern of stem-stress in the singular and end-stress in the plural, is already common in the RJaSO survey (Krysin 1974: 226, 230, 232); it is allowed as a permissible variant by Gorbačevič (1973) and is given as the only variant by Borunova *et al.* (1983), where the form фро́нты is identified as archaic and is not recommended.

The use of end-stressed plurals, overall, is more common in specialized, professional speech, where such stresses as тельца́ 'cells', масла́ 'oils', мыла́ 'soaps', шприцы́—шприцо́в 'syringes', спирты́—спирто́в 'alcohols' are found (Voroncova 1979: 122–3, 90).

The general tendency is for stress alternation to be lost as a marker of case difference, while there is a secondary, weaker tendency for stress alternation to be extended as a marker of number difference. As will be discussed in Chapter 3, as stress loses its disambiguating function, different case endings may emerge as markers of case and number distinctions; this compensatory tendency is particularly apparent in the growing number of masculine plurals in -á (see also Mustajoki 1990).

Other stress changes in noun declension

Since masculine nouns of the first declension have no ending in the nominative singular, it is not possible to tell from a nominative singular with final stress whether the word is stem-stressed or end-stressed, e.g. жук 'beetle', genitive жука́, but лук 'onion', genitive лу́ка. A number of nouns have changed over the recent history of the language from having stem-stress to having end-stress. For пруд 'pond', Avanesov and Ožegov (1959) allow only inflection-stress, and specifically condemn genitive пру́да,[9] although this earlier stress is the only one admitted by D. N. Ušakov (1935–40). Similarly, D. N. Ušakov (1935–40) allows

---

[8] Given the semantics of the word, it may be suggested that the change was catalysed by the events of several wars that were fought in the beginning of the century (the Russo-Japanese War and the First World War); as the word gained in frequency, it might have changed its stress by analogy with other end-stressed words.

[9] In Borunova *et al.* (1983), the form пру́да is given as permissible.

only stem-stress on мост 'bridge', characterizing genitive мостá as 'regional'; Avanesov and Ožegov (1959) give both мóста and мостá (in that order), and Borunova *et al.* (1983) give the two forms in the reverse order. The survey reported by Kolesov (1967: 99) includes у моста 'by the bridge' and к мосту 'to the bridge', with 198 informants preferring end-stress in the first case (and only 16 stem-stress), and 152 preferring end-stress in the second case (with 76 preferring stem-stress, and 3 allowing both).[10] The word гусь 'goose' is subject to similar variation and change in the singular, with genitive гýся or гуся́: while Avanesov and Ožegov (1959) specifically condemn the latter variant, in Kolesov's survey (1967: 99), 146 informants gave гуся́ and only 70 гýся, with 7 allowing both, suggesting that here again normative handbooks and current usage are out of step. The recommendations by Borunova *et al.* (1983) are more consistent with current usage: гуся́ is given as a permissible second variant.[11] Gorbačevič (1971: 68–9) found that all of his informants (more than 40) gave only end-stress for гуляшá 'goulash', for which Avanesov and Ožegov (1959) allow only genitive гуля́ша; in Borunova *et al.* (1983), both forms are listed, though гуля́ша is given first.[12] The latter word is a borrowing; however, masculine borrowings in general have been observed to acquire stem-stress in the genitive singular. This has been tentatively explained by the relative freedom enjoyed by loan-words: there seems to be less need for them analogically to follow other words (Voroncova 1979: 95–6). Though they may be free from semantic analogy, loan-words still tend to follow the formal analogy with existing words, and this reasoning, therefore, does not explain the predominance of end-stress on loan-words.

A large number of masculine nouns, most of which are monosyllabic, underwent the shift from stem-stress to end-stress. For example, the word грош 'penny; small coin' (from Polish *grosz*) had stem-stress in the nineteenth century (*SAR* 1806–22); this stress pattern is retained in the saying не было ни грóша, да вдруг алтын 'from rags to riches'. In the modern language, however, the only acceptable stress otherwise

[10] The figure of 3 is actually quoted for к мóсту which occurs twice, but by comparison with the layout of the other entries it seems that the second occurrence of к мóсту is an error for к мóстý.

[11] In general, the stress change of this particular word is complicated by the existence of the set phrase как с гýся водá 'like water off a duck's back', which may hinder the switch to the end-stressed variant.

[12] A particularly complex picture is presented by words in -аж; for details, see Jiráček (1969) and also Ožegov (1947), Voroncova (1979: 114–15).

is гроша́.[13] Similarly, the word шут 'jester' is end-stressed in the modern language but retains its original stress in the expression какого шу́та 'what the heck'. The overall number of words that underwent such change is close to a hundred (Voroncova 1979: 106–7). Semantic factors play a crucial role in this development: as shown by Zaliznjak (1977: 108–14), the words of this type belong to several clearly delineated semantic groups, such as names of animals (слон 'elephant', морж 'walrus', кит 'whale'), names of occupations (шут), names of signs, symbols, letters, and monetary units (грош, туз 'ace'), and some others. Pragmatic factors (see p. 76) are also relevant for the development of end-stress: the use of end-stress signals greater familiarity with the word, while the use of stem-stress indicates that the word is perceived as alien or exotic. Accordingly, the number of end-stressed genitives is greater in specialist use and in various jargons. For example, the standard language requires root-stress for the genitive of шар 'balloon; ball' (ша́ра); meanwhile, шара́ is used by players and fans of billiards; the slang word хип 'hippie' (late 1960s) has root-stress in the speech of older people (хи́па) and end-stress in the speech of younger people (хипа́), for whom this is an indication of familiarity with the word and the concept (Zaliznjak 1977: 74, 76).

The number of masculine nouns that underwent the change from end-stress to stem-stress is far smaller, for example, вопль 'scream', гон 'chase', кров 'shelter', воск 'wax', терн 'thorn' (Voroncova 1979: 111). It is possible to view these nouns as a semantic group, too, since many of them denote mass entities or abstract concepts; however, other words, for example, змей 'dragon', лях 'Pole', смерд 'serf' are also in this group. All these words, clearly, are infrequent in the language, and some of them, for example, лях, смерд, are becoming even less frequent due to their status as historicisms. This decrease in the frequency of use is an important reason for the shift to stem-stress.

Prepositions and Prefixes

(i) Stress on prepositions

In Russian, a number of combinations of preposition plus noun take the stress on the preposition; this feature was probably inherited by Russian from Proto-Slavonic and was also widespread in Old Russian

---

[13] This stress is first attested in *SCSRJa* (1847), which indicates that the tendency towards the shift of stress started in the nineteenth century.

(Voroncova 1979: 135–7 and references there). The prepositions that commonly attract stress include без, за, из, на, по, под. In the nineteenth century this practice was still much more widespread than in the twentieth century, and examples are found which would be quite impossible nowadays, such as this one from Griboedov's *Горе от ума*, II.vii (1823–8):[14]

> Молчалин нá лошадь садился
>
> Molčalin was mounting the horse

However, even in nineteenth-century verse many doublets are found, with the same poet using stress now on the preposition, now on the noun; thus Lermontov uses both нá берег and на бéрег 'to the shore', where the traditional standard is still the former (Gorbačevič 1971: 86; 1972). In current usage, the tendency to replace preposition stress by stress on the noun is continuing; thus Avanesov and Ožegov (1959) and Borunova *et al.* (1983) allow both нá берег and на бéрег (in that order), and Superanskaja (1959: 161) notes that of her informants, 87 preferred на бéрег, only 27 нá берег, with 32 hesitating.

With some combinations of preposition plus noun, stress is found on the noun in the literal meaning of the expression, and on the preposition in other meanings. One such example sanctioned by the normative handbooks is за гóрод(ом) 'beyond the town, city' versus зá город(ом) 'to/in the suburbs'. For a number of combinations where the traditional standard is with preposition stress, differentiation of this kind is common in practice (Superanskaja 1959: 161–2). For instance, Avanesov and Ožegov (1959) give only на стéну 'onto the wall', while many of Superanskaja's informants distinguished the literal meaning на стéну from лезть нá стену 'go up the wall', in the sense of 'become irritated' (this latter variant is acknowledged in Borunova *et al.* (1983)). Overall, however, the situation is more complex (*Русская грамматика* 1980: i. 527). Thus, the preposition за 'beyond, behind, for' attracts stress if it has the spatial meaning 'over, behind' (e.g. зайти зá угол 'to turn round a corner'), temporal meanings (e.g. зá день 'through the day' or 'a day before'), or the meaning 'at, by' (e.g. схватить зá руку 'grasp by the hand').

The preposition на 'on' attracts stress if it indicates direction towards a localization, for example, сесть нá пол 'sit down on the floor', взять нá руки 'to lift'; the stress is on the noun if a more abstract direction is

---

[14] In this particular example, the presence of a set phrase нá конь 'mount' may be an additional factor.

implied, for example, посмотреть на дверь 'to look towards/at the door'. The preposition по 'on, over, at' attracts stress if it is used in the meaning 'over, through', for example, гулять пó полю 'to walk in the field', плавать пó морю 'to navigate the sea'; the noun is stressed if the preposition has a more abstract meaning (e.g. тоскá по мóрю 'longing for the sea') or if the preposition indicates a more localized point (e.g. ударить по нóсу 'hit somebody on the nose').

Stress on the preposition is impossible altogether if the preposition and the noun are separated by other words, governed by this noun, for example, by an adjective; thus, the only possible stress pattern in the expressions из мѝлого дóма 'from sweet home', по сѝнему мóрю 'over the blue sea', is with the secondary stress on the adjective and primary (main) stress on the noun. Similarly, if the noun is followed by a dependent or is linked to another noun, the stress does not shift to the preposition; thus, по льдý Фѝнского залѝва 'over the ice of the Finnish Bay', по снéгу и льдý 'on snow and ice' (Zaliznjak 1980: 72).

An exception to this is the combination of preposition, simple (non-compound) numeral, and noun: in such a combination, the stress can be on the preposition and the noun; thus, Borunova *et al.* (1983: 679) give such examples as нá два гóда 'for two years', нá пять рублéй 'for five roubles'. However, the educated spoken language tends to avoid this stress pattern, replacing it with the stress on the numeral and noun, which is consistent with a general trend of eliminating the prepositional stress variant (see also below).[15] In numerical expressions where the numeral is higher than ten or is a compound form, the stress is invariably on the numeral and the noun, e.g. за двáдцать двá часá 'in twenty-two hours'.

A large number of combinations of preposition plus noun allow stress variation, for example, ѝз виду and из вѝду 'out of sight', дó дому and до дóму 'to the house', зá плечи and за плéчи 'by the shoulders', бéз вести and без вéсти 'without a message' (the stress on the preposition is obligatory in пропáсть бéз вести 'to be missing in action'), нá зиму and на зѝму 'for winter' (*Русская грамматика* 1980: i. 527–30). The general tendency of Russian in the twentieth century has been towards the elimination of stress on the preposition; thus, a number of combinations where stress is still on the preposition are either considered

---

[15] In numerical expressions denoting approximate quantity, where the noun must precede the numeral, stress on the preposition is still the predominant variant; thus, лéт нá пять 'for approximately five years' is still a more common variant than лéт на пять (Zaliznjak 1980: 73).

archaic (for example, по́ свету 'over the world') or have been fossilized in set expressions, such as пропа́сть бе́з вести above or брать за́ ду́шу 'to be touching'. This tendency observed in CSR is consistent with the fact that stress on the preposition is more characteristic of the northern dialects than of the innovatory southern dialects, so here we have another example of encroachment of a southern dialect feature into the standard language; though here again, the loss of preposition stress also means a reduction in the amount of stress alternation. Accordingly, those word combinations where stress remains on the preposition often develop specialized meanings or turn into set phrases, e.g. туго́й на́ ухо 'deaf', рука́ о́б руку 'hand in hand' (for a detailed discussion, see Voroncova 1979: 137–66).

(ii) Stress on verbal prefixes

Similar to stress on prepositions is stress on the prefix of a number of verbs with monosyllabic roots in the past tense and past participle passive (excepting the feminine form with final stress), e.g. про́дал (feminine продала́, neuter про́дало, plural про́дали) 'sold', cf. дал (дала́, да́ло,[16] да́ли) 'gave'. Although there is some variation even in nineteenth-century literature, for the most part the traditional standard, with prefix stress, was then usual (Voroncova 1979: 175). In current usage, there is a tendency for this to be replaced by stress on the root of the verb, particularly where the meaning of the prefixed verb is literally the sum of the meaning of prefix plus root, e.g. отдать 'give away', but less so where this is not the case (e.g. продать 'sell'), or where the root does not exist as a separate word (e.g. принять 'accept'). Pirogova (1967: 19) describes the result of a questionnaire completed by 75 students, which included the stress of past masculine singular and plural отдал, отдали 'gave away', прожил, прожили 'lived through', and past plural продали 'sold', in all of which the traditional standard is with prefix stress. Root-stress was preferred by 57 informants for отдал, 61 for отдали, 38 for прожил, 45 for прожили, and 34 for продали. Until recently, many normative handbooks allowed only the traditional standard, with prefix stress; thus, *SSRLJa* (1948–65) allows прожи́л as a colloquial variant, but gives only о́тдал, without comment, although Pirogova's survey suggests that отда́л is in fact

[16] Until recently, the standard stress variant was да́ло; this variant is given as the only correct one in Avanesov and Ožegov (1959). Borunova *et al.* (1983) as well as Ožegov (1972) cite both stress variants as permissible.

more widespread than прожи́л. In Avanesov and Ožegov (1959), the root-stressed variants of these verbs are cited as colloquial alternatives; Borunova *et al.* (1983) give both variants as permissible, starting with the prefix-stressed variant in each case.

Root-stress in such verbs clearly has the effect of reducing the amount of stress alternation. Also, root-stress seems to be associated with southern dialects; thus, the results of the RJaSO survey (Krysin 1974: 265) for нали́л 'filled by pouring', отпи́л 'took a sip', при́был 'arrived', зада́ли 'set (a task)' show that for each of these items root-stress was reported significantly more frequently by informants from southern Russia than by those from northern Russia. Another factor responsible for the rise of root-stressed variants is the fact that many prefix-stressed forms, especially those of the infinitive, are *prostorečno*, for example, на́чать 'begin', при́нять 'accept'.[17] The influence of the infinitive on the other elements of the verbal paradigm is particularly strong because the infinitive is used as a citation form; in a hyper-correct manner, speakers try to avoid the prefix stress even where unnecessary.

The tendency towards root-stress is most apparent in the past tense masculine, and root-stress is consistently found in early twentieth-century poetry (Voroncova 1979: 175–81), to an even greater extent than in the current standard and possibly reflecting imitation of non-standard speech. A few verbs that steadily retain stress on the prefix include созда́ть (со́здал) 'create', убы́ть (у́был) 'depart', прокля́ть (про́клял) 'damn', запи́ть (за́пил) 'start drinking', and verbs derived from -мере́ть (e.g. за́мер 'froze') and -пере́ть (e.g. о́тпер 'unlocked').

In the past tense feminine, two competing tendencies are observed, one towards root-stress, the other tendency, which is much stronger, towards end-stress. For example, the former tendency is reflected in the verb избы́ть (избыла́) 'exhaust, use up', for which Avanesov and Ožegov (1959) specifically indicate that root stress is unacceptable, and the latter tendency determines the end-stress on the form отбыла́ (Avanesov and Ožegov (1959) cite both о́тбыла and отбы́ла as not recommended). The spread of end-stress in the feminine, in turn, has been influencing the development of past tense neuter forms, both with and without prefixes, for example, оторвало́ 'tore off' and the stress variant дало́ mentioned above (see also n. 15). The active rise of end-stressed neuter forms is a relatively recent phenomenon (Voroncova

---

[17] Both these forms occurred regularly in the speech of the Soviet leader Mikhail Gorbačev, who combined features of southern dialects and of *prostorečie* (for a more general characterization of Gorbačev's speech, see Kostomarov 1994: 46, 207).

1979: 183–5), and such forms are more apparent in non-standard varieties (Voroncova 1979: 185–6). The increasing number of end-stressed forms in the neuter certainly contributes to the analogical levelling in the paradigm. One might also expect the rise of end-stress among prefixed past plurals. Though this phenomenon is commonly observed in *prostorečie*, there are few examples of stabilized end-stressed prefixed plurals in the standard language.[18,19]

Stress Changes in Conjugation

(i) Verbs in -úmь

Verbs of the second conjugation with infinitive in stressed -и́ть either have fixed stress throughout the present tense (e.g. говори́ть 'speak', first person singular говорю́, second person singular говори́шь) or have end-stress on the first person singular only and stem-stress on all other forms (e.g. води́ть 'lead', вожу́, во́дишь).

In current usage there is considerable variation with a large number of verbs in -и́ть,[20] and there is a general tendency for verbs without stress alternation to move into the class of verbs with stress alternation. For instance, Grot (1891–5) cites дружи́ть 'be friends' as having only fixed stress, while allowing both fixed and mobile stress with вари́ть 'cook' and грузи́ть 'load'; Trubetzkoy (1934: 41) criticizes да́рит, пла́тит as provincialisms, unacceptable in the Moscow standard. In current usage all these verbs are commonly root-stressed in the relevant forms, and Borunova *et al.* (1983), while acknowledging end-stress as an archaic variant for грузи́ть, дари́ть, дружи́ть, cite only the root-stressed form for вари́ть.[21] This comparison between Grot's standard and the standard

---

[18] Voroncova (1979: 186) cites the verb поплыли́ 'floated', which probably gained widespread acceptance due to the well-known poem by Mixail Isakovskij *Катюша*: 'Расцветали яблони и груши, | Поплыли́ туманы над рекой . . .' 'Apple and pear trees were in bloom, | Clouds of mist were floating above the river . . .'. This development is even more unusual given that the unprefixed plural плы́ли retains root stress.

[19] Strom (1988) provides detailed information on stress variation of prefixed verbs, based on reading experiments, and contrasts different explanations of the tendencies observed.

[20] The situation is complicated by the fact that derivatives of verbs need not belong to the same class as the verb from which they are derived: thus сади́ть 'plant, seat' has stress alternation, but сади́ться 'sit down' does not; води́ть 'lead' does, but руководи́ть 'supervise, control' and води́ться 'be friends with' do not. A comprehensive account of the stress of verbs in -ить is given by Voroncova (1959; 1979: 204–36), with numerous examples from nineteenth-century and contemporary verse, and the results of surveys.

[21] The treatment of дружи́ть in normative handbooks is, however, rather confusing:

of the late twentieth century[22] shows that the switch to stress alternation is almost complete.

Revealing light can be thrown on the normativity of various verbs in -ить with mobile stress by examining the qualifications given to forms with mobile stress in Avanesov and Ožegov (1959). For варить, where nineteenth-century usage allowed fixed stress, mobile stress is given without any comment. For дарить, where Grot (1891–5) allows only fixed stress, mobile stress is recommended, and fixed stress qualified as 'archaic'. For грузить, where nineteenth-century usage allowed both fixed and mobile stress, mobile stress is given, but fixed stress is qualified as 'permissible'. For дружить, where Grot allows only fixed stress, fixed stress is recommended and mobile stress 'permissible'; as noted above, current usage overwhelmingly favours mobile stress. For звонить 'ring; call on the phone', only fixed stress is allowed, and mobile stress is specifically condemned; this verb has become something of a shibboleth with normative grammarians, being one of the most often cited examples of a word which is frequently wrongly stressed, although from the informant responses in Kolesov (1967: 109) it is doubtful whether mobile stress is so widespread with this word (141 informants gave звони́т, 53 зво́нит, 11 both forms); some recent dictionaries permit mobile stress, though only as a colloquial form (SPU 1971–2; Gorbačevič 1973); in Borunova *et al.* (1983), зво́нит is vaguely characterized as 'not recommended'.

In such verbs, the northern dialects tend to favour fixed stress,[23] the southern dialects the innovatory mobile stress (Kasvin 1949). As generally with stress, a further distinction can be drawn between the western (north-western) and eastern dialects (Zaliznjak 1985). Though overall restructuring of stress in the history of Russian is quite complex (Zaliznjak 1985: 356–62, 380–1), the recent changes that have taken place and are taking place in the stressing of verbs in -ить can be interpreted as evidence of the eastern and southern dialects encroaching on

---

SSRLJa (1948–65) describes дружи́т as *prostorečno*; Avanesov and Ožegov (1959) describe it as 'permissible'; Ožegov (1972) allows both дружи́шь and дру́жишь in that order; SSRLJa (1991–) cites дружи́шь as archaic; while Ageenko and Zarva (1984), usually conservative in their attitude towards the norm, cite only дру́жишь, without comment. Of the informants in the RJaSO survey (Krysin 1974: 232), 94.4 per cent preferred дру́жишь, which is reflected in the recommendations by Borunova *et al.* (1983).

[22] Note that until recently, normative handbooks still treated грузи́ть, дари́ть, дружи́ть, вари́ть as having fixed stress.

[23] This feature of the northern dialects seems to be an unusual archaism within the Slavonic language-area as a whole; the South Slavonic languages have reflexes of a stress pattern more like that of southern Russian dialects here.

the north-western standard. The role of southern dialect influence is particularly clear here because the effect of this change is to increase the amount of stress alternation within the paradigm, rather than to reduce it, as has been the case in most of the stress changes examined earlier in this chapter. The southern dialect influence has here been a much more potent factor than analogical levelling.[24]

In addition to this geographical difference, pragmatic factors also play an important role in the choice between fixed and mobile stress: learned, less frequent words tend to retain fixed stress, while everyday words acquire mobile stress; in Russian Church Slavonic, the usual rule is for fixed stress, which is also consistent with the predominant stress pattern of northern Russian. Thus we find contrasts like просвети́ть 'shine through' with mobile stress and просвети́ть 'enlighten' with fixed stress,[25] and измени́ть 'change' with mobile stress but видоизмени́ть 'modify' with fixed stress.[26] In a number of cases, variants with fixed and mobile stress have become lexicalized. For example, коси́ть (ко́сишь) 'mow, cut' has mobile stress, and коси́ть (коси́шь) 'squint' has fixed stress; the relatively infrequent чини́ть (чини́шь) 'do, make' (e.g. чини́ть препятствия 'impede') has fixed stress, and the commonly used verb чини́ть (чи́нишь) 'repair' has mobile stress (Voroncova 1979: 220–1).

Similar variation is found with present participles active and past participles passive of verbs in -ить, although overall end-stress is commoner with these forms than with forms of the present tense (perhaps because the former are more learned forms). Where stress variation is still allowed for present participles active, the variants are distinguished stylistically: the stem-stressed variant is associated with a poetic, elevated style; for example, хва́лящий 'praising', дра́знящий 'teasing'.

In a growing number of cases, stress has become a disambiguating factor in distinguishing past participles passive from the corresponding adjectives, for example, from дари́ть 'present', да́ренный (participle) and дарёный (adjective). In writing, participles are known to differ

[24] The statistics cited in Krysin (1974: 265) show that in general southerners are more likely than northerners to favour mobile stress, though for the examples cited the difference is not particularly significant.

[25] Other forms of these two verbs also show differences between Church Slavonic and native Russian variants: in the sense 'shine through' the first person singular of the future is просвечу́, the past participle passive просве́ченный, and the imperfective просве́чивать; the corresponding forms in the sense 'enlighten' are просвещу́, просвещённый, просвеща́ть.

[26] Fixed stress for видоизмени́ть is given by most dictionaries, although Ageenko and Zarva (1984), surprisingly, give only mobile stress.

from adjectives in having double н in the suffix (*Русская грамматика* 1980: i. 298). However, this rule is far from universal: first, there are a number of adjectives that have double н in the suffix (*Русская грамматика* 1980: i. 298, 671); second, it is often hard to decide whether a form is adjectival or participial, e.g. у́лица, мощённая булы́жником 'street paved with cobble-stone' (*Русская грамматика* 1980: i. 666; Borunova *et al.* 1983: 699).[27] In some cases, stress distinguishes two lexical items both of which have lost their participial characteristics, for example, располо́женный 'located' (adjective, from past participle passive from расположи́ть 'locate, situate') and расположённый 'benevolent'; новоро́жденный 'new-born' (adjective) and новорождённый 'new-born, infant' (noun).

The number of verbs in -и́ть with mobile stress is also being increased, though to a lesser extent, by the shift of a number of verbs which originally had stem-stress in the infinitive into this class (Gorbačevič 1974).[28] In the nineteenth century, for instance, the usual stress was у́дить (у́жу, у́дишь) 'fish', whereas nowadays it is уди́ть (ужу́, but still у́дишь). For a number of verbs where Avanesov and Ožegov (1959) and Borunova *et al.* (1983) give only stem-stress, end-stress in the infinitive is in fact common in contemporary speech and verse, e.g. пригубить 'take a sip', принудить 'compel', приструнить 'take in hand'.[29] For the verb искриться 'sparkle', the variant искри́ться is qualified as *prostorečno* by *SSRLJa* (1948–65), as 'permissible' by Avanesov and Ožegov (1959), and as the first of the two accepted variants in Borunova *et al.* (1983); of Gorbačevič's 258 informants (students at Leningrad State University) only 25 gave the traditional stress и́скриться (Gorbačevič 1974: 11).

(ii) Verbs in unstressed -ить

Stem-stressed verbs in -ить normally retain this stress throughout the paradigm, including the past participle passive, for example, напо́лнить

---

[27] For other examples, see Kolesov (1967: 111–12), Krysin (1974: 232).

[28] This article also notes a small number of verbs which have undergone the reverse change (e.g. current уско́рить 'speed up' for older ускори́ть) and a number of other infinitives where the recommendations of normative handbooks do not correspond to current usage, e.g. ржа́веть 'rust' (ржаве́ть common in contemporary speech and verse), ба́ловать 'spoil, pamper' (балова́ть preferred by 195 of Gorbačevič's 247 informants). See also Voroncova (1979: 210–27).

[29] For this latter verb, Borunova *et al.* (1983) cite the end-stress form as 'not recommended'.

'fill up'—напо́лненный. In a small number of verbs, however, the older form of the participle, under Church Slavonic influence, had stress on the suffix, for example, засне́жить 'to cover with snow' (attested in nineteenth-century Russian but archaic in the twentieth century)— past participle passive, заснежённый, озло́бить 'embitter'—past participle passive озлоблённый. In these cases, the shift in stress reduced the amount of stress alternation; in the modern language, only stem-stress is acceptable, thus засне́женный, озло́бленный. Another example of such stress levelling is the past participle passive of уни́зить 'humiliate': while the modern standard has the stress on the root (уни́женный), the older form is унижённый (cited as permissible but archaic in Borunova *et al.* (1983)). This latter stress variant is used in the title of Dostoevskij's *Унижённые и оскорблённые* 'The Insulted and the Injured' (note that with the stress on the suffix, the two participles rhyme).

(iii) Reflexive verbs

In the masculine singular past tense, a number of monosyllabic verbs and their derivatives, and also роди́ться 'be born' (though only in the perfective aspect) have, in accordance with the traditional standard, stress on the reflexive particle, e.g. начался́ 'began', роди́лся́ 'was born', взялся́ 'set to (work)', обнялся́ 'embraced'. In nineteenth-century literature this stress was in general adhered to, cf. in Puškin's *Сказка о царе Салтане* (1831):

> Сын на ножки подня́лся,
> В дно головкой уперся́ . . .
>
> The son rose to his feet,
> Pushed against the bottom . . .

However, there are exceptions, too, as in Puškin's *Евгений Онегин*, I. ii (1823):

> Онегин, добрый мой приятель,
> Роди́лся на брегах Невы . . .
>
> Onegin, my good friend,
> Was born on the banks of the Neva . . .

In current usage, many such verbs have lost the possibility, or at least the requirement, of stress on -ся. Thus обнялся́ is qualified only as 'permissible' by Avanesov and Ožegov (1959), and given by only 20 per

cent of the informants in the RJaSO survey (Krysin 1974: 232). Взялся́
is described as archaic by Avanesov and Ožegov (1959) and by
Borunova *et al.* (1983), and in the survey reported in Kolesov (1967:
115) 169 informants gave взя́лся, 19 взялся́, and 8 both forms.
Avanesov and Ožegov (1959) list both роди́лся and родился́ (in that
order);[30] of Kolesov's informants (1967: 115), 178 gave роди́лся, 12
родился́, 8 both forms (though it is not clear whether these informants
distinguished in their replies between perfective and imperfective
роди́ться, since the latter has only роди́лся). Only a few verbs still
require stress on -ся, e.g. начался́ (given by 100 of Kolesov's 194
informants as the only possibility, and as a variant by a further 13).
Overall, the comparison of the twentieth-century language with
nineteenth-century poetry shows that the number of verbs with stress on
the reflexive particle is steadily decreasing (Voroncova 1979: 186–9).
Furthermore, the difference in recommendations given by Avanesov and
Ožegov (1959) and by SPU (1971–2) confirms that this tendency is very
active in the modern language (Voroncova 1979: 190).

In the feminine singular of such verbs there is no problem, since stress
is on the last syllable in both reflexive and non-reflexive forms (e.g.
взяла́, взяла́сь). With the neuter singular form and plural form, however, a similar stress alternation exists in the traditional standard, with
stem-stress in the non-reflexive (e.g. взя́ло,[31] взя́ли), but end-stress in
the reflexive (взяло́сь, взяли́сь). Change has been much slower here
than in the masculine singular, although here too there has been a
tendency to lose the stress alternation in the plural by having stem-stress
in the reflexive form too; many such forms are given in Avanesov and
Ožegov (1959), though usually as permissible (дожда́лись 'waited
for', придра́лись 'found fault'), or colloquial variants (напи́лись 'got
drunk', созда́лось 'was created').[32] From the informant responses quoted in Kolesov (1967: 114) and Krysin (1974: 232) придра́лись is much
commoner than придрали́сь, дожда́лись somewhat commoner than
дождали́сь, напи́лись and напили́сь about equally common, while
созда́лось is preferred to the traditional form создало́сь by under 20
per cent of those questioned. Lack of stress alternation in such verbs is

---

[30] In Borunova *et al.* (1983), the variants are listed in the opposite order.

[31] In the second half of this century, end-stress of the neuter form, long attested in the
spoken language, found its way into the standard; thus, Borunova *et al.* (1983) list both
stress variants for a large number of verbs (cf. да́ло above).

[32] In Borunova *et al.* (1983), these two forms are no longer identified as colloquial;
instead, in each case, the stem-stressed form is listed as a second permissible variant,
labelled 'additional' (дополнительно).

again characteristic of the southern dialects (see the statistics in Krysin 1974: 265).

Stress Changes in Adjective Declension (Short Forms)

(i) Feminine singular

Such forms from non-derived adjectives, and also from adjectives with the suffixes -н-, -л-, -к-, preceded by a consonant, usually have end-stress, for example, мила́ 'nice', проста́ 'simple', верна́ 'faithful'. However, a number of suffixed adjectives are exceptional in having stem-stress; for the most part these are more learned adjectives, though in practice the application of this criterion is rather subjective (Gorbačevič 1971: 79–80), e.g. ве́чна 'eternal', пра́здна 'idle'. Until recently, normative handbooks recommended, as the only or preferred form, end-stress; meanwhile, in current usage one finds stem-stress very frequently, even as the preferred form (Gorbačevič 1971: 79–81). Thus Avanesov and Ožegov (1959) give only склонна́ 'inclined', but of the 222 informants polled by Kolesov (1967: 106), 206 gave скло́нна, 15 склонна́, and 1 both forms. Borunova *et al.* (1983) list both stress variants for склонна, giving the end-stressed form first.

The general rise of stem-stress in feminine short adjectives, characteristic of CSR, is acknowledged in Zaliznjak (1980) and Borunova *et al.* (1983); although both dictionaries allow stem-stress for a greater number of adjectives than was done by their predecessors, they still consider this stress a variant, parallel to end-stress, rather than the only standard. Some examples of adjectives allowing both end- and stem-stress: гне́вна́ 'furious', четка́/чётка 'precise', квела́/квёла 'weak, stale', сто́йка́ 'resilient'. As is indicated in Borunova *et al.* (1983: 691), the shift of stress to inflection in feminine short-form adjectives is a relatively new phenomenon in CSR, which normative handbooks were slow to recognize.

(ii) Plural forms

The traditional rule for Russian short-form adjectives in the plural was to have the same stress as the neuter singular short form: жа́рки 'hot' (cf. жа́рко), хороши́ 'good' (cf. хорошо́). However, many such adjectives, even within a conservative conception of the standard, allow variants with stem-stress and end-stress. Thus for во́льны 'free' and сильны 'strong' Avanesov and Ožegov (1959) allow both variants (citing the stem-stressed variant first); Borunova *et al.* (1983) give the same recommendations for the first word but identify си́льны as archaic though permissible. For бодры 'alert, cheerful', горды 'proud', and просты 'simple', Avanesov and Ožegov (1959) cite the end-stressed variant as a permissible alternative; for all these adjectives, Borunova *et al.* (1983) give the end-stressed variant first and identify го́рды and про́сты as archaic. While Avanesov and Ožegov (1959) allow only the stem-stressed forms of круглы 'round', прямы 'straight', туги 'tight', and храбры 'brave', Borunova *et al.* (1983) give both the end-stressed and stem-stressed variants (in that order) for круглы, прямы, and храбры, and, in the opposite order, for туги.

All of these are adjectives where Šapiro (1952) already found preference for the end-stressed variant. Similarly, Kolesov (1967: 105) found that his informants preferred end-stress in all cases examined where the normative handbooks allow alternatives, and even in some cases where they do not (e.g. близки 'near');[33] only with стары 'old', where Avanesov and Ožegov (1959) give стары́ as permissible, was there preference for the older form ста́ры.

Overall, the data obtained in surveys and the comparison between the orthoepic dictionaries reveal the tendency for the increasing number of short-form adjectives in the plural with mobile stress; starting from the middle of the twentieth century, there seems to be a slight preference for end-stress.

Stress and Derivational Morphology[34]

(i) Nouns in -граф, -лог, -метр[35]

Nouns with these suffixes started entering Russian from French in the eighteenth century. In the earlier period they almost always followed the French stress pattern, with final stress; thus, in Puškin's *Евгений Онегин*, I. vi (1823):

> Он знал довольно по-латыне,
> Чтоб эпигра́фы разбирать
>
> He knew enough Latin
> To figure out epigraphs.

---

[33] However, Borunova *et al.* (1983) allow both близки́ and бли́зки.

[34] The general problem of variant stresses in derived words is treated by Red′kin (1966).

[35] See further Superanskaja (1968: 147–61).

Towards the end of the nineteenth century, most words of this group transferred to having penultimate stress, and most of the numerous new creations connected with technological developments were also given penultimate stress. Grot (1891–5) is the first dictionary to list the penultimate stress variants widely.

Nearly all nouns in -граф, whether referring to people or things, have penultimate stress in current usage, e.g. фото́граф 'photographer', авто́граф 'autograph', пара́граф 'paragraph', although there are a few exceptions, like телегра́ф 'telegraph', полигра́ф 'polygraphist'.[36] For some of these words, however, final stress was widespread, if not the rule, in the nineteenth century: nineteenth-century dictionaries give only автогра́ф, and even both editions of *SSRLJa* (1948–65 and 1991–) still give this as an archaic alternative; фоногра́ф 'phonograph' is not noted in the nineteenth-century dictionaries, and twentieth-century dictionaries all give фоно́граф but L. Tolstoj's pronunciation фоногра́ф is preserved on the record *Голоса писателей*.[37]

For nouns in -лог, a distinction must be made between those referring to people and others. For those referring to people, the older standard was for final stress (thus Puškin uses филоло́г 'philologist' and физиоло́г 'physiologist'), whereas in contemporary usage and normative handbooks most have penultimate stress, with the exception of генеало́г 'genealogist', and минерало́г 'mineralogist'.[38] Grot (1891–5) is the earliest dictionary to list penultimate stress as a regular alternative to final stress (though Dal´ (1880–2) gives био́лог 'biologist'), and D. N. Ušakov (1935–40) still lists some final stresses as alternatives (e.g. метеоро́лог 'meteorologist').

Words in -лог referring to inanimate entities have been subject to the same tendency, though to a lesser extent, and with many words of this class the stress variants go back two hundred years. Thus nineteenth-century and many twentieth-century dictionaries give both диало́г and диа́лог 'dialogue', which latter is already considered archaic by Avanesov and Ožegov (1959); in the first half of the twentieth century, диа́лог was cultivated by specialists in literature, as also was occasionally моно́лог 'monologue', for which the dictionaries allow only

[36] Final stress is obligatory in borrowings from German where -граф occurs in a different meaning, namely 'earl', 'count' (e.g. ландгра́ф 'landgrave').

[37] The word is now archaic, having been replaced successively by граммофон, патефон, and the current проигрыватель 'hi-fi'.

[38] Note that these words end, exceptionally, in -алог, not -олог. Avanesov and Ožegov (1959) warn against the pronunciation минеро́лог; *SAR* (1806–22, the relevant volume having appeared in 1814) gives минера́лог.

монолóг (Superanskaja 1968: 153).[39] Каталог 'catalogue' has been
subject to similar variation, though here it is the stress каталóг that is
cultivated by librarians; каталóг is the only form recognized by
Avanesov and Ožegov (1959) and by Borunova *et al.* (1983); the survey
cited by Superanskaja (1968: 153) noted overwhelming preference for
катáлог, though of the informants polled by Kolesov (1967: 108) 99
preferred катáлог and 98 каталóг. Некролóг 'obituary' is another
word where Avanesov and Ožegov (1959) and, more recently, Borunova
et al. (1983) allow only final stress, but where the survey reported in
Superanskaja (1968: 154) shows overwhelming preference (89.5 per
cent of informants) for penultimate stress. The variation between penultimate and final stress in this word is acknowledged in Zaliznjak (1980).

Nouns in -метр, excepting those that are measures in the metric
system, have undergone the same general change: thus термометр
'thermometer' is given in most nineteenth-century dictionaries as
термомéтр, while modern dictionaries give only термóметр. With the
names of measures in the metric system, however, current normative
handbooks allow only final stress (киломéтр 'kilometre', миллимéтр
'millimetre'), although penultimate stress is common in vernacular,
uneducated, speech. The famous metallurgist and member of the
Academy of Sciences I. P. Bardin, when asked whether one should say
киломéтр or килóметр, replied: 'It depends on the time and place. At
a meeting of the Praesidium of the Academy—киломéтр, otherwise
academician Vinogradov will curl his face up. But at the Novotul´skij
factory, of course, килóметр, otherwise people will think Bardin is
giving himself airs' (Kostomarov and Leont´ev 1966: 5).

(ii) Verbs in -ировать[40]

In current usage, the overwhelming majority of verbs with this suffix are
stressed -и́ровать, although those in -ировáть include many common
verbs, and the partition into two classes is essentially arbitrary. In the
nineteenth century there were far fewer verbs in -ировать, and the
majority of such verbs that did exist were stressed on the last syllable.
This was consistent with the general Gallicization of loan-words in late
eighteenth- and nineteenth-century Russian: loan-words were known

---

[39] With several words, non-standard stresses are cultivated by certain professional
groups, e.g. компáс 'compass' among sailors, харáктерный 'characteristic' among
actors (Gorbačevič 1973).

[40] See further Voroncova (1967; 1979: 237–48).

and used primarily by educated people who were often bilingual in Russian and French, and even if a word was borrowed from a different language, final stress was used as a sign of the word's borrowed status. Thus, the pronunciation of Shakespeare's first name was Вильям throughout the nineteenth century and the shift of stress to the first syllable did not occur until the 1920s. Likewise, the influence of French borrowings in -*eur* affected the stress on similarly sounding words even if their origin was other than French, for example, вахтёр, borrowed from German (*Wachter*).[41] (See also Chapter 5.)

The shift away from final stress in borrowings started in the late nineteenth century, often under the influence of German and often in more technical, specialized borrowings. One large group of such specialized borrowings was represented by verbs in -ировать, whose number increased dramatically as the many new coinages resulting from technological developments were adopted by the language. These verbs typically had antepenultimate stress and soon other verbs, already known by the language, were undergoing the shift from final to antepenultimate stress. Some idea of the change can be gained by looking at the stress given for буксировать 'tow' in various dictionaries: *SCRJa* (1847) gives only буксирова́ть; Grot (1891–5) gives both stresses, as does D. N. Ušakov (1935–40); Avanesov and Ožegov (1959) give only букси́ровать, and specifically condemn final stress; Borunova *et al.* (1983) do not even mention the possibility of final stress.[42] One of the rare instances where the shift of stress was in the opposite direction is the verb тренировать 'coach': while D. N. Ušakov (1935–40) allows stress variation (трени́рова́ть), the modern norm prescribes the ultimate stress (Borunova *et al.* 1983). Similarly, while final stress was unacceptable for the verbs пломбировать 'fill' and гофрировать 'crimp; goffer' in the beginning of the twentieth century, it has now become the only one permissible (Voroncova 1979: 246; Bogatyrev 1985: 165–6).

With many verbs in -ировать, there is variation between final and antepenultimate stress in current usage. Two such verbs are преми́ровать 'award a bonus to', and нормировать 'standardize', where nearly all dictionaries allow only премирова́ть, нормирова́ть (Avanesov and Ožegov (1959) and Borunova *et al.* (1983) specifically

---

[41] The stress variant ва́хтер is labelled by modern normative handbooks as either archaic or *prostorečno*.

[42] Occasionally, the past participle passive may retain the earlier stress even when the other forms have changed, e.g. дистилли́ровать 'distil', but дистиллиро́ванный 'distilled'; see the discussion of verbs in -ить earlier in this chapter.

condemn премировать), although Gorbačevič (1966) notes that in speech it is the antepenultimate stress that predominates, and Voroncova (1979: 247) notes that for both verbs the stress variant in -и́ровать has gained wide acceptance. The form премировать is admitted as a permissible variant by Rozental´ (1964: 120) (but not in earlier editions of this work), SPU (1971–2), and Gorbačevič (1973). Though admitted by some dictionaries, the form with antepenultimate stress is apparently more colloquial, probably merging on *prostorečno*.

A number of words in -(из)ировать, most of them borrowings, undergo a different kind of change, where the suffix is replaced by the suffix -(из)овать; for example, легализи́ровать and легализова́ть 'legalize', индустриализи́ровать and индустриализова́ть 'industrialize', скандализи́ровать and скандализова́ть 'scandalize', вульгаризи́ровать and вульгаризова́ть 'vulgarize'; also, the analogically formed большевизи́ровать and большевизова́ть 'Bolshevize', советизи́ровать and советизова́ть 'Sovietize'. The verbs in (из)овать replacing verbs in -(из)ировать invariably have final stress. In general, the switch from -ировать to the shorter -(из)овать is indicative of a greater degree of nativization of the borrowing, but there are a large number of idiosyncrasies (Graudina *et al.* 1976: 310–12).

Words with Secondary Stress

As was mentioned in the beginning of this chapter, a number of Russian compound words can occur with the so-called secondary stress (in Russian linguistic terminology, вторичное or побочное ударение). As a rule, secondary stress precedes primary stress; accordingly, the shape of the initial component of the word plays a crucial role in determining whether or not the secondary stress will occur. Though in general variation is possible, depending on such pragmatic factors as the tempo of speech or emphasis (Kalenčuk 1993: 11), there are several tendencies that can be recognized.

Many compound words characteristically used by a certain professional group are pronounced without secondary stress by members of this professional group (indicating familiarity with the word), and with secondary stress outside this group; for example, элѐктроте́хника and электроте́хника 'electrical engineering', фòтосни́мок and фотосни́мок 'photograph' (Zaliznjak 1980: 10; Borunova *et al.* 1983: 683). Similarly, bookish compound words tend to have secondary stress, for example, клятвопреступле́ние 'perjury'; this is again a manifestation of lesser familiarity with a word.

If a compound word includes, as its non-final component, a truncated word or an abbreviated word, it normally requires secondary stress. As will be shown in the next chapter, the Russian language in the twentieth century developed a large number of abbreviations; accordingly, a large number of new compound words arose that bear secondary stress; for example, про̀фсобра́ние 'trade union meeting',[43] па̀ртсобра́ние 'party meeting', агѝтбрига́да 'propaganda team'. If a word includes several truncated words or abbreviations as its components, several secondary stresses are possible, for example, Со̀винфо̀рмбюро́ 'Soviet Information Agency', а̀утосѐротерапи́я (Ageenko and Zarva 1984: 53) 'administration of self-therapy with sulphuric medications'. Similarly, secondary stress falls on the first component of the so-called hyphenated compounds unless they are perceived as regular compounds (see Chapter 3).

Secondary stress is common in words with the Russian prefixes после- 'after' and сверх- 'excessive', for example, свѐрхъесте́ственный 'supernatural'; it is also found in words with borrowed prefixes архи-, анти-, ультра-, супер-, транс-, контр- (Borunova *et al.* 1983: 683), for example, а̀нтиобще́ственный 'antisocial'.

The overall tendency is for the loss of secondary stress in nativized words; representative of this tendency are words with borrowed prefixes де- and ре- : in many of such words, the stress on the prefix was, until the 1940s, indicated by the hyphenation of the prefix in writing. For example, in Mariètta Šaginjan's *Гидроцентраль* (1928–48) we find де-монтировать 'disassemble'. As words with these prefixes become more a part of the lexicon, the stress on the prefix disappears; thus, Borunova *et al.* (1983: 684) indicate that secondary stress does not occur in such words as демобилиза́ция 'demobilization', дешифро́вка 'deciphering', реорганиза́ция 'reorganization'.

Intonation

The study of Russian intonation has been concerned primarily with the principles of synchronic description and their application to teaching spoken Russian as a second language (e.g. Bratus 1972; Čeremisina 1989). Some studies focus on the role of intonation in conveying the

---

[43] However, профсою́з 'trade union' has only main stress.

communicative structure of the utterance (Pavlik 1977). In synchronic descriptions, it is customary to differentiate between several basic tonal contours or numbered intonational constructions (abbreviated as IK, from Russian интонационные контуры, ИК), proposed by Bryzgunova (1977)[44] and also discussed in detail in Odé (1989), Svetozarova (1982).[45] An important distinction between these contours consists in their distribution in final and non-final syntagms or, from a different standpoint, in functionally complete and functionally incomplete contextual segments (Schallert 1990: 60–1). According to Bryzgunova (see *Русская грамматика* 1980: i. 99–111; 1980: ii. 100), IK-3, IK-4, and IK-6, all of which include a rising or a high tonal component, can be used in non-final (incomplete) segments. (See Figs. 1–6.)

Two common contours, IK-3 and IK-4, differ in the degree of conversational overtones: IK-3 is generally considered to be more casual and conversational, while IK-4 is viewed as more official (*Русская грамматика* 1980: i. 101–2, 118). Bryzgunova describes IK-4 as typical of the speech of radio and television announcers (дикторская речь). The percentage of IK-4 (and its variants) is higher in the speech of the older generation, especially in the speech of intellectuals (Nikolaeva 1977: 86). As shown by the data in Buning and van Schoonveld (1960: 35–6, 58–9), this contour was retained as most frequent declarative contour by *émigré* speakers in the middle of this century.[46]

With regard to IK-3, the general tendency of the contemporary language has been towards its use as the major type of nexal intonation (Schallert 1990: 60–4), and the appropriateness of this contour in incomplete syntagms may explain its conversational character: spontaneous, unplanned speech normally includes more incomplete sentences than the so-called codified spoken language represented in дикторская речь. Accordingly, by controlling tonal variations a speaker of CSR is able to switch registers or functional styles (see also Nikolaeva 1977: 83–4).

In completed declarative syntagms, e.g. Погóда улýчшилась 'The weather improved', there seems to be a generational difference in the

---

[44] The sections on intonation in the Academy Grammar (*Русская грамматика* 1980: i. 96–122; ii. 89, 99–100, 103, 105, 109–10, 115–16, 118–19) were also written by Bryzgunova.

[45] See also Baldwin (1979: 3–15), for a brief review of studies of Russian intonation.

[46] The speaker interviewed by Buning and van Schooneveld had other characteristics that had become either archaic or rare in the Russian language spoken in the Soviet Union in the 1950s, when the study was conducted. For example, she had overall hard pronunciation of the reflexive particle (Buning and van Schooneveld 1960: 57, ex. (91)) and used some obsolete words and expressions.

Там холодно

Fig. 1 IK-1: a fall in the tonic syllable followed by a low-level continuation in the post-tonic syllable(s) (if any).

Когда он придет?

Fig. 2 IK-2: a fall in the tonic syllable preceded by a rise in the pretonic syllable and followed by a low-level continuation in the post-tonic syllable(s) (if any).

Он предупредил их?

Fig. 3 IK-3: a sharp rise in the tonic syllable followed by a fall in the post-tonic syllable(s) (if any).

Внимание!

Fig. 4 IK-4: a deep fall in the tonic syllable followed by a high-level continuation in the post-tonic syllable(s) (if any).

Какой ветер!

Fig. 5 IK-5: a sharp high-fall on two tonic syllables followed by a low-level continuation in the post-tonic syllable(s) (if any).

Народу набежало!

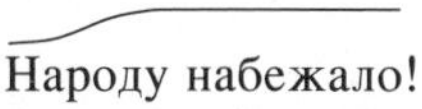

Fig. 6 IK-6: a gradual rise in the tonic syllable followed by a high-level continuation in the post-tonic syllable(s) (if any).

realization of IK-1 (rise-fall): younger speakers have a higher initial rise
and tend to prolong the final post-tonic syllable, while older speakers
show a tendency towards a more levelled intonation with the reduction
of final post-tonic syllables (Nikolaeva 1977: 82–3 n. 13).[47] The generational distinction correlates with the difference between the Moscow and
Leningrad intonation: the Leningrad intonation is more conservative
(Nikolaeva 1977: 82). This is another instance of what V. V.
Vinogradov (1938: 439) called 'the struggle between St Petersburg and
Moscow for the norms of Russian pronunciation': the Moscow pronunciation is typically more innovatory and tends to win over the competing variants.

The question of overall intonation change in the history of Russian
has been studied much less. Intonation change is examined by Ceplitis
(1974), who differs from the authors cited above in adopting a very comprehensive approach to intonation: as intonation parameters, he includes
frequency, length, pitch, pausing, intensity, range, loudness. His study is
based on the changes undergone by Russian theatre pronunciation since
the end of the nineteenth century. Overall, the standard Russian intonation in the twentieth century has increased the proportion of rising syntagms, which is consistent with Schallert's observations. The pause can
be used to convey the logical structure of the text or its emotive component (Ceplitis 1974: 82); in the structural division of the text, the long
pause has a separative function, and the short pause serves to connect
text constituents (Peškovskij 1956: 458). The long pause is also typical
of the emotive function. The twentieth-century language has tended to
eliminate the long pause and indiscriminately use the short pause in all
functions.

According to Ceplitis, the intensity and the auditory loudness of
spoken standard Russian have increased dramatically in the twentieth
century; his conclusion is based on the comparison of early gramophone
records (e.g. *Голоса писателей*, mentioned above, p. 95) and contemporary speech. The relevance of loudness as a tonal parameter is also
noted by Baldwin (1979: 26–7);[48] he indicates that loudness and lexical

---

[47] Nikolaeva (1977: 80) indicates that she studied ten standard speakers, representing
Moscow and Leningrad pronunciation, but does not specify their age. Given the time of
the study, we can assume that the older speakers are closer to OM and OPb, while the
younger speakers represent the norm of the 1950s onwards. Cf. a similar distinction
between the norms of the first and second half of the twentieth century in Panov (1990: 13,
15–22).

[48] Baldwin, however, argues against including loudness in the underlying parameters
of Russian intonation (1979: 200).

stress do not necessarily coincide, which seems to be an innovatory feature, too.

Another emerging tendency, probably related to the increase in intensity, concerns the placement of emphatic stress. While it was typical of the nineteenth-century language to place the emphatic stress (or the so-called emphatic stress, Russian логическое ударение) only on the focus of contrast,[49] the contemporary language tends to include adjacent words under the same stress (Raspopov 1961: 119; Nikolaeva 1977: 90). This extension of emphatic stress has prompted Zinder (1960: 292) to suggest that it should be treated as a separate intonation type (emphatic or emotive intonation), rather than accent.

As methods of speech recording and speech analysis advanced, more and more samples of spoken Russian became available, primarily in recorded speech over the radio, in spoken cinematography (since the mid-1930s), and later on television and tape-recordings. However, this vast material still awaits further investigation.

---

[49] Such placement was still characteristic of the *émigré* speech studied by Buning and van Schooneveld (1960: 73–84).

3 Morphology

Gender

The gender of many Russian nouns has changed in the period since 1917. The largest specific group consists of those affected by the change from masculine to common or varied gender—a change motivated by the new roles of Russian women in Soviet society. This phenomenon is of such proportions that we have allotted a separate chapter to it (Chapter 6).

There have been other kinds of gender-change, however, which, in addition, have had more effect on the overall grammatical system of Russian since they involved change of declension. Usually, for a time, two variants of the same word existed simultaneously, belonging to two different genders and two different declensions. But while the lexical meaning of both variants is the same, they are often distinguished stylistically, socially, or functionally. The standardizing pressures operating in the Soviet period have substantially reduced the number of such variant pairs, establishing as correct only one gender or the other.

(i) Masculine-feminine variation

Among the nouns whose gender has recently changed a prominent place is occupied by borrowings. In many cases their gender had been unstable ever since they were first borrowed and has only recently been stabilized. In particular, a large number of words which in the nineteenth century were found as both feminine and masculine are now found in only one or other of these two genders.

In 1914–15 Černyšev published a list of nouns of unstable gender (1914–15: 119–41), but his notes describing certain variants as *prostorečno*, 'archaic', 'rare', etc., show that in some cases stability was already very close. A large number of his words are given without comment, however, which means, according to his own statement (1914–15: 123), that both (or all) forms quoted were at that time equally acceptable. They include the following words which are all recent borrowings: бакенбард—бакенбарда 'side-whisker', бисквит—бисквита 'sponge-cake', ботфорт—ботфорта 'jackboot', вуаль 'veil' (masculine or feminine), желатин—желатина 'gelatine', жираф—жирафа 'giraffe', зал—зала 'hall', клавиш—клавиша 'key' (piano), манер—манера 'manner', мётод—мётода 'method', ниш—ниша 'niche', рельс—рельса 'rail', рояль 'grand-piano' (masculine or feminine), санаторий—санатория 'sanatorium', табурет—табуретка 'stool', эполет—эполета 'epaulette', эстафет—эстафета 'relay-race'. Other words, either native Russian or earlier borrowings, in Černyšev's list include: брызг—брызга 'splash', валенок—валенка 'felt-boot', глист—глиста 'worm', дрязг—дрязга 'squabble', жар—жара 'heat', жниво—жнива 'stubble', начал—начало 'beginning', овощ—овощь 'vegetable', округ—округа 'region', плевальник—плевальница 'spittoon', поверток—повертка 'screw-driver', пролаз—пролаза 'dodger', прохлад—прохлада 'coolness', псалтырь—псалтирь 'psalter' (both masculine and feminine), ставень—ставня 'shutter', щиколоток (щиколок)—щиколотка (щиколка) 'ankle', ярем—ярмо 'yoke', яства—яство 'victuals'. Other nouns of varied gender include ботинок and ботинка 'shoe', занавес and занавесь 'curtain', станс and станса 'stanza', фарс and фарса 'farce', ферзь (masculine or feminine) 'chess queen' (see *Русская грамматика* 1980: i. 470), туфель and туфля 'dress shoe'. (See also Graudina *et al.* 1976: 65–70.)

By the 1930s things had changed considerably, as can be seen from the entries for these words in D. N. Ušakov (1935–40), where we frequently find only one of the two (or more) variants given by Černyšev. By omitting their variants D. N. Ušakov gives, for example, exclusive approval to the following: бисквит, вуаль (feminine), желатин, жниво, клавиш, начало, ниша, плевальница, прохлада, щиколотка and щиколка, яство.

By this time, moreover, many pairs of variants were no longer equally acceptable. The following forms, though included by Ušakov, are noted as 'archaic': бакенбард, ботфорта, округа, пролаз, рояль (feminine), санатория, эстафет, ярем. Others are described as *prostorečno*: манер (occurring only in fixed phrases, e.g. таким манером 'in such a way'), рельса.

Despite the general move towards stability indicated by these examples, there were still many nouns of unstable gender in the 1930s, some of which have since been stabilized. Several of the unstable nouns in D. N. Ušakov are recorded in only one gender in subsequent dictionaries such as Ožegov (1972):

D. N. Ušakov (1935–40)	Ožegov (1972)
банкнот—банкнота	банкнот
валенка—валенок	валенок
глюкоз—(more often) глюкоза	глюкоза
жираф—жирафа	жираф
фильм—фильма	фильм
эполет—эполета	эполета

See also Graudina (1980: 33–5).

The pace at which gender changes (i.e. at which one variant supplants another) varies considerably. An example of rapid change is provided by the loan-word фильма (from English 'film'), which appeared in Russian in the early 1920s and was soon followed by the masculine variant фильм.[1] Both were in use in the 1920s and 1930s, but even by the end of the 1920s the masculine form was predominant (Krysin 1968: 85; Gorbačevič 1971: 156–7). Nearly all recent change has tended to reduce the number of variants; the emergence of new forms in the twentieth century has been a rare occurrence. However, an example is provided by стропа́ 'sling'; in D. N. Ušakov (1935–40) and Ožegov (1972) we find only строп, but nowadays both genders are acceptable as standard (Bukčina 1970; Gorbačevič 1973).

In the language of the late twentieth century, some words are still vacillating between two genders. Several types can be distinguished here: some names of animals, most of them recent borrowings (e.g. какаду 'cockatoo'); doublets of which one form is more professionally specialized (e.g. аневризм—аневризма 'aneurysm', катаракт—катаракта 'cataract', компонент—компонента 'component', парафраз—парафраза 'paraphrase'); abbreviations, which will be discussed in the next section; a number of gender-unstable words that have to be given as a list; and words of the so-called common gender.

With regard to names of animals, their gender assignment is motivated by the actual sex of the animal, for example: шимпанзе влез/влезла на дерево 'the chimpanzee climbed (masc./fem.) the tree' but шимпанзе родила (not родил) детеныша 'the chimpanzee gave birth (only fem.) to a baby' (Iomdin 1990: 85–6).

Next, mention must be made of the professional specialization of certain gender variants, e.g. компонента 'component' (mathematics, physics, chemistry—Butorin 1969), желатина (photography—

[1] However, Fessenko (1955: 71) mention a 1939 publication where the feminine variant is still used (Terskij, *Этнографическая фильма*).

Gorbačevič 1973; 1978: 141). Although non-specialist dictionaries give only компонент, желатин, the feminine variants are in no way non-standard but simply restricted to specialist use. Спазм—спазма 'spasm' and аневризм—аневризма also show a rudimentary tendency towards professional specialization as masculine (Gorbačevič 1973; *Русская грамматика* 1980: i. 471).

The following words in the modern language seem to show actual variation in gender, with no semantic differences and minor or no stylistic[2] differences between the two genders: вольéр—вольéра 'open-air cage', вы́хухоль (masculine or feminine) 'musquash', скирд—скирда 'hay-stack', псалтырь (feminine or masculine) 'psalter', авеню (feminine or neuter) 'avenue' (Graudina *et al.* 1976; *Русская грамматика* 1980: i. 471; Gorbačevič 1978: 139). In addition, a number of words, normally used in the plural, because they denote paired or multiple entities, are of unstable (masculine or feminine) gender in the singular; for example, the latest Academy Grammar still allows both бакенбард and бакенбарда 'side-whisker' (pl. бакенбарды), ботфорт and ботфорта 'jackboot' (pl. ботфорты), манжет and манжета (pl. манжеты) 'cuff', ставень and ставня (usu. pl. ставни) 'shutters', арабеск and арабеска (pl. арабески) 'arabesque' (*Русская грамматика* 1980: i. 471); for all these nouns, however, the feminine form is slightly more prevalent. The instability of the gender in all these words is undoubtedly related to the fact that they are seldom used in the singular.

The instability appears to be particularly great in the case of masculine and feminine nouns whose nominative singular ends in a soft consonant (i.e. soft stem with null ending), for here the morphological manifestations of gender are restricted to certain oblique cases and to the singular. Nevertheless, here too there has been a movement towards greater stability in the twentieth century. For example, госпиталь '(military) hospital', портфель 'briefcase', профиль 'profile', рояль 'grand-piano', which in the nineteenth century and early twentieth century occurred as either feminine or masculine, are now only masculine. (The change in gender was in some cases linked to change in stress; see Superanskaja 1965*a*: 48–9.) Formerly feminine табель is now masculine, except in reference to Peter the Great's табель о рангах 'Table of Ranks'. The gender of шампунь 'shampoo', which formerly fluctuated (e.g. in D. N. Ušakov 1935–40), is now considered to be

---

[2] For some words, gender distinction is paralleled by a stylistic distinction; thus, лебедь 'swan', while normally masculine in the modern standard language, can occur as a feminine noun in poetry.

masculine (Ljustrova and Skvorcov 1972: 48; Ožegov 1972), and the common use of this word as feminine is now identified as *prostorečno*.

The following, on the other hand, have now been stabilized as feminines, although in the nineteenth century they could also occur as masculines: антресоль 'mezzanine', вуаль 'veil', дуэль 'duel', диагональ 'diagonal', кадриль 'quadrille', мигрень 'migraine', модель 'model' (Superanskaja 1965*a*: 49–50).

In speech, however, nouns may well occur with a gender other than that prescribed officially, as may be seen from the fact that guides to usage find it necessary to emphasize that портфель, рояль, тигр 'tiger', толь 'roofing tar', тюль 'curtain lace', шампунь, etc., are not feminine and that бандероль 'package', мигрень, модель, плацкарта 'reservation in sleeping-car', etc., are not masculine. (Masculine плацкарт is in common colloquial use, where it also has the meaning 'sleeping-car'; cf. Jazovickij 1969: 19; Gorbačevič 1973.)

(ii) Neuter gender

We have so far dealt mainly with changes in the distribution of masculine and feminine genders. Changes affecting the neuter seem to have been relatively few in number. A few indeclinable loan-words which in the nineteenth century might have masculine (e.g. кашне 'scarf', портмоне 'wallet', пальто 'overcoat', боа 'boa scarf', какао 'cocoa', контральто 'contralto', рагу 'ragout') or feminine (e.g. шоссе 'highway') gender have subsequently become neuter. After going through a period in the 1920s and early 1930s when they could be either masculine or neuter авто 'car', кино 'cinema', радио 'radio', такси 'taxi', метро 'underground railway' have now settled down as neuters, though the non-standard use of такси as masculine was still occasionally encountered until the 1960s (Krysin 1968: 81; Gorbačevič 1971: 161 n.; Gorbačevič 1973). The use of the word метро as a masculine noun, apparently due to the influence of метрополитен, is attested in a popular song of the early 1930s (N. Bogoslovskij, *Песня старого извозчика*):

> Но метро мелькнул стрелою быстрою,
> Сразу всех он седоков очаровал.

> But the underground railway rushed by as a quick arrow
> And immediately enchanted all the riders.

D. N. Ušakov (1935–40) already cites метро as a neuter noun.

Until recently, the word виски 'whisky' varied between masculine and neuter; in Graudina (1980: 34), the masculine form is declared non-standard, and *MAS* (1981–4) gives only the neuter (in the spoken language, this word also occurs as a plural form). Instability acknowledged by normative works is still encountered in the word динамо 'dynamo' (feminine or neuter), cf. *MAS* (1981–4). Before rushing to the conclusion that the neuter gender has been resistant to change in the Soviet period, however, we should take a look at the generally somewhat unsteady state of this gender. In some dialects it is absent, in others only weakly represented, and it has been argued that even in the standard language it is in the initial stages of corruption (Mučnik 1963*b*: 55). Statistics prepared by Mučnik underline its weakness (1963*b*: 57): of the 33,952 nouns in the modern dictionaries examined, 15,600 (46 per cent) were found to be masculine, 13,884 (41 per cent) feminine, but only 4,468 (13 per cent) neuter.[3] Even more ominous is the fact that of the post-1914 innovations in D. N. Ušakov (1935–40) only 10 per cent are neuter. This appears to indicate a state of general decline.

One aspect of the general weakness of the neuter gender is the tendency for recent borrowings which are neuter in standard Russian to acquire other genders in non-standard varieties. But it is not only the neuter that is involved in such divergences from the standard. The loan-words which came pouring into Russian in the early twentieth century have often acquired non-standard genders in the vernacular, which certainly had its effect, if slowly, on the standard. The feminine appears to have been particularly popular, as may be seen from the following examples occurring in the speech of characters in Soviet literature (Mučnik 1963*b*: 58 n.): митинга (for митинг 'meeting'), социализма (for социализм 'socialism'), литра (for литр 'litre'). Feminines are also well represented among forms recorded in Jaroslavl´ *gubernija* in 1923: кила (for кило 'kilo'), емпа (for ЕПО (Единое потребительское общество) 'united consumers' society'), закса (for ЗАГС (from отдел записи актов гражданского состояния) 'registry office') (Seliščev 1939: 68–9). There is a general tendency for borrowings in dialects to be feminine whenever the stem ends in a sonant preceded by another consonant (Seliščev 1939: 77). This explains the gender of социализма, механизма, кадра, литра, метра. The tendency of stem-stressed neuters to become feminine (e.g. for повидло 'jam' to be feminine повидла) is a result of *akan´e*.

All the deficiencies of the neuter group notwithstanding, at least one

---

[3] How nouns of common gender were allocated is not stated.

word, and a very common one, has almost completed its shift from masculine to neuter; it is the word ко́фе 'coffee'. Borrowed from English or from Dutch (*koffie*) in the beginning of the eighteenth century, the word originally had the form ко́фий or ко́фей, which allowed one to identify it as a masculine noun, by analogy with other nouns in -й.[4] The form in -й is commonly found in eighteenth- and nineteenth-century language; *SAR* (1806–22) lists only the form кофе́й. The analogy with чай 'tea' was probably a contributing factor that added to the stability of кофе́й (ко́фий) in nineteenth-century language; the two words were sometimes juxtaposed in folklore (ча́ю-ко́фию). The form ко́фе, the rise of which is due to pronunciation reduction of the unstressed final segment, is cited as primary in *SRJa* (1895–1927); the word кофе́й (ко́фий) is explained by reference to ко́фе. In *SSRLJa* (1948–65), кофе́й (ко́фий) is still cited but as *prostorečno*; other dictionaries (e.g. Ožegov (1972)) do not even mention it. The spread of the form ко́фе, which resembles other nouns in the neuter, created a conflict between the form and the earlier masculine gender of the word. As an attempt to resolve the conflict, ко́фе was increasingly used as a neuter noun in spoken Russian. Normative handbooks, however, were very slow and reluctant in acknowledging this change and stubbornly insisted on the masculine; the first mention of neuter, as a permissible variant alongside with masculine, occurs in the Academy Grammar (*Русская грамматика* 1980: i. 469); see also Zaliznjak (1980) and Borunova *et al.* (1983).

The change in the gender of ко́фе shows that, in the stabilization of gender, two types of analogy, notional and formal, play an important role and may sometimes conflict with one another. The evolution of ко́фе as a neuter noun is apparently due to formal analogy. Likewise, formal analogy is responsible for the stabilization of such words as портмоне́ 'wallet' or сопра́но 'soprano' as neuters. The above-mentioned use of такси́ as a masculine noun was motivated by the notional association between this word and the masculine noun автомоби́ль 'automobile'. The later stabilization of this word as neuter is due to the formal analogy or, more precisely, the absence of other masculine nouns in -и. The notional parallel between the word галифе́ and the generic *plurale tantum* брю́ки 'trousers' motivates the declining use of the former as a neuter noun and the reinterpretation of it as a plural (Gorbačevič 1978: 145). A number of gender mistakes made by

---

[4] There is, however, some evidence that the form ко́фе has existed since the late seventeenth century (Fasmer 1986–7: ii. 355).

Russian schoolchildren and recorded in N. N. Ušakov (1957) are due to notional analogy: thus, the feminine gender of картофель 'potatoes' in на сковородке жарилась картофель is the result of the interference of the common colloquial feminine word картошка 'potatoes'. Overall, formal analogy plays a greater role in the stabilization of gender in CSR than the association between the unstable word and a generic word, which is also known to affect the choice of gender (Corbett 1991).

Compared with the state of affairs presented by Černyšev (1914–15), the number of nouns of unstable gender in the standard language nowadays is small, especially if we restrict the list to those that are really equally acceptable in all respects. As we narrow the list down we tend to find disagreement between the normative authorities, but differences of opinion are minimal viewed in the light of the overall state of greater stability already reached. Nevertheless, in Russian schools, the problem of correcting non-standard genders used by pupils remains. It is sometimes discussed by Soviet teachers in their specialist publications. N. N. Ušakov (1957), for example, records mistakes made in written work by pupils from various areas including the *oblasti* of Moscow, Novosibirsk, Gor´kij. Some of the forms are familiar to those who know the history of the words in question, for example, лицо закрыто вуалем 'the face is covered with a veil', etc. The fact that Tolstoj and Turgenev treated вуаль as masculine must be disconcerting to the teacher who has to explain that nowadays it is only feminine. Many of the incorrect formations encountered by teachers have never been used in literature, however, and can only be understood from a knowledge of the pupils' local dialect;[5] for example, in тела (singular) потеряла гибкость 'the body lost its flexibility', the neuter тело is reanalysed as feminine due to *akan´e*.

(iii) Common gender nouns

Gender confusion also occurs over nouns of common gender ending in -a, for example, сирота 'orphan', соня 'sleepy-head', неряха 'sloven', зануда 'bore'. The number of such words varies dramatically between different authors: V. V. Vinogradov (1947: 71–9) lists about a hundred such words, in Graudina *et al.* (1976: 76–7), the number is over 200, and Zaliznjak (1980) lists about 400 such words (including derived ones). According to the codified rules, common gender nouns are masculine

[5] On the problems of Russian teaching in areas where the local system differs from the standard, see Tekučëv (1974: 157–72).

when they refer to male persons; however, agreements such as ты такая большая неряха (with неряха 'sloven' applied to a boy) are not uncommon and, though sometimes condemned (Jazovickij 1969: 20–1), are often approved (Gorbačevič 1973: 515), at least in colloquial Russian (Rozental´ and Telenkova 1972: 304). As shown in Zaliznjak (1967: 67–9) and Iomdin (1990: 80–5), common gender nouns are not uniform from the lexical and grammatical standpoint. Words such as сирота, соня, коллега 'colleague', самоучка 'self-made person', скряга 'miser' are grammatically masculine when they denote males and feminine when they denote females; they determine agreement accordingly. The other group of common gender nouns is comprised mostly of expressive words such as неряха, тупица 'dunce', разиня 'gawk', растяпа 'muddler', сластена 'sweet-tooth', тихоня 'demure person'. If these words refer to females, they must be of feminine gender (thus *моя сестра ужасный обжора 'my sister is a terrible glutton' is ungrammatical); if they refer to males, they can be of either masculine or feminine gender, for example, ты такой неряха or ты такая неряха 'you are such a sloven' referring to a male.

(iv) Gender and declension of stump-compounds, hyphenated compounds, and acronyms[6]

Our attention so far has been directed to the gender of nouns most of which were already in existence by the turn of the century and also that of a few more recent borrowings. The picture has been one of accelerating standardization. We turn now to the question of certain twentieth-century innovations which Russian has formed from its own resources.

The gender of stump-compounds (Russian сложносокращенные слова, cf. Pavlovskaja 1967) has posed no special problems. They acquire the gender appropriate to their form: собес is masculine (though социальное обеспечение 'social security', from which it is derived, is neuter), зарплата (from заработная плата) 'wages' is feminine, ликбез is masculine (though ликвидация безграмотности 'abolition of illiteracy' is feminine).

Hyphenated compounds or hyphenated noun co-ordinates (Russian сложносоставные слова) pose gender problems only when their components are of different genders, for example, кресло-кровать 'armchair sleeper'. When the compound is no longer perceived as an

---

[6] For definitions of stump-compounds and acronyms and for details of formation, see below.

occasional formation, the fusion of its components becomes greater; in pronunciation, this is commonly signalled by the elimination of secondary stress, and in morphology by the fact that the first component is no longer declined as a separate word.[7] As such fusion occurs, the gender assignment is determined, formally, by the last component of the word; for example, плащ-палатка (feminine) 'cape-tent', штаб-квартира (feminine) 'headquarters', альфа-распад (masculine) 'alpha-decay', жар-птица (feminine) 'firebird'. In those hyphenated compounds where both components decline,[8] gender is typically determined by the first component, which is viewed as informationally more salient (Gorbačevič 1973; 1978: 151; Graudina *et al.* 1976: 175–6); for example, платье-костюм (neuter) 'two-piece dress', диван-кровать (masculine) 'sleeper sofa'. In hyphenated compounds denoting people, however, more variation is observed (Graudina *et al.* 1976: 177–8).

Acronyms, on the other hand, have introduced new problems to the gender system. Those in which the names of the letters are retained (e.g. МТС [emte'es] (from машинно-тракторная станция) 'machine and tractor station', ЦК [tse'ka] (from центральный комитет) 'central committee') are indeclinable—just as the names of letters in other circumstances are indeclinable—and take their gender from the central noun of the phrase for which they stand. Hence, МТС is feminine; ЦК is masculine. Declined forms (e.g. в эмтээ́се) are nowadays possible only in non-standard Russian, though in the 1920s they might also be encountered, rarely, in literary usage (Seliščev 1928: 159, 165; Alekseev 1961: 67–8; Mučnik 1964: 168).

It is possible for the other main type of acronym, i.e. that in which the sounds of the letters are pronounced, to take its gender in accordance with the same principle. It is thus possible for ГЭС [ges] (гидроэлектростанция) 'hydro-electric power station' and НОТ [not] (научная организация труда) 'scientific organization of labour' to be feminine, for МИД [mʲit] or [mʲid] (Министерство иностранных дел) 'Ministry of foreign affairs' to be neuter, and for РОНО [ro'no] (районный отдел народного образования) 'regional department of public education' to be masculine. There are, however, conflicting tendencies. Conflict arises from the fact that acronyms, having their own morphological propensities, tend to acquire a gender appropriate to their form, and this may be different from the gender of the central noun of the phrase for which they stand. Since acronyms constitute a fair

[7] Exceptions to this are discussed in Bukčina and Kalakuckaja (1974: 59–60).
[8] See Wade (1992: 81) for a brief overview of declension of hyphenated compounds.

proportion of all Soviet neologisms, the amount of new instability they have introduced (measured in numbers of words) may even outweigh the movement towards stabilization in the gender of other words. For example, ЖЭК [ʒek] (жилищно-эксплуатационная контора) 'housing management office', has the appearance of a masculine noun of the same type as век, человек, etc., and this word is in fact very often used in the same way, being declined ЖЭКа, ЖЭКом, etc. On the other hand, контора is feminine. Consequently, ЖЭК may alternatively be feminine, in which case it is not declinable. This particular word remains unstable to the present day, but many acronyms of this type have stable gender, especially those that were formed during and immediately after the Revolution. At that time new acronyms came into wide use (and also disappeared) so quickly that often their users had never heard the phrases from which they were derived. In those circumstances gender could be determined only on morphological grounds. Therefore КЕПС [kʲeps] (Комиссия по изучению естественных производительных сил России) 'Commission for the Study of the Natural Productive Forces of Russia', for example, was masculine and declined:

Поэтому монографическое изучение, предпринятое КЕПС'ом,[9] более чем своевременно . . .(*Печать и революция*, 1923, 4: 184)

Therefore, the comprehensive study undertaken by KEPS is more than timely . . .

Like many other institutions of the 1920s, КЕПС has long since been defunct and forgotten, but other acronyms of that time have survived and acquired stable gender:

(i) The gender of НЭП (Новая экономическая политика) 'New Economic Policy', which dates from 1921, fluctuated for a year or two between masculine, motivated by the form of the acronym, and feminine (motivated by the head-word политика) before settling down as a declined masculine. It is attested (declined) in a letter from Lenin to Molotov dated 23 March 1922 (Panov 1968: iii. 62). G. O. Vinokur (1929: 125) also uses it as a masculine declinable noun: есть в «гражданин» кое-что от НЭПа 'there is something in the word гражданин that reminds one of NEP'. In Soviet history textbooks of the second half of the century, the acronym is invariably masculine (and is often used without capitalization), for example: В соответствии

---

[9] In quotations from sources of the 1920s we reproduce the apostrophe and full stop used with acronyms (cf. p. 115).

с определением сущности нэпа . . . (Genkina 1954: 499) 'In accordance with the definition of the essence of NEP . . .'.

(ii) The word вуз (высшее учебное заведение) 'institution of higher learning' has existed as a declined masculine since the early 1920s. In its early years it was not always declined, however, though non-declension would be impossible nowadays:

Наибольшее число стипендий русским учащимся в В.У.З. Германии выдается организацией: „Europäische Studentenhilfe". (*Печать и революция*, 1923, 2: 262)

The majority of scholarships awarded to Russian students in German institutions of higher learning are funded by the organization 'Europäische Studentenhilfe'.

Основная цель его—объединение разрозненных действий отдельных ВУЗ'ов, рабфаков и организаций в области издательской деятельности. (ibid. 3: 304)

Its main goal consists in unifying the uncoordinated activities of individual institutions of higher learning, workers' educational departments, and other organizations as far as publishing is concerned.

In the 1920s there was much inconsistency in the morphology of acronyms. It is not unusual to find discrepancies on one and the same page in publications of that period. Nevertheless, the main tendency then was for acronyms ending in a consonant to become declined masculines.

Declinability is correlated with the question of gender: the declension of feminines or neuters ending in a hard consonant would conflict with the existing declension system. It is said that there are certain acronyms which must be feminine because of the gender of the underlying phrase and that to treat them as masculines (and thus to decline them) is *prostorečno* (see Gorbačevič 1971: 164, and particular entries in Gorbačevič 1973). This is true, for example, of ГЭС (гидроэлектростанция) 'hydroelectric power station', ВАК (Высшая аттестационная комиссия) 'Higher Attestation Commission', and ООН (Организация объединенных наций) 'United Nations Organization'. Despite the efforts of editors and language planners to establish order, however, disorder persists.

A recent case is that of the name for the Pacific railway link, a gigantic construction effort of the 1970s–early 1980s, Байкало-Амурская магистраль 'Bajkal–Amur Railway', abbreviated as БАМ [bam]. Since the head-word of the expression, магистраль 'main-line', is feminine and the acronym ends in a hard consonant, БАМ, according to the normative handbooks, should have been indeclinable, by analogy

with such words as the above-mentioned ГЭС or ТЭЦ (тепло-
электрическая центральная (станция)) 'thermo-electrical power
station' (Graudina 1980: 151). Indeed, the early occurrences of БАМ in
the Soviet press were non-declined, as in the newspaper *Вечерняя
Москва* for 28 September 1974: Москвичи призывают отлично
обслуживать стройки БАМ 'The Muscovites are calling for excellent
service at the construction sites of the BAM'. However, by the beginning of 1975, both the press and the spoken language concurred in using
БАМ as a declined masculine noun, probably due to the particular frequency of the locative phrase на БАМе (Graudina 1980: 152; Wade
1992: 41).[10]

The only type which cannot, whatever its gender, decline in standard
Russian is that ending in a vowel, e.g. РОНО (see above), ГАИ
(государственная автомобильная инспекция) 'state department of
motor vehicles', НАТО 'NATO' (a borrowed and transliterated
acronym),[11] including a few of a mixed type composed of both syllables
and initials such as сельпо (сельское потребительское общество)
'village consumers' society' (real meaning 'village shop'), самбо
(самозащита без оружия) 'unarmed self-defence'. Despite their
absolute indeclinability, however, there is much uncertainty as to
gender: РОНО fluctuates between masculine and neuter, ГАИ and
самбо between feminine and neuter.

These problems evolved, together with the acronyms themselves, in
the Soviet period, and there are no signs of any language-planning
initiative to settle them. There is not even consistency between various
normative works. For example, НОТ (see above) is masculine in D. N.
Ušakov (1935–40) and Ožegov (1972), but feminine, or 'colloquially'
masculine, according to Gorbačevič (1973).

Particularly significant is the fact that even acronyms which by either
criterion are masculine, like МХАТ (Московский художественный
академический театр) 'Moscow Arts Theatre', СЭВ (Совет
экономической взаимопомощи) 'Council of Economic Mutual Aid',
ОВИР (отдел виз и регистрации (иностранцев)) 'visa office', frequently appear non-declined both in print and in standard speech; in the

---

[10] Construction of the railway was actually started in the 1930s but later abandoned
because of the Second World War. The long-forgotten acronym was revived when construction was restarted in the 1970s. Earlier, the acronym БАМ occurs, in the masculine,
in the 1956 memoirs of Nikolaj Zabolockij: Царство БАМа встречало нас . . . 'The
kingdom of the BAM was welcoming us' (Zabolockij 1990: 671).

[11] The full version differs from the acronym entirely (Североатлантическая
(военная) организация) but is hardly ever used.

1960s–1970s, non-declension was given a degree of official approval (Gorbačevič 1973: 516–17).[12] Another source of confusion over the issue of declension is that a number of acronyms show a varying degree of declinability in different cases. Overall, the tendency to decline acronyms is more pronounced when they occur in the prepositional case or in the prepositional dative and is the weakest when acronyms are in the genitive; for example, в ОВИРе 'in OVIR' but сотрудник ОВИР 'an official of OVIR'.

The appearance of a class of words of masculine gender fitting the masculine declension pattern yet not declined can be a development with serious implications. It is best interpreted as a form of hyper-correction (comparable to the non-declension of эхо—see the next section). There will always be a tendency for all acronyms ending in a consonant to be treated equally, owing to their paradigmatic relationships.

Analyticity in the Nominal Paradigm

Indeclinable nouns

The most distinctive feature of grammatical change in the twentieth century has been the growth of analyticity—the increasing tendency for the grammatical meaning of words to be expressed by their context rather than their form and for the expression of separate meanings by separate words that can be used on their own, in isolation. An obvious aspect of this tendency is the growth of indeclinability among nouns. With the increase in the number of indeclinable nouns in the twentieth century growing account has to be taken of them in describing the morphological system. In the nineteenth century they were so few in number as to be merely peripheral to the system as a whole. That is now no longer the case.

A large proportion of indeclinables are borrowings of neuter gender, like депо 'depot', фото 'photo', бюро 'office, bureau', пальто 'overcoat', which have nothing in their structure to prevent them from being declined, as may be demonstrated by comparing them with such declined nouns as вино 'wine', нутро 'interior', лето 'summer'. The non-declension of the former group of words is, therefore, a convention.

[12] It is surmised that acronyms would be declined even less in print, were it not for the vigilance of editors (Panov 1968: iii. 63). However, spoken standard language clearly favours the declension of such abbreviations (Zemskaja 1987: 79).

Some, but not many, were borrowed as long ago as the eighteenth century, including депо and бюро. The habit of not declining them grew up in the first half of the nineteenth century among the upper class, but declined forms too, such as на бюре, на фортепиане are attested from that period (Bulaxovskij 1954: 81). Only certain members of the intelligentsia and upper class, owing to their knowledge of Western languages, were conscious of the foreign origin of these words, and it was only in upper-class circles that they were not declined (Kudrjavskij 1912: 93, quoted in Panov 1968: iii. 49; Karcevskij 1923: 55; Superanskaja 1965*b*: 119). But even the educated strata did not consistently observe non-declension (Černyšev 1914–15: 116); as late as 1934 N. S. Trubeckoj (born Moscow 1890, emigrated 1919) stated that for his generation (and, presumably, for his class) declension was normal though 'somewhat *prostorečno*' (Trubetzkoy 1934: 37; (1987: 95)).

The vast majority of the population were ignorant of the Western languages from which these words came, and, on the rare occasions when they knew and used such words, they declined them. At the time of the Revolution non-declension of neuter loan-words had acquired prestige among the ruling class, but to the illiterate masses it was unknown or (if known) incomprehensible. It would therefore have been quite possible in the early years of Soviet power to codify declension of these words as standard, approximating Russian practice to that of most other Slavonic languages. Only a small minority of the population would have been offended.

After 1917, however, non-declension continued its progress under the impetus of the pre-Revolutionary prestige structure. And so, when in the 1960s, as part of the RJaSO project, a survey was carried out in which 1,500 Russians were asked: 'Do you accept the possibility of declining . . . nouns . . . of the type пальто, депо?' only 3 per cent said 'Yes'. The actual text of the replies received indicates that most of the informants were quite indignant at the thought of declining them (Panov 1968: iii. 50–5).

Nevertheless, declined forms of these words may still be heard in Russia, though more commonly in the country than in the towns. (We are not, of course, speaking of their use by speakers of standard Russian for humorous or ironic effect.) The assumption made in Panov (1968: iii. 50) that even the 3 per cent who said 'Yes' do not actually use declined forms tells us more about the social make-up of the sample than about the survival of declension among the population as a whole. In any case, the RJaSO survey was not aimed at non-standard Russian.

Mučnik draws the following conclusions from the survey: 'In the modern Russian language без ведро and без пальта are to an equal degree impermissible infringements of the grammatical norms' (Panov 1968: iii. 55). But there is, in fact, an important difference, for без ведро is not recognizable as any kind of utterance known to the Russian speech community. There is no question as to whether ведро is declinable or not (and no surveys have been thought necessary to test public opinion on that point). On the other hand, the question whether пальто, кино 'cinema' (and other similar neuters) should decline or not is a real one, for declined forms, though non-standard, do occur, however much displeasure they may cause (Čukovskij 1963: 23–7; Timofeev 1963: 158–60). They occur, moreover, in literature, both in the speech of characters (to convey social information) and (rarely) for expressiveness in the author's own words (Mučnik 1964: 178). The indeclinable plural бигуди 'curlers' shows a tendency to decline, even in print, e.g. бессонная ночь с бигудями на голове 'a sleepless night with your hair in curlers' (quoted from a provincial newspaper by *Заметки крохобора*, 1976).[13]

We have so far considered only those indeclinable borrowings whose structure is such that they might decline but for the prescriptive rule which says they may not. There are also some borrowings which simply do not fit into the Russian morphological system, such as такси 'taxi', рагу 'ragout', конферансье 'master of ceremonies', мадам 'madam', виски 'whisky', меню 'menu'. There are some which are placed outside the system by their stress only, e.g. ателье 'tailor's shop; studio', желе 'jelly', портмоне 'wallet', жюри 'jury; panel of judges'. (Declined soft-stem neuters, except those ending in -ьё, are virtually all stem-stressed in the singular.)[14] In the nineteenth century and earlier, loan-words which did not immediately fit into the system were adapted to make declension possible, producing such forms as желей (masculine), мадама (feminine) (Černyšev 1914–15: 116–17). The same, or similar, processes operated, and probably continue to operate, in non-standard varieties, but there is a dearth of information on what happens to indeclinables in non-standard Russian, apart from the fact that the пальто type declines like other neuters. Panov (1968) and Mučnik (1964) only give examples from fiction and poetry, including бюро, пианино, and танго as declined feminines, такси declined as a plural, etc.

---

[13] A column in *Литературная газета* (quoted from No. 27, 1976, p. 6).
[14] Such exceptions as житие́, бытие́ are very distinctly Church Slavonic.

The emphasis on non-declension has had an interesting secondary effect on the morphology of эхо 'echo', which, in the singular, was until recently nearly always declined. In recent times (contrary to the advice of dictionaries) it has shown a tendency not to decline (Panov 1968: iii. 47 n.; Vomperskij 1964). The results of hyper-correction are also seen in the non-declension of declinable acronyms (see p. 116) and in reluctance in scientific texts and the press to decline new technical terms and personal names (Superanskaja 1965*b*: 119). Planned language change (i.e. the decision taken by nineteenth-century grammarians not to decline the пальто type) has led to new planning problems. Mučnik appositely describes indeclinables as 'an open flank in the Russian declensional system (which on the whole is synthetic) for the penetration of analytical elements' (Panov 1968: iii. 45).

Another case of hyper-correct non-declension is the non-declension of titles when applied to a woman; this includes the non-declension of the standard Soviet form of address/title товарищ, e.g. говорят о товарищ Ивановой, and such titles as профессор, директор, депутат. This usage is condemned by normative works (e.g. Jazovickij 1969: 94–6), but is encountered in both speech and writing. Another factor contributing to the non-declension of such words is the fact that the frequent use of the title leads to its desemantization and loss of grammatical properties of an independent noun; such a title becomes formally indivisible from the name it modifies. The desemantization of the title товарищ is confirmed by the fact that in spoken Russian it sometimes does not decline even when used as men's titles, for example с товарищ Сергеевым (see further Chapter 7). Also, spoken Russian normally treats kinship names such as тётя, дядя as the indeclinable part of a compound noun that they form with the name they modify, for example, тётя Маринины дети 'aunt Marina's children'.[15]

Declension of personal names

The majority of Russians have surnames which in their masculine nominative singular form end in -ов, -ев, -ин, or -ский and are therefore declined according to established paradigms. In the use of most other surname types, however, there is considerable inconsistency. This affects the names of some Russians (and of other citizens of the former Soviet Union with Russian-suffixed names) and foreigners. Theoretically, all names which fit into the morphological system are

---

[15] See also the section on indeclinable adjectives below.

capable of being declined, but in practice they are sometimes non-declined. Resistance to declension is particularly strong among bearers of surnames which have appellative homonyms, e.g. Жук (жук 'beetle'), Крыса (крыса 'rat'), Медведь (медведь 'bear') and, being motivated by the desire to distinguish the name from the appellative, is accepted by some guides to usage (Ljustrova and Skvorcov 1972: 55).[16] However, the non-declension of various other declinable names may sometimes be seen, especially in the press, e.g. . . . наградил Коровкевич Николая Владимировича (*Вечерняя Москва*, 6 October 1954, quoted in Superanskaja 1965*b*: 121) 'granted an award to . . .'; экспедиция под руководством кандидата исторических наук Вячеслава Канивец (*Вечерняя Москва*, 10 November 1964, quoted in Kalakuckaja 1984: 171) 'expedition headed by Candidate of History . . .'. But it is a practice that is censured by normative handbooks (Superanskaja 1965*b*; Superanskaja and Suslova 1981; Kalakuckaja 1984), which require that male surnames ending in a consonant or in consonant followed by -a be declined (Superanskaja and Suslova 1981: 173; Kalakuckaja 1984: 184–6). However, contrary to this recommendation, there is a firmly established tradition of not declining French surnames ending in -a, such as Дюма 'Dumas', Золя 'Zola', etc., and this despite the fact that there is nothing in their form to prevent declension.

The question of inconsistencies in the declension of surnames (of which a good overview is given in Superanskaja and Suslova (1981) and in Kalakuckaja (1984)) cannot be overlooked in the general discussion of increasing analyticity which is clearly evidenced by the growing tendency not to decline certain groups of surnames (Kalakuckaja 1984). Particular attention must be given to the surnames of Ukrainian origin ending in the suffixes -ко and -енко. There are three possible declension patterns: (i) like neuters ending in -о (as in Ukrainian), (ii) like feminines and masculines ending in -a (the result of *akan'e*, though those with stressed ending such as Франко́ are included), (iii) non-declined. Type (i) is now the rarest and although used, for example, by Čexov in *Дуэль* (1891), was already considered abnormal by Černyšev (1914–15: 85–7). However, throughout the nineteenth century this type was predominant (Kalakuckaja 1984: 40–2). The main problem, both in

---

[16] Superanskaja and Suslova (1981: 173) and Kalakuckaja (1984: 115–34) treat these surnames as declinable when they belong to males. Stress pattern is another effective way to distinguish the surname from the appellative homonym: while the appellative word can have mobile stress (e.g. жук—жуку́), the surname has fixed stem-stress (Жук—Жу́ку) (Kalakuckaja 1984: 50, 120–6).

Černyšev's time and subsequently, has been fluctuation between declension and non-declension, and although he considered either expedient acceptable, prescriptive works have sometimes insisted on declension. The RJaSO survey conducted in the 1960s showed an overwhelming majority (about 95 per cent) in favour of non-declension, increasing from approximately 90 per cent in the oldest age-group to approximately 96 per cent in the youngest. The breakdown by profession showed more resistance among writers and journalists (11 per cent favouring declension) than in any other professional group (Krysin 1974: 194–6). Although these figures are based not on objective observation but on the subjects' assessment of their own behaviour, they cast serious doubt on Superanskaja's assertion that the declined forms are colloquial and the non-declined forms characteristic of the official style (Superanskaja 1965*b*: 126–7). Officialdom's preference for non-declined forms (both of these and of all types of name whose declension might lead to muddle) is well known and understandable. Owing to the difficulty or impossibility of deducing the nominative from an oblique case, it is only . reasonable to use non-declined forms of unusual names in official documents. But the tendency not to decline names ending in -ко and -енко appears to be general and has been increasing throughout the twentieth century.

Another group of surnames that lost their declension in the twentieth century are names in -их, -ых, -ово, -ево. These names normally declined in the nineteenth century (Kalakuckaja 1984: 148–9, 22–3). The declension of names in -ово becomes rare by the end of the nineteenth century, probably because such surnames were rare themselves (Unbegaun 1972: 18, 173); thus, the name of the famous Russian linguist N. N. Durnovo (1876–1937) does not decline.[17] The surnames in -их, -ых (for example, Ти́хих, Черны́х, По́льских) resisted the non-declension tendency for a longer time. While normative grammars characterize these surnames as non-declinable (*Русская грамматика* 1980: i. 506; Rozental´ 1971: 169), instances of their declension can be found in the press as late as in the 1970s (Kalakuckaja 1984: 144–5). The declension of these surnames is qualified as *prostorečno* (Rozental´ 1971: 169). See also Graudina *et al.* (1976: 150–65).

---

[17] Surnames in -аго, for example Жива́го, Мертва́го, originated as orthographic variants of surnames in -ово (the latter representing the pronunciation variant); their spelling follows the Church Slavonic pattern (Unbegaun 1972: 18, 174). These surnames were already indeclinable in the nineteenth century.

Declension of place-names

With the exception of those ending in -o, such as Глазго 'Glasgow', Токио 'Tokyo', Сан-Франциско 'San Francisco', foreign place-names are traditionally regarded as declinable if they conform to the existing declension patterns. Non-declension incurs disapproval, but in the case of certain morphological types it is quite clearly increasing (Kalakuckaja 1970: 233–42), which is another sign of growing analyticity.

Among Russian place-names those with the suffixes -ово, -ево, -ино, such as Шереметьево, Щелково, Останкино, behave inconsistently, but it is only in Soviet times that they have developed a tendency not to decline. Černyšev remarks on certain particularities of such names, but does not mention the possibility of not declining them (1914–15: 185). Instructions issued by the authorities during the Second World War forbidding the declension of place-names in dispatches and documents to avoid confusion left a deep and lasting effect. During the war non-declined forms were used in the press (Mirtov 1953: 105) and although normative works did not accept it, the tendency not to decline them grew.[18]

The survey conducted by the RJaSO team to test the preferences of Russians on this point produced figures of 31.9 per cent in favour of non-declension and 61.9 per cent in favour of declension. These figures relate to test sentences including the names Щелково and Болшево. In the case of the place-name Пушкино, however, 72 per cent favoured non-declension. All the names tested showed increasing support for non-declension in each succeeding age-group, so that whereas, for example, only 27.2 per cent of the age-group born before 1909 used the non-declined dative of Щелково, it was used by 39.5 per cent of those born after 1939 (Panov 1968: iii. 60–1). These figures show the rapid growth of a feature which before the Revolution was unknown and which, until recently, was rejected by all normative works. The latest Academy Grammar acknowledges the tendency of such names to be non-declined in spoken language, in professional speech, and in the press; however, it still recommends declension as the norm (*Русская грамматика* 1980: i. 505–7). In Gorbačevič (1990: 77–8), the non-declension of 'some geographical names' (Gorbačevič gives three examples: Переделкино, Останкино, Репино) is presented as a given.

---

[18] For non-declension of place-names when accompanied by a generic appellation in apposition, e.g. город Москва, see pp. 163–5.

Changes in Case Endings

(i) Masculine genitive singular

The principal function of the morpheme -y in the masculine genitive singular is to indicate the partitive, e.g. две чайные ложки сахару 'two teaspoonfuls of sugar', дайте нарзану! 'give me some Narzan mineral water'. But it is also used in certain other contexts, e.g. из лесу 'out of the forest', со страху 'out of fear', ни разу 'not a single time', час от часу 'more and more, increasingly'. To differentiate this form from the regular genitive in -a, Zaliznjak (1967: 44–6, 281–4) identifies the -y form as the second genitive. In 1914–15 Černyšev observed that -a was replacing -y (1914–15: 27), and during the Soviet period this tendency continued. The use of -y has become increasingly rare, and some instances in nineteenth-century literature would not be acceptable in present-day Russian, e.g. болит от морозу лоб (Gogol´, *Шинель*, quoted in Gorbačevič 1971: 171) 'the forehead is aching in the frost'. Even by Černyšev's day there was much fluctuation, and there are today many environments where -a is acceptable, but would not have been in the nineteenth century. Despite the decline of this distinction popular normative guides continue to insist on the use of the second genitive (Jazovickij 1969: 21–2; Gorbačevič 1971: 172 n.).

Statistical analysis of texts of various kinds shows a rapid falling off of -y forms among partitive genitives between 1900 and the 1960s (Panov 1968: iii. 177–200). General decline, but at a slower rate, is indicated by the results of a self-assessing survey, although comparison of the survey data with that collected by objective observation of the forms used by customers in food shops suggests that some Russians may consciously prefer -a forms yet unconsciously use -y (Panov 1968: iii. 190–200; Graudina 1966).

In its partitive meaning, the second genitive is still used in quantificational expressions, especially those of indefinite quantity (побольше сахару 'more sugar', немного кипятку 'a little boiling water'), in negative phrases that require genitive (не осталось крахмалу 'there is no starch left', не хватает сыру 'there is not enough cheese'), with verbs in на- that indicate the multiplicity of the subject or object referent (навалило снегу 'there fell much snow', наносил copy 'he brought in much rubbish'); in all these uses, the second genitive alternates with the first genitive (Zaliznjak 1980: 71). Often the use of the second genitive creates the effect of a lower, colloquial style, and very few words, most of them names of substances, can still take the second genitive without such a stylistic effect (Zemskaja 1983: 116).

Outside the partitive meaning, the second genitive is used in certain prepositional constructions, for example, с разбегу 'in a running dive', без спросу 'without permission', where it also alternates with the first genitive, for example, nowadays we encounter both без спору and без спора 'indisputably', со страху and со страха 'out of fear', etc. (for a comprehensive list, see Graudina *et al.* 1976: 122). Texts from the early twentieth century contain prepositional constructions such as для запаху 'for (better or spicier) smell', вместо сахару 'instead of sugar', до пару 'to steam'. This type was described by Černyšev, though he already regarded the -y genitive with для and y as archaic (1914–15: 20). By the 1930s such constructions had disappeared (Panov 1968: iii. 182).

The -y type is most stubborn of all in partitive constructions with diminutives, particularly in dialogue, e.g. хотите чайку? 'would you like some tea?' (from чаёк, diminutive of чай 'tea') (Paus 1995). Diminutives of names of foods (чаёк, кофеёк 'coffee', медок 'honey', сахарок 'sugar', коньячок 'cognac', квасок 'kvass', лучок 'onions', кефирчик 'kefir') and some other nouns (ледку 'ice', табачку 'tobacco') comprise a small and dwindling class of words which as yet cannot take their partitive genitive in -a (Gorbačevič 1973: 512; 1978: 179; Graudina *et al.* 1976: 123; Zaliznjak 1980: 71).

(ii) Masculine prepositional singular

The prepositional singular ending for the majority of masculine nouns is -e, but after the prepositions в and на certain masculines take the so-called second prepositional case in -y, always stressed (Zaliznjak 1967: 43–4, 284–7; 1980: 69–70), e.g. в углу 'in the corner', на берегу 'on the bank'. There are also some nouns which after these prepositions may take either -e or -y.[19]

Some of the words which at the beginning of the twentieth century could take either ending can now take only one or the other. There has been a movement towards greater uniformity, as may be seen by comparing the words quoted by Černyšev as taking either ending (1914–15:

[19] The second prepositional case is also attested for some feminine nouns ending in -ь, where it differs from the first prepositional by the end-stress (e.g. бровь 'eyebrow'—на брóви/на брови 'on the eyebrow') and for two neuter nouns (забытьё 'oblivion', полузабытьё 'half-consciousness').

30–3) with those in modern guides to usage (such as Gorbačevič 1973). Whereas at the time of the First World War ад 'hell', берег 'bank', год 'year', дым 'smoke', лес 'forest', остров 'island', сад 'garden', угол 'corner' (among others) could take either -e or -y (though in most cases one was already more common than the other), the present-day standard is: в аду, на берегу, в году, в дыму, в лесу, в саду, на углу but на острове. The alternation between the first and the second prepositional can be explained by the morphophonemic shape of the word (the second prepositional is commonly found in monosyllabic nouns, including nouns with a fleeting vowel, and nouns characterized by mobile stress).[20] Pragmatic factors, discussed in Chapter 2 above, also play a role in the choice between the first and the second prepositional: abstract nouns or nouns used in an abstract meaning often take the second prepositional, while nouns denoting non-abstract entities form the first prepositional; for example, хмель 'hop-plant; drunkenness, tipsiness' forms the first prepositional in the concrete meaning (в хмеле 'in the hops') and the second prepositional in the abstract meaning (во хмелю 'tipsy, drunk').

Some of the words which were unstable in 1915 are still unstable, e.g. в отпуске and в отпуску 'on leave' are both still acceptable. Sometimes there is disagreement as to the present standard: the information on порт 'port' and пруд 'pond', for example, in Gorbačevič (1971: 176) and Gorbačevič (1973) is conflicting. Even new instability has arisen in a few cases: в цехе and в цеху 'in the shop', в меде and в меду 'in honey' (formerly only в цехе, в меду) (Graudina *et al.* 1976: 134–7).

The use of the second prepositional is determined by the specific meanings of the prepositions в and на (Zaliznjak 1980: 70). The preposition в takes the second prepositional case in the meanings 'inside', 'within a localization' (в шкафу 'in the cupboard', в степи 'in the steppe', в дыму 'in smoke', в плену 'in captivity') and in the meaning 'abundantly covered with' (весь в снегу 'all covered with snow', в долгу как в шелку 'up to the neck in debt (lit.: in debt as in silks)'). The following meanings of на require the use of the second prepositional: 'on the surface of' (на лугу 'in the meadow'), 'under the circumstances of' (на балу 'at a ball');[21] 'manufactured with the use of' (на спирту 'based on alcohol'). It seems that the lexicalization of some phrases with the second prepositional case is motivated by the prevalent

---

[20] For details, see Zaliznjak (1967: 286–7; 1977: 76).

[21] Cf. in Puškin's *Евгений Онегин* (1824), III. xxviii: Не дай мне Бог сойтись на бáле . . . 'God forbid that I encounter at a ball . . .'

use of a certain noun with в or на in one of these meanings. For example, the expression в снегу means either 'inside a snow-drift' or '(covered) with snow', which are probably the most frequent instances of reference to snow in speech; accordingly, this makes the alternative в снеге extremely rare. The RJaSO survey recorded that in locative contexts less than 3 per cent favoured в снеге (Krysin 1974: 177).

The RJaSO survey also included the prepositional singular of мед, отпуск, цех; the picture produced by the other words shows that, lexicalized expressions as the ones mentioned above notwithstanding, the younger the speakers the less likely they are to use the second prepositional forms (Krysin 1974: 177, 250).

(iii) Masculine nominative plural

Continuing a tendency from the nineteenth century, the number of nouns with nominative plural in -á has increased still further. Among the words which Černyšev quotes as taking either -ы or -á in the nominative plural are: директор 'director', инспектор 'inspector', закром 'corn-bin', округ 'region', провод 'wire', профессор 'professor', сорт 'sort', том 'volume' (1914–15: 63).[22] Ožegov (1972) gives only: директора, инспектора, закрома, округа, провода, профессора, сорта, тома.

It has been shown that the expansion of plurals in -á is related to the expansion of words with mobile stress which have end-stress in oblique cases (Durnovo 1971; Zaliznjak 1967: 223–7; Voroncova 1979: 91–2). As mobile stress develops, there is a growing need to differentiate between the forms of the singular and those of the plural, and the innovatory plural -á assumes the disambiguating role. Since it also attracts stress, the use of the -á ending is an important factor in paradigm levelling. Incidentally, normative handbooks often acknowledge end-stress in oblique cases of the plural prior to recognizing the -á plural; for example, such words as крендель 'pretzel', соболь 'sable', трюфель 'truffle' are accepted as having end-stress by Avanesov and Ožegov (1959), but the recommended plural forms are only крендели, трюфели (Zaliznjak 1967: 226; Voroncova 1979: 92). Meanwhile, the plurals кренделя, трюфеля are commonly found in *prostorečie* and in the professional usage of confectionery workers; for the word крендель, the existence of the set phrase выписывать (выделывать)

---

[22] Černyšev already regarded these -ы forms as archaic and advocated their replacement.

кренделя 'stagger, lurch' is an additional factor in favour of the á plural. The latest orthoepic dictionary (Borunova *et al.* 1983) seems to have closed the gap between the standard language and non-standard varieties: it cites both кренделя and крендели (in that order), соболя and соболи (in that order), трюфеля and трюфели (in that order).

Some of the -á plurals already known to Černyšev, however, such as офицера 'officers', консула 'consuls', лектора 'lecturers', are still not accepted in standard Russian. On the other hand, certain forms not even mentioned by him were sometimes approved later: бухгалтера 'book-keepers' (still colloquial, but *prostorečno* in the 1930s), лагеря 'camps' (semantically distinguished from лагери 'camps' in the ideological sense). Many further plurals in -á have appeared but remained non-standard: выбора 'elections', инженера 'engineers', etc. The difference between the standard and the colloquial language is clear from the following statistics: normative grammars and dictionaries list about 300 plurals in -á (Graudina *et al.* 1976: 118–19; Worth 1983: 257), and in non-standard varieties of Russian the number of plurals in -á is about 650 items (Ivanova 1967; Shapiro 1985: 173; Voroncova 1979: 90).

Despite the productivity of the type, some of the earlier known plurals in -á have fallen out of use, e.g. факторá 'factors' (now only фáкторы), гетманá 'hetmans' (now only гéтманы) (for a full list, see Zaliznjak 1967: 225–7; 1977: 74–5; Voroncova 1979: 94–6). Often the shift from -á/-я́ to -ы/-и can be explained by a less frequent use of the respective word: for example, this happened with the word гетман, due to changed historical conditions (see also Zaliznjak 1977: 93). This is another manifestation of the effect of pragmatic factors (ibid. 1977: 74–7): more common words acquire the innovatory plural, while less frequent words retain or even shift to the more conservative plural in -ы. For some words, the transition from the -á/-я́ plural to the more conservative -ы/-и plural is still in progress: one such word is лекарь 'medicine man, healer', for which the plural in -я́ and the end-stressed plural in general are considered archaic though still acceptable (Borunova *et al.* 1983).

As in the nineteenth century, plurals in -á are particularly characteristic of professional varieties (T. A. Ivanova 1967: 64). Professional plurals include: торта 'cakes' (used by confectioners),[23] плана 'plans' (used by draughtsmen), супа 'soups' (used in the catering trade)

---

[23] A group of confectionery workers from various parts of the USSR who visited Nottingham in September 1968 referred to themselves as кондитера (non-standard). (Personal observation by G. Stone.)

(Čukovskij 1963: 14). The nautical terms боцмана 'boatswains', лоцмана 'pilots', штурмана 'navigation officers', etc., are non-standard in non-nautical use, but in the Soviet Navy were officially codified (T. A. Ivanova 1967: 65; Suleržickie 1967: 69). Further evidence of the professional specialization of the -á type is provided by the RJaSO survey, which shows that while the greatest overall tendency to use these forms is exhibited by industrial workers, it is the white-collar workers who most favour бухгалтера 'bookkeepers' and инспектора 'inspectors'. Most significant of all, perhaps, is the fact that journalists and writers, though overall less likely than any other social category to use these forms as a whole, are more likely than any other category to use the form редактора 'editors' (Krysin 1974: 186, 251).

Despite the efforts of these same editors to regulate the nominative plural in -á, it continues to expand at the expense of the -ы type. Two examples of rapid change are the twentieth-century loan-words трактор 'tractor' and бункер 'bunker', whose plurals in the 1930s were still тракторы and бункеры (D. N. Ušakov 1935–40). Ožegov (1972) gives both трактора and тракторы, but only бункера. The RJaSO survey shows that the younger the speakers the more likely they are to prefer трактора (Krysin 1974: 251). However, this word is not typical of the survey as a whole, which shows varying tendencies. Though the general statement holds good that the number of words with nominative plural in -á is growing, some of the words surveyed (инспектор, кондуктор 'conductor', прожектор 'searchlight', редактор, сектор 'sector', слесарь 'locksmith', токарь 'turner') show a decreasing propensity to take -a in each succeeding age-group.

(iv) Genitive plural

A number of masculine nouns which in the nineteenth century formed their genitive plural in -ов now take the zero ending. The following semantic categories are affected:

  (a) Fruit and vegetables, e.g. помидор 'tomato', апельсин 'orange'.
  (b) Units of measurement, e.g. грамм 'gram', вольт 'volt'.
  (c) Members of human groups, including nationalities (e.g. грузин 'Georgian') and military units (e.g. драгун 'dragoon').
  (d) Objects occurring mostly in pairs, e.g. носок 'sock', сапог 'boot'.

Černyšev gives a list of 27 words which in his time took the zero ending, and 11 more for which he considered zero archaic. They include no fruit or vegetables. However, observations carried out in Russian shops in 1962–3 showed that the zero forms predominated overwhelmingly in the case of абрикос 'apricot', апельсин 'orange', баклажан 'egg-plant', гранат 'pomegranate', мандарин 'tangerine', помидор 'tomato'. Not a single instance of апельсинов or баклажанов was recorded. Only in the case of банан 'banana' was the balance different: 33 instances were recorded of бананов, 11 of банан. Answers to the RJaSO questionnaire on апельсин, баклажан, мандарин, and помидор confirm a general preference, but with smaller majorities, for the zero ending (Panov 1968: iii. 82–3). The data presented in Graudina *et al.* (1976: 125–8) and Graudina (1980: 91, 183, 279) confirm the preference for the zero ending.

Some units of measurement, especially electrical units such as вольт 'volt', ампер 'ampere', ватт 'watt', and ом 'ohm', had already acquired stable genitive plurals with zero ending by the first decade of the twentieth century (Graudina 1964*b*: 217). A few, however, are still unstable. It seems that граммов and килограммов never occur in speech, but owing to the insistence of normative works they are commonly used in writing (Panov 1968: iii. 80–1). The treatment of гектар 'hectare' is similar.

The movement towards the zero ending among names of members of human groups is extremely slow and irregular. Although грузинов, for example, is not acknowledged by D. N. Ušakov (1935–40) or Ožegov (1972), the RJaSO survey conducted in the 1960s showed that over 20 per cent of subjects born in the 1940s still preferred it. Башкиров, though admitted by D. N. Ušakov (1935–40) and preferred by nearly 38 per cent of subjects born in the 1940s, is rejected by Ožegov (1972) and Gorbačevič (1973). Партизанов, which was still accepted by D. N. Ušakov (1935–40), is described as 'archaic' by Gorbačevič (1973). The other military terms are nearly all historicisms.[24] A statistical analysis of 65 ethnonyms in written sources from the 1890s to the 1950s, mostly of very low frequency and therefore low stability, shows a small overall increase (6.2 per cent) of zero forms (Panov 1968: iii. 73–9; Graudina 1964*a*: 199–206; 1980: 279).

The paired objects сапоги 'boots', валенки 'felt boots', носки 'socks', чулки 'stockings' also exhibit a gradual movement towards the zero ending. In the nineteenth century these words could all take their

---

[24] Кадет had zero in the meaning 'cadet' but (usually) -ов in the meaning 'Constitutional-Democrat' (from the abbreviation КД). The military and political meanings were sometimes confused, however (Jakobson 1921: 30; Karcevskij 1923: 21).

genitive plural in -ов, though the zero form also occurred. The -ов forms survived into the Soviet period and, for a time, they were still recognized as standard. But at the present time only носков survives. The RJaSO survey shows a growing preference for genitive plural носок among the younger informants, and this form is acknowledged as grammatical in Zaliznjak's dictionary (1980). The recent (post-1930s) loan-words кеды 'keds, plimsolls', гольфы 'knee-high stockings', колготы (колготки) 'tights' (from Czech *kalhoty*) tend to follow the same pattern (Panov 1968: iii. 81–2).

Change in the genitive plural of feminine nouns has been restricted to those of the first declension whose stems end in soft or palatal consonants, some of which can take the ending -ей. The general tendency is for -ей to be replaced by a zero ending. Some of the -ей forms, such as пустыней, бурей, каплей (genitive plural of пустыня 'desert', буря 'storm', капля 'drop'), though used in the nineteenth century, were already archaic by the early twentieth century (Černyšev 1914–15: 97). Among the nouns for which -ей was still acceptable then but is now archaic are: петля 'loop', сплетня 'gossip'. On the other hand, the zero genitive of свеча 'candle', having been approved by normative works until the 1950s, has now been replaced by свечей (Gorbačevič 1971: 193–5). The form with the zero ending is retained in the set expression игра не стоит свеч 'not worth the trouble'.

Until the time of the First World War the neuter плечо 'shoulder' also took either -ей or zero in the genitive plural, but in the Soviet period плечей soon became archaic. Among certain neuters with nominative singular in -ье such as кушанье 'food, dish', поместье 'estate', платье 'dress', угодье 'fertile land', устье 'mouth (of river)', there was vacillation between -ьев and -ий in the genitive plural until the early twentieth century. In the case of all the words quoted, Černyšev regarded both variants as acceptable, but by the 1930s, кушаний, поместий, угодий, on the one hand, and платьев, устьев, on the other, were established as the only correct forms. The masculine подмастерье 'apprentice' showed similar instability before 1917, but since then the variant подмастерьев has ousted подмастерий.

(v) Instrumental plural

Certain instrumental plurals in -ьми which early in the present century were still acceptable (Černyšev 1914–15: 79–80, 95) are now archaic or defunct, viz. зверьми (зверь 'beast, animal'), плетьми (плеть 'lash'), сетьми (сеть 'net'), свечьми (свеча 'candle'), костьми (кость 'bone'). Only дети 'children', люди 'people', дверь 'door', дочь 'daughter', and лошадь 'horse' may now take instrumental plural in -ьми (V. V. Vinogradov *et al.* 1960: i. 170; Švedova 1970: 385; *Русская грамматика* 1980: i. 503). The form костьми is retained in the expression лечь костьми 'to fall in battle; to outdo oneself'.

The forms дверями, дочерями, лошадями are permissible according to the Academy Grammar (Švedova 1970: 385), though the latter two are described as *prostorečno* by Gorbačevič (1973). There are minor areas of disagreement between the normative authorities in their evaluation of -ьми forms, but all are agreed that детями and людями are nonstandard (Jazovickij 1969: 24).

(vi) Vocative

Nouns, particularly names, ending in unstressed -a/-я have developed a special form with zero ending used in address, especially to attract the hearer's attention. Instead of Нина, Коля, мама, гражданка, etc., the forms Нин!, Коль!, мам!, гражданк!, etc., are used. Composite address forms such as дядь Петь! (from дядя Петя), Никит Петрович (from Никита Петрович), Анн Ивановн or, in allegro speech, Ан Иван (from Анна Ивановна) are equally affected, and there is at least one plural: ребят! (from ребята 'lads'). Especially common is the duplicated type Коль, а Коль! (Švedova 1970: 575).

Such vocative forms are used by speakers of standard Russian, but they are colloquial and are not even recognized by the latest Academy Grammar (*Русская грамматика* 1980). Zemskaja (1987: 77) specifically indicates that the vocative form is alien to the codified spoken language (see also Bolla *et al.* 1970: 558; Zemskaja 1973: 157; 1983: 114–15; Superanskaja 1973: 230; Dulewiczowa 1983). Truncated vocative forms were in existence before 1917 (Vinogradov *et al.* 1960: ii. 2. 125), but it seems likely that their use has increased in the last half-century.

Adjectives

(i) Hard or soft

A few adjectives which in the nineteenth century could have either hard or soft stems (e.g. давний/давный 'of long ago', дальний/дальный 'distant')[25] now belong exclusively to the soft type. Cases where different types of stem are associated with different meanings are very few, cf. горний (poetic and slightly archaic) 'sublime, heavenly' and горный 'related to mountains, mountainous'. Generally speaking, the hard variants were already defunct by the early twentieth century (Černyšev 1914–15: 163–6), but a few cases of instability survived into the Soviet era, e.g. бескрайный/-ий 'boundless', междугородный/ -ий 'intertown; long-distance', искренный/-ий 'sincere', внутрен- ный/-ий 'interior'. Since the 1930s искренний, внутренний, and бескрайний on the one hand, and междугородный on the other, have tended to predominate (however, in the feminine, there is still significant variation between the standard междугородная and the more frequent in colloquial speech междугородняя). Related to this is the tendency for the soft adverbs внутренне and искренне to replace внутренно and искренно (Gorbačevič 1971: 199–201).

(ii) Indeclinable adjectives

Since before the Revolution Russian has had indeclinable adjectives, such as бордо 'claret, deep red', беж 'beige', электрик 'intense bright blue' but only in Soviet times have they become numerically important enough to be treated as a grammatical category (Šmeleva 1966: 27; Panov 1968: iii. 105–7). Even so the Academy Grammars have given them scant attention; for example, the Academy Grammar (*Русская грамматика* 1980: i. 556) justifies this by indicating that most such indeclinable adjectives are specialized terms. Meanwhile, we now have such common noun phrases as час пик 'rush hour', цвет беж 'beige colour', стиль модерн 'modern style', картошка (картофель) фри 'pommes-frites', in which only the noun is inflected according to case and number. The number of phrases increases dramatically if we include names of languages and ethnic groups, many of which appear as inde- clinable adjectives, for example, язык коми 'Komi language', народы банту 'Bantu peoples', словарь эсперанто 'Esperanto dictionary', эсперанто–русский словарь 'Esperanto–Russian dictionary'.

The view is also held that units such as гор- 'town, city', гос- 'state', парт- 'party', used in stump-compounds, e.g. горсовет 'city council', партбилет 'party card', are really invariable adjectives (Panov 1968: iii. 120).

---

[25] The variant дальный belonged to the OM pronunciation (Timofeev 1963: 212).

(iii) Possessive adjectives

Possessive adjectives ending in -ов/-ев and -ин may, according to prescriptive grammars, take short or long case endings in the genitive and dative masculine and neuter singular. For example, старухин 'old woman's' may decline as старухина or старухиного in the genitive, and as старухину or старухиному in the dative. Such adjectives, which may be derived from animates only (principally persons), are in any case stylistically restricted and of low frequency in the written standard.

Even in the nineteenth century the long forms were already in use in literature, and Černyšev, although he considered them incorrect, quoted a number of examples from well-known writers (1914–15: 183). Since then the short forms have become ever rarer, until today only the long forms can be regarded as normal (Gorbačevič 1971: 202).

Numerals

One of the facts of modern Russian grammar indicative of growing analyticity is the tendency not to decline certain cardinal numerals, especially in compound forms. Černyšev was aware of a general tendency for cardinal numerals not always to decline as required by the normative rules (1914–15: 196), a fact which appears to have disturbed him very little. The tendency not to decline numerals, which is known to some Russian dialects, increased during the Second World War, fostered to some extent, apparently, by officialdom (Mirtov 1953: 105). Non-declension is especially common among mathematicians (Panov 1968: iii. 88–9). In general, normative works still insist on declension, except in the case of compound numerals, which colloquially may be declined only partially.[26] Usually the last element only is declined in colloquial Russian, e.g. с шестьсот семьдесят двумя иллюстрациями 'with 672 illustrations'; more rarely, only the initial component of the numeral is declined, e.g. с двумя тысячами четыреста семьдесят

[26] In the 1960s and onwards, even some compound numerals, mostly those denoting hundreds, start occurring as indeclinable if they are followed by a noun: for example, in the Soviet news telecast *Время* of 12 July 1988, the announcer used the phrase с восемьсот самолётов 'with 800 airplanes'; the Academy Grammar (*Русская грамматика* 1980: i. 578) condemns as non-standard уничтожили более четыреста фашистских танков 'destroyed over 400 Nazi tanks'. Though this usage is still completely non-normative, it indicates that the tendency not to decline compound numerals is further increasing in the modern language.

человек 'with 2,470 people' (see also Graudina 1980: 238–44; *Русская грамматика* 1980: i. 579; Mel´čuk 1985: 222–5, 237–9; Wade 1992: 206). In more formal styles the whole numeral is declined (V. V. Vinogradov *et al.* 1960: i. 369; Rozental´ and Telenkova 1972: 210).[27]

Verbs

(i) Present stem

Certain first-conjugation verbs of the non-productive type which contains the vowel -a in the infinitive but loses it in the present tense (such as писать 'to write', пишу, пишешь, etc.) have acquired variant present tenses formed by analogy with the productive type which retains the vowel (e.g. знать 'to know', знаю, знаешь, etc.). They include the following:

алкать	'crave'	мурлыкать	'purr'
брызгать	'splash'	мыкать(ся)	'live miser- ably'
двигать	'move'	плескать(ся)	'splash'
жаждать	'thirst, crave'	полоскать(ся)	'rinse'
капать	'drip'	прыскать(ся)	'sprinkle'
колыхать(ся)	'sway'	рыскать	'roam'
крапать	'drip'	тыкать(ся)	'poke'
кудахтать	'cackle'	хлестать	'lash'
махать	'wave'	хныкать	'whimper'
метать(ся)	'throw'	щипать(ся)	'pinch'

(reflexive: 'rush about')

An investigation carried out in 1948 led to the conclusion that there was preference for the unproductive variants, even where the dictionaries indicated a movement towards the new type (Istrina 1948: 8–11). Long before this, however, Černyšev had indicated that for a number of these verbs he regarded both types as equally acceptable, including the following: капать, колыхать, кудахтать, махать, мурлыкать, мыкать, мяукать 'mew', плескать, полоскать, прыскать, стонать 'moan' (1914–15: 294–8). Since then certain variants have ceased to be acceptable, and this can be seen from the discriminations made in Soviet

[27] See also pp. 153–4.

dictionaries. Ožegov (1972), for example, describes каплю, мычу, стонаю as archaic; махаю, мурлыкаю, плескаю, полоскаю as colloquial; and does not even acknowledge the existence of колыхаю, кудахтаю, мяучу, прыщу (see also Gorbačevič 1978: 167–70; Il´ina 1980: 122–4).

The RJaSO survey in the 1960s included questions on колыхаться, махать, брызгать, капать, and showed a growing preference for the productive type in each succeeding generation. But (except for капает, which was supported by a majority in all age-groups) only a minority favoured the new type, even in the youngest age-group (Krysin 1974: 203). The variation of conjugation between the unproductive type and the productive type with the -a- stem is acknowledged in Zaliznjak (1980: 141) and Borunova *et al.* (1983), who follow Zaliznjak's dictionary. According to the latest normative handbooks, the verbs listed above differ in the degree of acceptability. Thus кудахтать is still accepted only in the unproductive conjugation and прыскать only in the productive one; for жаждать, only the gerund is formed productively (жаждая); двигать, in the non-productive conjugation, means 'to motivate, to cause to act' and, if conjugated productively, 'to move (physically)'.

(ii) Past stem

A number of verbs with infinitives in -нуть have two possible forms in the past tense and past participle, e.g. умолкнуть 'fall silent' can have умолк or умолкнул, and умолкший or умолкнувший. Other verbs of this type are: блекнуть 'dim', избегнуть 'avoid', прибегнуть 'resort (to)', сохнуть 'dry,' меркнуть 'fade', глохнуть 'die away', достигнуть 'reach', хрипнуть 'become hoarse', гибнуть 'perish', вторгнуться 'invade', виснуть 'hang'. The recommendations of dictionaries are inconsistent, but there appears to be a tendency to describe as archaic several -ну- variants which in reality are still in use. For example, сохнул, умолкнул, and померкнул are given as archaic in D. N. Ušakov (1935–40), but quoted without comment in Ožegov (1972). Some of the variants in -ну- approved by Černyšev (1914–15: 244–7) are now quite definitely obsolete, such as исчезнул 'disappeared', зябнул 'shivered', but quite a number are still in use, albeit rarely in some cases. Overall, though, forms without -ну- are becoming more productive in the language (Gorbačevič 1978: 164–6; Il´ina 1980: 126–8).

(iii) Biaspectual verbs

The majority of biaspectual verbs are either borrowings or have been derived from borrowed elements, e.g. атаковать 'attack', организовать 'organize', госпитализировать 'hospitalize'; non-borrowed biaspectual verbs include казнить 'torture, execute', ранить 'wound', молвить 'say, utter', велеть 'order', наследовать 'inherit', and some others (*Русская грамматика* 1980: i. 591–2). Because problems of communication arise (мы наследуем, for example, may mean 'we shall inherit' or 'we are inheriting'), there has been a tendency to treat the simple verb as imperfective only and create a new perfective by means of a prefix, e.g. унаследовать. Alternatively, the simple verb may be treated as only perfective, in which case a secondary imperfective is produced by suffixation, e.g. организовать—организовывать. The problem was noted by Černyšev (1915: 226–8) and the high degree of instability which now exists is reflected in the disagreement among various normative works in their classification of such verbs. As a rule, the secondary formations are not easily accepted as standard (e.g. заатаковать either 'begin to attack' or 'attack thoroughly', использовывать 'make use of' are non-standard), but there are several recent formations which have been given approval (e.g. отредактировать 'edit', сорганизовать 'organize') (Mučnik 1961; Gorbačevič 1971: 218–23).

Word Formation

(i) Productivity of suffixes

The deverbative suffixes -льщик and -щик (-чик), which in the nineteenth century could form primarily nouns meaning persons, now show a tendency to form nouns meaning things too,[28] e.g. зондировщик (1957) 'aeroplane for probing the atmosphere', бензозаправщик 'petrol tanker', сеноподборщик 'hay collector'. In some cases, one and the same form can be ambiguous, denoting both a person and a tool, for example, трубоукладчик 'pipe-layer'. Because the suffix -чик was traditionally used in the formation of nouns meaning persons, its use in the formation of nouns denoting things may still cause ambiguity; one example is the so-called правило буравчика 'corkscrew rule,

---

[28] This is to be distinguished from the process of resemanticization producing e.g. счетчик 'meter' from счетчик 'teller'.

Ampere's rule', taught in Soviet high-school physics and commonly thought to refer to the scientist who formulated it, while in actuality including a noun meaning 'corkscrew, gimlet'. Also -тель, formerly used to form nouns referring to either persons or things, shows an increasing ability to form those meaning things or locations (Panov 1968: ii. 170–90), e.g. разбрызгиватель 'sprinkler', вытрезвитель 'sobering-up station', (закрытый) распределитель '(closed) distribution office'.

From the beginning of the century onwards the suffix -ка has been extremely productive, forming nouns from both verbs and adjectives, e.g. маёвка 'pre-Revolutionary illegal May Day celebration', майка 'sleeveless shirt', буденовка 'Red Army helmet', семилетка 'seven-year school', пятилетка 'five-year plan', обезличка 'lack of personal responsibility', уравниловка 'wage-levelling', неувязка 'lack of co-ordination', скрепка 'paper clip', авоська 'mesh shopping bag' (from авось 'perhaps'),[29] похоронка 'notification of death in the battlefield' (in the Second World War), and the more recent кофеварка 'coffee-maker', стыковка 'space docking'. Though it had been in use long before the twentieth century, the suffix -ка appears to have been at its most active in non-standard varieties, especially the speech of students (Seliščev 1928: 175) and in educated spoken language (Zemskaja 1992: 50, 154). Its extended representation in the standard language stems from the general readjustment of social and functional varieties resulting from changes in the structure of social control (Janko-Trinickaja 1964b: 27–9). Many -ка formations now recorded in dictionaries are still qualified as 'colloquial' or *prostorečno* (Rojzenzon 1966: 110–11; Gornfel´d 1922: 56–7; Natanson 1966: 182; Panov 1968: i. 67–9; Lopatin 1973: 46–7; Zemskaja 1992: 50, 154).

During the first years of Soviet power there was a remarkable burst of activity by the previously unproductive suffix -ия to designate various social groups and areas—regional, political, or professional. In 1918 the area held by the Bolsheviks was called Совдепия by their opponents, but later this name was used by the Bolsheviks themselves (Pavlovskaja 1967: 16). At about the same time Скоропадия (from the name of Hetman Skoropadskij) and Красновия (after General Krasnov) came into existence (Seliščev 1928: 184). The Soviet state or system was called коммуния. To the Komsomol and Pioneers the names комсомолия and пионерия were given. Worker, peasant, and military correspondents (as groups) were referred to as рабкория, селькория, рабселькория, военкория. So quickly did most of these words fall out of use, however, that they were never recorded in dictionaries. The only exceptions are комсомолия, пионерия, инженерия 'engineers', which continue in rare use to the present day but with a very specific literary stylistic colouring. The suffix is now once again unproductive (Mis̓kevič 1967; Rojzenzon and Agafonova 1972; Protčenko 1975: 125).

The borrowed nominal suffix -изм has been increasingly popular in the language of the twentieth century. In the nineteenth century, the norm prescribed the use of this suffix only with Romance roots; Russian roots and stems were supposed to attach the suffixes -ость and -ство (this meant, for example, that the normatively acceptable name of Bolshevism had to be большевичество, not the current большевизм).[30] By the end of the nineteenth century this normative rule was effectively violated, and this opened the flood gates to numerous formations in -изм. The latest Academy Grammar (*Русская грамматика* 1980: i. 181) indicates that this suffix is primarily used in the formation of scientific and political terminology; the popularity of the suffix is confirmed by the fact that it is widely used to form new words from Russian stems, for example, жестокизм 'cruel attitude' and even from phrases, as in селявизм (from French *c'est la vie*) (Zemskaja 1992: 187). (See also Chapter 5.) The suffix often forms words that have parallels in abstract nouns formed with the help of the suffix -ость or -ство, differing from these in that the former denote a tendency or trend, for example, прогрессизм 'progressive approach' and прогрессивность 'progressive nature' (Zemskaja 1992: 187). The spread of -изм is accompanied by the increasing use of the suffix -ист, denoting persons, for example, прогрессист.

(ii) Acronyms and stump-compounds

We know of no totally new word-formation model originating in the Soviet period, though the productivity and functions of certain word-forming elements have varied. However, the method of producing words like ГЭС, загс, колхоз, нарком, the very name of the Soviet Union (СССР), etc. from initials or segments of other words is usually thought of as a specifically Soviet procedure. Certainly, a very large number of Soviet neologisms have been formed by this process, but it actually originated before 1917. Even before the First World War a few such

[30] Granovskaja (1983: 63).

words were in existence, some connected with politics, like эсер (с.-р., социалист-революционер) 'Socialist-Revolutionary', кадет (конституционалист-демократ) 'Constitutional-Democrat', others with commerce, such as Лензото (Ленское золотопромышленное товарищество) 'Lena Gold-Mining Company', and Монотоп (монополия топлива) 'Fuel Monopoly', and they were then already in colloquial use (Jakobson 1921: 10). Polivanov ((1927) 1974: 183–4) mentions the now obsolete правоучение (право на обучение) 'study permit' as an innovation of the 1900s–1910s, known to any student of that period. At that time, however, this procedure was merely peripheral to the established word-formation system. During the First World War its convenience for use in telegrams became apparent to the military and certain conventions were set up for use in communications: Военмин (Военное министерство) 'Ministry of Defence', командарм (командующий армией) 'army commander', etc. (see also Chapter 5, section 'Lexical change, 1900–17').

During 1917, even before October, a number of new political terms were formed by this method: совдеп (совет депутатов) 'soviet of deputies', армком (комиссар при армии) 'army commissar', исполком (исполнительный комитет) 'executive committee', Викжель (Всероссийский исполнительный комитет союза железнодорожников) 'All-Russian Executive Committee of the Union of Railwaymen'. After October it was an ideal way of forming the many new words needed to make manageable the titles of many new institutions which came into existence during the first years of the new regime.

Compounds of this type are known by the Russian terms аббревиатура and сложносокращенное слово. In English they are called 'stump-compounds', 'clips' (Ward 1965: 156 ff.; Wade 1992: 42), but we prefer to restrict this term to those actually made of stumps, and refer to the others (made of initials) as 'acronyms'. The following types may be distinguished:

1. Stump-compounds proper, i.e. those in which segments of words—or stumps—are used. The latter are usually, but not always, syllables, e.g. колхоз (коллективное хозяйство) 'collective farm'.

2. Acronyms, i.e. those in which initials are used,[31] subdivided into:

---

[31] Wade (1992: 40–1, 80–1) distinguishes alphabetisms, i.e. acronyms consisting of initial capital letters. However, it should be borne in mind that some current alphabetisms were earlier spelt without any capitalization, for example, нэп (now НЭП). Ward (1965: 161–2, 268–9) recognizes a subset of initial-words.

(*a*) Those consisting of the names of the letters,

e.g. КПСС [kapee'ses] 'CPSU', СССР [eseses'er] 'USSR', ОРЗ [oer'ze] (острое респираторное заболевание) 'acute respiratory disease'

(*b*) Those consisting of the sounds of the letters,

e.g. загс [zaks] 'office of the registrar', БАМ [bam] 'Baikal-Amur Railway'.[32]

3. Mixed compounds combining stumps with the names or sounds of the letters, e.g. гороно (городской отдел народного образования) 'city department of public education'.

Immediately after the Revolution there were a few cases of the names of letters being spelt out, e.g. чека (чрезвычайная комиссия) 'Emergency Committee', цека (центральный комитет) 'Central Committee', but these are exceptional.

Stumps may also occur independently, e.g. зав (заведующий) 'chief', зам (заместитель) 'deputy', спец (специалист) 'specialist', but they are not very numerous and are often colloquial. The production of new words by this method is also mainly a post-1917 phenomenon, but it too originated before the First World War with the appearance of экс (экспроприация) 'expropriation' (Karcevskij 1923: 47).

In the first few years of Soviet power certain easily recognizable stumps were especially productive, e.g. агит- 'propaganda', парт- 'party', полит- 'political', проф- 'professional', культ- 'culture', гос- 'state', сов- 'Soviet', соц- 'socialist', etc. The stump -ком- can stand for a number of full words: Коминтерн (Коммунистический интернационал), комбед (комитет бедноты), нарком (народный комиссар), краском (красный командир). But homonymy is kept within bounds by certain positional restraints (Jakobson 1921: 14).

From 1917 to the end of the 1920s the stump-compound proper predominated over the acronym as a means of creating words. The fact that pre-Revolutionary phrases could be given a Revolutionary air by abbreviation was convenient, e.g. сберегательная касса 'savings bank' had existed before the Revolution, but сберкасса was new. In the same way the old Донецкий бассейн 'Donets Basin' became the new Донбасс.[33]

[32] In several abbreviations, the two subtypes compete (for example, США 'USA' has the pronunciation [si^e ʃi^e 'a] and [sʃa] or [ʃʃa]) or even combine: thus, ФРГ 'Federal Republic of Germany' was pronounced as [fi^e er'ge] (Ageenko and Zarva 1984), though the name of the first letter is [ef].

[33] It is significant that the Whites, having rejected the new orthography and the reform of the calendar, could not quite resist the stump-compound: note their добрармия (добровольческая армия) 'voluntary army' (Jakobson 1921: 13, 30). Altogether,

However, so many new words were being created that objections were voiced, particularly in the press, where the ironic and humorous possibilities of this model were not overlooked (Jakobson 1921: 12). More and more incomprehensible words were added to the vocabulary until the mid 1920s, when a certain moderation in their use can be observed (Seliščev 1928: 168), and from 1930 onwards there was a distinct reduction in both their use and production (Panov 1968: ii. 92). There ensued a period of stabilization, during which a number of stump-compounds fell out of use, e.g. домзак (дом заключения) 'prison', шкраб (школьный работник) 'teacher',[34] дензнак (денежный знак) 'banknote', стенгаз (стенная газета) 'wall newspaper' (replaced by стенгазета). In the 1930s and 1940s the proportion of new acronyms to new stump-compounds increased (Panov 1968: ii) and this tendency continues.

Both stump-compounds and acronyms (especially the latter) tend to be structurally irregular. They may, for example, contain combinations of sounds not occurring in other words. Consequently, in the 1960s and 1970s, there were attempts to create forms which are structurally conventional, e.g. лавсан (a synthetic fibre named from the initials of Лаборатория высокомолекулярных соединений Академии наук СССР), БАМ (Байкало-Амурская магистраль), and even to make them coincide with existing words: БУЗА (боевой устав зенитной артиллерии) 'anti-aircraft artillery field manual' (cf. буза 'row'), СУП (строевой устав пехоты) 'infantry drill manual' (cf. суп 'soup'), etc. (Ickovič 1971, 1972). One of the levelling tendencies is the positioning of stress on the final syllable of the acronym (*Русская грамматика* 1980: i. 255). The irregularity, however, remains and increases slightly because of the growing tendency to render foreign abbreviations by abbreviations of the Russian translation equivalent; for example, the official name of the Star Wars (Strategic Defense Initiative, SDI) developed during the Reagan presidency was translated and subsequently abbreviated in Russian as СОИ (стратегическая оборонная инициатива)—despite the semantic difference between the American English *initiative,* used here in the meaning 'plan, programme', and the

though, the practice of creating excessive abbreviations was condemned by the *émigré* circles, who maintain this attitude until now (Rževskij 1951: 9–10). A famous Russian poet Georgij Ivanov, who emigrated to France after the Revolution, was quoted as rejecting a country with the 'telegraph name' USSR (страна с телеграфным названием СССР). (Personal communication by Sofia Bogatyreva.)

[34] On the early use of this word, see Seliščev (1928: 160–2); in the contemporary language, this word is retained, as purely colloquial, with negative connotations.

Russian инициатива, which can only denote the ability to follow through with a plan. The resulting acronym СОИ, which resembles a plural noun, immediately joined the ranks of words of unstable gender; in colloquial speech, it was changed to СОЯ, by analogy with соя 'soybean'. Similarly, the acronym НЛО, which appeared in the 1970s, is based on the first letters of the exact translation of the English UFO (Unidentified Flying Object)—неопознанный летающий объект.

In some cases, stump-compounds and acronyms can undergo suffixation, cf. the pre-Revolutionary эсерствовать 'to associate oneself with the Socialist-Revolutionary Party (эсеры)'; the more recent КГБшник or кэгэбешник, кэгэбист (кэгебист) 'KGB employee', from КГБ plus -ник or -ист; эсемка 'computer', from СМ (эсем) (acronym of счетная машина 'computing machine') plus -ка (Zemskaja 1992: 50), гэдээровский (from ГДР—Германская Демократическая Республика) 'made in the GDR' (Wade 1992: 41). Such suffixed formations are typically colloquial (*Русская грамматика* 1980: i. 256; Zemskaja 1992: 50).

4   Syntax

THE subject-matter of this chapter may be divided into two main parts: syntactic variation and syntactic stylistics. The first is similar to the subject-matter of most of the rest of the book, in that it deals with syntactic variants—different syntactic means of expressing the same meaning—where the choice between the variants impinges on the question of which syntactic forms are admissible in the current standard. Except for a few detailed points, there are no surveys of educated syntactic usage comparable to those for pronunciation, stress, or morphology (e.g. the RJaSO survey): the material on syntactic variation is thus rather less comprehensive than on these other components of the language, although much material has been gathered on change in standard written usage, and on deviations from the codified standard in speech and writing (Graudina *et al.* 1976; Ickovič 1982; Zolotova 1973, 1974*a*, 1976, 1979, 1982; Zemskaja 1973, 1981, 1987).

Verbal Government

In a large number of instances, the case or preposition required after a particular verb is arbitrary, not following from the meaning of that verb; in many instances, one even finds synonymous or nearly synonymous verbs requiring different constructions, e.g. предупредить о 'warn about', but предостеречь от, or платить за and оплачивать + accusative 'pay for'. In many such instances where the particular case or preposition governed by a verb is arbitrary, there have been shifts in standard usage between nineteenth-century and current practice, while in other cases one finds variation in practice even where this variation lies outside the current standard.

(i) Accusative objects, oblique objects, and objects with prepositions

In Russian, there are three possible forms for the object of a verb: in the accusative case, in one of the other prepositionless oblique cases (genitive, dative, or instrumental), or with a preposition. Among verbs whose object case is not determined semantically, there has been some tendency over the recent history of the language for oblique objects to be replaced by accusative objects or objects with prepositions. For instance, the verb благодарить 'thank' in nineteenth-century literature is often found with the dative case object, because of its association with дарить which requires the dative object; in current usage only the accusative is standard (Gorbačevič 1973). A number of verbs which took the genitive in the early nineteenth-century usage now require a preposition, e.g. бежать от 'avoid', скучать по and, alternatively, скучать о 'miss; long for', трепетать перед 'tremble before', надеяться на 'rely on, hope for' (Gorbačevič 1971: 229–30; Graudina 1980: 30). In general, these changes in standard usage were completed during the nineteenth century.

This tendency has even been extended to a number of reflexive verbs, which according to the traditional standard can never occur with a direct object, but which in current usage, especially colloquial usage, often do occur with an accusative object. Traditionally, слушаться 'obey' takes the genitive, but the accusative is common in colloquial speech, and Butorin (1966) cites a number of examples with an accusative object from literature, commenting that this usage can no longer be considered a gross violation of the norm; according to the latest Academy Grammar (*Русская грамматика* 1980: ii. 35), the use of the genitive with слушаться is archaic.[1] Butorin cites similar examples for some other reflexive verbs, including бояться 'fear' (though only colloquially, for instance in direct speech in literature, and especially with animate objects), and дождаться 'wait for' (only with animate objects).

Several verbs take an object in either the accusative or the genitive, with subtle semantic differences between the two. With such verbs there is again a tendency in current usage for the accusative to oust the genitive. In the nineteenth century, the verb ждать 'wait' regularly took the genitive case, while nowadays both accusative and genitive are found, even in literature, with concrete nouns (in particular names of means of transport, e.g. ждать поезда/поезд 'wait for a train', and names referring to people, e.g. ждать сестру/сестры 'wait for one's

---

[1] This calls into question the claim often made, e.g. by Ickovič (1968: 28; 1974), that new forms violating general models of the language cannot, in principle, be accepted as standard, since the pattern reflexive verb plus direct object is a clear violation of a general model in the traditional standard. Butorin (1966) also discusses the increasing acceptability in the standard language of the accusative as object of the category of state, e.g. слышно музыку 'music is audible', видно деревню 'a village is visible'.

sister');[2] with abstract nouns, however, the genitive is still preferred by
most normative handbooks, though examples with the accusative are
found, e.g. ждать покорно беду—нет, это, извините, не в моем
характере 'to wait submissively for misfortune—no, forgive me, that's
not my character' (Polozov, *Хождение за три моря*, quoted by
Gorbačevič (1971: 234)). A similar change has occurred with искать
'look for', though here the earlier standard is for the accusative case
when referring to specific individual objects, and the genitive when
referring to abstracts, although the current tendency is to allow both the
accusative and the genitive with more general and abstract nouns, the
accusative being used particularly when reference is to a specific
instance of the abstract concept. In addition, the accusative/genitive
contrast with искать conveys the difference between a definite and
indefinite object, for example, искать свое место (в театре) 'look for
one's seat (in a theatre)' but искать места 'look for a job' (Prokopovič
et al. 1981: 17). The tendency towards the use of the accusative object
is particularly evident in the use of interrogative pronouns: according to
Prokopovič *et al*. (1981: 17), the difference between чего он ищет? and
что он ищет? 'what is he looking for?' is hardly perceptible in the
modern language. (See also Graudina *et al*. 1976: 33–42.)

Related to the general tendency for oblique objects to be replaced by
other kinds of object is the tendency towards lower frequency of the
partitive genitive,[3] and the genitive of negation. The latter subsumes the
direct object of a negated verb, e.g. я не встретил сестры 'I didn't
meet my sister', and the subject of a negated intransitive verb, as in
ответа не пришло 'no answer came'. Both subtypes of the genitive of
negation are on the decline in the contemporary language: they are
becoming replaced, accordingly, by the accusative of negation (я не
встретил сестру) and by the nominative (ответ не пришел) (*Русская
грамматика* 1980: ii. 325–6, 415–18, 430); similarly, the genitive is on
the decline as the object of an infinitive dependent on a negated verb
(*Русская грамматика* 1980: ii. 322).[4] Though there are a series of

[2] Borras and Christian (1984: 25–6) indicate that the usage of the accusative with verbs
such as ждать 'is a feature of spoken, rather than written Russian'. See also Wade (1992:
97–9).
[3] One use of the partitive genitive, the 'genitive of temporary use', is impossible in
current usage, though still found in nineteenth-century literature, e.g. одолжить
карандаша 'lend a pencil' (sc. for a while) (Ickovič 1968: 57–8).
[4] Exceptionally, Ickovič (1968: 63–5) claims that the genitive of the direct object of an
infinitive dependent on a negated verb, as in он не хотел читать этой книги 'he did not
want to read this book', is on the increase, though without quoting the statistical basis of
this claim. Mustajoki (1985: 62–9, 149–58), based on the analysis of the literature and his

semantic and syntactic factors that determine the choice between the accusative and the genitive of object under negation (Mustajoki 1985; Mustajoki and Heino 1991; Ueda 1992: 4–128), the decline of the genitive of negation is commonly explained by the influence of colloquial Russian, where the tendency to avoid the genitive of negation as well as the lexically governed genitive is even more pronounced (Prokopovič *et al.* 1981: 16–17; Zemskaja 1981: 166). One of the few constructions where the genitive of negation remains relatively stable is that with the so-called 'stressed' negation, as in я не видел никаких чашек 'I haven't seen any cups' or никаких детей здесь не бегает 'no children run around here' (Mustajoki 1985: 49–53; Pesetsky 1982: 40).

Overall, the genitive seems to be the weakest case as far as coding of the object is concerned in modern Russian: not only is it replaced by the accusative, as shown by the above examples, but also by the instrumental, for instance, with such verbs as гнушаться 'disdain', брезгать (брезговать) 'be squeamish about', исполниться, преисполниться 'fill with' (in the figurative sense), разжиться 'obtain' (*Русская грамматика* 1980: ii. 36). The genitive object with the verbs беречься 'take precautions against', робеть 'be timid' is replaced by a prepositional object, e.g. беречься от гриппа 'take precautions against the 'flu', робеть перед строгим отцом 'quail before a strict father' (Rozental´ 1986b: 14, 195).

Prepositional objects have been effectively replacing objects in the instrumental that occur with verbs of motion; such objects denote either the location of motion (идти садом 'go through a garden') or the means of transportation (ехать поездом 'go by train') (see also Mrazek 1964: 33, 38, 88, 98, 143 for other examples). Though normative handbooks still recommend the use of the instrumental object, the tendency is towards expressing the name of location by the preposition по plus dative, for example, идти по саду. In the expression of transportation means, the prepositions в and на with the prepositional case are becoming more common, for example, ехать трамваем/в трамвае/на трамвае 'go by the trolley'. The combination в plus prepositional case is considered more acceptable; на is also permitted in the standard language, especially if the vehicle is a closed one, so that passengers travel inside it, e.g. лететь на самолете 'fly by plane' (Prokopovič *et al.* 1981: 21). That the prepositional construction is ousting the instrumental of means of transport is also evident from the fact that names for

own statistical experiments, shows convincingly that the genitive of negation is undergoing a decline in this type of construction as well.

new means of transport, such as aircraft or spacecraft, occur with prepositions but not in the instrumental case, e.g. лететь на дирижабле,
на космическом корабле 'fly in a dirigible, a spaceship', ехать в
карете скорой помощи/на скорой помощи 'ride in an ambulance'
(Graudina 1980: 105).

The dative object is replaced by a prepositional object, for example,
with the verbs благоволить 'regard with favour' and довлеть 'prevail
over, dominate': the former still takes the dative, but with the preposition к, the latter takes the instrumental phrase with the preposition
над. While the prepositionless objects are still accepted as normative
by some sources (Rozental´ 1986b: 15, 45), others cite these types of
objects as obsolete.

Although the general trend has been from oblique objects towards
accusative or prepositional objects, there are a few verbs that have
undergone the reverse change. In many instances this has been determined semantically, e.g. with руководить 'lead, be in charge of',
дирижировать 'conduct (orchestra)', which used to take the accusative
or dative in the nineteenth century, but now require the instrumental,
like other verbs with the general meaning of 'control', e.g. управлять
'control', править 'reign' (Prokopovič *et al.* 1981: 18).[5]

In the nineteenth century the verb писать 'write' could take an indirect object with the preposition к, as in Lermontov's *Валерик* (1840):
Я к Вам пишу случайно . . . 'I write to you by chance . . .'. In
current usage this indirect object, like other indirect objects (e.g. after
давать 'give') takes a simple dative: Я Вам пишу/Я пишу Вам.[6, 7]
Some other instances are more clearly just exceptional: льстить 'flatter'
takes the dative in current usage rather than the accusative of the nineteenth century, although the earlier construction remains in the expression льстить себя надеждой 'flatter oneself with hope'. Касаться
'touch, concern' takes a simple genitive in current standard usage,
although in the nineteenth century it also occurred, because of French
influence, with the preposition до (and less commonly with к, or with a
prepositionless dative) (Gorbačevič 1971: 230–1), and the construction
with до is still common in current non-standard usage (Gorbačevič
1973). One verb, следить 'track, keep an eye on' has shifted from

---

[5] Дирижировать still occurs with the accusative in musicians' jargon (Zolotova
1974b: 150).

[6] Note also the variation in word order: in the twentieth century, the occurrence of pronouns after the verb in the present or future tense has become much more common.

[7] The noun письмо 'letter' still allows both constructions: письмо (к) другу 'letter to
a friend'.

taking an accusative object to taking за with the instrumental, though the older construction survives in the literal sense of 'track' in hunters' jargon (Gorbačevič 1971: 229–30).

The trend away from verbs taking prepositionless objects in an oblique case is one that has operated, slowly, throughout the history of Russian and other Slavonic languages.[8] The overall tendency is towards a situation like that of Bulgarian, or English, where there is only a two-way distinction among object types: those with prepositions and those without; this is therefore consistent with the general trend towards analyticity, so obvious in the contemporary Russian language.

(ii) Analogy and object cases

Where the case of the object of a verb (or adjective or noun, especially deverbative noun) is arbitrary, then there is likely to be pressure for a change in this case from semantically similar verbs that take a different case. Thus we have already noted verbs like руководить 'be in charge' and дирижировать 'conduct' which have shifted to take an instrumental object, parallel to other verbs with the general meaning of 'control'. Most of these analogical changes have their origin in the spoken language, and many of them remain outside the bounds of standard usage.[9] Thus, under the influence of платить за 'pay for' one finds оплачивать за instead of оплачивать with the accusative of the object; under the influence of приговорить к 'sentence to' one finds осудить к instead of осудить на; under the influence of the large number of verbs expressing informational content which take the preposition о 'about', one finds указать о instead of указать plus accusative or указать на 'indicate' (for other examples, see Prokopovič *et al.* 1981: 49–54).

In some cases, however, the frequency of the newer form, and its use by writers, suggests that there may be reasons for accepting that a change in the standard has taken place. Thus the traditional government of the verb поразиться 'be astounded' is with the instrumental, and this certainly remains as a possible construction. However, many other verbs expressing surprise take the dative case, e.g. удивиться 'be surprised', изумиться 'be astounded', and under their influence поразиться is also found with the dative, even in literature. In many recent normative

---

[8] See Sjöberg (1964) for Old Church Slavonic, Bobran (1974) for Polish (in comparison with Russian), Timberlake (1974) for Slavonic in general.

[9] For a full discussion, with numerous examples, see Švedova (1966).

handbooks, the dative case is cited as a possibility after поразиться: thus Ožegov (1972) cites both поразиться известию 'be astounded at some news' and поразиться красотой героини 'be astounded at the beauty of the heroine' without comment; Gorbačevič (1973) recommends the instrumental, but cites the dative as 'permissible'. Similarly, the verb возлагать/возложить 'lay upon' traditionally takes two objects, one in the prepositionless accusative, the other in the accusative with the preposition на, e.g. возложить венок на могилу 'lay a wreath upon a grave'. In modern usage, however, возложить can also occur with the dative object introduced by preposition к, e.g. возложить венок к могиле Неизвестного солдата 'to lay a wreath upon the grave of the Unknown Soldier', or the genitive object with the preposition у (возложить венок у могилы . . .). Prokopovič *et al.* (1981: 54) explain this extension of verbal government by the change in the actual practice of laying wreaths: in addition to positioning the wreath upon a gravestone, it can also be put next to it or next to a monument, which is reflected in the verbal government.

Nominal and Adjectival Government

A number of nouns that, in the nineteenth century, took the object in the dative now commonly take the object in the genitive, for example, цена 'price', начало 'beginning', предел 'limit', причина 'reason', корень 'root', доказательство 'proof', итог 'sum'. Though the objective genitive is more common with these nouns than the objective dative, the latter is retained in a number of set expressions, for example, знать цену людям 'to be aware of human nature', назначить цену товарам 'to set the price of merchandise', положить конец беспорядкам 'to put an end to rioting' (Prokopovič *et al.* 1981: 28).

Several words that earlier required the dative object can no longer take this object and take only the objective genitive, for example, план 'plan', чертеж 'blueprint', проект 'project', парад 'parade' (Prokopovič *et al.* 1981: 28–9), e.g. праздничный парад войск 'military parade in observance of a national holiday'.

Possessor genitive and possessor dative are both possible with objects denoting body parts and clothing, occurring with sense perception verbs and such verbs as пожать (руку) 'shake a hand', прострелить 'shoot through'; cf. the following example from Gogol´'s *Мертвые души* (1842): с четверть часа тряс он руку Чичикова и нагрел ее страшно 'for about half an hour he was shaking Čičikov's hand and warmed it up terribly' *versus* он тряс гостю руку 'he was shaking the guest's hand'. According to Prokopovič *et al.* (1981: 29–30), the use of the possessor genitive is increasing in twentieth-century Russian; however, this observation is challenged by the material discussed in Apresjan (1974: 34–5, 269–70).[10]

The genitive replaces the instrumental case after the adjective полный 'full'; cf. the use of both cases by Puškin:

> На берегу пустынных волн
> Стоял он, дум великих полн
> (*Медный всадник*, 1833)
>
> On a deserted wave-swept shore
> He stood, filled with lofty thoughts

and:

Полный тревожными мыслями, я вошел в комендантский дом. (*Капитанская дочка*, 1836)

Filled with anxious thoughts, I entered the commander's house.

Though modern dictionaries still allow the instrumental case (for example, listed as the second option in Zaliznjak 1980), the use of the genitive is by far more common (Prokopovič *et al.* 1981: 33).

Similar to the tendencies observed in verbal government, there is a tendency in twentieth-century Russian to replace adnominal and adjectival objects without a preposition by prepositional objects. This is due to the general increase of analyticity in the language as well as to analogy.

The noun надежда 'hope' in the nineteenth century normally occurred with the prepositionless genitive, e.g. in Puškin's *Стансы* (1826): В надежде славы и добра . . . 'in the hope of glory and grace'. In the modern language, надежда takes the object in the accusative introduced by the preposition на. The noun прогноз 'forecast', especially 'weather forecast', traditionally requires the genitive (прогноз погоды), although by analogy with other nouns expressing informational content it is also found with the preposition о 'about', and also with относительно 'relative to'; Gorbačevič (1973) recommends the genitive, but cites as 'permissible' the variants with о and относи-

---

[10] The claim made in Prokopovič *et al.* (1981: 30) is also questionable in the light of the frequent use of the possessor genitive in nineteenth-century literature, cf. the example from Gogol´ cited here.

тельно.[11] In the nineteenth century, контроль 'control' occurred only with the preposition над; in current usage it is also found with за + instrumental (cf. наблюдение за 'observation', надзор за (also над) 'supervision'), and with the genitive (cf. проверка + genitive 'check'). All three variants are listed, without comment, in Gorbačevič (1973). Gorbačevič (1971: 239–40) again permits all three variants, but suggests semantic and stylistic differences among them: both над and за are used with deverbative nouns indicating a process, while над is preferred with other nouns (thus контроль над/за работой 'control over work', but контроль над финансами '. . . finances', контроль над поставщиками '. . . suppliers'), and the genitive is used primarily in official and technical language. It is not coincidental that of the three permissible variants, the genitive is most restricted to specialized, written language: this is another instance of growing analyticity in twentieth-century Russian.

The extent to which native speakers can be uncertain in practice of standard usage in some of these instances is well illustrated by L. Čukovskaja's *В лаборатории редактора* (Moscow, 1963), quoted and criticized by Švedova (1966). Čukovskaja condemns such contaminations as катастрофа самолета (cf. гибель самолета, крушение самолета 'the wreck of the plane' and катастрофа с самолетом 'the plane disaster'), смириться с 'resign oneself to' (cf. смириться перед 'resign oneself to' and примириться с 'reconcile oneself with'), but then uses in her own text constructions that violate the traditional standard in just this way: испуг перед разнообразием естественных интонаций 'fear of the variety of natural intonations' (for испуг + genitive, cf. боязнь перед 'fear of'), чутье к языку 'feel for the language' (for чутье языка, cf. чувствительный к языку 'sensitive to language').

Another representation of the tendency towards analyticity is the increasing tendency to avoid nominal objects governed by a number of nouns, most of them abstract; such nominal complements are replaced by infinitival objects or clausal objects introduced by a conjunction. For example, the noun обещание 'promise' took either a genitive object or an infinitival object in the nineteenth century, cf. in Puškin's letter to his brother Lev (22–3 April 1825): Благодарю за обещание предисловия 'Thank you for the promise of the preface', and in

---

[11] This work also cites another variant, прогноз на + accusative, presumably under the influence of указание на 'indication'; this variant is qualified as incorrect.

Дубровский (1833) обещание вскоре увидеться 'the promise to meet again soon'. In the modern language, the former government is obsolete, and the noun обещание can take either the infinitive, or the clause introduced by the conjunction что; the latter type of government is especially common in colloquial speech.

Preposition Government

(i) по

In current usage the preposition по followed by a numeral with distributive meaning takes either the dative or the accusative of most numerals, e.g. по пяти or по пять 'five each'; exceptions are the numeral 'one', which is always in the dative, and the numerals 'two', 'three', 'four', 'two hundred', 'three hundred', 'four hundred', which are always in the accusative (for a formal account, see Mel´čuk 1985: 221–2, 443–4, 487). For the other numerals, the traditional standard required the dative case (i.e. по пяти), a requirement that remained virtually unchallenged until the early twentieth century. For the numeral 'hundred', the old dative сту was used (пó сту), rather than the newer dative form ста used in other constructions;[12] for the indefinite numerals such as много 'much, many', мало 'little, few', несколько 'some', сколько 'how many', again a special dative form in -у was used (по многу 'many each'). During the twentieth century, there has been a tendency for these dative forms to be replaced by accusative forms.[13] D. N. Ušakov (1935–40) still considered the newer forms like по пять to be *prostorečno*, but most current dictionaries admit both forms, though qualifying the citation form as colloquial. An exception is 'hundred', where only the newer form, по сто, corresponds to the current standard (Avanesov and Ožegov 1959; Borunova *et al.* 1983).

The survey reported in Panov (1968: iii. 93–4) tends to confirm this picture. Only 3 per cent of those asked preferred по сту to по сто. Only

---

[12] D. N. Ušakov (1935–40) does, however, recommend пó ста (which would be identical in pronunciation with пó сто); he considers по сту *prostorečno*, and does not mention по сто.

[13] Perhaps more accurately, by citation forms, since nominative and accusative of these numerals are alike, and the use of the citation form can be seen as part of the general trend towards analyticity. For further details of the changes, with examples from literature, see Butorin (1964).

5 per cent preferred по сорока to по сорок; сто and сорок tend to behave alike morphologically, although Avanesov and Ožegov (1959) and Gorbačevič (1973) still recommend по сорока, qualifying по сорок as 'colloquial'. For numerals declined like пять, the percentage of informants preferring the dative varied from 8 per cent to 25 per cent. For the indefinite numerals there were more informants preferring the dative forms: 26 per cent for по нескольку, 29 per cent for по скольку, and 56 per cent for по многу, the last being the only example where the majority favoured the dative. The greater retention of the dative in indefinite numerical expressions is explained by the interference of the adverbials помногу, понемногу, (мало-)помалу, where the -y ending is the only one possible.

We may conclude by referring the reader to a note in the September–October 1974 issue of the *Association of Teachers of Russian Newsletter,* discussing linguistic aspects of the Russian commentary on a Davis Cup tennis match between the USSR and Czechoslovakia, in which both umpire and commentator used по пятнадцать and по пятнадцати 'fifteen all', по тридцать and по тридцати 'thirty all' indiscriminately in calling the score.

There have been some other minor changes in the use of cases after по between nineteenth- and twentieth-century usage.[14] For instance, in its basic meaning of motion across a surface, по regularly took the prepositional case of personal pronouns in the nineteenth century, whereas in current usage pronouns, like nouns, stand in the dative (по нему 'across it', rather than по нём); the prepositional here was still required by D. N. Ušakov (1935–40), but is qualified as *prostorečno* by Gorbačevič (1973). After verbs of grieving like тосковать по 'yearn for', current usage has the dative of nouns; the use of the prepositional case of nouns is not uncommon in the nineteenth century.

(ii) Other prepositions and expressions with the prepositional function

The case required after a number of other prepositions has also changed during the recent history of the Russian language. Thus вопреки 'despite' took the genitive case in the nineteenth century, whereas now it requires the dative. Благодаря 'thanks to' could take the accusative, whereas nowadays only the dative is possible; as noted above (p. 145),

---

[14] For details, see Astaf´eva (1974: 20–5), Gorbačevič (1973), Iomdin (1991).

of the variants found earlier with the verb благодарить it is the accusative that has triumphed. Gorbačevič (1973) considers the accusative after благодаря to be archaic. One preposition whose usage is not completely stabilized is между 'between', at least in the sense 'between like objects'. In current prose fiction and scientific writing preference is clearly for the instrumental, except in a few set phrases (читать между строк 'read between the lines', между двух стульев 'between the devil and the deep blue sea'), although the genitive, common in earlier periods of the language, is still to be found in recent fiction; Gorbačevič (1973) quotes the following sentence from G. Markov's *Соль земли*: на земле между стволов было тихо 'on the ground among the tree-stumps it was quiet'. In fact, the only normative recommendation made in Gorbačevič (1973) is that with the instrumental one usually finds между and with the genitive usually меж; this seems to be too non-partisan an assessment, since the preference in current non-stylized prose is clearly for между and the instrumental.

Such variation in prepositional government can also lead to the appearance of variation where previously there was none. Thus, in both nineteenth-century and current standard usage согласно 'according to' requires the dative. Gorbačevič (1973) condemns the use of согласно + genitive as incorrect. Mazon (1920: 54) refers to 'the adoption by the language of administration and official prose of the incorrect construction of согласно with the genitive'. In addition to the dative and archaic accusative, благодаря is also found with the genitive in nonstandard usage.

The expression в адрес '(addressed) to' normally takes the genitive case, e.g. в адрес советской делегации поступили сотни взволнованных писем (*MAS* 1981–4: i) 'hundreds of concerned letters were sent to the Soviet delegation'. However, in the modern language, this expression is often found with the dative, e.g. в адрес Верховному Совету был подан проект (news telecast *Время*, 17 November 1985) 'a proposal was submitted to the Supreme Soviet'. The appearance of the dative case is due to the analogy with the regular prepositionless dative, which is required with the cognate verb адресовать 'address' and the verbs 'send', 'submit'.

The preposition навстречу 'towards' derives from the desemanticized adverb навстречу, which in turn derives from the nominal phrase на встречу plus genitive. In the beginning of the nineteenth century, the adverb and the nominal phrase were still competing, cf. their use by

Puškin (note that there is also variation in the spelling of the preposition and the noun as two separate words or as a single word):

> На встречу бедного певца
> Прыгну́ла Оленька с крыльца
> (*Евгений Онегин* (1827), VI. xiii)
>
> Dear Olga leaped off the porch to meet the poor poet.

and

> Жители вышли к нему навстречу (*Капитанская дочка*, 1836)
> The locals came out to meet him.

The noun phrase took the genitive and the adverb took the dative, due to the analogy with and actual presence of the preposition к 'to' (examples from nineteenth- and early twentieth-century literature are given in Čerkasova 1967: 39–40). In the modern language, the nominal expression на встречу + genitive has become obsolete, and the increasing tendency has been for the preposition навстречу to occur without к; for example, Gorbačevič (1973) allows the combination к + dative after навстречу, as a rarer form, and Ožegov (1985) gives several illustrative examples, all of them without к. The grammatical classification of навстречу is, however, still variable: while Ožegov (1985) characterizes it exclusively as an adverb, more recent dictionaries distinguish between the adverb and the preposition (Borunova *et al.* (1983)). Čerkasova (1967: 40) views it as a non-stabilized preposition.

К вопросу о (по вопросу о) is another expression that seems to be evolving into a preposition, with the meaning 'regarding, concerning something'. For example, Ožegov (1985) cites по вопросу о as an expression occurring 'in the function of a preposition'; many other dictionaries, including *MAS* (1981–4) do not identify its grammatical characteristics. The word вопрос 'question, point, issue, matter' can take either a prepositional object or a prepositionless genitive;[15] meanwhile, к вопросу and по вопросу no longer occur without о in the contemporary language; that this change is relatively recent can be seen from the comparison of the titles of Čumakova (1970) and Klinskaja (1957), where the latter uses the now archaic genitive. The preposition к вопросу о is particularly common in official and scientific style.

---

[15] The genitive object is required if the word вопрос is used in a more specialized meaning 'subject of concern', cf. вопрос жизни и смерти 'matter of life and death' and вопрос о жизни и смерти 'question about life and death'.

Agreement

(i) Conflict between semantic and grammatical agreement

There are several instances in Russian where the semantic and grammatical gender or number of a noun phrase are at variance, for instance in the use of the masculine noun врач 'doctor' in referring to a woman doctor, or the use of the grammatically singular words много 'many', большинство 'majority', in referring to a plurality of entities. In Russian, as in many other languages (including English), there is some variation within normative usage in such cases, over whether agreement with such nouns should be on a semantic or a grammatical basis. For example, in equational sentences with the predicate быть, оказаться, стать in the past tense followed by the predicate nominative, there is variation in the gender or number of this predicate: the gender/number can be determined either by the subject or by the predicate nominal, e.g. его спокойствие (subject, neuter) было (neuter) личина and его спокойствие была (fem.) личина (predicate noun, fem.) 'his tranquillity was a mask'; главное наше оружие было топор и лопата and главное наше оружие были топор и лопата 'our main weapons were an axe and a spade' (*Русская грамматика* 1980: ii. 284). In such cases, the form of the verb is typically determined by the gender and number of the subject, but agreement based on the gender or number of the predicate noun is also acceptable and seems to be gaining ground. This reflects the change from the traditional standard in the nineteenth century, which was grammatical agreement with the subject, towards more variation at the present time.

Conflict between semantic and grammatical agreement for gender is further dealt with in Chapter 6, and the present section is concerned with those instances where a conflict can occur between semantic and grammatical agreement for number.

Conflict between semantic and grammatical number agreement occurs in Russian where the subject of the sentence has plural reference, but is either:

(i) a numerical expression (e.g. пять солдат 'five soldiers'), including an indefinite numeral expression with the neuter singular form of the indefinite numeral (e.g. много солдат 'many soldiers') and a distributive numerical expression with the preposition по (e.g. по пять солдат 'five soldiers each');

(ii) a collective noun with quantitative meaning (e.g. большинство солдат 'the majority of the soldiers', ряд суждений 'a series of judgements');[16]

(iii) a conjoined noun phrase (e.g. солдат и офицер 'a soldier and an officer') or a comitative expression consisting of nominals linked with the preposition с 'with' (e.g. солдат с офицером '(lit.) soldier with the officer');

(iv) disjoint noun phrase with the conjunctions ни . . . ни 'neither . . . nor', ли . . . ли 'either . . . or', (или) . . . или '(either) . . . or' (Wade 1992: 490, 493).

The traditional standard in constructions involving types (i), (ii), and (iv) is for the predicate to stand in the singular, i.e. to agree grammatically with the subject, and this is by and large adhered to in nineteenth-century literature, though there are occasional examples that go counter to the general principle, such as the following from Lermontov, quoted in Rozental´ (1971: 217): несколько дам скорыми шагами ходили взад и вперед по площадке 'several ladies were walking back and forth across the landing with rapid steps'.

During the course of the late nineteenth and twentieth centuries there has been a tendency for semantic agreement to become more widespread, so that in current usage both singular and plural predicate forms are in principle possible with all such numerical, collective-quantitative, conjoined, and comitative subjects. For example, Graudina *et al.* (1976: 31) indicate that sentences such as преподавалась (fem. sing.) математика и физика and преподавались (pl.) математика и физика 'Mathematics and physics were taught' are equally possible. Though there are no inviolable rules prescribing when the singular is to be used and when the plural is to be used, there are certain tendencies which determine preference for one or the other form. These tendencies are analysed in detail by Corbett (1983: 94–156), who shows that animacy and the linear order of the subject and the predicate play an important role in the choice of the agreement form. Thus, animate subjects are more likely to take semantically motivated plural agreement than inanimates, for example, ряд лиц направили свои предложения (news telecast *Время*, 18 April 1986) 'a number of persons addressed their suggestions', but ряд опытов был проведен (*Правда,* 31 March 1985, p. 2) 'a series of experiments was conducted'. Next, subjects that pre-

---

[16] In Russian, unlike (British) English, grammatical agreement prevails with collective nouns that do not have quantitative meaning, e.g. молодёжь 'youth', армия 'army', правительство 'government', although occasional deviations can be attested (Mullen 1967: 48–9). Semantic number agreement with such collective nouns is found in Old Russian and in regional dialects (Borkovskij and Kuznecov 1965: 352–8).

cede the predicate are more likely to determine plural (viz. semantically motivated) agreement than those subjects that follow the predicate, cf.

Авдеев со своим ведомым чуть было не отправили (pl.) на тот свет фон Манштейна

and

фон Манштейна чуть было не отправил (sg.) на тот свет Авдеев со своим ведомым

Avdeev and his co-pilot almost sent von Mannstein to the other world (Corbett 1983: 140–1).[17]

The choice between grammatical and semantic agreement is also determined by definiteness, which is a covert category in Russian; definite noun phrases are more likely to determine semantic agreement. Thus, a numerical expression modified by a demonstrative can determine only semantic agreement: Эти десять человек уже ушли (not ушло) 'These ten people have already left'; meanwhile, a numerical expression of an indefinite quantity can determine only grammatical agreement, cf. уехало (not уехали) всего человек десять 'Only about ten people left' (Iomdin 1990: 77; see also Mel´čuk 1985: 95–8).

Similarly, the plural is more likely with verbs of action, or where the various individuals subsumed under the subject noun phrase act independently. As demonstrated by Corbett, the major tendency characteristic of Modern Russian, Russian in the twentieth century in particular, consists in separating the notional characteristics (such as animacy, agentivity, definiteness) and subject-before-predicate position as the independent factors that could determine the choice of the plural agreement. While earlier, the plural agreement was possible only if both sets of factors were at work, in the modern language, either factor can determine plural agreement (Corbett 1983: 131).[18]

Another instance where semantic and grammatical agreement compete concerns the agreement determined by the polite (formal) Вы,[19] addressing one person. Regardless of the singular or plural reference, Вы determines the plural form of the verb and of the short predicate

---

[17] Since some types of subjects, particularly distributive noun phrases with по and numerical expressions such as пять солдат, often follow the predicate, introducing new information, they are commonly associated with singular agreement (see also Corbett 1983: 219).

[18] See also Mullen (1967), Skoblikova (1959); a detailed set of normative guide-lines, based on tendencies of the type noted in these two works, is given by Rozental´ (1971: 213–19).

[19] To distinguish it from the plural вы, this pronoun is capitalized in spelling.

adjective, e.g. Вы ошибаетесь and Вы неправы 'you are mistaken'. Meanwhile, long adjectives occurring with the polite plural take semantic agreement, with the gender distinction where it is relevant, e.g. Вы заботливый and Вы заботливая 'you are caring (masc./fem.)'; Я считаю Вас добрым/доброй 'I consider you kind (masc./fem.)'. However, in the spoken language deviations from this rule occur (Corbett 1983: 24–8).

(ii) Adjective case after numerals

The numerals два 'two', три 'three', четыре 'four' require a following noun to be in the genitive singular, irrespective of gender. However, an adjective agreeing with such a noun does not stand in the genitive singular, but in either the nominative (accusative) or the genitive plural, e.g. два новые/новых дома 'two new houses', две новые/новых книги 'two new books'. In discussing the relative frequency of nominative and genitive adjectives, it is necessary to treat separately on the one hand masculine and neuter nouns, and on the other feminine nouns.

With masculine and neuter nouns the overwhelming preference in current usage is for the genitive. In a statistical survey of contemporary literature, Suprun (1957: 73) found that over 80 per cent of the relevant examples contained the adjective in the genitive case. In nineteenth-century literature, the nominative was quite usual in such constructions, e.g. только две звездочки, как два спасительные маяка, сверкали на темно-синем своде 'only two stars, like two safety beacons, sparkled on the dark-blue vault' (Lermontov, *Герой нашего времени* (1838–41), *Тамань*). For the modern language, the genitive is given as the only admissible form by Rozental´ (1971: 230) and as the more frequent form by the latest Academy Grammar (*Русская грамматика* 1980: ii. 56).[20]

The situation is much more complex with feminine nouns, and there has even been disagreement as to the direction of the recent trend: Bulaxovskij (1952: 315) and Suprun (1957: 75, 79) claim that the nominative is becoming more common, whereas V. V. Vinogradov *et al.* (1960: i. 373–4) say that the nominative is the older form. According to the latest Academy Grammar (*Русская грамматика* 1980: ii. 57), both forms are acceptable, and no distinction between them is made.

---

[20] However, the nominative remains the preferable form if the adjective precedes the numeral, e.g. потерянные четыре дня 'the four lost days' (*Русская грамматика* 1980: ii. 56).

Certainly the nominative is very frequent in nineteenth-century literature, e.g. три скользкие, мокрые ступени вели к ее двери 'three
slippery, wet steps led to her door' (Lermontov, *Герой нашего времени*
(1838–41), *Бэла*), and it is the nominative rather than the genitive that
is recommended as the preferred form by most normative handbooks;
thus V. V. Vinogradov *et al.* (1960: i. 372–3) say that such adjectives
usually stand in the nominative, but that this can no longer be considered
the sole norm.[21] Gorbačevič (1973), in the articles две and четыре,
simply describes the genitive plural as less usual; the article три makes
no gender distinction, qualifying the nominative-accusative plural as
'rarer' in general. As a striking instance of the inconsistency that can be
found in current usage, even written usage, we may note that in an
article in *Вопросы языкознания* (1974, no. 1), we find on p. 20 the
phrase две исходные конструкции 'two initial constructions', and in
the next sentence, two lines below, две производных конструкции
'two derived constructions'. Despite all the variation, it seems that the
nominative is more typical of higher styles and dominates in poetry. The
use of the adjective in the genitive is more economical in terms of the
concord between the case of the modifier and the modified noun, and,
as in many other instances, the ongoing change is more apparent in the
spoken language or lower styles of the written language.

Interpretation of the Subject of a Gerund

In standard Russian, the understood subject of the gerund (also known
as adverbial participle; Russian деепричастие) and the subject of the
main clause must be identical, as in Возвращаясь из школы, мальчик
потерял ранец 'Going home from school, the boy lost his back-pack';
hence, Возвращаясь из школы, у мальчика пропал ранец is
ungrammatical because the two subjects are different (*Русская
грамматика* 1980: ii. 182–3; Wade 1992: 389–91). This rule of precise
coreference between the two subjects is relatively new to Russian:
violations are common in the language of the eighteenth and early
nineteenth centuries (Borkovskij and Kuznecov 1965: 351; Borkovskij
1978: 117, and further references there; Yokoyama 1980).[22] Some

---

[21] In two instances, however, the genitive plural is recommended: after the prepositions
на and по, and where the noun in question distinguishes genitive singular and nominative
plural by stress alone (Graudina *et al.* 1976: 32–3).

[22] Later in the nineteenth century, L. Tolstoj stands out among other Russian writers in
excessive violations of this rule; for example, in *Война и мир* (1863–9): Накурившись,

evidence in favour of the stabilization of this rule comes from the fact that Čexov, in his *Жалобная книга* (1884), uses the violation of this rule in order to create a humorous effect of apparently illiterate speech:

Подъезжая к сей станцыи и глядя на природу в окно, у меня слетела шляпа.

On approaching the railway station and while observing the scenery out of the window, my hat fell off.

In twentieth-century Russian, two tendencies are becoming increasingly prominent in the interpretation of the subject of a gerund. The first tendency concerns the subject of the passive, which, despite its subject status, is severely constrained in its ability to be coreferential with the subject of a gerund. Thus, the Academy Grammar cites the following example as non-standard: Пройдя в космосе сотни тысяч километров, сигналы были . . . приняты обсерваторией 'Having passed through hundreds of thousands of kilometres in space, the signals were received by the observatory' (*Русская грамматика* 1980: ii. 182). The Academy Grammar explains the unacceptability of such examples by the fact that the syntactic subject here corresponds simultaneously to the subject of a state and object of an action. Though this explanation has been criticized as much too categorical (Kozinskij 1983: 18), the syntactic fact that the subject of the passive clause cannot be coreferential with the subject of a gerund remains unchallenged.[23]

The second tendency concerns the so-called dative experiencer or dative of the subject (дательный субъекта) and is opposite to the restrictive tendency just described: sentences where the dative phrase is coreferential with the subject of a gerund seem to be gaining in acceptability if the predicate taking the dative phrase also takes an infinitive. For example: играя черными, чемпиону не удалось захватить инициативу (*Русская грамматика* 1980: ii. 183) 'as he was playing black, the champion failed to seize the initiative', or знакомя меня с коллекцией, ей трудно было скрыть восхищение (Ickovič 1974: 97) 'while acquainting me with her collection, she experienced difficulty hiding her delight'. The acceptability of such constructions improves when more lexical material separates the dative phrase and the gerund;

между солдатами завязался разговор 'Having smoked, the soldiers started a conversation.' This can probably be explained by the idiosyncrasies of Tolstoj's style and also by the influence of French syntax.

[23] Note that coreference with the subject of the passive gerund with the auxiliary будучи is possible: будучи окружен, гарнизон продолжал сопротивляться 'being besieged, the garrison continued fighting' (Kozinskij 1983: 18).

for example, у вас будет возможность лучше узнать страну, путешествуя пешком 'you will be able to know the country better travelling on foot' is more acceptable than путешествуя пешком, у вас будет возможность лучше узнать страну (Kozinskij 1983: 45). Another factor contributing to the spread of such constructions is the indefinite reading, under which the dative experiencer in the main clause is unspecified, e.g. не установив причины напряженности, невозможно эффективно разрешить конфликт 'it is impossible to resolve a conflict effectively without establishing the reasons for tension' (*Русская грамматика* 1980: ii. 182). While normative handbooks disagree as to whether constructions with a specified dative experiencer are acceptable (see Rappaport (1984: 36) for an overview), constructions with the unspecified dative are commonly accepted as normative (Ickovič 1974: 99).[24]

Analyticity and Apposition

Different aspects of the trend towards analyticity in the Russian language are discussed in various parts of this book; in particular, indeclinable words, i.e. words which are inherently indeclinable, irrespective of their syntactic role in the sentence, are treated in Chapter 3 on morphology. The present section will look at syntactic aspects of analyticity: certain words are inherently declinable, i.e. in general they can and do decline, but in certain syntactic constructions they are, or may be, indeclinable. The constructions in question are where the declinable word occurs in apposition to, or as an attribute to, some word which is declined (or is itself indeclinable).

Even in traditional usage there are many examples of this kind, in particular where the title of a literary, musical, or other work stands in apposition to the noun describing the genre to which it belongs, or where the proper name of some organization stands in apposition to the generic name for organizations of that kind; the title or proper name is usually written in guillemets, e.g. роман «Евгений Онегин» 'the novel *Evgenij Onegin*', опера «Пиковая дама» 'the opera *The Queen of Spades*', газета «Правда» 'the newspaper *Pravda*', кинотеатр «Россия» 'the *Rossija* cinema', кафе «Космос» 'the café *Kosmos*'. With the preposition в 'in', these appear as: в романе «Евгений

---

[24] A review of other constructions with a non-subject controller of the gerund is given in Rappaport (1984: 37–67).

Онегин», в опере «Пиковая дама», в газете «Правда», в кинотеатре «Россия», в кафе «Космос». Where the generic term is omitted, then declension of the title or proper name is usual: в «Евгении Онегине», в «Пиковой даме», в «Правде», в «России», в «Космосе». The declension of a proper name is particularly common if this name occurs in the prepositional or genitive case; in the accusative, the tendency is much less clear and seems to vary depending on the length of the proper name and its actual components. Cf. читал «Евгения Онегина», купил «Правду», смотрел «Три сестры» (possible «Трех сестер»), «Мертвые души» (but not «Мертвых душ»). One of the functions of the use of the generic term in such expressions can be seen in a desire to retain unaltered the citation form of the work or institution referred to. The data in Graudina *et al.* (1976: 174) and Graudina (1980: 148–9, 278) confirm this tendency.

With many other kinds of apposition, however, there is an increasing trend away from a traditional standard which requires declension towards indeclinability. This can be seen particularly clearly with geographical names in apposition to generic terms, such as город Москва 'the city Moscow', река Волга 'the river Volga', остров Мальта 'the island Malta', планета Венера 'the planet Venus'. The question that arises concerning standard usage is whether one should say, for instance, with the prepositions в 'in', на 'on': в городе Москве or в городе Москва, на реке Волге/Волга, на острове Мальте/Мальта, на планете Венере/Венера. The traditional, nineteenth-century standard was for declension of the proper name in such constructions. Most current normative handbooks recommend declension in certain instances, indeclinability in others, and occasionally allow either declension or indeclinability indifferently.[25] As with proper names as titles, specific groups of toponyms seem to differ with regard to declinability; further, different styles may also differ in their treatment of declinability: as shown in Graudina (1980: 158), in the press place-names are commonly declined (80.4 per cent of all cases in her sample).

While the recommendations of these handbooks do not always correspond to current educated usage, in particular in that both variants are often found in educated usage where only one is recommended by the handbooks, yet still the tendencies noted there are essentially the same as those observed in practice. For instance, the handbooks recommend declension of names in apposition to город 'town', and in practice в

---

[25] See, for instance, Superanskaja (1965*b*: 137–43), Rozental´ (1971: 236–7); apart from a few points of detail, their recommendations coincide.

городе Москве is still commoner than в городе Москва. Rozental´
(1971: 236) allows (and seems even to recommend) indeclinability of
little-known town-names, citing the example в городе Мина 'in the
town Mina', where the Saudi Arabian town of Mina is unlikely to be
known to the Russian reader, and в городе Мине would leave it unclear
whether the town was called Mina or Min; Superanskaja (1965*b*: 137–8)
criticizes this practice. Rozental´ also recommends the distinction
between в городе Кирово 'in the town Kirovo' and в городе Кирове
'in the town Kirov'.[26] The indeclinable forms here and elsewhere have
undoubtedly been fostered by the practice in military communiqués, and
also to a lesser extent in other administrative documents, of leaving
place-names in their citation form and accompanying them by a declined
generic term. At the other extreme, names of islands (especially if not
well known) in apposition to остров, and names of planets in apposition
to планета, are usually indeclinable, and this is the recommendation of
both handbooks cited. Janko-Trinickaja (1964*a*: 303–4) cites examples
of the names of planets in apposition to планета, and indeclinable, but
notes also the following example from Nikolaj Gumilev's poetry, where
Венера declines: на далекой звезде Венере солнце пламенней и
золотистей 'on the faraway star Venus the sun is more fiery and
golden'. With many other generic terms both declension and non-
declension are found, indeclinability tending to be preferred where the
proper name is unfamiliar, where it is composed of an adjective plus
noun, and where it differs in gender from the generic term. Janko-
Trinickaja (1964*a*: 304) notes that in all these cases, nineteenth-century
and early twentieth-century usage preferred declension, the only widespread exceptions being a few generic geographical terms (e.g. станция
'station') in technical or administrative works relating specifically to rail
and water transport.

In the examples considered so far there has been a single proper name
corresponding to the generic name, but often there is a series of proper
names corresponding to a single generic name, as in совместный
полет «Союз–Аполлон» ' "Sojuz–Apollo" joint flight'.[27] Here both
'Sojuz' and 'Apollo' are essential to the concept of the joint flight.

[26] He does not discuss в Кирово (see Rozental´ 1971: 87–8). According to Graudina
(1980: 156–9), the indeclinable form is rapidly becoming obsolete in the modern language.
However, the opposite view is held by Gorbačevič (1990: 77–8), who claims that the
indeclinable form has been gaining ground.

[27] The use of indeclinables in such constructions has been studied in detail by Janko-
Trinickaja (1966a), from which many of the examples below are taken. See also Iomdin
(1990: 66–8).

Particularly frequent examples of this construction in current usage are with a series of geographical names indicating an itinerary (e.g. магистраль Абакан–Тайшет 'the main Abakan–Tajšet line, line from A. to T.'), a series of personal names indicating a meeting (e.g. встреча Брежнев–Форд 'the meeting (between) Brežnev (and) Ford', матч Карпов–Каспаров 'the Karpov–Kasparov (chess) match'), and a series of numbers indicating a relation, for instance a score (e.g. со счетом четыре : пять 'with a score of 4 : 5'). Such examples are characteristic of current usage, but were rare in the nineteenth and early twentieth centuries. Thus even in the *Вестник министерства путей сообщения* (*Bulletin of the Ministry of Communications*) at the end of the nineteenth century it was common to find explicit expressions of the type прямое беспосадочное сообщение Варшавы с Москвой 'direct communication without change between Warsaw and Moscow', Витебско–Орловское шоссе 'the Vitebsk–Orel highway', even though it is precisely in official documents of the Ministry of Communications that indeclinable geographical names in apposition to generic names are most frequent in the nineteenth century (Janko-Trinickaja 1966*a*: 177).

A further instance of the spread of analyticity in appositional constructions concerns numerals in apposition, but here the distinction is not simply between declined and indeclinable forms, but between the ordinal form (which must then agree with its noun) and the cardinal form (which is then invariable, in the citation form), e.g. номер третий and номер три 'number/room three'.[28] In the written language such constructions usually appear with the numeral written in figures, in which case the written form номер (abbreviated №) 3 is ambiguous as to whether it should be read as ordinal третий or cardinal три. It is not certain, for instance, how Čexov himself read the title of his short story *Палата № 6* 'Ward 6'. In a number of instances from the late nineteenth and early twentieth centuries, however, we do have the numeral written out in full, or explicit indication of the ordinal form by means of the orthographic device 3-й for третий. Thus in a letter from Korolenko to Čexov we find explicit reference to Палата № 6-й (Janko-Trinickaja 1964*a*: 305).[29] The ordinal was the usual form until the 1920s, when

[28] The form нумер was still used in the beginning of the twentieth century, but is completely obsolete now and is retained only in derivatives such as нумеровать 'enumerate'.

[29] Where the expression номер plus numeral occurs in apposition to another noun, номер itself is always indeclinable, and the point at issue is whether or not the numeral agrees with the preceding noun (whether or not this is номер), i.e. whether it is cardinal or ordinal. The fullest treatment of this problem is Janko-Trinickaja (1964*a*).

usage began to fluctuate, leading to the present situation where the cardinal form predominates. Janko-Trinickaja (1964*a*: 305) quotes examples from the 1920s where both cardinal and ordinal forms are found in the same work, with apparently no difference between them. Panov (1968: iii. 90–1) notes a small majority in a survey of 100 informants for the cardinal in палата № 3 'ward 3' (54: 46), and a large majority for the cardinal in из дома № 1 'from house No. 1' (90: 10).

The inclusion of the word номер is by no means a necessary feature of such constructions, so that in addition to в квартире номер двадцать семь 'flat no. 27' one can have simply в квартире двадцать семь ог в квартире двадцать седьмой (also в двадцать седьмой квартире); with such examples, Panov (1968: iii. 91) notes a preference for the ordinal (with this particular example, 59: 41). Product names with numerals without номер are common with products that have appeared in several different versions, e.g. aeroplanes, such as ТУ-164, ИЛ-86, satellites and spaceships, such as Салют-4, which are usually read with cardinal numerals, although Janko-Trinickaja (1964*a*: 307–8) observes that in the professional jargon of pilots, etc., ordinal forms are used. With such product names the overwhelming majority of informants in the survey discussed in Panov (1968: iii. 90–1) preferred the cardinal numeral (92: 8 for самолетом ТУ-104).

Although current usage tends towards the cardinal forms, this is not to say that the ordinal forms are not found, indeed one often finds both almost side by side: thus Maršak's poem *Мистер Твистер* (1933) has on the one hand номер девятый 'room nine' and номер десятый 'room ten', and on the other номер сто девяносто 'room 190'. In such examples, the numeral in question may be a conditioning factor, the cardinal being particularly preferred if the numeral is high or complex. It is doubtful whether anyone would read паспорт № 379205 with an ordinal numeral, rather than a series of cardinal numerals. The use of fractional house numbers is another factor militating against the ordinal, since it is simply impossible to form an ordinal from a fraction, e.g. Волхонка, дом 18/2 (read: дом восемнадцать дробь два), which happens to be the address of the Russian Language Institute of the Russian Academy of Sciences.

With these examples one may compare the frequent current use of an expression of measure in the citation form in apposition to the expression of the parameter of which it is a measure, e.g. двигатель мощностью 35 (тридцать пять) лошадиных сил 'motor of power 35 h.p.', глубина 300 (триста) метров 'depth of 300 metres', ров

глубиной 3 (три) метра 'ditch 3 metres deep' (Zolotova 1974*b*:
161–75). The more traditional form is with the preposition в, i.e.
мощность в 35 лошадиных сил, глубина в 300 метров/в 3 метра,
although the forms without в are more frequent in current writing and
speech. Gorbačević (1973), in the article высота 'height', lists the
following, without any further comment, though in this order: дом
высотою в двадцать метров, дом высотою двадцать метров
'house 20 metres high'.[30] According to Graudina (1980: 52–3), all
constructions denoting length, height, weight, temperature, and other
measurable characteristics are losing the preposition в, which is indicative of increasing analyticity. This process has become particularly
apparent since the 1960s, and analogy between different parametric
expressions plays an important role in the emergence of the new type.

Predicate Cases

In Russian, predicate nouns can stand in either the nominative or the
instrumental, while predicate adjectives stand in either the short form,
the nominative long form, or the instrumental long form. Over the whole
history of Russian, there has been a tendency for the instrumental to
encroach upon the nominative (Mrazek 1964: 209–15), and for the long
form to encroach upon the short form (Gustavsson 1976);[31] this process
is by no means complete, and normative and pedagogical handbooks
still have to list the criteria that require or favour one or other of these
forms,[32] but in the recent history of the Russian language we can see
some reflections of this general change away from nominative and short
forms, in particular in constructions where nineteenth-century usage
allowed the nominative or the short form (as an alternative), but where
current usage does not. We shall be concerned here only with instances
where there has been a shift in usage, and not with the general problem
of the choice among the predicate variants.

[30] Of course, the very choice of the -ою ending for the instrumental case indicates
orientation towards older norms: in the current language, the choice of -ою over -ой
denotes deliberate archaization or poetic style (*Русская грамматика* 1980: i. 489).

[31] Overall, the opposition of long-form and short-form adjectives cannot be described in
a uniform way: as shown, for example, in Gustavsson (1976), Zemskaja (1973: 200–14),
different subtypes of adjectives behave differently with regard to this contrast.

[32] In dialects and in colloquial speech the use of the short and long adjectives, in
particular, is markedly different from their use in the written language, with much more
use of long forms; cf. Zemskaja (1973: 196–214), and references cited there.

(i) Predicate nouns after быть in the past tense, future tense, conditional, and imperative

Most normative handbooks, including V. V. Vinogradov *et al.* (1960: vol. ii, bk. 1, 421–2, 428–9), and the latest Academy Grammar (*Русская грамматика* 1980: ii. 283), say that the difference between the nominative and the instrumental of a nominal predicate is that between permanent and temporary characteristic, e.g. Пушкин был великий поэт 'Puškin was a great poet', but в то время я был студентом 'at that time I was a student'. Timberlake (1993: 862) describes this contrast in terms of a pure unrestricted description (predicative nominative) and 'the slightest hint of restriction on the predicative function' (predicative instrumental).

V. V. Vinogradov *et al.* (1960: vol. ii, bk. 1, 422) note that in nineteenth-century literature the nominative was also possible for a temporary characteristic, e.g. конечно, мы были приятели 'of course, we were friends' (Lermontov, *Герой нашего времени* (1838–41), *Максим Максимыч*), i.e. they note a shift of usage in favour of the instrumental. In a detailed study of the use of the nominative and instrumental in recent literature, including political and other non-fictional literature, Křížkova (1968: 213–14) finds no strong confirmation for the alleged semantic distinction between permanent and temporary characteristics, but rather a stylistic distinction: in more colloquial texts the nominative is more frequent than in non-fictional texts, in particular political texts.[33] Thus while overall the nominative case was used on average in 12.8 per cent of relevant instances, it did not occur once in *Материалы XXII съезда КПСС (Materials of the XXII Congress of the CPSU)*, occurred in 2.1 per cent of instances in *Из жизни древней Москвы (From the Life of Ancient Moscow)*, in 4.1 per cent of instances in *Pravda*, in 31.1 per cent of instances in Leonid Leonov's novel *Русский лес* (1950–3), and in 61.5 per cent of instances in Valentin Kataev's novel *Белеет парус одинокий* (1936). Thus, while there may have been some shift between nineteenth-century and current usage, the variation within current usage, dependent largely upon style, is itself immense (see also Zolotova 1964).

According to the latest Academy Grammar (*Русская грамматика* 1980: ii. 283–4), the predicate instrumental after the verb быть in the

---

[33] The trend in the current written language to replace the predicate nominative by the instrumental is more advanced than in the colloquial language; whereas the trend to replace short adjectives by long adjectives is more advanced in the colloquial language. For a statistical account restricted to fiction, see Rœed (1966).

past tense is more common, especially in the written language; the use of the predicate instrumental is considered stylistically more neutral. Though the Academy Grammar does not mention any direct analogy, it treats the use of the predicate instrumental in the past tense together with the predominant use of this form in the future and in the non-indicative.

In current usage the instrumental is virtually obligatory after the future tense, conditional, and imperative of быть, although the use of the nominative here is not uncommon in the nineteenth century, e.g. он решил, что женитьба на Элен была бы несчастье 'he decided that the marriage to Hélène would be a disaster' (L. Tolstoj, *Война и мир* (1863–9), quoted in V. V. Vinogradov *et al.* (1960: vol. ii, bk. 1, 425)). As an illustration of the variation found in the nineteenth century, we may note the use of the instrumental and nominative in successive lines of Lermontov's *К*** (Мы случайно сведены судьбою)* (1832):

> Будь, о будь моими небесами,
> Будь товарищ грозных бурь моих . . .
>
> Be, oh be my heavens,
> Be the companion of my thunderous storms . . .

See also Iomdin (1990: 65).

(ii) Predicate nouns after other copular verbs in the present and past tenses

With other copular verbs, with the general meaning of being (e.g. являться 'be'), seeming (e.g. казаться 'seem'), or becoming (e.g. стать 'become'), current usage has the instrumental of a predicate noun (*Русская грамматика* 1980: ii. 286–7). In nineteenth-century literature, the nominative is also found, e.g. я грубиян считаюсь 'I am considered a boor' (A. N. Ostrovskij, *Гроза*, I. i (1859)).

(iii) Predicate adjectives after verbs other than быть

The morphological possibilities for adjectives as predicate to быть are essentially the same in current usage as in the nineteenth century, although again there are widespread divergences depending on style in current writing (Nichols 1981: *passim*; Ueda 1992: 129–98).[34] After other verbs, however, whether they are copular (like стать 'become') or not (e.g. verbs of motion and position like вернуться 'return', прийти

---

[34] Cf. the statistics in Křížkova (1968: 219).

'come', стоять 'stand'), current usage allows only the long form of the adjective (nominative or instrumental), whereas the short form is not infrequent in nineteenth-century literature, e.g. я стал раздражителен, вспыльчив, резок, мелочен 'I have become irritable, irascible, abrupt, petty' (Čexov, *Иванов*, I. iii. (1887–9)). In addition, there seems to be a current trend towards the instrumental. In the 1970s one of the authors of this book witnessed a generation fight within a Moscow family over the acceptability of автобусы идут переполненными 'buses travel crowded', with mother rejecting this variant and son accepting it; both accepted the nominative, автобусы идут переполненные. In the spoken language, the preference for the nominative in such cases remains quite strong (*Русская грамматика* 1980: ii. 289, 291).

Usage of Prepositions

(i) *B and на*

Although the difference between the prepositions в 'in' and на 'on' in general corresponds to that between position in an enclosed space and position in an unenclosed space, more specifically on the surface of an unenclosed space, there are several instances where the choice of one or other of these two prepositions is essentially arbitrary; such differences between в 'in' and на 'on' with the prepositional case are paralleled by similar differences between в 'into' and на 'onto' with the accusative, and из 'out of' and с 'off' with the genitive. Such arbitrary uses of the distinction can give rise to doubts and arguments about standard usage, and there have been some shifts in standard usage since the nineteenth century, most typically in the encroachment of на upon в. More widespread use of на is characteristic of non-standard speech, and of the professional jargon of certain occupations: thus sailors usually say на флоте for standard во флоте 'in the navy', cinematographers на киностудии for standard в киностудии 'in the film studio'.[35] One of the ways to describe the differences between в and на that would otherwise remain unexplained is to interpret в as emphasizing location *per se* and на as the preposition emphasizing the function of a particular

[35] An additional factor is that in many dialects the difference between из and с is lost, giving rise to с or з in both meanings, thus reducing the degree of differentiation between the two series. Another common confusion in non-standard usage is between от and с in time expressions, e.g. магазин работает от 11 до 19, instead of . . . с 11 до 19 'the shop is open from 11 to 19'.

location (e.g. Wade 1992: 427, 434–5). The interpretation of на as the preposition emphasizing the function of a location or event explains its use with names of theatrical performances and other entertainments, meetings, etc., e.g. на концерте 'at the concert', на концерт 'to the concert'. However, в концерте and в концерт are found throughout the nineteenth century, and Gorbačevič (1973) considers them obsolescent, rather than archaic, citing both ходить на концерты 'go to concerts' and был в концерте 'was at a concert' from Žuxovickij's *Я сын твой, Москва*.

Names of streets in current usage require the preposition на, e.g. на улице Горького 'on/in Gor´kij Street', на Невском проспекте 'on Nevskij Prospekt'. In the nineteenth century, both в and на are found. With the word переулок 'alley' there is variation in current usage between в/на переулке, and similarly with proper names of alleys containing переулок; the traditional form is в переулке, reflecting the fact that a narrow alley is more of an enclosed space than a broad street (cf. in Puškin's *Евгений Онегин* (1827–8), VII. xxxix. 40: У Харитонья в переулке 'in an alley by St Chariton'),[36] but Gorbačevič (1973: 320) cites на переулке as a permissible alternative to the recommended form в переулке, and the same work on p. 50 gives both forms, in the order в, на переулке, without comment. Still, in the modern language the form with в remains more acceptable, and на переулке may be used for humorous effect. This is probably due to the fact that the choice between в and на with names of streets and other urban locations is usually determined by the extra-linguistic knowledge of how wide and open the street is: names of wider and more open locations take на (thus, we invariably find на проспекте 'on a prospect', на бульваре 'in a boulevard', на площади 'in a square', на шоссе 'on a highway'), while names of narrow, enclosed spaces take в, hence в переулке, в тупике 'in a blind alley', в сквере 'in a small public garden'.[37] Related to this is the difference, observed in the nineteenth century, in the choice of preposition for streets in Moscow and those in St Petersburg: Moscow streets invariably took в,[38] while in St Petersburg some took в while others took на (Astaf´eva 1974: 30, referring to observations by N. Greč in 1840). Indeed, St Petersburg, with its architecturally planned and structured

---

[36] In Moscow of the nineteenth and early twentieth century, residents identified their habitation by its proximity to a church where they were parishioners.

[37] The variant на сквере is permissible.

[38] The apparent exceptions occur where names of Moscow streets derive from names of neighbourhoods or regions, e.g. на Арбате (see also Wade 1992: 426).

streets and squares, had predominantly wide and open prospects, while Moscow was famous for its small cosy alleys and streets.

The use of на prevails, in a much more definite manner, in another example where there is variation, namely, в/на кухне 'in the kitchen'. The traditional form is again в, with на as the newer form. Gorbačevič (1971: 253) notes that in current speech and writing на is much more frequent, and was preferred by the majority in a survey he conducted; Gorbačevič (1973) cites both variants, and lists на first. One of the authors of this book has been corrected by Russians for saying в кухне. In this particular case, в and на seem to differ as a spatial preposition and the one emphasizing function (see above).

In at least one case the existence of competing norms has led to a semantic differentiation in the standard language, namely with двор 'courtyard', where во дворе means literally 'in the courtyard', e.g. машины стояли во дворе 'the cars were standing in the courtyard', and на дворе 'outside, out of doors', e.g. in Pasternak's *Про эти стихи* (1920):

> Какое, милые, у нас
> Тысячелетье на дворе?
>
> Friends, what millennium is it out there?

In the literal sense of out of doors, на дворе seems in any case to have been largely replaced in current urban usage by на улице, literally 'on the street'.

A number of examples where на, and even more so с, are heard in current usage are, however, clearly outside the current standard, e.g. на клубе 'in the club', с клуба 'from the club'.

However, in some instances the development has been the reverse of this, на being replaced by в. For instance, with the names of towns we find examples in the nineteenth century like: царь вернулся на Москву 'the tsar has returned to Moscow', where nowadays only в Москву would be possible. Expressions like поезд на Москву and especially билет на Москву are still possible, but differ somewhat in meaning from поезд в Москву, билет в Москву 'the Moscow train/ticket, the train/ticket to Moscow'. The choice of на simply states that the train or other transportation is going in the Moscow direction, not necessarily the whole way to Moscow, and the speaker's attention is probably focused on the fact that it stops at various intermediate points even if it does terminate in Moscow. Next, Gorbačevič (1973) characterizes на деревне 'in the village' as incorrect, for current standard в деревне while noting that на деревне was possible in the nineteenth century, and is still occasionally found as a stylistically marked form, especially in the possessive expression, e.g. у нас на деревне 'in our village'.

The tendency for в to be replaced by на particularly in colloquial speech has led to a certain extent to a rearguard action being fought against на in certain constructions, as a hyper-correction. For instance, the use of на with enclosed means of transportation (e.g. на автобусе 'by bus') is quite acceptable according to the traditional standard when emphasis is on the means of transport rather than on position in the particular vehicle (when в автобусе is required); in the former case, на автобусе is synonymous with the more archaic автобусом 'by bus'. However, many native speakers of Russian, under the influence of normative pronouncements against на in other constructions where both в and на may be heard, maintain that на автобусе is impossible in this sense, but can only mean literally 'on (top of) the bus'. Although the origin of this stricture is a misunderstanding of normative pronouncements, it will be interesting to observe if the belief in the unacceptability of на автобусе 'by bus' will be sufficient to effect a change in usage, more especially standard usage, with time.

(ii) по

Russian has a number of traditional constructions for expressing a relation of purpose, or simply some general, unspecified relation, between one noun and another, such as a noun followed by a genitive (программа литературы 'literature syllabus'), a noun followed by a prepositional phrase (автомат для продажи сигарет 'cigarette-vending machine'), a noun preceded by an adjective (шахматный чемпионат 'chess championship'), or a compound noun (мастер-технолог 'foreman-technician'). One of the relevant prepositional phrases is with the preposition по and the dative, as in товарищ по школе 'school-friend'. In present-day Russian, this preposition is tending to take over from the other means outlined above, so that one often comes across expressions like: программа по литературе, автомат по продаже сигарет, чемпионат по шахматам, мастер по технологии.[39]

---

[39] The standard discussion, with numerous examples from the Soviet press, is Švedova (1966: 40–52); see also Gorbačevič (1971: 247–50), Graudina *et al.* (1976: 42–50), and Iomdin (1991), where a large number of examples are presented. Švedova, incidentally, says little about the normativity of such constructions, apart from criticizing obvious instances of redundancy.

The preposition по has the great advantage, in such constructions, that it has no lexical meaning of its own, but can serve simply to express the most general kind of relation between the two nouns.[40] In a number of instances this construction is a useful addition to the complement of relational constructions in the language, but in many other instances this is not so, and it is in such cases that normative grammarians have tended to inveigh against the innovation.

In some constructions the inclusion of the по phrase is simply redundant, e.g. магазин по продаже уцененных товаров 'shop for the sale of reduced-price goods' (shops can be expected to sell things, so one needs only магазин уцененных товаров 'reduced-price goods shop', with the traditional genitive construction), работа по продаже газированной воды 'work in selling mineral water' (here работа 'work' is redundant, and продажа газированной воды on its own suffices).

In some instances, however, there is no real alternative to по, and here normative grammarians seem agreed that the spread of this construction should be evaluated positively. For instance, although инженер по технике 'technology engineer' is redundant, this is not so if one needs to specify what kind of technology or techniques are involved, as in инженер по технике безопасности 'engineer concerned with safety management'. It is not possible to form a compound noun of the type мастер-технолог if one of the components is an adjective plus noun rather than just a noun on its own, and there is no other compact construction to express this general relationship. Since the noun лифт 'lift, elevator' has no derived adjective, there is again no real alternative to механик по лифтам 'lift mechanic'. Although Россия 'Russia' has the derived adjective российский 'Russian' (relating to the Russian state) and the related русский 'Russian', the expression специалисты по России 'Russia specialists' is not synonymous with российские/русские специалисты. Other such examples quoted by Švedova (1966: 41–2) include эксперт по борьбе с колорадским жуком 'expert in the fight against the Colorado beetle', почтальон по доставке телеграмм 'postal carrier who delivers telegrams'.

In addition to occurring with nouns, по also occurs frequently after

---

[40] Popova (1974: 184) suggests that for this reason the use of the preposition по should be encouraged by normative grammarians, although she is looking specifically at a more restricted range of uses of по, namely where it relates a specific kind of work activity to a more general description of that kind of work, e.g. помощь по переработке кукурузы 'help in sorting maize'.

verbs, particularly in order to give a more specific description of a verb describing some work activity more generally, e.g. принять меры по сохранению молодняка 'take measures for the preservation of saplings', работать по истории боев в нашем крае 'work on the history of the battles in our area'. Popova (1974: 183–4) takes a positive attitude towards the spread of по in such constructions, though many other normative grammarians are particularly opposed to the spread of по to constructions where there is already a different established standard (in these cases, принять меры для, работать над). With this one might compare Gorbačevič's criticism (1971: 248) of the book-title *Футбол. Указания судьям и игрокам по правилам игры* (*Football: Instructions to Referees and Players Concerning the Rules of the Game*), where the traditional standard clearly requires указания на правила. Compare the discussion of changes in verbal government, pp. 144–9.

Syntactic Stylistics

Syntactic stylistics is one of the most important areas in which to study the relations among the various styles in the process of the 'democratizing' of the Russian language in the Soviet period, whereby constructions that had previously been inadmissible in the written language come to be acceptable (often via journalistic practice), and on the other hand constructions that had previously been considered literary, high style, filter down into the lower styles. As an initial example, we may note the history of the conjunctions раз 'if, once' and поскольку 'in so far as'. Раз was originally colloquial but, though still predominating in colloquial style, is now to be found in stylistically neutral writing. Поскольку originated, in this meaning, as a bureaucratic form, but is now much more widely acceptable in the written language, in addition to being common in speech (Rogožnikova 1966).

Many of the examples to be discussed, especially those spread by journalism and popular science, are of deviations from what had hitherto been standard syntactic practice in the direction of a more expressive language. Although many of these expressive devices can be found occasionally in pre-Revolutionary journalistic writing, it is only during the Soviet period that they have become at all widespread, initially as stylistically marked devices, though increasingly, with greater use, losing their stylistic markedness and becoming ordinary features of journalistic style.[41] As illustrative material, we have cited examples from *Известия* of late July and early August 1975.

(i) Question and answer sequences

One of the most salient differences between colloquial speech and the written language, particularly in such variants as the language of scientific writing, is the high frequency of question and answer sequences in the former. Thus the inclusion of question and answer sequences in the written language is an obvious way of making it more expressive, closer to the spoken language. There is, of course, a certain artificiality in this stylistic device, since in a newspaper article or piece of popular scientific writing the writer both asks the question and gives the answer (indeed, he usually assumes that his addressee does not know the answer—this is a device for presenting information, rather than for eliciting it), but none the less it can serve to create a closer rapport between writer and audience. In the issues of *Известия* examined this device occurs so frequently that it seems almost to have lost any stylistic markedness, having become one of the usual ways of presenting information in all but the most formal pronouncements. In an article on the Moscow Film Festival in the issue of 24 July 1975 we find: Чем дорог нам Московский фестиваль? Прежде всего тем, что на его экранах в течение двух недель можно увидеть как бы весь мировой кинопроцесс . . . 'Why is the Moscow festival so dear to us? Above all because on its screens we can see in the course of two weeks the whole world cinematographic process . . .'. An article in the issue of 27 July 1975, discussing the relation between superior and subordinate, bears a question as title: Как стать любимым? 'How can one become loved?', to which the whole article is an answer. The article contains a number of more specific questions and answers such as: А какая же здесь сухость и строгость? Здесь налицо отеческая мудрость и прямо-таки материнская нежность. 'And what dryness and strictness is there here? Here we are faced with fatherly wisdom and veritable motherly tenderness.' The issue of 3 August 1975 contains an article on tourism and ecology: Кто палит леса? Вытаптывает травы? Распугивает зверье? Люди. 'Who sets fire to forests? Tramples

---

[41] For further treatment of the problems discussed below, and examples from newspapers, starting mainly from the 1960s, see Popov (1964), Ivančikova (1966), Popov (1966), Prokopovič (1966), Švedova (1966), Uxanov (1966), Panov (1968: iii. 233–366), Prokopovič *et al.* (1981), Solganik (1973), Formanovskaja (1978).

grass? Frightens the animals? People.' The issue of 5 August 1975 has an article about the effect of industrial waste on a forest: Какого цвета хвоя может быть у сосны? Мы тоже думали: зеленая . . . А она в здешнем лесу—белая. 'What colour can the needles of a pine-tree be? We also thought: green . . . But in the local forest they are white.'

(ii) Parcellation

In colloquial speech, whether in Russian or English, the normal syntactic structure of a sentence is often dislocated in such a way that certain elements of the sentence are added to the end of the rest of the sentence and separated from it by a pause, i.e. added as an afterthought, e.g. *He's already gone. To see his grandmother.* Such dislocation is perfectly normal in speech, where the speaker may not plan the whole sentence in advance, and has no chance to correct what has already been said by erasing it and constructing the sentence again from the beginning. These constraints are not present in writing, and the use of such dislocations can therefore serve as a stylistic device. In current Russian linguistic work they are referred to as парцелляция 'parcellation' (the separate, dislocated parts being парцелляты, or присоединительные конструкции 'connective constructions'). Such constructions are rare in nineteenth-century writing, at least outside of the reported speech of characters (Ivančikova 1966: 12), but are very characteristic of current journalism, in particular.[42] The article already quoted above on the effect of industrial waste on a forest bristles with such examples: Гражданка Д. сделала несколько неверных шагов. С дворовой дорожки за ограду, где росла небольшая ель 'Citizen D. took a few unsteady steps. From the courtyard path through the fence, where a small fir-tree grew'; . . . о том, что нужно беречь природу, она знала из самых различных источников. В том числе из фельетона «Злоумышленники» . . . '. . . she knew from the most varied sources that one should protect nature. Including from the article "The Ill-Intentioned" . . .'; Оглянемся назад. Всего на восемнадцать лет. 'Let us look back. A mere eighteen years'; Он намерен сделать здесь пожарный водоем. В нескольких километрах от Волги.

---

[42] The frequent use of parcellation is often attributed to the satirist Mixail Zoščenko, who himself attributed it to Viktor Šklovskij. In reality, however, the first person to introduce parcellation, primarily into journalistic style, was Vlas Doroševič (1866–1922), a famous Russian journalist, who was known as the 'king of the feuilleton' and the creator of the 'short-line style' (стиль короткой строки) (Čudakova 1972: 47–9).

Для охраны лесов, которые целеустремленно уничтожает подведомственный ему завод. 'He intends to make a fire-brigade reservoir here. A few kilometres from the Volga. To protect the forests which the factory under his supervision is purposefully destroying.' (This last example contains two dislocations.)

The above examples illustrate parcellation of elements without any conjunctions. In general, parcellation is common between those segments that represent co-ordinate structures, linked without a conjunction (Formanovskaja 1978: 173–5). However, parcellation is also found in those cases where a non-initial construction is introduced by a conjunction, particularly causal conjunctions потому что 'because', так как 'because, as', e.g. Он посматривал сбоку на Динку Абажур . . . и ему было приятно это посматривание. Потому что он чувствовал, что Динка Абажур была в эти минуты в его власти (Ju. Trifonov, *Обмен*, quoted by Rudè (1990: 68)). 'He was glancing sideways at Dinka Abažur and he was enjoying glancing at her. Because he felt that in those moments Dinka Abažur was at his mercy.'

As shown by Formanovskaja (1978: 173–4), parcellation becomes particularly common if the conjunction is in the communicative focus of the sentence, which is signalled by the words только 'only', лишь 'only', наверно(е) 'probably', даже 'even', ведь 'indeed' (cf. p. 184 for an example), e.g. Почему вспомнилась эта древняя история?... Наверное, потому, что первая, она отпечаталась навеки (Ju. Trifonov, *Старик*, quoted by Rudè (1990: 69)). 'Why did this ancient story come back?... Probably because it was the first such one and was imprinted in his memory forever.'

Occasionally, parcellation can cross over a paragraph, for example:

А собирателю перлов народного творчества следует знать поэзию хотя бы в объеме массового песенника.

Ибо проколы происходят от некомпетентности...

Meanwhile, a person collecting folklore gems should know poetry, at least at the level of a popular book of songs.

Because lack of competence results in 'flops'... (*Литературная газета*, n.d., quoted in Formanovskaja 1978: 176).

The use of parcellation outside co-ordinate structures, where it most likely originated, confirms the expansion of this phenomenon in written styles of contemporary Russian.

(iii) Thematic nominative

In colloquial speech, another kind of dislocation frequently found is that whereby the noun phrase expressing the topic of conversation, irrespective of its syntactic function in the sentence, is presented at the beginning of the sentence, separated from it, in its citation form (i.e. nominative case); in the most typical instances, the topicalized (thematic) noun is then repeated, in the appropriate syntactic form, in the body of the sentence, usually as a pronoun, as in English: *Children. You never know what they'll be up to next.* Such examples have become very frequent in contemporary journalistic and popular scientific styles, as in the article on cups for sporting events in *Известия* of 12 August 1975: Кубки, кубки! Сколько ныне их в футболе. 'Cups, cups! How many of them there are nowadays in football.'

Sometimes, instead of the thematic noun phrase being repeated in full or as a pronoun, its semantic content is repeated by the inclusion of some semantically related expression in the main sentence, as in this example from the same article: Кубки, кубки. Приятно видеть, сколько наших команд ныне включились в спор на этих популярных европейских турнирах. 'Cups, cups. It is pleasant to see how many of our teams have now entered the fray at these popular European tournaments', where the idea of the cup or prize is subsumed in на этих турнирах 'at these tournaments'. Another straightforward example is to be found in *Известия* of 5 August 1975, in an article on Bhutan: Традиции. Они сильны в Бутане, где власть . . . верховного ламы почти равносильна власти монарха. 'Traditions. They are strong in Bhutan, where the power . . . of the head lama is almost equal to the power of the monarch.'

According to Švec (1971: 50), thematization of this kind became particularly common in the 1950s and 1960s. It is likely that the increasing amount of daily information forces journalists to devise new techniques of compressing this information and offering their readership immediately recoverable headlines. The use of predicateless structures is an effective means of conveying such information, and the fact that the above techniques are typical of the current press is, therefore, not accidental.

(iv) Nominative sentences

Most of the stylistic devices discussed so far in this section have parallels in colloquial speech, which is generally characterized by so-called situational ellipsis,[43] although some of them can also be found, though less frequently, in expressive writing of the nineteenth century, for instance in rhetorical poetry. The next stylistic device to be discussed is one that is essentially foreign to the spoken language, but is found traditionally in higher styles of the written language (especially poetry; Popov (1966: 83–4)), namely the frequent use of so-called nominative sentences (номинативные предложения). These are sentences consisting solely of a noun phrase in the nominative case, and used to set the scene for some action or series of actions. An example is to be found in *Известия* of 12 August 1975, where a football match is introduced by the paragraph: 9 августа 1975 года. Москва. Центральный стадион имени В. И. Ленина. 70.000 зрителей. '9 August 1975. Moscow. The V. I. Lenin Central Stadium. 70,000 spectators.' With this form of scene-setting there is no specification of tense (i.e. not: было 9 августа . . . 'it was 9 August . . .').

In earlier periods this technique was largely restricted to the stage instructions at the beginning of a scene in a drama. As noted by Popov (1966: 89–92), it is not uncommon in current prose writing to find long chains of such nominative sentences, each of which may consist of a long noun phrase with various attributes. He suggests, moreover, that one possible influence on the spread of nominative constructions is their use in film scenarios (ibid. 1966: 79–81). In current usage they are frequent with some (by no means all) writers (ibid.: 83), still rare in the spoken language, and common in newspaper reporting.

(v) Verbal nouns

In many constructions in Russian, it is possible to use either some form of a verb, or the abstract noun derived from that verb (verbal noun), e.g. я привык наблюдать такие явления 'I have grown accustomed to observing such phenomena', and я привык к наблюдению таких явлений 'I have grown accustomed to the observation of such phenomena'. In most instances where both verbal and nominal constructions are possible there is a stylistic difference between them: the nominal

---

[43] In addition to the devices described above, colloquial Russian has a number of other devices which are not found in the written language, at least not outside dialogue, such as the thematic nominative not taken up in the body of the sentence, which then lacks an expected syntactic constituent, e.g. Толстой я прочла 'Tolstoj I've read', Красные мои не знаешь где туфли? 'Have you seen my red shoes?' See Lapteva (1976: 119–36), Formanovskaja (1978: 161–2); Zemskaja (1973: 241–64; 1981: 191–227; 1987: 138–45, 150, 162–74).

construction is more characteristic of scientific, political, and bureaucratic language, whereas the verbal construction is more usual in other
styles, especially in speech.

The spread of nominal constructions in bookish styles is very marked
in the recent history of Russian, as of many other European languages.
In his article «Глагольность как выразительное средство»,
Peškovkij criticizes nominal constructions as indicative of bureaucratic
style and calls upon the literary language to go 'back to the verb'
(Peškovkij 1959 (1925): 101–11). Meromskij (1930: 52–3) notes that
'rural speech is characterized by the primacy of the verb, where the
townsman would tend towards use of the noun', i.e. this stylistic change
was more widespread in urban than rural usage, the former being generally more susceptible to the influence of scientific, political, and bureaucratic language. Meromskij quotes a statistical analysis by M. Gus, Ju.
Zagorjanskij, and N. Kaganovič, showing that out of 648 phrases in
Рабочая газета, an urban newspaper, where both noun and verb would
be possible, the noun is used in 38.5 per cent of them; in the rural
newspaper *Беднота*, the corresponding figure is only 4.4 per cent.
Prokopovič (1966) also supports the view that the spread of nominal
constructions is a recent phenomenon in Russian, indicative of increasing analyticity. This conclusion as well as the observation that nominal
constructions are typical of the so-called 'intellectual' styles (scientific,
bureaucratic) is challenged by Gak (1976) who notes that such constructions were common in Old Russian and that in the contemporary
language they can be found in stylistically varied contexts. According
to Gak, the main reason for using nominal constructions consists in
their ability to downplay or background the subject of the action (e.g.
кто-нибудь возражает?—есть ли возражения? 'are there any
objections?') and to express those shades of meaning that would be
impossible in the verbal construction (e.g. раздался резкий теле-
фонный звонок but not резко позвонили 'a sharp telephone ring was
heard'). This analysis, which does not, however, question the analyticity
of nominal constructions, helps explain the wide spread of nominal constructions in modern Russian fiction.

Comparing the norm and non-standard varieties, in particular
prostorečie, Ickovič (1974: 44–60) notes that in current non-standard
usage there is a tendency for verbal nouns governed by a verb or noun
to be replaced by infinitives, contrary to standard usage, e.g. препятствует вести наблюдения for препятствует ведению наблюдений
'prevents the carrying out of observations'. In his corpus there are some

200 examples of violation of the standard in this direction, and only two examples of violation in the other direction, e.g. умение выбора формы for умение выбрать форму 'ability to choose the form' (Ickovič 1974: 45–6). He concludes that the verbal noun tends to win out in scientific and administrative language, partly also in journalistic language, whereas the infinitive is tending to become more widespread in other styles, perhaps as a reaction against the proliferation of verbal nouns, which is often criticized in normative handbooks.

(vi) Hypotaxis and parataxis

The general discussion of the syntax of the complex sentence is beyond the scope of this book, partly because the data on such syntax are generally scarce and even less is known about the changes undergone by the language in this sphere. We would like, however, to discuss the relationship between paratactic and hypotactic linkage of clauses which plays an important role in syntactic stylistics (V. V. Vinogradov 1980 (1922): 31–7).

Overall, parataxis (clause linkage without conjunctions) is predominant in the spoken language, particularly in its non-standard varieties. In the standard language, the opposition of clause linkage with and without conjunctions is often used for stylistic purposes. The frequency of paratactic constructions in colloquial standard and in non-standard language explains the use of parataxis in literary imitations of this language, particularly in dialogue (Černuxina 1976; Formanovskaja 1978: 34, 62; Širjaev 1986: 137–51), for example, in V. Rozov's play *Традиционный сбор* (quoted in Širjaev 1986: 144):

Смотрю я на тебя и думаю—нет, не выдержишь ты испытания славой . . . И все жду—кто-то придет и скажет: он самозванец, король голый.

I am looking at you and keep thinking that you won't survive the test of fame . . . I keep waiting for someone to get here and say: he is an impostor, a naked king.

Another function carried out by paratactic constructions in poetry and fiction is that of the vivid presentation of the material, designed to create the illusion of the reader's close observation and co-participation in the events (Širjaev 1986: 156–8).

In other functional styles, parataxis is used for the expression of causal and comparative relations between clauses; this function is characteristic of scientific and official style. For example (from Širjaev 1986: 165),

А торопиться надо было. Ведь важна не только температура, но и скорость работы: исследователь, словно хирург, не может медлить: вырванные из живого организма митохондрии быстро . . . теряют свои качества.

And it was, indeed, necessary to hurry. Not only the temperature but the pace of work, too, played an important role: the researcher, just like a surgeon, cannot afford to linger: the mitochondria removed from the live body quickly lose their qualities.

The absence of conjunctions is compensated for by the increasing use of discourse particles such as ведь 'indeed' (as in the excerpt above), же 'indeed', a 'and, but', and others. The study of such particles has just begun; see, for example, Boguslavskij (1985).

5   Vocabulary

Motivation of Change

The reflection in language of extra-linguistic reality is easier to demonstrate on the lexical level than on any other, and the social motivation of linguistic change is consequently most easily demonstrated by change in vocabulary. The appearance of new things, concepts, qualities, activities, etc., is always accompanied or quickly followed (and sometimes even preceded) by changes in the lexical system. New words appear and old words change their meaning, often reflecting the changes in the outside world. But, as we have mentioned already, language varies not only along the scale of time, but along social, functional, and regional scales, too. Lexical innovation can therefore operate in many different ways, including the transfer of words and meanings from one variety to another.

Many of the new Russian words which came into use during the Soviet period closely reflected, and owed their existence to, the new social and political structures. Words such as загс 'registry office', совхоз 'collective farm', нарком 'people's commissar', made their first appearance in the Soviet period and as a result of the new political system. On the other hand, there are many new words that have arrived on the scene in this century whose arrival can scarcely be attributed to the Soviet system. This type includes, for example, вертолет 'helicopter', танк 'tank', компьютер 'computer', регби 'rugby', коммюнике 'press-release', the last attested already in the second half of the nineteenth century (Granovskaja 1983: 65).

There is, in addition, a third type: those words which existed in Russian before 1917 but which are nevertheless regarded as particularly characteristic of the Soviet period. Many of them before the October Revolution were severely restricted both territorially (being mainly urban), and, above all, socially. The use of most of the philosophical, political, and economic vocabulary of the revolutionary movements of the nineteenth and early twentieth centuries was restricted to participants in those movements and to certain social spheres either connected with or interested in such movements. The users of such words lived mainly in towns, but in addition, of course, many revolutionaries spent years in emigration. There are thus many words of this kind which were attested before the turn of the century (in some cases many years earlier) or before the revolutionary years but which only came into widespread popular use after 1917. Such words as агитация 'agitation, propaganda', альянс 'alliance', демократия 'democracy', демонстрация 'demonstration', депутат 'deputy', коллегия 'board', коммуна 'commune', ликвидация 'elimination', лозунг 'slogan', резолюция 'resolution', совет 'council', штрейк-брехер 'strike-breaker', for example, penetrated the vocabulary of the working class and peasantry only after the 1917 Revolution, though they had existed before that in the language of certain social groups. Similarly, the pre-eminently Soviet words большевик 'Bolshevik' and меньшевик 'Menshevik' came into existence soon after the Second Congress of the Russian Social Democratic Workers' Party, held in London in 1903, when the split occurred between the supporters of Lenin (who claimed to be in the majority—большинство) and the rest (the alleged minority—меньшинство),[1] but it was not until after 1917 that they came into use among the whole population. Several contemporary observers of the linguistic events following the Revolution noted the growing use of foreign words by ever widening spheres of users after (and only after) 1917 (Barannikov 1919: 77; Karcevskij 1923: 22–3; Seliščev 1928: 30–5). Even in the press (which was one of those restricted areas where the number and frequency of loan-words was already comparatively high) their frequency in political articles appears to have shown a slight but significant increase (Krysin 1965a: 129–31).

The fact that much of the characteristic vocabulary of the early Soviet period is first attested before 1917 and only subsequently entered the personal vocabularies of the vast majority of the users of Russian underlines one of the weaknesses of historical lexicology: the attestation of words in texts often reveals nothing of their actual use. Some words of the kind referred to above are attested even as early as the seventeenth (e.g. демократия, депутат) and eighteenth (e.g. альянс, демонстрация) centuries. If we could map their social distribution in the same way as regional isoglosses can be shown on dialect maps, we should find that throughout their two centuries or so of use in Russian they occupied a very small area indeed. Strictly speaking we cannot describe such words as Soviet neologisms, yet to the greater part of the Russian language community that is precisely what they were (Černyx 1929: 50).

---

[1] Ironically, the actual numerical representation of the factions was just the opposite (see Broido 1987 for details).

The social spread of many of these words began with the Revolution of 1905, but it was only in 1917 that the flood-gates were opened wide. Such words were originally restricted to those who may be described as politically unorthodox and constituted a distinctive attribute of their language separating them from other users of Russian. The nineteenth-century novelists provide evidence of this. Leskov in his novel *Некуда* (1864), for example, parodies the characteristic speech of young nihilists in the 1860s (Šor 1929: 52). But still more useful is the picture given by L. Tolstoj in *Воскресение* (1899) of the revolutionary Vera Efremova (quoted from Černyx 1929: 52):

Речь ее была пересыпана иностранными словами о пропагандировании, о дезорганизации, о группах, и секциях, и подсекциях . . . (*Воскресение*, Part 1, Chapter 55

Her speech was interspersed with foreign words about propagandizing and disorganization, about groups and sections and subsections . . .

An important factor in the borrowing of West European words was the fact that revolutionaries had long-standing links with the West. Many of them had been in exile abroad, sometimes for many years. The theoretical works on which their ideologies were based were written in and had been translated from West European languages. It is thus not possible to say how far the Western words borrowed in the seventeenth, eighteenth, and nineteenth centuries had a continuous independent existence within the Russian speech community, and to what extent they were renewed and reinforced by renewed Western contacts. Emigration was undoubtedly an important factor. André Mazon, who was in Russia during the whole of 1918 and the first weeks of 1919, was in no doubt as to its effect on the Bolshevik leaders (Mazon 1920: pp. i–ii). On the other hand, it is known that Western words abounded in the speech of even those revolutionaries who had not been abroad, a fact which led Černyx to conclude that the role of emigration in this process had been greatly exaggerated (1929: 52). It is certainly true that some of the political words which came to the fore in 1905–17 had a history in Russian going back to the time of the French Revolution. Some, in fact, were particularly associated with the French Revolution and for that very reason were revived by Russian revolutionaries, for many of whom the French Revolution was the model event (Seliščev 1928: 21–2; Černyx 1929: 54).

In the following sections, we will present the major tendencies of lexical change over the consecutive periods in the twentieth century: as this presentation will show, in each period, lexical changes were motivated by social change and by changes in the everyday life of people, associated primarily with technological innovations and global changes. After examining the actual change, we will discuss the motivation for change and the types of change that occurred during the twentieth century.

Periodization of Change

Lexical change, 1900–1917

The beginning of the century witnessed rapid technological and social developments which resulted in the appearance of a number of new words in the Russian language, most of them borrowings. The very approach to borrowings underwent significant changes in the end of the nineteenth and the beginning of the twentieth century. The first element of change concerned the status of French. In the nineteenth century, French was the indispensable language of the educated class, comprised mostly of the nobility; many Russian writers, for example, were bi-lingual in French and Russian, and Gallicisms are not infrequent in the prose of Puškin or L. Tolstoj. In the second half of the nineteenth century, as education became more open to other classes, many representatives of *raznočincy*, children of the clergy, and even peasants gained formal education; this changed the composition of the educated class and intèlligentsia (Müller 1971), with the number of people who grew up speaking French decreasing. As a consequence, the level of obligatory knowledge of French, compared to the time described in *War and Peace*, also decreased (Polivanov 1931: 29). Poetic Gallicisms and neo-Gallicisms still constituted an important element of the speech of some of the Silver Age authors (I. Annenskij, A. Belyj, A. Blok) but were becoming increasingly removed from the general usage.[2] As a manifestation of the opposite tendency, some non-poetic loan-words from French gained ground in the twentieth-century language, for example (цвет) электри́к 'bright blue (colour)'.

The beginning of the twentieth century was the time of unprecedented technological development, with the spread of telephone, photography, cinema, aviation, automobiles. In the names of new artifacts, French competed with German and English; thus, one of the early verbs for

---

[2] Accordingly, some neo-Gallicisms popular in the beginning of the century drop out of use by the 1920s, for example, вертиж 'bemusement', демимоденткa 'demi-mondaine'.

taking photographs was кодачить (from the trade mark 'Kodak'). German was popular in the 1900s and early 1910s, in particular among Socialists and Marxists (Filin 1981: 218–20); however, it fell out of grace during the First World War, owing to the anti-German feelings aroused by the war, but these had little lasting effect (see below in this subsection). English was clearly perceived as a fashionable language, and this gave rise to early loan-words such as фильма/фильм 'film', рэг-тайм 'ragtime', джаз 'jazz', бойкот 'boycott', бум 'boom', стэнд/стенд 'stand', (лаун-)теннис 'tennis', which were retained or revitalized[3] throughout the century, to be later joined by many other words that indicate the increasing role of English as a prestigious source of new loan-words (Filin 1981: 210–13). Despite the general acceptance of loan-words, many of which were associated with the new techno-logical concepts, there was at least one case where the borrowed names were abandoned, early on, in favour of the Russian words; these were the words related to aviation. The general public and many artists, espe-cially the Futurists, were fascinated by aviation in the first decades of the century. The original names that Russian used to describe this field were French borrowings (Filin 1981: 218, 230); however, by the late 1920s, the words авиатор (from Fr. *aviateur*), аэроплан (from Fr. *aéroplane*) had been replaced by the Russian летчик and самолет.[4] Cf. the following remarks by Anna Axmatova and Viktor Šklovskij:

Говорил, что его интересовали авиаторы (по-теперешнему— летчики)... (A. Axmatova. *Амедео Модильяни*, 1959–64)

He used to say that aviators (or, as they now say, pilots) interested him . . .

Тогдашнее (в 1910 году) имя самолетов—аэроплан. (V. Šklovskij. *Жили-были*, quoted in *SSRLJa* (1991–))

The contemporary (in 1910) name of planes—aeroplane.

The word аэроплан has been considered archaic since the 1960s (Ožegov 1972); *SSRLJa* (1991–) characterizes аэроплан and авиатор as *becoming archaic* (устаревающие).

Calques were also used to avoid direct borrowing, and among the

---

[3] Some of the words listed here (e.g. джаз, скетч, стенд) were known to a very limited number of speakers, which explains why they are sometimes treated as borrowings of the 1930s (see, for example, Krysin 1968: 82 ff).

[4] The word самолет was not new: it is cited in *SCRJa* (1847). The situation with the word летчик is less clear: the word is first cited, without any comment, in D. N. Ušakov (1935–40) and it has sometimes been attributed to Velimir Xlebnikov. Though Xlebnikov was indeed fascinated by aviation and created a number of neologisms with the root лет- (Stepanov 1975: 130–3; Vroon 1983: 153–61), летчик was not one of them.

calques of the late nineteenth and early twentieth centuries are небоскреб 'sky-scraper', работодатель 'employer' (from Germ. *Arbeitsgeber*), скоросшиватель 'folder' (from Germ. *Schnellhefter*) (Filin 1981: 226–32).

Oriental languages became a new source of loan-words in the nineteenth and early twentieth centuries; the interest in the 'exotic' vocabulary was motivated on the one hand by neo-Romanticism and Symbolism in literature, and on the other by the emerging journalistic style, where allegory (the so-called Aesopian language) played an important role. Territorial expansions of the Russian Empire also played a role in securing such loan-words as чадра 'veil; chador', паранджа 'yashmak; garment including face covering, worn by Muslim women', сакля 'shack, hovel', кишлак 'village in Central Asia', which sounded both romantic and exotic in the first decades of the twentieth century. The Russo-Japanese War (1904–5) brought about some borrowings from Japanese, most of them short-lived (Filin 1981: 225–6).

The revolution of 1905 became a turning-point in the 'politicization' of the general vocabulary; in particular, it accelerated the slow spread of existing loan-words to new social spheres. Among the examples given by Seliščev of words known for their increasing popularity at this time are: аграрный 'agrarian', аграрник 'one condemned for participation in agrarian disturbances', баррикады 'barricades', бастовать 'strike', бойкот, фракция 'faction' (Seliščev 1928: 28). Newspapers and political speeches were responsible for extending the vocabularies of their audiences; but when assessing the role of newspapers we should not forget the low literacy rate at this time and the fact that it was not destined to rise significantly until the 1920s. But even for the few who could read, the increase in new vocabulary (mostly of foreign origin) was already a problem. Words were being introduced to the press faster than the reading population could digest them. Symptomatic of this state of affairs is the unusually large number of small dictionaries and vocabularies published during the first two decades of the twentieth century, explaining words of foreign origin, related principally to political and economic matters (Krysin 1968: 62). Konduruškin's dictionary (1917), for example, is actually subtitled 'an aid to reading the newspapers'.

The war years 1914–18 saw a drop in the rate of borrowing. Those foreign words that were borrowed at this time were mostly connected with the war (Karcevskij 1923: 39; Krysin 1968: 63). There were also manifestations of a nationalistic purism: attempts were made to reject certain existing loan-words of German origin. However, the projected replacement of бутерброд 'slice of bread and butter' by хлеб с маслом and of плацкарт(а)[5] 'place in sleeping-car' by спальное место came to nothing (Barannikov 1919: 74). Здравница 'health resort, sanatorium', which originated during the war, reportedly on the initiative of Nicholas II to replace the loan-word санаторий/санатория 'sanatorium', has survived (Karcevskij 1923: 61), but the two words only overlap semantically. Demands that the German loan-word фельдшер 'medical assistant' be replaced by лекарский помощник were at least temporarily successful, though the motivation in this case was not simply nationalistic but also based on class considerations (cf. p. 223). The renaming of certain towns, e.g. Санкт-Петербург 'St Petersburg' as Петроград 'Petrograd',[6] was another aspect of this puristic tendency.

The rapid political change in the 1905–17 period had its toll on a number of words that immediately became obsolete, e.g. вечник 'a person convicted to life in penal servitude', халупник 'deserter (in the First World War)';[7] often, these were names of political factions, some of them based on the name of the leader, for example, активец 'armed hooligan', гвоздевец 'follower of the social chauvinist Gvozdev'. Some of these words survived into later periods, but in a different meaning; for example, черносотенец originated in the early 1900s as the name of a member of a political group Черная сотня 'Black Squadron' but later changed its meaning to 'ultra-nationalist; anti-Semite'; in the latter meaning, the word still exists in the contemporary language. Likewise, the deverbative noun разрядка 'discharge', derived from разряжать(ся), was coined probably in the 1880s in the Šlissel'burg Fortress, where a number of political prisoners were kept; it was then used in the expression разрядка нервной энергии 'need for peace of mind' (Granovskaja 1983: 54). It survived into the twentieth century and experienced a revival, primarily as a political term denoting détente, in the 1970s (Kotelova 1984).

Of course, words that had no political denotations were also subject to change. In Chapter 3, several acronyms that fell out of use by the early 1920s were already mentioned. The word серник 'match' was ousted

---

[5] According to Krysin (1968: 63 n.) this word was masculine at that time, but Barannikov (1919: 74) has плацкарта.

[6] Since the change was made by imperial decree and reflected tsarist chauvinism, the old name was partially revived in the left-wing press after the Revolution (Jakobson 1921: 9).

[7] From халупа 'hut', alluding to hiding in a secluded place.

by its close synonym спичка (Granovskaja 1983: 59). A number of words underwent semantic and stylistic change. For example, the word кабала lost the meaning 'nonsense, rumours', attested by V. Dal´ (1880–2), and has been retained only in the meaning 'hard labour, bondage'; accordingly, the phraseological expression возводить на кого-л. кабалу 'spread rumours about someone' also fell out of use. The word антик 'antique' lost the meaning 'old-fashioned person'; адвокатура, which originally denoted either law as a profession or lawyers as a group, has retained only the former meaning (Granovskaja 1983: 58–9).

Finally, the beginning of the century witnessed the creation of numerous acronyms and stump-compounds, some of which were already mentioned in Chapter 3. The First World War played an important role in increasing the number of acronyms, particularly in military language: the acronyms and stumps were needed to speed up communication (via telegraph) between the units. Some of the new acronyms were not particularly euphonic, which did not add to their popularity, e.g. наштаверх (начальник штаба верховного главно-командующего) 'Chief of the Military Operations Headquarters', штадив (штаб дивизии) 'division headquarters'; for some reason, the acronyms in the navy were much more accepted, and some of them have been in use since the First World War, e.g. подлодка (подводная лодка) 'submarine', эсминец (эскадренный миноносец) 'destroyer' (see also Fessenko 1955: 22).

Lexical change, 1917–1927

This period, especially its second half, is often characterized as revolutionary in the development of modern Russian vocabulary. However, apart from a large number of stump-compounds and acronyms, the lexical change did not accelerate and in fact reflected the same tendencies that were already present in the preceding period (Filin 1981: 311–12). The major difference, however, between this period and the first two decades of the twentieth century consisted in the mass spread of vocabulary previously limited to certain speech varieties: many professional, technological, political words became part of more general vocabulary. This was accompanied by semantic re-analyses and meaning shifts, which will be discussed below.

(i) *Borrowings*

The revolutions of 1917 did not accelerate the rate of borrowing. It remained particularly low during the first decade of Soviet power, and the number of loan-words first attested in this period is surprisingly small. They include: дансинг (1923) 'dance-hall' (Eng. or Fr. *dancing*), докер (1925) 'docker' (Eng. *docker*), конферансье 'master of ceremonies' (Fr. *conférencier*), такси (1926) 'taxi' (Fr. *taxi*), фокстрот (1923) 'fox-trot' (Eng. *fox-trot*), шезлонг 'deck-chair' (Fr. *chaise longue*),[8] сервис (Eng. *service*). (For further examples, see Krysin 1965*a*: 121–5; 1968: 70–1; Granovskaja 1983: 54–5.) The shift from French to English as the source language of borrowings actively continued in the 1920s.

Not only the small number but also the areas of human activity covered by these words come as something of a surprise. How are we to explain the fact that in a time of political events unique in the history of mankind the Russian language was borrowing words like конферансье, фокстрот, or шезлонг? The answer is to be found in the fact that the vocabulary was simultaneously enlarging itself from another source—from native elements using new word-formation models (Krysin 1968: 72) and from the semantic extension of existing words. Loan-words originating in this period are simply so few in number that they are not in any way typical. At the same time, it is important to remember that this was a period when loan-words from the preceding years were being digested by the masses (Karcevskij 1923: 39; Krysin 1968: 63–4). New words were not being borrowed by Russian from non-Russian sources, but within the Russian speech community existing loan-words were being borrowed from one social variety to another. This shift in borrowing techniques involved, for example, the loan-words from non-Slavonic languages of Russia, some of which were mentioned in the preceding section (*Lexical change, 1900–1917*). These words were adapted by the general social and political discourse and subsequently lost the exotic connotations they had in the earlier period. For example, in the 1920s, the expression сбросить чадру (паранджу) '(lit.) take off the veil' shifted from the earlier meaning of unveiling to that of becoming emancipated, and the word кишлак was commonly used in the expression революционный кишлак 'Revolutionary remote point' (see also Granovskaja 1983: 55).

---

[8] This word, however, is attested in nineteenth-century literature; for example, it is used by K. Stanjukovič, though in a slightly different spelling (see the quote below, p. 227). In the period described here, the word was probably brought back into active use or reborrowed.

Russian linguists working in the 1920s were aware of the necessity of observing social variation in vocabulary. Their attention was drawn not so much to the moment of birth of some new formation as to its spread (Černyx 1929: 62; Krysin 1965a: 125). The fact that certain loan-words were known to some social strata and not to others is attested in a number of ways. First, there are recorded instances of their inaccurate use, some even in writing. In 1928 the Soviet satirical magazine *Крокодил* (no. 15) published the following example from a notice displayed in a chemist's shop: В виду острого дефекта хинина в СССР отпуск товаров прекращен. (Quoted by Černyx 1929: 50) 'In view of an acute defect of quinine in the USSR the issue of goods is discontinued'. This demonstrates confusion between дефект 'defect' and дефицит 'shortage'.

(ii) *Folk-etymology*

Secondly, the fact that many words were new to their users is shown by folk-etymological interpretations. The term folk-etymology is applied to the creation of new forms or meanings, often resulting from language contact, when users of a given variety begin to use words from another variety without understanding their meaning. The new word may acquire a new form (to make it appear to have some kind of etymological motivation), or it may acquire a new meaning (to link it semantically with existing words of similar form). The emergence of such words is characteristic of situations of cultural transfer, when not only the word but also the referent is unfamiliar to the receiving group. This was the situation in early revolutionary Russia, when many words relating to new concepts were taken into use by new users (Šor 1926: 94, 127), either in the rural population or among non-native speakers of Russian, for example, speakers of Turkic languages in Central Asia or Yiddish speakers that moved out of the Pale of residence (Kreindler 1982; 1985).

Many of the folk-etymological innovations of the early Soviet period were recorded by contemporary observers and they testify to the social and linguistic upheaval at that time. The following were noted during the first ten years or so of Soviet rule: бубличное место for публичное место 'public place' (being linked to the familiar бублик 'bagel, bread-roll' instead of unfamiliar публика 'public'); космомолец for комсомолец 'member of Komsomol' (linked to косо 'askew' and молиться 'pray'); купиратив for кооператив 'co-operative' (linked to купить 'buy') (Šor 1926: 94); скупилянт, скупиляция for спекулянт 'speculator', спекуляция 'speculation' (linked to скупить 'buy up') (Barannikov 1919: 79), and скопилянт for спекулянт 'speculator' (linked to скопить 'amass') (Jakobson 1921: 9); переле- тарий for пролетарий 'proletarian' (linked to перелетать 'fly over, hop'), пример-министр for премьер-министр 'prime minister' (linked to пример 'example'), леворуция for революция 'revolution' (linked to лево- 'left' and рука 'hand, arm'), ликтричество, ликс- триство for электричество 'electricity' (possibly linked to лик 'image (esp. religious)') (Barannikov 1919: 79); элементы 'elements' for алементы 'alimony', дистанция 'distance' for инстанция 'instance (legal)' (Seliščev 1939: 76). In some country districts пробольшевики 'pro-Bolsheviks' was understood as meaning противобольшевики 'anti-Bolsheviks' (Karcevskij 1923: 63). Šor quotes the interesting case of куманист for коммунист 'communist', occurring in a North Russian tale, where it is derived from the dialect word куманика 'cloudberry' (1926: 94).[9] A number of distorted words and phrases that occurred in the proletarian press in the early years after the revolution can be found in I. Bunin's *Окаянные дни* (1920–5) (Bunin 1982: 122–4, 127–9, 138–45, 147, 170).

(iii) *Problems of understanding*

In certain other changes of meaning there is no apparent similarity between the two forms involved, and the motivation of change is consequently obscure. Often, a formerly unfamiliar word was acquired in a very narrow meaning, based on the concretization of the actual meaning. In a sense, this process is similar to folk-etymology; the difference between folk-etymology and semantic concretization is that the latter does not affect the actual shape of the word. A list of such partially understood words is given by Seliščev (1928: 214–18); it includes, for example, кандидат 'alternate' (for 'candidate'),[10] конференция 'place for speeches' (for 'conference'), республика 'new rule' (for 'republic'); спектакль 'comedy' (for 'performance').

The word сознательный 'conscientious' underwent both semantic and stylistic changes, summarized in the following way by the Soviet writer P. Nilin:

Это слово «сознательный» было в те годы в большом ходу. Им как

---

[9] Another possible source for куманист might have been the word кум/кума 'god-parent'.

[10] Seliščev (1928: 215) cites the actual explanation obtained for this word: когда выбирают лишнего 'when the unnecessary person is chosen'.

бы награждали человека. Сознательный—значит, понимающий, осо-
знающий, с какими трудностями связано построение нового мира, и
готовый пойти на любые жертвы в преодолении трудностей. (Quoted in
Šmelev 1964: 7)

This word, сознательный, was very popular in those years. It was as if a
person were awarded this word. Сознательный means 'understanding, aware
of the difficulties accompanying the construction of the new world, and ready to
make whatever sacrifices are needed in overcoming those difficulties'.

The opposite semantic re-analysis, from a concrete to a more abstract
meaning, was also attested in the 1920s. It was recorded, for example,
that in parts of the countryside персонально 'personally' was understood as редко 'rarely' (Šor 1926: 127) and серьезный 'serious' as
хороший 'good' (Šafir 1927: 131).[11]

One can only speculate on the precise origins of these new meanings,
but the way in which a shift from a particular to a general meaning could
produce the opposite of the intended message in a given utterance is
demonstrated by the story of an argument between Maksim Gorʹkij and
another man as to whether the common people could understand the
slogan Религия—опиум для народа 'Religion is the opium of the
people'. They decided to ask a Red Army man on guard: Что такое
опиум? 'What is opium?' The reply was: Знаю . . . это лекарство 'I
know . . . it is medicine'. It is not known whether it was merely co-
incidence that дурман 'dope' was later used in this slogan instead of
опиум (Šklovskij 1925: 29–31).

Some contemporary observers, such as Seliščev (1928, 1939), aimed
simply to record the linguistic facts they heard and saw before them.
Others, however, were concerned with practical problems. Šafir (1924,
1927), for example, was concerned with the press and the task of
writing in words which would be understood by workers and peasants,
both those who, in the 1920s, were beginning to read for themselves, and
those who still relied on others to read the newspapers aloud to them. In
1923 he carried out surveys and experiments to discover whether
peasants could understand the words being used in the press, and dis-
covered that in many cases they could not. His survey of 64 Red Army
men (who, presumably, reflected the general make-up of the population
and were thus mainly peasants) showed a high degree of ignorance of
certain words. Among the words with which Šafir's informants showed

[11] For a more general overview and a comprehensive list of abstract nouns in the
language of the first half of the twentieth century, see Jelitte (1990).

a particularly low degree of acquaintance are the following (1927: 131–2): система 'system', ультиматум 'ultimatum', регулярно 'regularly', элемент 'element', авторитет 'authority', инициатива 'initiative', реклама 'advertisement', меморандум 'memorandum', репарации 'reparations', официально 'officially'. His survey also covered industrial workers in Voronež, however, and their knowledge of words used in the newspapers was much greater.

In order to assist correspondents to make their language more accessible to the masses Šafir published lists of words often not understood and accompanied them by better-known Russian equivalents. His point was that the language of the press should be closer 'to the colloquial language' (1927: 130).

The amount of difficulty experienced by the newly literate in understanding the newspapers was a constant topic of public debate in the 1920s and it engaged the attention of leading political figures (Špil´rejn *et al.* 1928: 8). This was not a new problem: both before and after the October Revolution politicians and correspondents had used synonyms or explanations to make political terminology comprehensible. The following examples of this method are taken from the 1920s (Seliščev 1928: 29–30): Эта модификация, это изменение тактики . . . (*Правда*, 29 May 1924) 'This modification, this change of tactics . . .'; Стимул (побуждение) к борьбе . . . (*Известия*, № 295, 1924) 'stimulus (inducement) to struggle . . .'; Сбалансировка (уравновешение) бюджета . . . (*Правда*, № 65, 1926) 'Balancing (equalizing) of the budget . . .'.

We have no way of telling precisely at what rate and in which directions vocabulary formerly restricted to privileged groups spread to other sections of the population, but things were undoubtedly moving fast in the late 1920s and early 1930s. It is characteristic of this volatile period that only three years after Šafir was expressing dismay at the extent to which words were still not known among the peasantry, another observer (Meromskij 1930) was registering his admiration for the skill with which the rural correspondents (селькоры) of the central *Крестьянская газета* were using loan-words which 'formerly would have sounded very unusual in the mouth of a peasant' (1930: 99–100). To Meromskij it was evident that a flood of words which before the Revolution had had what he calls a 'restricted learned and urban sphere of dissemination' had in the last few years poured into the everyday speech of the village, 'Europeanizing' it (1930: 100–1). He describes the surprise of the members of an agitation and propaganda expedition to the village of Nenaševo (Paxomovo *rajon*, Tula *gubernija*) in 1928 on discovering that all the children there knew the word компот 'stewed fruit', which had until recently been known only in the central parts of towns (1930: 108).

An important agency for spreading literacy and education in the early years of Soviet power was the Red Army, and the tests of passive vocabulary carried out among men of the Moscow garrison in 1924–5 (Špil´rejn *et al.* 1928) showed that knowledge, especially of socio-political vocabulary, increased rapidly during the time spent in the army (1928: 112–13).

(iv) *Derivation*

The number of actual borrowings dating from the early Soviet period may be small, but between the February Revolution and the beginning of the first Five-Year Plan (1917–28) the vocabulary was growing fast by forming new words from elements already present in Russian.

The method of forming new words from initial letters or from stumps is especially characteristic of this period. Although it had been used before 1917 the number of words produced in this way was small. From 1917 onwards the productivity of this type increased out of all proportion to what had gone before. (See also Chapter 3, p. 142.) A good part of these innovations had a relatively short life span, however, and it has been estimated that most of those created in the 1920s (a particularly productive period) have since fallen out of use (Ward 1965: 157). The following examples of this type originating in the first decade of Soviet power constitute only a tiny fraction of the total number (a number of these acronyms have achieved the status of symbols of the time, some of them quite sinister):

(i) Using initials: вуз (высшее учебное заведение) 'higher educational institution', ГПУ (Главное политическое управление) 'Central Political Administration', НЭП (Новая экономическая политика) 'New Economic Policy', МАПП (Московская ассоциация пролетарских писателей) 'Moscow Association of Proletarian Writers', РСФСР (Российская Советская Федеративная Социалистическая Республика) 'Russian Soviet Federative Socialist Republic', ЦИК (Центральный Исполнительный Комитет) 'Central Executive Committee', чека (ЧК) (Чрезвычайная комиссия по борьбе с саботажем) 'Cheka' (the precursor of the KGB), каэр (контрреволюционер) 'counter-revolutionary'.

(ii) Using stumps: Госиздат (Государственное издательство)

'State Publishing House', зарплата (заработная плата) 'wages', исполком (исполнительный комитет) 'executive committee', Истпарт ((Комиссия по) истории (Коммунистиической) партии) 'Commission on the History of the Communist Party', истмат (исторический материализм) 'historical materialism',[12] комбед (комитет бедноты) 'Poor Peasants Committee', Коминтерн 'Comintern', партбилет (партийный билет) '(Communist) Party card', пролеткульт (пролетарская культура) 'proletarian culture', Персимфанс (первый симфонический ансамбль) 'First Symphonic Ensemble', рабкор (рабочий корреспондент) 'worker correspondent',[13] совхоз (советское хозяйство) 'state farm', совзнак (советский (денежный) знак) 'Soviet bank-note'.

The creation of acronyms in this period was perceived by many as the progressive way of expanding the vocabulary and activating the social dimension of the language; many acronyms were perceived as 'ideologically meaningful' (Krjučkova 1976: 14). On the other hand, the acronyms and stump-compounds, many of them being *ad hoc* creations, obscured the language and were communicatively opaque. This difficulty in understanding, together with the perception of acronyms as alien to the Russian vocabulary, contributed to the decline in the number of acronyms by the end of this period and in later periods (Alekseev 1963: 159; S. I. Vinogradov 1983).

At the same time new words were continuing to be coined by conventional methods: by affixation and compounding whole words. One of the derivational processes characteristic of the 1920s consisted in forming Russian words with borrowed affixes. One such early formation was старостат 'council of elders' (alternatively, совет старост), which was formed in the days of the February Revolution, probably by analogy with секретариат 'secretariat'. This word was praised by G. Vinokur, who parted company with language purists by approving of its compact shape and its appropriateness (Granovskaja 1983: 54 n. 6). Other words that were similarly formed in the 1920s included станковист 'machine-tool operator', кулакизация 'spread of kulaks', военизация 'militarization',[14] советизировать 'sovietize', царизм 'tsarism', антисниженцы

---

[12] Later changed to the full form исторический материализм; the stump-compound истмат, however, continued to be actively used in students' speech until the exclusion of this obligatory course from university curricula in the early 1990s.

[13] Cf. also селькор 'rural (peasant) correspondent', mentioned above.

[14] Unlike милитаризация, which has been used only with negative connotations, this word had a positive shade of meaning, as, for example, in the seemingly tautological военизация армии 'modernization and activization of the army'.

'opponents of price reduction', архиневерно 'extremely incorrect'.[15]
The process also involved loan-words, both long-adopted and recent, for
example, типизация 'stereotyping', инструктаж 'instruction',
фордизация 'acquisition of Ford automobiles' (Granovskaja 1983: 54).

Other affixal derivations first attested in the period 1917–25 include:
аллилуйщик 'one who overpraises', беспризорник 'homeless child,
waif', субботник, воскресник 'Saturday, Sunday of voluntary work
without pay', ленинец 'Leninist', керенщина 'Kerenskyism;
Alexander Kerenskij's followers',[16] партиец '(Communist) party
member', продуктовый 'grocery' (adjective), митинговать 'hold
meetings', проработка 'collective discussion, criticism', чрезвычайка
'Cheka'. The suffix -ец (-овец, -евец), which appears in ленинец,
партиец, seems to have been particularly active in this as well as the
preceding period, producing such nouns as впередовец 'follower of the
newspaper *Vpered*' (1911), оборонец 'advocate of active military
policies in the First World War', пораженец 'advocate of defeatist
policies in the First World War', правленец 'member of the board
(правление)', лишенец (лишенный избирательных прав) 'person
denied voting (and other social) rights because of non-proletarian origin'
(Seliščev 1928: 171–2).

In the same period the following compounds were coined: бело-
гвардеец 'White Guard', красноармеец 'Red Army man', красно-
гвардеец 'Red Guard', правозаступник 'lawyer',[17] Ленинград
'Leningrad'. Close to the compound words are hyphenated compounds
(see Chapter 3, p. 112), consisting of two nouns, for example: изба-
читальня 'reading room in a peasant village', крестьянин-самоед
'peasant on individual property', портной-квартирник 'home-based
tailor' (Seliščev 1928: 170–1).

The new acronyms and stump-compounds were themselves capable
of being used to form further new words by affixation: исполкомство-
вать, комсомолец, комсомольский, нэпман, нэпач, чекист.
(These examples all date from 1917–25.)

[15] The prefix архи- was particularly favoured by Lenin (Seliščev 1928: 53), which
probably affected its popularity in the early years after the October Revolution and its
immediate decline thereafter.
[16] This word was retained in Russian *émigré* literature, though in a different meaning:
'political weakness, political apathy' (Granovskaja 1983: 60).
[17] Replaced адвокат which, owing to its class connotations, was abolished (1918), but
later restored (1922) (Karcevskij 1923: 59–60).

(v) *Semantic change*

There is also the question of semantic change as a means of enlarging the vocabulary. Among the many new meanings which arose in this early part of the Soviet period are: абитуриент 'university candidate' (formerly 'secondary-school-leaver'), бригада 'work-team; study team' (formerly only 'work-team on train'), молодняк 'young people' (formerly 'saplings'), чистка 'purge' (formerly 'clean-up'), чиновник 'bureaucrat' (formerly 'civil-servant' only), смычка 'union (especially of workers and peasants)' (formerly 'juncture'),[18] уплотнить 'confiscate part of someone's residence putting in new residents' (formerly 'make denser') and the related самоуплотнение 'voluntary acceptance of additional residents' (Seliščev 1928: 170, 187, 195). Numerous examples of such words are given in Seliščev (1928: 192–7). Certainly, there is no clear line between the semantic change in the examples given here and the semantic re-analysis discussed in subsection (iii) above: granted that a critical mass of language users adopt the semantic concretization or generalization of a given word, this word can undergo semantic change as well.

(vi) *Historicisms*

With the overthrow of the old regime and the disappearance of many tsarist institutions the status of the words referring to them changed. While, for example, the words городовой 'policeman', дума 'duma, council', земство 'zemstvo', столоначальник 'table-master', жандарм 'gendarme', экзекутор 'seneschal', фрейлина 'maid of honour', did not disappear from the language, new circumstances meant that the frequency of such words was bound to fall, providing conditions for their eventual disappearance, at least from the active vocabulary of most speakers. Such words are sometimes called историзмы 'historicisms' by Russian linguists (Zarickij 1990). Further examples of words which fell into this category, either immediately in 1917 or in the following decade, are: губернатор 'governor', казначейство 'exchequer', стражник 'constable', полицейский 'policeman', государь 'sovereign', государыня 'sovereign lady', наследный 'hereditary', князь 'prince', камер-юнкер 'gentleman of the chamber', лицей 'kind of a grammar school', гувернёр 'tutor', гувернантка 'governess', бонна 'nursery-governess', гимназия 'grammar school', посол 'ambassador', посольство 'embassy', аттестат зрелости 'school certificate', градоначальник 'governor of a town, mayor', министр

[18] See Bezděk *et al.* (1974: 100).

'minister', товарищ министра 'deputy minister', министерство 'ministry', воскресник 'Sunday-school pupil (or teacher)'.[19]

Some of these words were later reinstated (e.g. посол, посольство, министр, министерство) and some continued to have referents in other countries. Thus the word царь continued to be used to refer to the king of Bulgaria, полицейский to refer to foreign police, губернатор to governors of American states, etc.[20]

The process opposite to the development of historicisms was the revival of certain words that, until the revolutionary period, existed as historicisms themselves. During the early years after the 1917 Revolution, one of the most prominent changes in this sphere concerned the revival of names associated with the French Revolution of 1789 and the Paris Commune of 1871 (Altajskaja 1960: 18), e.g. террор 'terror', (революционный) трибунал '(revolutionary) tribunal', комитет 'committee', комиссар 'commissar' and its derivatives (see also Seliščev 1928: 157). Changes in the use of the latter word in the twentieth century are particularly instructive.

The words министр 'minister' and министерство 'ministry', which had been used both by the Provisional Government in early 1917 and in tsarist times, were abolished as a planned measure to break with the past. The decision was taken at a meeting of the Central Committee in the Smol´nyj Institute during the night of 24–5 October 1917, while the outcome of the Revolution was still uncertain. According to Miljutin (who made notes of the discussion) the word министр 'smelt of bureaucratic stuffiness' and the question of replacing it was discussed. Trockij proposed народный комиссар 'people's commissar', which pleased Lenin and was approved by all. The proposal that the new government should be called Совет народных комиссаров 'Council of People's Commissars' came from Kamenev, and it was with that name that it was formed on 26 October (Miljutin 1918). The ministries were called народные комиссариаты, which in accordance with the current trend soon became наркоматы. Народный комиссар became нарком and Совет народных комиссаров became Совнарком (also abbreviated CHK). The titles of the individual commissars and commissariats were also made into stump-compounds: Наркомпрос (Народный

[19] Cf. Karcevskij (1923: 60). The new воскресник 'Sunday of voluntary work without pay' (see p. 200) is too remote in meaning for this to be regarded as semantic change.

[20] The presence of historicisms in the modern Russian vocabulary is evidenced by the fact that many of them were vigorously revived in the late 1980s and early 1990s: many secondary schools assumed the name гимназия or лицей, the emergence of Russian Royalists brought back the word наследный, etc.

комиссар(иат) просвещения, Народный комиссар(иат) по просвещению) 'People's Commissar(iat) of Education', Наркомзем (Народный комиссар(иат) земледелия) 'People's Commissar(iat) of Agriculture', Наркомвнудел (Народный комиссар(иат) внутренних дел) 'People's Commissar(iat) of Internal Affairs', which came to be better known as НКВД, etc. The compounds all refer to either the commissar in question or his commissariat. Other types of abbreviation were also used. The words комиссар and комиссариат were not new. Not only had they been used in the eighteenth and nineteenth centuries, but комиссар was also used under the Provisional Government. Subsequently, after nearly 30 years of being applied only to ministers and ministries of other countries, министр and министерство were reintroduced by the Soviet government (1946), while нарком and Наркомат passed into history.

(vii) *Archaisms*

To be distinguished from historicisms are true archaisms, i.e. words which virtually have ceased to be used—even to refer to past events. They include: дантист 'dentist' (now зубной врач), лавка and лабаз 'shop' (now магазин), нервический 'nervous' (now нервный), and the two demonstratives сей and оный characteristic of chancellery language before 1917 (Jakobson 1921: 9). However, the vocabulary always seems to acquire new words faster than it discards old ones, and the number of words which have become truly obsolete since 1917 is small. Curiously enough, they include a fair proportion of words created in the 1920s and 1930s, e.g. желдорога (железная дорога) 'railway', лимитрофы 'independent states formerly part of the Russian Empire',[21] правозаступник 'lawyer' (see p. 200), дормезный 'outdated', викжелить 'to manœuvre, in politics', лакированный коммунист 'insincere communist' (Granovskaja 1983: 57), редиска 'anti-Bolshevik who pretends to sympathize with the communist cause' (based on the colour metaphor: white inside, red outside).[22] The latter word was brought back into popular, though colloquial, use in the early 1970s, with the appearance of the film *Бумбараш*; it subsequently shifted in meaning to 'rascal'.

---

[21] Cf. the recent coinage ближнее зарубежье 'near abroad' for the former non-Russian Soviet republics that became independent after the break-up of the Soviet Union in 1991.

[22] Cf. an interesting parallel in American English slang, where *oreo*, the trade name for a chocolate cookie with a vanilla cream filling, is a pejorative name for a black person who is part of the predominantly white establishment (Barnhart *et al.* 1990: 362).

In some cases it is only a certain meaning that has become obsolete, e.g. возразить, formerly 'reply', now only 'object' (Kalinin 1971: 106), покойный, formerly 'quiet' (replaced in this meaning by спокойный), now only 'deceased', американец, formerly 'practical, energetic person', now only 'American', маргариновый, formerly 'unnatural, sham', now only 'margarine' (adjective), афишный, formerly 'pretentious, bright', now only 'pertaining to hoardings' (Granovskaja 1983: 57–8).

(viii) *Renaming*

The new political system in the country had its most visible effect on geographical names and ethnic names. The renaming trend did not start immediately after the Revolution but, rather, after the Civil War; the rate of change was greatly accelerated with the renaming of such a major city as Petrograd to Leningrad in 1924. Though the renaming of geographical names is beyond the scope of this book (some examples can be found in Fessenko 1955: 68–77; Veksler 1968; Nikonov 1965), we would like to stop here at the changes undergone by ethnic names in the early years after the Revolution.

Two major factors were responsible for changes in ethnic names: avoiding derogatory names and using self-denominations if available. For example, in the nineteenth and early twentieth centuries, the native population of Turkestan (Central Asia) was often referred to as сарты; while originally this Turkic borrowing from Old Indic meant 'merchant' and was applied to the urban population of Central Asia (Fasmer 1986–7), it gradually acquired pejorative connotations, to such an extent that some authors, erroneously, identify it as 'dog' (Fessenko 1955: 70). The word was abandoned, in the early 1920s, in favour of the ethnic names узбек 'Uzbek' and тюркмен (later туркмен) 'Turkmen'. The word жид 'Yid' was replaced by the neutral еврей 'Jew', and the names хохол '(lit.) tuft of hair' and малоросс 'little Russian', both used to refer to Ukrainians, were officially condemned and replaced by украинец 'Ukrainian'. The Peterburgian чухонец, derogatory name for Finns and Estonians,[23] was replaced by финн and эстонец. The very word инородец '(lit.) alien-born', which had been widely used to refer to national minorities of Russia until 1917, was condemned as chauvinistic; no single word was found to replace it, but gradually the expressions малые народы 'minor peoples' or народы и народности

---

[23] For example, in Puškin's *Медный Всадник* (1833): приют убогого чухонца 'the dwelling of a humble Finn'.

CCCP 'peoples and ethnic groups of the USSR' evolved. The replacement of Russian names by self-denominations brought about the following changes: вотяк became удмурт 'Udmurt', остяк—ханты
'Khanty', черемис—мари 'Mari', ламут—эвен 'Even', etc. Most of
the replacement words had existed in Russian prior to the period in
question, but in a very restricted usage.

Lexical change, 1928–1938

During the First Five-Year Plan (1928–33) the number of loan-words
increased; they include the following: аттракцион (1935) 'show, entertainment', комбайн (1933) 'combine', контейнер (1932) 'container',
танкер (1933) 'tanker', траулер (1933) 'trawler', троллейбус (1933)
'trolley-bus', джемпер (1932) 'jumper', автострада (1930s) 'motor-
way', демпинг (1930) 'dumping', коктейль (1933) 'cocktail'. (For
further examples, see Krysin 1968: 85–126.) It is worthy of note that by
the late 1920s English had become the predominant source of borrowings.

By the middle of the 1930s, with the tightening of Stalin's regime and
related to that alienation from the West, the number of borrowings
decreased and the very attitude to everything foreign became increasingly negative. This attitude was reflected even in the development of
negative connotations of the Russian word заграничный 'foreign,
overseas' (Papernyj 1985: 60–1). The increasing control of the state
over many aspects of everyday life, including censorship and language
planning, was also an effective tool in monitoring the number of new
borrowings in the press and literature. In 1926 the Soviet state started
monitoring population migrations within the country, the policy which
was concluded by 1932 with the introduction of internal passports and
residency registration (прописка). These measures helped control the
mass migrations of the early post-Revolutionary period and certainly
had their effect on the slower accumulation of new vocabulary.

At the same time, of course, the old word-formation processes were
adding to the vocabulary, producing such innovations as the above-
mentioned прописка and also: авоська 'mesh shopping bag',[24]
встречный (план) 'counter-plan', глубинка 'remote point', грузовик
'lorry', вертолет 'helicopter', коллективизация 'collectivization',

---

[24] From авось 'perhaps': people carried this light small bag in the hope they might find
something to buy.

раскулачивать 'dekulakize', стахановец 'Stakhanovite',[25] пятилетка 'five-year plan', уравниловка 'wage-levelling'.

The number of new acronyms and stump-compounds was drastically reduced by comparison with the preceding decade. Among those that did arrive on the scene at this time were: MTC (1928) (машинно-тракторная станция) 'machine and tractor station', детсад (1932) (детский сад) 'pre-school, kindergarten', универмаг (*c.*1930) (универсальный магазин) 'department store'. However, given names became a new area of the unprecedented spread of acronyms in the late 1920s–early 1930s. Though the trend started in the early 1920s, with such pioneer names as Тролебузина (from Троцкий, Ленин, Бухарин, Зиновьев), it clearly peaked up in the period described here, with such popular names as Вилен(а) (from В. И. Ленин), Влад(и)лен(а) (from Владимир Ленин), Эрлена (from the name of the first letter—эр—in революция plus Ленин), Стален (from Сталин and Ленин). Some new proper names were also allusions to existing names, for example, Дима (from диалектический материализм 'dialectical materialism') or Гертруда (from герой труда 'Hero of Socialist Labour', the title introduced in 1927) (Papernyj 1985: 150, 97). Related to the tendency of creating acronym proper names was the trend to read the names of political leaders backwards; the most popular of such anagrams became the female name Нинель (from Ленин).[26]

With the new administrative division of the country, a few more pre-Revolutionary words lost currency: волость '*volost´* (small rural district)', уезд '*uezd* (district)', губерния '*gubernija* (province)'.

The picture of lexical change at this time begins to be complicated by the revival of some words which had been deliberately abandoned in 1917. They include certain items from the old, English-based military terminology, such as лейтенант 'lieutenant', майор 'major', полковник 'colonel', интендант 'commissary'.

Lexical change, 1938–1945

In the period from the beginning of the Third Five-Year Plan (1938) to the end of the Second World War (1945) the most easily distinguished group of lexical innovations is composed of words connected with the

---

[25] From the last name of the person who started the trend of working with extra productivity (Staxanov).

[26] A number of people born in the late 1920s and in the 1930s, later, in the 1960s, had their names changed away from such 'politicisms'; for example, Идея 'idea' was changed to the more conventional Ида, Владлен to Владислав, etc.

War. The majority of them were very specifically connected with military matters and short-lived. They include a number of German loan-words, such as: блицкриг 'blitzkrieg' and полицай 'member of the local population (in occupied areas) serving in the Nazi police'. In general, the attitude towards German loan-words during this period was understandably negative, and the tendency was to use German words related to the War if they had negative connotations, as the words above.

Probably the only German loan-word from this period to acquire a general meaning and remain in use after the War is ас 'ace' (Ger. *As*), which first referred to German pilots but later to Soviet aces, too. Eventually, it came to be applied to ace performers of other kinds (Kožin 1961: 196–7; Krysin 1968: 127). The English loan-word бульдозер (early 1940s) 'bulldozer' has also survived from the War period.

The outstanding characteristic of the War years 1941–5 is the drop in the rate of lexical borrowing by comparison with the preceding period (Krysin 1968: 126), which had seen the appearance of a fair number of loan-words, including the following: диверсант (1939) 'saboteur', велюр (1940) 'velour', грейпфрут (1939) 'grapefruit', гангстер (1941) 'gangster', телетайп (1940) 'teletype', роллер (1939) 'scooter', призёр (1939) 'prize-winner', перманент (1939) 'permanent wave', газовать (1939) 'accelerate' (*prostorečno*).

The tendency to avoid German loan-words during the War was compounded by the severe censorship of information pertaining to the War; in particular, words denoting military defeats and set-backs were carefully avoided. A dramatic example of such avoidance is the word котел '(lit.) cauldron' which during the Second World War developed the meaning 'encirclement'. The use of the word in this figurative meaning was clearly a calque of the German *Kessel* 'cauldron; encirclement'. While the word окружение 'encirclement' and its derivatives were widely used in the spoken language, military dispatches and accounts of the Second World War consistently used the more opaque котел.

Native formations relating to the War include катюша 'Katjuša rocket-projector', ГКО (Государственный комитет обороны) 'State Defence Committee', дзот (дерево-земляная огневая точка) 'log pill-box', дот (долговременная огневая точка) 'pill-box', СМЕРШ (Смерть шпионам) 'Military Counter-Intelligence (lit.: Death to Spies)', ОСНАЗ ((войска) особого назначения) 'special purpose formations'.

While the reluctance to borrow foreign words could be explained by a greater awareness of national pride during the War, it seems, in fact, that not only borrowing but lexical innovation of all kinds was restricted during the War. Apart from the single word гангстер there appear to be few innovations dating from 1941–5 except those motivated by the military events. An interesting innovation of the period is the semantic extension of the word броня 'armour; shell'; during the War years, the word acquired the meaning 'warrant securing the retention (e.g. of residence)'.[27] The meaning was retained after the War and Ožegov (1972) already lists this word as a homonym to броня in the meaning 'shell, armour'. The derived verb бронировать 'to secure the retention, possession of smth.' also followed; it soon acquired the related meaning 'to reserve', in which it has been used since the War.

The negative attitude to borrowings was related to another tendency that became apparent during the War and continued into the next period, viz. the revival of certain archaisms. Thus, the word Россия and its derivatives, which were avoided as chauvinistic in the earlier decades of Soviet society, returned as the name of the country, even more widespread than СССР (Fessenko 1955: 115–18). Even the more archaic Русь was revived; the Soviet national anthem (written by S. Mixalkov and R. Èl´-Registan), which in 1944 replaced the 'Internationale', included the following lines:

> Союз нерушимый республик свободных
> Сплотила навеки великая Русь . . .

Great Russia has brought together an unbreakable union of free republics . . .

There were also a number of more neutral revivals, viz. посол 'ambassador', посольство 'embassy', гвардия 'guards', офицер 'officer', and names of military ranks (see below).

The increased number of archaisms, some of which were actual Church Slavonicisms or resembled those, led to suggestions that the language was subject to a renewed influence of Church Slavonic and Old Russian elements (Ožegov 1951: 32; 1953). However, this was a relatively superficial phenomenon, limited to certain functional styles (press, poetry). The orientation of these styles towards archaic vocabulary can be explained by the need for greater differentiation between the elevated and lower styles. Apart from a small number of markedly archaic words, many of which soon fell out of use, this trend hardly had any long-lasting effect on the development of the language.

---

[27] The colloquial бронь, viewed as *prostorečno* by the normative handbooks, has been widely used since then.

Lexical change, 1946–1955

The reluctance to borrow foreign words was even stronger after the War, in the late 1940s and early 1950s. These were the years of the Struggle against Cosmopolitanism, when efforts were made to restrain borrowing and to 'purify' the language by rejecting existing loan-words. When Ožegov's one-volume dictionary *Словарь русского языка* made its first appearance in 1949, it was condemned for including such foreign words as аббревиатура 'abbreviation', бекар 'natural (music)', диакритический 'diacritic', диатонический 'diatonic', лозунг 'slogan' (Rodionov 1950). Even a number of popular names of foods were changed: французские булки 'French rolls' were renamed городские булки 'town rolls', the sweets called американский орех 'American (Brazil) nuts' became южный орех 'southern nuts', брауншвейгская колбаса 'Braunschweig wurst' was renamed московская колбаса 'Moscow wurst', the generic name цукаты 'candied fruit' was abandoned in favour of киевская смесь 'Kiev assortment'. In the same sweep of change, the name of the Café «Норд» in Leningrad was changed to «Север».

Because of the Cold War, this period differed from the earlier periods discussed above in the increasing hostility towards the United States and Western Europe, which resulted in the rise of negative attitudes towards English borrowings. It was proposed that бульдозер and the names of certain other mechanical implements be replaced, though the replacement words sometimes retained borrowed affixes (e.g. автоструг instead of автогрейдер 'autograder'). A number of sports terms of English origin actually were changed: половина игры replaced тайм 'half', вратарь replaced голкипер 'goalkeeper',[28] угловой (удар) replaced корнер 'corner', полузащитник replaced хавбек 'half-back', вне игры replaced офсайд 'off-side' (Krysin 1968: 141). All these words, with the exception of половина игры, actually replaced the earlier loan-words and have remained in active use until the present time. The basket-ball terms фол and фолить (Eng. *foul*) were abandoned but found their way back into the language, being first recorded in the early 1970s (Kotelova 1984).

Despite all efforts, however, a few new borrowings did appear: аллергия (1949) 'allergy', адаптер/адаптор (1954) 'gramophone pick-up', драндулет (1949) 'jalopy', бойлер (1950) 'boiler', гандбол

---

[28] Вратарь with this meaning had, however, existed since 1908 (Faktorovič 1966), though it had not previously succeeded in replacing the English loan-word.

(1954) 'handball', дзюдо (1954) 'judo', кросс (1949) 'cross-country', офис (1949) 'office', робот (1948) 'robot'; the latter word, invented by the Czech writer Karel Čapek, was borrowed indirectly, from English.

Neologisms arising from internal word-formation processes in this decade include: болельщицкий (1954) (from the earlier болельщик 'fan'), витаминизировать (1951) 'vitaminize', стиляга 'teddy-boy' (Kostomarov 1959*a*).

Lexical change, 1956–1969

The relaxation in relations with the outside world that came with Stalin's death in 1953 did not have much immediate effect on the vocabulary. By the late 1950s, tourism was made possible, cultural and scientific contacts with other countries were established or re-established, and knowledge of their way of life grew. An increase in the rate of borrowing foreign words, however, does not become noticeable until the 1960s. The following borrowings all date from the late 1950s: акваланг (late 1950s) 'aqua-lung', геофизик (1956) 'geophysicist', круиз (1957) 'cruise', шорты (1959) 'shorts', колготки (early 1960s) 'tights' (from Czech *punčoškové kalhoty*);[29] the latter word underwent subsequent back-formation to колготы. The rate of borrowing increased in the 1960s and the following appeared: аутсайдер (1963) 'outsider', бадминтон (1963) 'badminton', бармен (1960) 'bartender', бикини (1964) 'bikini', битник (1964) 'beatnik', дизайнер (1966) 'designer', компьютер (1966) 'computer', лазер (1958) 'laser', секс (1963) 'sex', твист (1961) 'twist', хула-хуп (1964) 'hula-hoop', хобби (1964) 'hobby'. The word (не)коммуникабельность '(lack of) communication', adopted in the late 1960s (Zemskaja 1992: 13–15), boosted the popularity of the borrowed suffix -абель- (from -*able*), which started being added, though mostly in the spoken language, to Russian roots, cf. читабельный 'readable', смотребельный 'pleasant to see'. The Chinese Cultural Revolution of the 1960s, which received wide (and negative) coverage in the Soviet press, brought at least two new words into Russian, дацзыбао '(wall) slogans' and хунвейбин 'Red Guard' (Borunova *et al.* 1983).[30]

The treatment of the phonetic shape of loan-words also underwent change in this period. The nineteenth and the early twentieth centuries

[29] See Kalakuckaja (1966: 213–15).
[30] These words, however, are not acknowledged in Kotelova and Sorokin (1971) or in Kotelova (1984), probably for extra-linguistic reasons.

were characterized by the tendency to transliterate the borrowed word (cf. лаун-теннис above); in the 1920s–early 1950s the adaptation of loan-words shifted towards transcription (cf. гандбол above), and since the late 1950s practical transcription has become increasingly popular (see also Superanskaja 1962; Dulewiczowa 1981; Kalakuckaja 1984: 6).[31]

The warming of political relations with foreign countries, symbolized most clearly by the 1957 Moscow International Festival of Youth and Students, was paralleled by the greater political freedom inside the Soviet Union. In particular, this was reflected in the new surge of population mobility, unknown in the 1930s and in the post-war period; the late 1950s and early 1960s are often characterized as the period of the 'tourist culture' (Papernyj 1985: 146). All these changes, both foreign and domestic, contributed to the rise of new words and to the semantics of such new formations. From its own resources Russian produced such words as: анонимщик (1959) 'writer of anonymous letter', бескомпромиссность (1957) 'quality of being uncompromising', верхолаз (1957) 'steeplejack', скалолаз (1950s) 'rock climber', целинник (1950s) 'worker on the virgin lands (целина)'.

Lexical developments in the post-war years are well documented (Kotelova and Sorokin 1971; Bragina 1973; Kolomijec´ 1973; Kotelova 1973; Corten 1993), and it is clear that growth in the 1960s exceeded that of the 1940s and 1950s. Interestingly, some of the borrowings, primarily those from English, that became frequent in the 1960s, were actually the revived earlier borrowings of the 1920s, for example, дансинг 'dance hall', джаз 'jazz', шлагер/шлягер 'hit-song, popular song', скетч 'sketch', чарльстон 'charleston'.

The launching of the first sputnik in 1957 not only gave a new meaning to the word спутник (formerly only 'companion' or 'satellite') but initiated a whole new terminology (Bragina 1973: 9–83), including a number of verbs formed by analogy with the earlier приземлиться 'to land': прилуниться 'land on the Moon', приводниться 'land on water', примарситься 'land on Mars'. However, internal processes also produced several hundred new terrestrial words in the 1960s, including the following: блинная (1964) 'pancake bar', водолазка (1970) 'polo-necked sweater', грудник (1966) 'breastfed baby',

[31] To illustrate the difference between abstract transcription and practical transcription, the English 'h' is rendered as г in the former (cf. гандбол from *handball*) and as х in the latter (cf. холдинг-центр 'a kind of stock exchange', from *holdings* 'stocks'); similarly, O.Henry's name is О'Генри in Russian, while Aldous Huxley's surname is rendered as Хаксли.

общепит (1963) (acronym of общественное питание) 'public feeding organization', окномойка (1966) 'window-cleaning machine', показуха (1960) 'bluff, show-off', фарцовка (1965) 'illegal dealings in goods or currency bought from foreigners'.

Objections to the use of foreign words continued to be made occasionally even after the Struggle Against Cosmopolitanism had passed into history. The use of найлоны 'nylon stockings', то(у)ст 'toast', кар 'car', and the diminutive шортики 'shorts', in the speech of the (then) younger generation, and of оранжад 'orangeade', шорты 'shorts', and тренинг 'training' by translators was condemned by Kostomarov (1959*b*), but шорты and тост, as well as the related word тостер 'toaster', are now widely accepted. A reader's letter to *RR* (1972, 1: 156–7) complained about the loan-words хобби 'hobby' and сервис 'service', but no-one, apparently, has taken any notice. Lexical purism has since ceased to be an issue of any significance and apparently ceased to play a part in the Soviet language planning of the latest period.

Lexical change, 1970–1985

This period is also well documented (Kotelova 1983; 1984; 1987; Kulinič 1990; Zemskaja 1992; Corten 1993). The gap between the literary language and the spoken varieties, including educated slang (students' slang, professional jargons), became particularly apparent, partly because more colloquial words were admitted into works of literature and into the press; cf. a dictionary of vocabulary not listed in normative dictionaries (Milejkovskaja *et al.* 1988; 1990). It is unclear, though, whether the gap between the literary standard and the spoken language actually widened in this period or merely the awareness of the difference between the two variants grew. As in the discussion of the earlier periods, we will concentrate primarily on the standard language.

The number of borrowings, most of them from English, seems to decrease in this period, compared to the previous decade. Several reasons, not entirely unrelated, are responsible for such a decline. On the one hand, the language was saturated with a large number of recent loan-words, adopted in the late 1950s and in the 1960s, and the perception of loan-words was becoming more negative; the early 1970s witnessed a number of discussions in the press concerning the large number of loan-words in the language, particularly in specialized fields. For example, *Литературная газета* published a number of articles where loan-words were perceived as a negative phenomenon (N. T. Fedorenko. «Не перевести ли на русский?», 30 January 1974; N. Ignat´eva. «Наука для немногих», 2 February 1974; A. Petrova. «Не назвать ли кошку кошкой?», 13 March 1974). This campaign against loan-words can be compared with the struggle against acronyms and stump-compounds in the 1920s–early 1930s, which certainly contributed to the decrease in their number. On the other hand, the political climate of the 1970s–early 1980s was colder than at the time of Xruščev's 'Thaw' (Оттепель); this produced a harsher attitude towards foreign borrowings, including those already in the language. Accordingly, the excessive use of foreign words in the 1970s becomes a sign of dissent, for example, in student and hippie slang (Borisova-Lukašanec 1983; Rožanskij 1992).

New borrowings of this period include: биг-бит (1973) 'big beat', бидонвиль (1973) 'township' (Fr. *bidonville*), биеннале (early 1970s) 'biennial exhibition' (Ital. *biennale*), биотехнология (1972) 'bio-technology', икебана (late 1960s–early 1970s) 'flower arrangement' (Jap. *ikebana*), импичмент (1974) 'impeachment',[32] истеблишмент (early 1970s) 'establishment', карате (каратэ) (1967–70) 'karate', каскадер (1973) 'stunt-man' (Fr. *cascadeur*), консенсус (1973) 'con-sensus' (Lat. *consensus*, probably via Eng.), менеджмент (mid-1970s) 'management', нонконформизм (early 1970s) 'non-conformism', панк (1978) 'punk', свинг (1971) 'swing', фифти-фифти 'com-promise, tie', фломастер (1969–70) 'felt pen' (Eng. *flowmaster*). The sources of borrowings reflect the unending interest in the English-speaking countries as well as the discovery of Japan, through the eyes of several Soviet journalists and writers. Many new borrowings were deter-mined by the development of computer and video technology, and some of the words remained unstable, for example, чип and чипс (early 1980s) 'computer chip'. Due to rapid changes in the technological sphere, some borrowings appeared to be short-lived: for example, ком(м)одор (from the brand name *Commodore*) was widely used as the generic name for personal computers in the early 1980s but did not survive the competition with the earlier loan-word компьютер and the internal formation персоналка (from Eng. *personal computer*) (the latter has remained colloquial).

A number of borrowings entered the language equipped by Russian affixes, e.g. батник (1978) 'dress-shirt' (Eng. *button* and Russian suffix -ник), персоналка. Earlier borrowings acquired new meanings, which reflected the polysemy of the respective word in the source language, e.g. абсурд 'absurd' develops the meaning 'theatre of the absurd', банк

---

[32] Brought into the language by the press coverage of Watergate.

'financial bank' acquires the new meaning 'database'. Words of native origin were also actively involved in this process of semantic extension, e.g. the earlier acronym ширпотреб (from товары широкого потребления) 'mass production' acquired the negative meaning 'cheaply made'; наставник 'educator' added the new meaning 'worker supervising trainees'.

The low number of borrowings was compensated, in part, by the growing number of calques, both individual words and word combinations, e.g. заднескамеечник 'back-bencher', факторы риска 'risk factors', мозговая атака 'brainstorm', банк данных 'data bank', база данных 'data base'. A new tendency in this period consisted in translating the components of foreign acronyms and then creating new acronyms on this basis, for example, the above-mentioned НЛО (неопознанный летающий объект) 'UFO', СПИД (синдром приобретенного иммунного дефицита) 'AIDS' (early 1980s).

In general, the increasing productivity of foreign affixes, such as -дром, -тека, -визор, -трон, -мобиль, -абель-, which characterized the 1960s (Panov 1968; 1971*b*), was no less typical of this period. However, unlike the preceding decade, when words formed with these suffixes were mostly confined to specialized technological vocabulary, in the 1970s and 1980s they enter other styles, cf. веломобиль (late 1970s) 'pedal car', собакодром (1978) 'dog track'. The occurrence of the foreign affixes with native Russian words indicates that these affixes were becoming increasingly nativized.

Two of the most popular nominal affixes of the period are -ист and -изм. Both suffixes were borrowed into Russian in the eighteenth century and early on could occur with Russian stems (Jiraček 1971). In the earlier periods of the twentieth century, the suffix -ист was actively used, producing such words as чекист 'Cheka official', but in the 1970s and 1980s it no longer occurs with acronyms (Zemskaja 1992: 107). One of the notable new formations with -изм is the word вещизм (1970) 'materialistic outlook, consumerism, philistinism', formed by analogy with such words as алкоголизм 'alcoholism', идиотизм 'idiocy' (Volkov and Sen'ko 1983: 56; Zemskaja 1992: 22).

Affixation in general continued to play an important role in the formation of new words.[33] The word разрядка, mentioned above, became frequent in the political language of the 1970s as the name of détente (also разрядка международной напряженности 'relaxation of inter-

---

[33] A very good review of the new affixed words is given in Zemskaja (1992: 92–155); see also Glovinskaja (1975) on the suffix -ник.

national tension').The formation of new verbs, many of which pertain to technology, is based mainly on prefixation (Zemskaja 1992: 83–5, 205), e.g. перепрописать 'change residency registration', размонтировать 'dismount', подселять (late 1960s or early 1970s) 'lodge someone in a vacant room of another's residence'. (See also Bojarkina 1983.)

New Russian acronyms developed, many of them also based on foreign words or morphemes borrowed much earlier. Thus, in the early 1970s, the word универсам (универсальный магазин самооб-служивания) 'supermarket' was created, which quickly gained popularity by analogy with the earlier compound универмаг 'department store'.

A large group of new words in this period is represented by a combination of a truncated word and a full word, for example, видео-техника 'video technology', луноход 'lunar explorer', стереомузыка 'stereo music', сельхозоборот 'agricultural output', спортподготовка 'athletic fitness' (Zemskaja 1992: 52–60; Jachnow 1980; Kotelova 1984). In addition, continuing the trend that became apparent in the preceding decade, numerous new words were formed by compounding two words, often hyphenated in writing, e.g. смотр-конкурс 'pageant', театр-студия 'theatrical studio', ясли-сад 'day-care and pre-school centre'.

New words also appear due to substantivization of adjectives, for example, командировочный 'person on a business trip' and командировочные 'per diem allowance', первичная 'local party group', скорая 'ambulance'. Substantivized words can undergo further affixation, cf. первичная and первичка.

Areas of Lexical Change

From our broad chronological survey of lexical change we now turn to change in particular thematic areas. The links between social and lexical change are better demonstrated by dealing with particular areas in detail, concentrating the material by taking a higher proportion of all the words under each thematic heading.

(i) Politics and public administration

It was especially in the public and political spheres that deliberate steps were taken to replace old words by new ones. New institutions which might be externally similar to old ones, yet, being based on a new philosophy, were internally different from their predecessors, needed new names to symbolize their new content.

The early attempts following the February Revolution to set up a new organization which would maintain public order and protect life and property against crime involved the abolition of many words associated with the old police system: полиция 'police', полицейский 'policeman', городовой 'policeman', полиц(ей)мейстер 'police chief', пристав 'police officer', жандарм 'gendarme', жандармерия 'gendarmerie', участок 'police station'. (The last of these, участок, survives with other meanings.) To signify that the new organization was different from the tsarist police (despite external similarities) it was given the new name милиция 'militia', and its members the new name милиционер 'militiaman'. The fact that some people drew an analogy between the new and the old organizations is shown by the hybrid form милицейский (by analogy with полицейский), which Mazon heard in use in 1918–19 (1920: 29; also Jakobson 1921: 8). On the other hand, in the countryside the tsarist police system was little known, and it is, therefore, not surprising that the word милиция, though not properly understood,[34] was not associated with the tsarist police system. The abolition of стряпчий 'solicitor' and адвокат 'lawyer, barrister' was similarly motivated; only the latter was subsequently reinstated (1922).

Another deliberate break with the terminology of the old regime was the replacement in 1918 of посол 'ambassador' and посольство 'embassy' by the new compounds полпред (полномочный представитель) and полпредство (полномочное представительство). The new words served to distinguish Soviet diplomatic representation from that of all other states (which continued to be referred to by the old words), but they also resulted in technical difficulties as to protocol, and eventually, for the sake of convenience in international relations, посол and посольство were reintroduced by edicts dated 1941 and 1943 (Altajskaja 1960: 18). Полпред has survived, however, not in its original strictly terminological meaning, but with the general sense of 'representative', as shown in the following example of its use: Безымянный комбат стал символом, полпредом наших славных

---

[34] In 1925, the following definition was recorded in the Jaroslavl′ *gubernija*: мелицея, милицея—1) это . . . вроде красногвардейцев, только они не на войне, а в городе за порядком следят; 2) это туда заявление подают, когда о чем хлопочут (Seliščev 1928: 215) 'militia—1) this is . . . like the Red Guard but they enforce order in the town, not during the war; 2) this is where applications are submitted'.

командиров . . . (*Неделя*, 43, 21–7 October 1974: 6) 'The nameless battalion commander has become a symbol, a representative of our famous commanders . . .'.

The fact that the Party itself changed its name four times had certain repercussions. РСДРП (Российская социал-демократическая рабочая партия) 'Russian Social-Democratic Workers Party' was changed to РКП(б) (Российская Коммунистическая партия (большевиков)) 'Russian Communist Party (of Bolsheviks)' at the Seventh Party Congress in March 1918, and soon afterwards the form Компартия appeared, later being applied to foreign communist parties, too. Thus the word большевик, which had originated following the Second Congress of the RSDRP in London in 1903, was adopted as part of the title. A further change was made in 1925 at the Fourteenth Congress to ВКП(б) (Всесоюзная Коммунистическая партия (большевиков)) 'All-Union Communist Party (Bolshevik)' to take account of the fact that it was now the party of the Soviet Union, the USSR having come into being in December 1922, with the title Союз Советских Социалистических Республик 'Union of Soviet Socialist Republics', abbreviated as СССР. In 1952 the Nineteenth Congress changed it yet again, this time to Коммунистическая партия Советского Союза 'Communist Party of the Soviet Union', abbreviated as КПСС—the name which it retained till its last day. This latest alteration removed the word большевик and consequently a member came to be called коммунист, -ка 'communist', instead of большевик, -чка 'Bolshevik'. According to Ožegov (1972) коммунист, -ка now has only one meaning, viz. 'member of the Communist Party'. Meanwhile, большевик, -чка changed its meaning to refer to members of the Party before 1952 or, in a general way, to supporters of Bolshevism (Altajskaja 1960: 15–16). Clearly, changes that took place in the Soviet Union in the late 1980s and early 1990s should affect the meaning of the word коммунист, -ка.

The naming of new organs of government, administration of justice, and the Party at all levels has involved the creation of many new words, the majority of which are stump-compounds, such as:

(i) Party organs: партком (партийный комитет) 'Party committee', райком (районнный комитет) 'district committee', горком (городской комитет) 'town committee', etc.

(ii) Organs of justice: нарсуд (народный суд) 'people's court', облсуд (областной суд) '*oblast'* court', etc.

(iii) Government organs: сельсовет (сельский совет) 'village council', райисполком (районный исполнительный комитет) 'district executive committee' (known in the 1930s as РИК), горсовет (городской совет) 'town council', etc.

Terms relating to the territorial division of the USSR into administrative districts were affected by innovations made in the 1920s and completed with the division into *rajony* (районирование) of 1929–30. Thus the words волость, уезд, губерния disappeared, except in reference to the past, giving way to сельсовет (both a region and a government body), район, область, край. (The last three are old words with a new terminological meaning.) The office of губернатор 'governor' was abolished in 1917. The only function of this word nowadays is to refer to officials in other countries and in pre-Revolutionary Russia.

Owing to political and administrative changes since 1917 several words introduced in the early Soviet period have since fallen out of use. Some we have mentioned already; others are: комъячейка 'communist cell', батрачком 'farm labourers' committee', крестком 'peasants' committee', ревком 'revolutionary committee', реввоенсовет 'revolutionary military council'. The word совнархоз 'national economy council'—which Lenin said foreigners took to be a place-name and checked it in their railway guides (Rybnikova 1925: 115)—first came into existence in 1917. It has subsequently had an eventful career, for совнархозы were later abolished, reintroduced in 1957, and later abolished again (Meščerskij 1967a: 19).

A number of Soviet political terms later expanded their meaning and were applied equally to Soviet or foreign institutions. This is so, for example, in the case of исполком, компартия, комсомол.

The РКСМ (Российский Коммунистический Союз Молодежи) 'Russian Communist Union of Youth', founded in 1918, was known as the комсомол 'Komsomol' (Коммунистический Союз Молодежи 'Communist Union of Youth'), a title which was not affected by subsequent changes in the official name, first to РЛКСМ (Российский Ленинский Коммунистический Союз Молодежи) 'Russian Leninist Communist Union of Youth' in 1924 and then to ВЛКСМ (Всесоюзный Ленинский Коммунистический Союз Молодежи) 'All-Union Leninist Communist Union of Youth' in 1926 (Altajskaja 1960: 15). Both комсомол and its derivatives комсомольский, комсомолец, -ка (but not комсомолия, which was exclusively Soviet) were applied to communist youth organizations in other countries. For example:

Одной из главных задач, стоящих сейчас перед КПВ,[35] Дж. Голлан назвал работу по увеличению численности рядов партии и комсомола (*Правда*, 13 November 1974)

As one of the many tasks now facing the Communist Party of Great Britain, J. Gollan named the job of increasing the membership of the Party and the Komsomol.

The Soviet word исполком is also employed in this way:

Здесь состоялось заседание национального исполкома лейбористской партии, где была принята резолюция, критикующая проведение совместных маневров британского и южноафриканского флотов . . . (*Правда,* 4 November 1974)

A meeting of the national executive committee of the Labour Party has been held here, at which a resolution was passed criticizing the holding of joint manœuvres by the British and South African fleets . . .

(ii) Agriculture

The October Revolution took place in a predominantly agricultural country, and agricultural reorganization and modernization were from the beginning matters of prime importance. The Land Decree passed on 26 October 1917 proclaimed the abolition of private ownership of land, but it was only with the beginning of the First Five-Year Plan (1928) that collectivization was introduced. The word коллективизация, which still has only the specialized meaning 'collectivization of agriculture', came into existence a few years earlier, when the question first came under discussion (Seliščev 1928: 109). It was accompanied by колхоз 'collective farm' (1925), whereas совхоз 'state farm' is older, dating back to at least 1921.

The early Soviet years saw the specialization of бедняк 'poor peasant' and its collective correlate беднота 'poor peasantry', referring to a specific socio-economic category. The words provided the source of others, including комбед 'committee of poor peasants', the name given to committees organized throughout the RSFSR during 1918 to strengthen Soviet power in the villages (Rybnikova 1925: 114). Collectivization meant dispossessing the kulaks of land and equipment, a process which brought into being the verb раскулачивать (1929) 'dekulakize' (Ovsjannikov 1933: 222). Apart from the бедняк and

---

[35] Коммунистическая партия Великобритании 'Communist Party of Great Britain'.

кулак, the new social category of 'middle peasant', neither exploiting nor exploited, came under discussion, producing the new word середняк (1921) and its derivatives. To refer to those peasants who continued, as long as possible, to work alone without joining an agricultural commune the new noun единоличник 'individual farmer' (early 1920s) was derived from единоличный 'individual' (Šanskij 1963–82). In the late 1920s подкулачник came into use, meaning a middle or poor peasant who supported kulaks (Ovsjannikov 1933: 196). Since collectivization кулак, бедняк, середняк, раскулачивать have become historicisms. Also, батрак 'farm labourer', помещик 'landowner', and имение 'estate' had no referents in Soviet Russia, but they are still used with reference to other countries.

Essential to collectivization was mechanization, and state-owned machine and tractor stations serving the collective farms were set up throughout the country during the First and Second Five-Year Plans. This was the origin of the well-known abbreviation MTC 'machine and tractor station' (1928–58).

The use of machinery transformed Russian agriculture: by 1937 there were 450,000 farm tractors and 121,000 combine harvesters in use. The word трактор 'tractor' arrived round about the time of the Revolution: Šanskij (1963–82) and Kalinin (1971: 112) consider it an innovation of the Soviet era, but it is difficult to be sure. That many of its derivatives originated after 1917 is beyond dispute, however: тракторист,[36] -ка, тракторизация, тракторизм. The English loan-word комбайн 'combine harvester' arrived in the late 1920s (Krysin 1968: 96) and, similarly, led to a string of derivatives: комбайнер, -ка, комбайновый.

The training of agricultural experts and the application of their skills brought in: агротехник (агрономический техник) 'agrotechnician', агробаза (агрономическая база) 'agricultural station', and other stump-compounds with агро-. Further neologisms connected with agriculture are: сельмаш ((отдел) сельскохозяйственных машин) 'agricultural machinery department', посевкампания (посевная кампания) 'sowing campaign', мичуринец 'Michurinite', трудодень 'working day' (unit by which collective farmers' income was calculated).

---

[36] In his report to the Eighth Party Congress (1919) Lenin (lacking anything better) could only use the word машинист to refer to tractor drivers (Ovsjannikov 1933: 121).

(iii) Industry

Industrialization and urbanization have changed the Russian language not only by changing the social make-up of its users, but also by motivating change in the vocabulary. Modernization, new methods of production, and improved technology have been accompanied by the appearance of new words, many of which are restricted to specialized use. Many others, however, have entered the general vocabulary. In a country where the role of industry was so prominent in the media it is not surprising that the vocabulary of industry was well known. The prestigious role of industry in the 1920s–1930s is probably best illustrated by the fact that proper names Индустрий and Индустрия were popular at that time.

New methods in the organization of labour to increase productivity included the system of work-teams or 'brigades', introduced in the 1920s. The word бригада thus acquired a new meaning, for previously, apart from its military meaning, it had been applicable only to a team of workers running a train. Similarly, бригадир (a military rank in the eighteenth century) acquired a new meaning as 'leader of a work-team', and the derivative бригадничество came into existence to describe the brigade system (Ovsjannikov 1933: 38; Klinskaja 1957: 25), though it later gave way to the phrase бригадная система 'brigade system'. The term was so popular that it became used even in education where, in the 1920s, бригадная система обучения and бригадный метод обучения were introduced.

In 1929 workers of a machine-building factory in Leningrad introduced their own amendments, or counter-plan (встречный план), to the management's production plan, thereby increasing productivity. Counter-plans became a regular part of the industrial scene and the substantivized adjective встречный came into everyday use. Changes in industry in the 1920s also brought in: пятидневка 'five-day week' (replaced in 1932 by шестидневка 'six-day week'), непрерывка 'id.', норма 'norm', нормировка 'establishment of norms', остановка 'work stoppage', планировать 'plan', самотёк 'drift', обезличка 'lack of personal responsibility', диспетчер 'dispatcher'.

Words of common knowledge resulting from improvements in industrial technology include the following: грузовик (contracted from грузовой автомобиль) 'lorry', механизация 'mechanization', моторизация 'motorization', электрификация 'electrification', амортизатор 'shock absorber', автоматизация 'automation'.

(iv) The armed forces

In the armed forces, too, deliberate changes were made in terminology in order to symbolize the break with tsarism. Even the word солдат 'soldier', a long-time German borrowing, was rejected by the Red Army together with nearly all the pre-Revolutionary names of ranks; the rejection of this particular word was reinvigorated during the Second World War, as a manifestation of the opposition to everything German. When the Рабоче-крестьянская Красная Армия 'Workers' and Peasants' Red Army' was founded in 1918 the lowest rank was красноармеец. In the navy матрос 'seaman' was replaced by краснофлотец.

Ranks, as such, were abolished and replaced by the names of appointments. The word офицер 'officer' became obsolete and was replaced by командир 'commander' or красный командир 'red commander', abbreviated to краском. The names of ranks ефрейтор 'lance-corporal', бомбардир 'bombardier', сержант 'sergeant', прапорщик 'ensign', лейтенант 'lieutenant', поручик 'id.', капитан 'captain', майор 'major', полковник 'colonel', генерал 'general', fell out of use together with чин 'rank' and звание 'id.'.

Appointments in the new army were named as follows: командир отделения 'section commander', помощник командира взвода 'deputy platoon commander', командир взвода 'platoon commander', старшина роты 'company warrant officer', командир роты 'company commander', командир батальона 'battalion commander', командир полка 'regimental commander', командир дивизии 'divisional commander'. They were often abbreviated as комбат, комдив, комбриг, etc.

In 1935 the concept of rank and the word звание were revived, together with the words лейтенант, капитан, майор, полковник. In 1940 сержант and ефрейтор were reintroduced, followed in 1943 by офицер. By 1940, even before the Soviet Union was engaged in the War, the innovatory military rankings such as комбриг (командир бригады) 'brigade-commander', had been completely abandoned in favour of the English-based equivalent rankings, e.g. маршал 'marshal', полковник 'colonel', генерал 'general', etc. (Suvorov 1990: 63). As Stalin's personality cult found its particular reflection in awarding him the highest possible military ranks, the word генералиссимус found its way into the language during the Second World War (prior to that, this rank had been held by Aleksandr Suvorov at the end of the eighteenth century). After the War, in 1946, солдат made its come-back, and прапорщик 'ensign' returned in 1972 (Protčenko 1973: 13). In the navy адмирал (together with контр-адмирал 'rear admiral', etc.) returned in 1940; матрос was reinstated in 1946. The system of political command in the Red Army produced several new words, including политрук 'political instructor' (1919–42) and замполит 'political deputy'. The latter remained in use until the break-up of the Soviet Union.

Since 1917 денщик 'batman' has not been used, though words of similar meaning have had limited functions at times, viz. вестовой, ординарец. During the First World War there were nationalistic attempts to replace the German loan-word фельдшер 'medical assistant' with лекарский помощник (Barannikov 1919: 74). It was as part of the rejection of old discriminatory practices in the medical profession that this change actually took place (Meščerskij 1967a: 6), however, and the Red Army regulations retained ветеринарный фельдшер for veterinary assistants but introduced лекарский помощник to refer to medical personnel (*Устав* . . . 1918: 30–1). The new term was generally abbreviated to лекпом. During the 1940s фельдшер (and the colloquial фельдшерица) was reinstated and replaced лекпом both in the armed forces and in general use.

(v) Language and ideology: military metaphors, collective descriptions

There have been numerous attempts to demonstrate the effect of Soviet ideology on the Russian language, though often the authors simply fail to acknowledge language change which would probably have occurred regardless of the political system (Rževskij 1951; Fessenko 1955). For example, the loss of declension in numerals or the use of stump-compounds and acronyms are signs of growing analyticity and of the expanding language community, and critics of these phenomena find a strange ally in Lenin, who commented on the development of new acronyms by saying that Russian is evolving towards the same type as English (quoted in Gorbačevič 1990: 77). However, there are language areas where the influence of ideology is less disputable (for some discussion, see also Krjučkova 1976; Seriot 1985), and one such area is the use of military metaphors and military lexicon in relation to everyday life.

Indeed, since the 1920s, the political language of the Soviet period routinely used such words and expressions as: авангард 'avant-garde', армия 'corps' (e.g. армия учителей 'the teacher corps'), вахта 'enthu-

siastic work' (e.g. нести трудовую вахту 'to work honourably'),
гвардия 'guard', фронт 'front, site' (e.g. фронт строительства 'the
construction front (i.e. industry)'), торпедировать 'to torpedo' (e.g.
торпедировать переговоры 'torpedo talks (i.e. hinder negotiations)'),
дезертир 'deserter' (e.g. дезертир трудового фронта 'deserter from
the labour front'), борьба за 'fight for' (e.g. ударный фронт в борьбе
за увеличение производства сахарной свеклы 'the forefront in the
fight to increase sugar-beet production' (Bezděk *et al.* 1974: 99)),
буржуазный недобиток 'bourgeois sympathizer', враг народа 'an
enemy of the people', командир производства 'commander of production', огонь критики 'the fire of criticism', etc. One of the most
popular words became мобилизовать 'to mobilize' and мобилизация
'activization' (Zemcov 1985: 226–7), for example, мобилизовать
резервы 'to mobilize resources', мобилизация студенчества 'the use
of students (usu. in harvesting)'. (See also Fessenko 1955: 138.)

The excessive use of such metaphors has been explained by the perception of the opposition between the Soviet Union and the outside
world in military terms: the Soviet regime promoted the idea of world
revolution and of the ongoing struggle between socialism and capitalism
(Zemcov 1985: 13). The interesting fact, however, is that many of the
military words did indeed change their meaning and became partially
desemanticized in the process. In the first post-Soviet years, military
metaphors remained actively used and even new metaphors appeared
(Baranov and Kazakevič 1991: 8–11), which suggests that the adaptation of military metaphors to everyday life is far from complete.

It has been noticed that social conditions and social groups can
influence the choice of certain semantic interpretations of a polysemous
word; other interpretations do not necessarily become obsolete, they can
simply remain 'passive' (Pokrovskij 1959: 53; Krysin 1989: *passim*).
Such rearrangement of meanings occurred in the collective nouns народ
'people' (esp. советский народ 'Soviet people'.), массы 'masses',
трудящиеся 'working people'. The political understanding of народ as
a stable, ideologically pure collective was added to the interpretation of
this word in the early Soviet period; in the pre-Revolutionary language,
народ primarily had the meaning 'crowd, passers-by', still retained in
the colloquial language throughout this century. It is in this latter meaning that the word народ is used in Čukovskij's *Крокодил* (1917):

> А за ним-то народ и поет, и орет . . .
>
> And people behind him are singing and yelling . . .

The poem was criticized by Krupskaja primarily for 'lowering, through the use of linguistic means, the status of народ, which is completely unacceptable in children's literature' (N. K. Krupskaja. О крокодиле Чуковского. *Правда*, 1 February 1928, quoted in Baranov and Kazakevič (1991: 13)).

The excessive use of народ, массы in the official style led to a partial desemantization of these words, hence such tautological word combinations as народные массы 'popular masses, i.e. people'.

The representation of individuals as a collective also had a profound effect on the use of personal pronouns: in the Soviet period, it became increasingly inappropriate to use the first person singular я in a number of styles, and this led to the excessive use of мы, primarily as *pluralis modestiae* (Komtè 1990). (See also Chapter 7.)

Sources of Borrowings

Considering the question of foreign influence in Russian around the time of the Revolution, Mazon concluded that the contribution made by English had been minimal (1920: 17). Not very long afterwards, however, English became the largest single identifiable source of loan-words. At the same time, it must be admitted that there are cases of loan-words with possible models in several different European languages and that sometimes it is not possible to identify the source. The adjective превентивный 'preventive', for example, though described by Krysin (1968: 119) as a French or German borrowing, could well have its source in several languages, including English.

Not in every case are we able by some semantic or formal peculiarity of one of the models to identify it as the true source. Many Soviet borrowings can only be classified as Europeanisms, for example, the recent borrowings консенсус, мини, миди, макси. There is room for argument, for example, in the case of кемпинг, which Krysin (1968: 158) identifies as an English loan-word, though the fact that it means not 'camping' but 'camping site' makes some other language a more likely source, such as French, in which the latter meaning is present. But we are dealing in probabilities only.

Overall, the increasing role of English as the prestigious source of borrowings is evident in the course of the twentieth century. The significance of English has become so great that some recent formations in Russian, even those that use native elements, imitate the shape of

English words, for example, бéстер (1973), the stump-compound formed from the words белуга 'sturgeon' and стерлядь 'sterlet' and denoting the hybrid of these two fish species. The influence of English had an important effect on the accentological treatment of new loan-words. In the course of the nineteenth century and in the early twentieth century, it was common for loan-words to have ultimate stress, regardless of the stress the respective word had in the source language; this practice was due to French influence and was relatively unproblematic as long as most loan-words were actually from French. The diminishing role of French undermined this practice, and, under the influence of English, many new words retained the stress of the source language. As a result, some stress doublets appeared, for example, апартеúд (transliteration, stress as in French) and апáртхайд (practical transcription) 'apartheid'. Shakespeare's name, long known to Russian readers, changed from Вилья́м to Ви́льям and then Уи́льям; Ageenko and Zarva (1984) cite the latter form as standard, characterizing Вилья́м as 'traditional'. The recessive stress tendency even involved some French borrowings; for example, the appearance of the stress variant плáнер 'glider', mentioned in Chapter 2, is part of the same trend.

Internal borrowings

The vocabulary of the standard language has expanded by borrowing not only from other languages, but also from non-standard varieties of Russian itself. This internal process depends on changes in attitude towards non-standard words, which can consequently be accepted first in the colloquial and possibly later in the written standard.

   Some of the words which in the Soviet period have ceased to be non-standard are: балка 'ravine' (Kuznecova 1970), задира 'trouble-maker' (Kuznecova 1971), расческа 'comb' (Balaxonova 1967), фарцовщик 'dealer in goods bought illegally from foreigners' (Skvorcov 1972: 52–3),[37] халтура 'hack-work' (Skvorcov 1972: 53–4), шпаргалка 'crib'. (All these, except балка and расческа, are considered colloquial by Ožegov 1972.)

   Many non-standard words gained wide currency among the young people in the early 1920s. Several reasons were responsible for this spread of non-standard vocabulary, largely from the language of criminals (Polivanov 1931: 154; Seliščev 1928: 80; Fessenko 1955: 77–99): first, many young people considered these 'the language of the

---

[37] The word фарцовка was discussed above, see p. 212.

proletariat' (Seliščev 1928: 80); second, the new regime was clearly exploiting this vocabulary as part of its populist policy (for example, such words commonly appeared in the films of the 1930s); finally, with the devastation that followed the Revolution and the Civil War, a lot of homeless children (беспризорники) found themselves in the street, where the criminal jargon was extremely widespread. It is remarkable, however, that many non-standard words and meanings are still shown in Ožegov (1972) as *prostorečno*, e.g. барахло 'old clothes', буза 'row', липовый 'faked', мура 'nonsense', сволочь 'scum'. There are also several other, more recent words and meanings which Ožegov (1972) records as *prostorečno*, even though they are now sometimes used colloquially by educated speakers: доходяга 'emaciated person', дуриком 'uselessly', загорать 'to hang about', кореш, корешок 'friend', левый 'illegal', левак 'one who earns illegally on the side' (also левачить, левачество), мухлевать 'to fiddle', стукач 'informer', хохма 'joke'. The hypothesis that this is another area of discrepancy between normative recommendation and actual usage (cf. Chapter 1, p. 11) might be tested by a further survey on the lines of the RJaSO project.

Two other words deserve note here because they underwent change opposite to that just described: they were used by the language before the twentieth century and were revived as popular though colloquial words in the 1960s. One of these words, клёвый 'good, useful' (etymologically related to клевать 'peck, bite') was registered in *SAR* (1806–22) and was later attested in central Russian dialects by Dal´ (1880–2). Not acknowledged by twentieth-century dictionaries, it made an amazing come-back in the late 1960s as part of young urban slang and has been frequently used since then. It remains to be seen, though, whether it will become part of the standard vocabulary.

The other word, кейф 'pleasure'—and its derivative кейфовать (variant кейфствовать) 'to enjoy smth., to have a good time'—was borrowed from Arabic (probably via Ottoman Turkish or Persian). These words are cited in *SRJa* (1895–1927), where they are illustrated by several literary examples, including one from Stanjukovič's *Василий Иванович* (1886), where the verb кейфовать is still in quotes, which suggests its relative novelty in the language:

Через несколько минут Василий Иванович уже «кейфовал», беззаботно растянувшись в просторном лонг-шэзе у раскрытого окна ...

A few moments later, Vasilij Ivanovič was already enjoying himself, carelessly stretched out in a spacious deck-chair at the open window ...

By the middle of the twentieth century the word had become obsolete; it is cited as such by Ožegov (1972). However, the word was revived, though in a slightly different phonetic form (кайф, кайфовать), in the late 1960s and has been part of the colloquial language ever since.

Other languages of Russia and the Soviet Union

Although for a long time it was not formally proclaimed as the first or official language of the Soviet Union, Russian occupied a unique position in the USSR, and most users of the non-Russian languages also knew and used Russian. Over the centuries Russian has acquired many loan-words from its immediate neighbours, but in the Soviet period their influence was but slight if compared with that of Western European languages. On the other hand, the influence of Russian on the other languages of the Soviet Union is very strong (see Lewis (1972: 61–6, 293); Kreindler (1985), on the expansion of Russian in the Soviet Union).

The degree of interference is greatest at the local level, where many people daily use both Russian and the local language. In these circumstances loan-words occur not only in spoken Russian but also in local newspapers and books, in both original and translated literature. In the Russian-language press of Central Asia, for example, the following local words were observed in use in the 1930s: курултай 'congress', меджлис 'conference', аксакал 'village headman', раис 'chairman', мудир 'director', мактаб 'school', муалим 'teacher'. The total number of such words recorded by Mirtov (1941) is considerable, but none of them has been adopted in the standard language; this is partially reflected by the fact that a later dictionary of Turkic loan-words in Russian (Šipova 1976) lists mainly older borrowings, attested long before the twentieth century. Even those words from the other languages of the Soviet Union that have become part of standard vocabulary refer for the most part to strictly local, non-Russian phenomena. The Kazakh loan-word акын, for example, borrowed in the 1930s (Šanskij 1963–82), refers to a folk-singer or poet only of Central Asia. The Uzbek loan-word басмач borrowed during the Civil War (Šanskij 1963–82) refers to a member of a counter-revolutionary band in Central Asia at that time. Similarly, the Uzbek or Tajik loan-word дехканин 'peasant, farmer', first registered in 1926 (Šanskij 1963–82), relates only to Central Asia. Another Central Asian loan-word said to have been borrowed in the Soviet period (Meščerskij 1967a: 27) and having strictly local functions is кетмень 'type of hoe'. It should be added, however, that several pre-1917 borrowings which were once extremely exotic and little known have become more widely used in recent years, owing to greater familiarity with the Central Asian ethos resulting from tourism (and travel generally). Russian translations of Central Asian literature have also played a part in this process (Suprun 1963: 155). Among the examples is арык 'irrigation ditch' (first borrowed from the Turkic languages of Central Asia in the nineteenth century). (See also pp. 190, 193 on the semantic changes undergone by words кишлак 'village', чадра 'chador', паранджа 'yashmak; garment including face covering, worn by Moslem women'.)

Several Turkic borrowings gained wide acceptance in colloquial speech but are still viewed with suspicion by the normative dictionaries. For example, the word аксакал mentioned in the preceding paragraph has been used to denote general approval or admiration of someone since the late 1960s. The Turkic borrowing калым 'bride price' in the 1960s acquired the meaning 'bribe, money earned illegally on the side'; in this meaning, it also has derivatives калымить and калымщик, all qualified as *prostorečno* by normative dictionaries (e.g. Ožegov 1972). Another example of that very rare phenomenon, a word borrowed from one of the non-Russian languages since 1917 which has acquired a general (non-local) meaning, is provided by тамада 'master of cere-monies at a banquet', which comes from Georgian. Its earliest dictionary reference dates from 1937 (Meščerskij 1967a: 27).

The question of Ukrainian loan-words in the Soviet period is particu-larly difficult. Examples quoted by commentators often turn out to have been borrowed before the Revolution; others are of doubtful Ukrainian origin. Самостийность 'nationalistic independence' (Mazon 1920: 19) was borrowed from Ukrainian at about the time of the Revolution and has a firm place in the Russian vocabulary. But although Ožegov (1972) defines it without mentioning the Ukraine, in practice it appears to be applied only to Ukrainian affairs. A Ukrainian loan-word which is not restricted to a local meaning is хлебороб 'corn-grower', but it was borrowed and had ceased to be felt specifically Ukrainian before the beginning of the twentieth century. Its frequency seems to have increased in the Soviet period, however, and the morpheme -роб has been used to form the new (1930s) хлопкороб 'cotton-grower' (Krysin 1964).

There seems to be a marked desire among some investigators to prove the influence of other Soviet languages on Russian in the Soviet period (e.g. Beloded 1964: 476–7; Meščerskij 1967*b*: 23) despite the scarcity of examples. The fact that so far little evidence of this influence has been assembled, however, does not mean that it does not exist. The problems of detecting the results of interference between genetically closely related systems are notorious, and it is therefore quite possible that details of the influence of Ukrainian, in particular, have yet to be revealed.

6   Sex, Gender, and the Status of Women

Word-Formation[1]

Traditionally, Russian has distinct masculine and feminine forms for nouns that can refer both to men and to women, in much the same way as it has separate masculine and feminine adjectives, the main difference being that with adjectives the distinction is shown by inflection (declension), whereas with nouns it is shown by derivation, the latter being less regular in formation. Thus an Englishman is англичанин, an Englishwoman англичанка, and a Muscovite is either москвич or москвичка. Overall, the use of the feminine is normal in reference to a woman in classificatory nouns, e.g. names of nationality, and descriptive nouns such as кошатница 'cat-fancier' (masc. кошатник) (Timberlake 1993: 855), авантюристка 'adventuress' (masc. авантюрист).

With occupations and professions, however, pre-Revolutionary Russian society did not in general concede that the same profession could be carried out equally by both men and women. A few occupations, mainly of low status, could be carried out equally by both sexes, so that we find differentiated pairs like ткач—ткачиха 'weaver'.[2] In a number of instances where both the masculine and the feminine noun existed, the masculine name had a wider range of meanings or denoted a more prestigious occupation: for example, the currently archaic эконом had the meanings 'economical person; housekeeper' (Ožegov 1972; *MAS* 1981–4), while the currently archaic экономка had only the second meaning. (See also below on the pair секретарь—секретарша.) There were also a few occupations that were exercised only by women, so that there is no masculine equivalent of сестра милосердия 'sister of mercy', the pre-Revolutionary word for a (medical) nurse. But there was no term, for example, for a woman general, correlating with

[1] For other discussions, see Janko-Trinickaja (1964*b*; 1966*b*), Protčenko (1964; 1975: 189–213, 273–95; 1985: 280–315), Panov (1968: ii. 191–213), Jachnow (1980), Zemskaja (1992: 148–55).

[2] Cf. also the suppletive pair портной—швея 'tailor—seamstress', where the lower status of the female occupation is connoted; see below on портной—портниха.

the fact that there were no women generals. In traditional Russian usage there is a word генеральша, formed from генерал by adding the feminine suffix -ша. However, this does not mean a woman who is a general, but a general's wife. Particularly with such names as this, conferring on the bearer higher social prestige, only men could have such prestige in their own right; the woman's place was in the home, and at best she could enjoy the reflected prestige of her husband's rank.

During the twentieth century, this social system has changed radically. Even in the late nineteenth century, as a result of industrialization, many more women came to be employed in industry, mainly in unskilled jobs. In 1901 26 per cent of industrial workers were women, and by 1917 the figure was 40 per cent (quoted in Janko-Trinickaja 1966b: 170–1). Part of the increase in the years leading up to the Revolution was due to mobilization: many working men were fighting at the front, and their places were taken by women. A similar situation arose during the Second World War, when women took on various jobs that had previously been considered unsuitable for them. In some sectors women now far outnumber men, for instance in education and the health service. Thus there has been a radical change in social structure.

Less commonly, typically women's professions have become open to men. The term медбрат (from медицинский брат) is now used in hospitals for a male nurse, cf. медицинская сестра (abbreviated медсестра) 'nurse'. Дояр 'man who milks cows' is a back-formation from доярка 'milk-maid'.[3] Many of the masculine terms in such cases are circumlocutions: Rozental´ (1971: 165) notes переписчик на машинке 'typist' (cf. машинистка; машинист means 'railway engine-driver'). With many occupations that are felt to be essentially women's, specifically female forms tend to be used without any stylistic connotation, e.g. телефонистка 'switchboard operator', массажистка 'masseuse' (Gorbačevič 1973: 514), манекенщица 'model'.

The increase in the number of women taking up jobs previously restricted to men was most noticeable during the early years after the Revolution. During this period, the tendency was for women taking up these jobs to be referred to by specifically feminine-suffixed forms (Janko-Trinickaja 1966b: 178). The commonest such suffix is -ка added to the masculine form of occupational, political, and other nouns, e.g.

---

[3] Formation of masculine names based on names of women is generally a rare phenomenon in Russian; outside the names of professions, the following examples can be found: ведьма—ведьмак 'witch—warlock'; вдова—вдовец 'widow—widower' (note that in English, too, the formation is from the feminine to the masculine).

комсомолка 'member of the Komsomol', активистка 'political activist', агентка 'agent', женкорка 'women's correspondent' (cf. женкор, an abbreviation of женский корреспондент; most women's correspondents, if not all, were women). Some of these have since fallen out of use, for instance агентка and женкорка. In current usage, the suffix -ка is productive particularly in forming feminine forms from masculine words in -ист, -ец, -(ов)ик; the correlation -ист/-ка is the most frequent and most regular, too, e.g. геодезист—геодезистка 'geodesist' (the feminine noun is an innovation of the 1960s and is cited as such in Kotelova and Sorokin 1971).

There are certain difficulties in generalizing the use of -ка, in particular because this suffix has a number of other uses (Mučnik 1971: 222). Thus the word электричка has been pre-empted to refer to a kind of suburban train, and is not used as the feminine of электрик 'electrician';[4] similarly, столярка is a colloquial term for a joiner's workshop (cf. столяр 'joiner'). In one case at least, the earlier meaning of a word in -ка failed to prevent the development of the meaning 'female': the word in question is землянка (1965) (cf. землянин 'inhabitant of the Earth'). The word землянка also means 'dug-out', and one should probably treat these two words as homonyms. Secondly, it is felt inappropriate to use this suffix with occupations of higher prestige; the form славистка for a woman Slavist is unacceptable, and likely to provoke laughter from Russians; as the feminine of филолог 'philologist', филоложка is quite impossible, while филологичка is only marginally better,[5] and would be evaluated in the same way as славистка. Likewise, депутатка 'deputy', делегатка 'delegate' are colloquial at best.

The suffix -ка remains extremely popular in spoken colloquial Russian, where it produces a large number of new words, some of them *ad hoc* formations, for example, кофеинистка 'coffee-drinker' (Zemskaja 1992: 151; Zemskaja 1983: 108–9). This frequency of the suffix in non-standard varieties of Russian is partially responsible for the perception of words in -ка as stylistically unsophisticated (стилистически сниженные, see Zemskaja 1992: 151). This pertains even to

---

[4] Feminine derivatives ending in -ичка are stressed -и́чка, irrespective of the stress of the masculine form (Švedova 1970: 121); thus there would be no stress difference between электричка 'suburban train' and a feminine derivative of электрик.

[5] Gorbačevič (1973: 514) notes that forms like биологичка 'woman biologist, biology-teacher' (cf. биолог) are characteristic of schoolchildren's slang. For some time, in the 1920s–1950s, филоложка existed as a colloquial term for филология 'philology', especially as a university department.

those words that are accepted by normative dictionaries or dictionaries of new words, e.g. фотокорреспондентка 'newspaper photographer', ветеранка 'veteran', аспирантка 'graduate student', слабачка 'weak person' (all registered in the 1960s); юристка 'lawyer', фотожурнал-истка 'reporter-photographer', геодезистка 'geodesist' (all 1970), разведёнка (1982) 'divorcee'.[6] One of the few words in -ка that are stylistically neutral is интриганка 'plotter', probably due to the common perception of women as more likely than men to engage in intrigues and gossip. Stylistically neutral are also names of female athletes (see below) and names of nationality and place of origin, e.g. марсианка (cf. марсианин 'Martian'), the above-mentioned землянка. (See also below on place of origin names.)

For masculine nouns ending in -тель, -ник, -чик, -щик, the suffixes -ница (after -тель, or replacing -ник), -щица (replacing -чик and -щик) became widespread (Protčenko 1964: 109–17). In addition to traditional terms like учительница (cf. учитель 'teacher'), such neologisms arose as истопница (cf. истопник 'stoker'), наждачница (cf. наждачник 'sandpaperer'), никелировщица (cf. никелировщик 'nickel-plater'), гардеробщица (cf. гардеробщик 'cloakroom attendant'), водительница (cf. водитель 'driver'). The examples quoted give some idea of the sort of occupations concerned here: mainly highly specialized, but many of these unskilled or semi-skilled, with little or no social prestige attached. There are many such terms in the specialized vocabulary of any industry, and while most of them arose in the late nineteenth and early twentieth centuries, they continue in use to the present day. One of the recent formations which stands out among other words with the above suffixes is манекенщица 'model'; though the word манекенщик 'male model' is also attested, the predominance of female models makes the feminine form much more frequent. (Nevertheless, Ožegov (1972) lists манекенщик as the main entry, followed by манекенщица as the related word.) Likewise, names of female athletes are stylistically neutral, e.g. (горно)лыжница (cf. (горно)лыжник '(mountain) skier'). The terms for those receiving

---

[6] In the late 1980s the word бизнесменка 'businesswoman' appeared; so far it has remained colloquial. The emergence of бизнесменка is due to the analogy to such well-established words as спортсменка 'female athlete', рекордсменка 'record-breaker'. This is in turn related to the influx of English loan-words in -*man* (бармен, бизнесмен, конгрессмен, полисмен, рекордсмен, спортсмен, яхтсмен), which resulted in the recognition of -мен as a structural element (Krysin 1965*b*: 109). Female names, most of them colloquial, are derived either with the help of -ка or with the help of -ша (бар-менша).

education, especially those in elementary and secondary school, seem to call for gender differentiation, without apparent stylistic distinctions between the masculine and the feminine; cf. ученик—ученица 'pupil', третьеклассник—третьеклассница 'third former'. In fact, the use of the masculine noun to refer to a female schoolchild would be unacceptable: thus, моя дочь третьеклассник 'my daughter is a third-former (masc.)' is simply ungrammatical. It seems that the general productivity of the suffixes under discussion prevents or disfavours the use of masculine names in reference to females; as to the low status associated with a number of feminine names with these suffixes, these connotations derive from the low prestige of the respective occupations and not from the stylistic perception of the feminine noun. This distinguishes feminine nouns in -ница, -щица from those in -ша and -иха, examined in greater detail below.

The simple suffix -ица is rare in words of the class under discussion; the relevant examples include фельдшерица (cf. фельдшер 'doctor's assistant'), which is stylistically low, and the neutral певица (cf. певец 'singer').

The suffix -иня, which until the middle of the century was non-productive and limited to a few words (богиня 'goddess', графиня 'countess', герцогиня 'duchess'), has gained acceptance, since the 1960s, as the suffix deriving names of occupations from words in -лог and -г ; such names, however, remain colloquial and are often used to create a humorous effect, e.g. геологиня (cf. геолог 'geologist'), йогиня (cf. йог 'yoga practitioner') (Zemskaja 1992: 154). One of the most common words in -иня is шефиня (cf. шеф 'chief, boss, supervisor'), still colloquial.

The suffix -ья is used primarily to derive female names denoting inherent characteristic features, e.g. лгунья (cf. лгун 'liar'), болтунья (cf. болтун 'chatter-box'), вещунья (cf. вещун 'augur, prophet'); the noun попадья denotes the wife of an Orthodox priest (поп).

Less commonly foreign suffixes were used to derive feminine nouns, such as -есса in адвокатесса (cf. адвокат 'lawyer'), or -иса in инспектриса (cf. инспектор 'inspector'), аббатиса 'mother superior' (cf. аббат 'abbot'). These formations are now for the most part defunct, with one or two exceptions, e.g. поэтесса (cf. поэт 'poet'), актриса 'actress' (cf. актер 'actor'). It is interesting to ask why актриса in particular (alongside певица mentioned above) should have been retained as distinct feminine forms. In general, during the Soviet period it did not matter from the point of view of social function whether the holder of a job is a man or a woman. However, there are exceptions, equally determined by social convention.

One such case is that of actors and actresses: in most plays there are specifically male and specifically female roles, and actors or actresses are cast accordingly. Similarly in sport, there are usually separate men's and women's competitions, whence separate terms for female athletes, e. g. спортсменка 'athlete', волейболистка 'volleyball player', гандболистка 'handball player', кролистка 'crawl-swimmer', пловчиха 'swimmer', дискоболка 'discus-thrower'.[7] Women's athletics is essentially a twentieth-century phenomenon, so the words are largely post-Revolutionary creations. M. P. Sokolov, in his book *Конькобежный спорт* (Moscow, 1952, quoted by Mučnik 1971: 216) refers to women skaters in the beginning of the century (before the Revolution) as женщины-конькобежцы (this was then an unusual phenomenon), but to contemporary women skaters as конькобежки.[8] Nowadays the forms with preposed женщина 'woman' are common only where it is necessary to emphasize the unusualness of a woman doing something, e.g. женщина-космонавт 'woman cosmonaut' (though the word космонавтка also appeared in the 1960s, following the first space flight performed by a woman, Valentina Tereškova); женщина-президент 'woman president', женщина-премьер-министр 'woman prime minister'. However, once the necessary clarification has been made, such usage is avoided; for example, Margaret Thatcher was invariably referred to in the Soviet press as премьер-министр Великобритании, and Indira Gandhi as премьер-министр (Индии), e.g.:

Выступая по Всеиндийскому радио с обращением к народу, премьер-министр Индира Ганди рассказала о некоторых экономических программах (*Труд*, 3 July 1975, quoted in Kotelova (1984: 143))

Addressing the nation on the All-India Radio Service, prime minister Indira Gandhi described several economic policies.

The use of the word женщина is even less desirable with names of those occupations where women are numerically well represented: for example, in current Russian usage, женщина-врач tends to be as condescending and patronizing as 'lady doctor' in English.[9]

---

[7] Soviet sports terminology is discussed by Protčenko (1975: 168–214), with discussion of the use of masculine or feminine forms with reference to women (189–213).

[8] More recent examples of the use of женщина-конькобежец, and also of конькобежец with reference to a woman, are noted by Protčenko (1975: 200), alongside more frequent конькобежка; the examples are from newspapers in the early 1950s. D. N. Ušakov (1935–40) gives a feminine form конькобежица, not known to us from other sources.   [9] Cf. Lakoff (1973: 59–60).

Some professional names in Russian are adjectives used as nouns, and these of course easily form feminine equivalents: дежурный 'man on duty', дежурная 'woman on duty'; управляющий домом (домами)— управляющая домом (домами) 'manager of a block of flats' (both usually abbreviated to управдом). However, even here there is, with higher prestige professions, a tendency to use only the masculine form. Thus the head of a department in a university is, irrespective of sex, заведующий кафедрой.

Some masculine nouns resolutely refuse to allow derived feminine forms. One such word is товарищ 'comrade'.[10] The current tendency to use the masculine form for both men and women is often attributed partly to the influence of the increased frequency of this word, as the title of address without gender distinction, in the post-Revolutionary period. This general tendency seems to have arisen first in the speech of the intelligentsia around the turn of the century (Janko-Trinickaja 1966*b*: 181). During the early post-Revolutionary years the influence of the old intelligentsia became less prominent, and large numbers of special feminine forms were created. With the re-emerging importance placed on the standard language, the influence of the intellectuals became more noticeable again, so that the tendency initiated by them among themselves has become much more widespread, particularly with higher prestige occupations. There is no internal linguistic reason why a woman president should not be президентка, but in fact this form is not used. Although both герой 'hero' and героиня 'heroine' exist, there was only the one form Герой Советского Союза 'Hero of the Soviet Union' or Герой Социалистического труда 'Hero of Socialist Labour'; see also below on the title Заслуженный учитель.[11] While both пионер and пионерка exist, the solemn oath taken by children joining this youth organization was invariably: Я, юный пионер Советского Союза, перед лицом своих товарищей торжественно обещаю . . . 'I, a young pioneer of the Soviet Union, do solemnly promise before my comrades . . .' (Janko-Trinickaja 1966*b*: 196).

Likewise, despite the existence of the distinct words учитель and учительница, the award title in this predominantly female field in the Soviet Union was Заслуженный учитель 'Honoured Teacher'.

In certain cases, of course, the relevant factor seems to be not so much the prestige attached to the occupation as the expectation, at least from

[10] In the sense 'companion', there is an archaic feminine form товарка.
[11] But note мать-героиня, the title awarded to a woman who has mothered ten children or more, which is specifically female and feminine.

a relatively traditional viewpoint, that the occupation is primarily male. Thus although строитель 'construction-worker' belongs to a class of nouns—agentives in -тель—that readily form feminines in -ница, the word строитель is in fact used for a construction worker of either sex. If need arises to specify that the construction worker in question is female, the expression женщина (девушка)-строитель is used. (See Protčenko (1985: 313), on the words почтальон 'postal-carrier', письмоносец 'letter-carrier', which are similar to строитель in this respect.)

Part of the RJaSO survey tested whether people would normally, in official documents, use the masculine or feminine form to refer to women's occupations. In the test, described in Panov (1968: ii. 204–5), the informants did not know that they were being questioned specifically on this point. They were asked to give various pieces of information about themselves in the preamble to the questionnaire, including their own and their parents' occupations. The relevant replies were collected (own occupation for women informants, mother's occupation for all informants) and analysed. In 1,000 replies the nouns referring to women that appeared more than ten times are as follows: учитель(ница) 'teacher', студент(ка) 'student', преподаватель(ница) 'teacher, instructor', воспитатель(ница) 'educator, nurturer', лаборант(ка) 'laboratory assistant', продавец (продавщица) 'shop assistant', фельдшер(ица) 'doctor's assistant'. Of these, студентка was used 131 times, студент 23; in general, names of those undergoing education have distinct forms, and if anything it is surprising that some 15 per cent of the informants should have used the masculine form. Even as traditional a form as учительница was used in only about 60 per cent of the relevant cases (93: 63). For all the other words, the masculine form was used by the majority of those replying to the questionnaire. According to a survey done in Saratov, the use of masculine forms in reference to women is more common in Saratov than in Moscow (Zemskaja 1992: 155), which suggests the influence of territorial factors on the distribution of masculine and feminine names.

In Kalinin, during July 1975, the Hotel Seliger required trainee-waitresses, and advertised for them in the following terms:

Ресторан «Селигер» приглашает на работу в ресторан и его филиалы . . . учеников официантов (девушек в возрасте до 25 лет со средним образованием).

The *Seliger* restaurant invites to employment in the restaurant and its branches . . . trainee-waiters (girls aged up to 25 with secondary education).

Here, the parenthesis makes it clear that only female applicants are sought, so that although the reference is specifically to women, the author of the notice felt justified in using the masculine form ученик официанта 'trainee-waiter'. The variation in usage in such cases can be seen from the fact that further along the same street, the café «Русский чай» was advertising for официанток (accusative plural) 'waitresses', with the specifically feminine form.

For some of the suffixes that can be used to make feminine forms, there are additional sociolinguistic factors that have led to their loss of popularity in forming female occupation names. One of these suffixes is -иха. This was used, even before the Revolution, to form some names of female occupations, e.g. ткачиха (cf. ткач 'weaver'), повариха (cf. повар 'cook'), портниха (cf. портной 'tailor'). However, it was at least as widespread in its use to indicate the wife of someone holding a certain (usually relatively low) rank or job, e.g. купчиха (cf. купец 'merchant'), полковничиха (cf. полковник 'colonel'); in regional dialects it even forms wives' names from male forenames, e.g. Иваниха 'Ivan's wife' (Švedova 1970: 122; Unbegaun 1972: 22, 84, 108). In addition, it is the most productive suffix for forming female animal names, e.g. дельфиниха 'cow-dolphin', зайчиха 'female hare'. In the 1920s it was used quite widely to form female occupation names, allegedly without any particular stylistic nuance, e.g. слесариха (cf. слесарь 'locksmith'), шпиониха[12] (cf. шпион 'spy'), even члениха (cf. член 'member') (Janko-Trinickaja 1966b: 180–1).[13] The pair дворник—дворничиха 'janitor' remained in active use and did not develop any stylistic differentiation, probably due to the low social status of the occupation. In the course of time, however, it went out of use as a productive suffix, no doubt owing to the recollection that it is associated with the socially obnoxious practice of classifying a woman solely in accordance with her husband's position, perhaps even more so to the fact that the suffix is now associated in particular with female animals' names. The word врачиха, formed from врач 'doctor', is not listed as standard (not even colloquial standard) in current dictionaries, and is usually avoided, unless the downplaying semantics is deliberately intended. Interestingly, there are several recent words where this suffix

---

[12] Later replaced by шпионка.

[13] The claim that -иха was free of stylistic nuances becomes questionable in the light of the opposition курсистиха—курсистка 'student of women's higher courses', attested in the first two decades of this century; while курсистка was indeed neutral, курсистиха, found in letters and personal diaries, was pejorative (Zemskaja 1992: 153).

is used, e.g. пловчиха (cf. пловец 'swimmer') (Mučnik 1971: 216;
Protčenko 1975: 209–10). As already noted, with names of people
engaged in sport there is considerable pressure for having separate
masculine and feminine words, and in this case this pressure has overcome the prejudice against -иха. Protčenko (1975: 210) also notes a
rarer term гребчиха (cf. гребец 'rower').

The fate of the feminine suffix -ша, which typically occurs with
nouns ending in a sonorant or a sonorant followed by another consonant
(e.g. -нт), has been similar, except that in traditional usage this suffix
was even more restricted to indicating wives of holders of ranks or professions, e.g. генеральша (cf. генерал 'general'), фабрикантша (cf.
фабрикант 'factory-owner').[14] In the early twentieth century -ша was
also used for women exercising certain professions, e.g. авиаторша (cf.
авиатор 'airman'), without any stylistic markedness (Janko-Trinickaja
1966*b*: 173), and such forms became productive particularly in the
1920s: агитаторша (cf. агитатор 'agitator'), редакторша (cf. редактор 'editor').[15] In general, these have since fallen into disuse. Certainly,
with the jobs just mentioned, to the extent that the masculine forms are
still in use, they are used for both men and women. A few words in -ша
do survive in the current standard to indicate women's occupations, but
are used mainly in the colloquial standard. Examples are кассирша (cf.
кассир 'cashier'), секретарша (cf. секретарь 'secretary'), and less
commonly кондукторша (cf. кондуктор 'conductor'), маклерша (cf.
маклер 'broker'). A form like секретарша again reveals the social
classification of occupations into high and low prestige: this form would
be used only of a secretary in an office, a shorthand-typist; the secretary
of, for instance, a Party committee would be секретарь irrespective of
sex. Very few forms in -ша are now used in neutral style: exceptions are
a few typically women's occupations (e.g. маникюрша 'manicurist'
and педикюрша 'pedicurist'; маникюр 'manicure' and педикюр
'pedicure' refer to the processes); even in sports terminology, such
forms as партнерша 'partner', призерша (along with the alternative

---

[14] Forms in -ша with this meaning are no longer current in educated usage. The form
профессорша, which before the Revolution meant 'professor's wife', is now used colloquially for a woman professor (Švedova 1970: 123). For other colloquial forms in -ша see
Zemskaja (1983: 109); all such forms denote a woman holding a certain position or occupation, rather than someone's wife. The possibility of further spread of forms in -ша into
the standard language is indicated by the fact that such forms have recently begun to
appear in the literature; thus, Kostomarov, in the otherwise serious academic monograph,
uses дикторша телевидения 'TV announcer' without quotation marks or italics
(Kostomarov 1994: 41).

[15] The latter word has been retained by the language, though as extremely colloquial.

призерка) 'prize-winner' are considered colloquial (Protčenko 1975: 208).

In principle, the separate feminine forms are obligatory with nationality and place-of-origin names, like англичанка 'Englishwoman', москвичка 'woman from Moscow', and the above-mentioned марсианка, землянка. Occasionally, however, one finds the masculine forms even here, as in the example quoted by Janko-Trinickaja (1966*b*: 208) from a review in *Вечерняя Москва* (27 June 1964): Приятно рекомендовать читателям «Вечерней Москвы» нового автора и старого москвича. 'It is a pleasure to recommend to the readers of *Večernjaja Moskva* a new author and an old Muscovite.' The author in question is identified as V. Krupennikova. A relevant factor, not noted by Janko-Trinickaja, may be the presence in this example of the masculine noun автор 'author', the usual form even with reference to a woman (the noun авторесса is used to create a humorous effect or to indicate the speaker's low assessment of the person's writings). However, such examples may be indicative of the next area in which the traditional gender distinction will break down.

In current usage, then, the masculine form is unmarked for sex. Thus a state farm advertising for a tractor-driver would just say совхозу требуется тракторист without specifying sex, and it would be assumed that both men and women tractor-drivers are eligible. Just as we can use англичане to refer to the English as a whole, so we can use учителя to refer to teachers, men and women, as a whole. While англичане always allowed of this possibility, this has not always been true of учителя (Janko-Trinickaja 1966*b*: 188): in the early twentieth century it was more usual to say учителя (учители) и учительницы. Note also the semantic difference between она лучший учитель в школе and она лучшая учительница в школе, where the former means that she is the best of all the teachers, the latter that she is the best among the women teachers, i.e. учительница is specifically feminine, учитель is non-specific.

If we use a personal noun metaphorically to refer to a thing, then traditional usage recommended the use of the feminine form if the other noun was grammatically feminine, the masculine otherwise, i.e. опыт (знание)—лучший советчик 'experience (knowledge) is the best counsellor', but жизнь—лучшая советчица 'life is the best counsellor'. Numerous deviations from this traditional rule were due to the fact that a number of nouns, used in the predicative function, did not have feminine correlates, cf. время—лучший лекарь 'time is the best healer' and работа—лучший лекарь 'work is the best healer' (the word лекариха is at best dubious). The interference of such examples and the general tendency of using masculine as the unmarked gender resulted in the current trend to use the masculine form irrespective of the gender of the other noun, i.e. also жизнь—лучший советчик (Janko-Trinickaja 1966b: 209).

Overall, masculine remains in most cases the gender-neutral form in reference to females, especially with names of those occupations that enjoy higher social prestige (директор 'director', руководитель 'chief', депутат 'deputy', заведующий 'chairman'). That such a name is used in reference to a woman is recovered from the context; hyphenated compounds with the word женщина can be used, though with limitations (see above on женщина-президент). The use of the distinct feminine form to denote an occupation is permissible if the occupation is viewed as highly specialized or has low social prestige. Otherwise, the use of the distinct feminine form is often colloquial. Whether or not a feminine form is colloquial can be revealed by whether or not such a form can be used in directly addressing the bearer of the respective occupation; thus, while it is normal to say вы хорошая певица, няня, массажистка, лыжница, красильщица, официантка 'you are a good singer, nanny, masseuse, skier, dyer, waitress', it is inappropriate to address someone as хорошая музыкантша, редакторша, почтальонша, хирургиня, врачиха 'good musician, editor, mail carrier, surgeon, doctor'. (See Dement´ev (1954) for similar observations.)[16] The use of the masculine form, however, creates syntactic problems that are discussed in the next section.

Syntax[17]

In those cases where the masculine form is used for women, a further difficulty arises. Russian regularly requires gender agreement, for instance of singular past tense verb forms and adjectives. When the word врач refers to a woman, should one say врач пришел (masculine) or

---

[16] Protčenko (1985: 313–14) cites several counter-examples to this rule, all of them from *prostorečie*.

[17] For other discussions, see Corbett (1983: 30–41, 50–9), Protčenko (1961), Panov (1968: iii. 19–41), Mučnik (1971: 205–44); the last two references are essentially the same (both having been written by Mučnik), but Mučnik (1971) also contains a comprehensive bibliography.

врач пришла (feminine) 'the doctor arrived', молодой (masculine) врач or молодая (feminine) врач 'young doctor'?[18] There is a conflict felt by many Russians in using a feminine adjective or verb with reference to a masculine noun, and in using a masculine adjective or verb to refer to a woman—in other words, there is here a real conflict between natural gender (sex) and grammatical gender. It seems not to be true, contrary to the claim sometimes made, that forms like врач пришла are used because it is felt necessary to indicate the sex of the person referred to: if this were so, then we should expect discomfort equally with the present tense врач идет, whereas this is not the case (Janko-Trinickaja 1966b: 203–5). Janko-Trinickaja (1966b: 175) points out that in the early twentieth century one sometimes finds a masculine word referring to a woman as subject of a present tense verb, and the equivalent feminine form (even if otherwise avoided on stylistic grounds) as subject of a past tense verb, to avoid the conflict, as in this quotation from *Женский вестник* (1908, No. 3): Автор энергично восстает против фарисейства общества . . . Эпиграфом этой книги авторша взяла изречение . . . 'The author takes an energetic stand against the hypocrisy of society . . . As the epigraph of this book the author has taken the dictum . . .'.

In nineteenth-century usage, when grammatical and natural gender conflicted (e.g. with подлец 'scoundrel' applied to a woman), the grammatical gender prevailed. Widespread encroachment of natural gender agreement is a more recent phenomenon.

Informants for the RJaSO survey were asked whether they preferred врач пришел or врач пришла when speaking of a woman. The full results are given in Panov (1968: iii. 19–41) and Mučnik (1971: 228–44) and are also reviewed in Corbett (1983: 31–8). The majority of people asked preferred the semantically agreeing variant врач пришла (51.7 per cent) to the grammatical agreement as in врач пришел (38.6 per cent), with 9.7 per cent undecided. When the figures were broken down according to social groups, it emerged that within each social group except writers and journalists there was a majority for the semantic agreement, and even with writers and journalists the majority for the masculine form was small (50.7 per cent). The figures were also broken down according to age: only with the oldest group (born before 1909) was the grammatical agreement preferred to the semantic (49.8 per cent: 42.2 per cent), and preference for the feminine form was clearly greater

---

[18] Rothstein (1973) and Corbett (1983) discuss theoretical implications of the existence of these variants.

the younger the informant, except that the very youngest group (born 1940–9) showed slightly less preference than the group born 1930–9. Mučnik (1971: 234) suggests that this may be due to the influence of prescriptive grammar taught in school and still remembered by the younger informants, since prescriptive grammars still often condemn forms like врач пришла.

The influence of school was specifically tested by Wood (1980, quoted in Corbett 1983: 37–8) who surveyed law and philology students at Voronež State University (born 1959 and earlier) and schoolchildren in Voronež *oblast´* (born 1963–6). The figures in Wood's survey, compared to the data obtained for the youngest group in the RJaSO survey, suggest that the trend towards semantic agreement remained relatively steady in the students' group (the slight decline observed in the students' group is statistically negligible) and was on the increase in the schoolchildren's group (the students opted for наконец врач пришла 'finally, the doctor came' in 50 per cent of cases, the schoolchildren born 1963–4 in 63.6 per cent, and those born 1965–6 in 70 per cent of cases). However, as noted by Corbett (1983: 38), these figures may well be indicative of the distinction between town and country (the schoolchildren were from a village secondary school) rather than between different age-groups. The evidence that the older group is more likely to follow grammatical agreement comes from the comparison between the two groups of schoolchildren: while директор вошла в комнату 'the director entered the room' was allowed by 59.1 per cent of those born 1963–4, the younger schoolchildren (born 1965–6) approved of this sentence in 89.5 per cent of cases. As the older schoolchildren had been familiarized with the normative rules, this indeed suggests that schooling has an effect on judgements. It remains to be seen if normative recommendations have any long-term effect.

Those who replied to the RJaSO questionnaire were also invited to air their views on grammatical versus semantic agreement more discursively. The majority of views expressed were in favour of the feminine form, though some extreme views were expressed on both sides. Many writers were either outright hostile, or prepared to accept the feminine form only under pressure. Prescriptive grammar is a great area for airing one's prejudices: one worker replied that the masculine form should be used because врач есть врач 'a doctor is a doctor', irrespective of sex; another that the feminine form should be used because женщина есть женщина 'a woman is a woman', irrespective of profession (Mučnik 1971: 233). Perhaps the most intelligent comment came from the linguist V. Kudrjavcev: грамматика вступила в противоречие с жизнью 'grammar has come into conflict with life', although he continues: но пока я на стороне грамматики 'but so far I'm on the side of grammar' (Mučnik 1971: 231).

Where the common noun is accompanied by a proper name, then it is much more usual to have agreement with the natural gender. Thus V. V. Vinogradov *et al.* (1960: vol. ii, bk. 1, 510–11) hesitate to admit as grammatical the construction кондуктор дала билет 'the conductor gave a ticket', but recommend оперировала хирург Мария Григорьевна Каменчик 'the surgeon Marija Grigor´evna Kamenčik operated', and go so far as to make the strange recommendation that in such cases one should always insert a proper name. This fails to allow for the possibility that the speaker or writer may not know the name of the person under discussion.

A second question on the RJaSO questionnaire asked informants to choose between the variants у нас хороший бухгалтер and у нас хорошая бухгалтер 'we have a good accountant'. Here the overwhelming preference, for all social and age groups, was for the masculine adjective (69.9 per cent, with 25 per cent for the feminine adjective and 5.1 per cent undecided); the highest figure for the feminine adjective was from industrial workers (38.7 per cent), and from the age-group born 1940 and later (28.4 per cent), although there is in fact little variation among those born after 1910. The data in Wood's survey (quoted in Corbett 1983: 37) show that the preference for grammatical agreement was overwhelming among university students (of whom only 3.9 per cent accepted она известная скульптор 'she is a recognized sculptor'); the younger group showed a little more preference for semantic agreement (27.3 per cent of those born 1963–4 and 10 per cent of those born 1965–6),[19] which is still below the percentages obtained for the youngest group in the RJaSO survey.

The difference between the acceptability of the semantic agreement in the predicate and in the modifying adjective has been long noticed in the literature. Peškovskij, writing in the 1920s, noted that while a Russian might say товарищ вошла 'the comrade entered', he would hardly say уважаемая товарищ 'dear comrade' (quoted in Mučnik 1971: 243). Where such examples occur in literature, it is usually as a stylistic device, or to characterize spoken language, as in Voznesenskij's танцуй, моя академик! 'dance, my academician!' (Mučnik 1971:

---

[19] Wood's percentages are generally less reliable than those in the RJaSO survey since her sample of informants was considerably smaller.

241–2).[20] There are also numerous examples from literature and the press where a past tense verb is in the feminine form, but an attributive adjective is in the masculine form, e.g. избранный организатор пришла ко мне 'the elected organizer came to me' (*Коммунист* 1925, No. 4; quoted by Janko-Trinickaja 1966*b*: 192–4); the reverse is at best very rare, and we know of no actual examples (see Švedova 1970: 555).

Different normative handbooks give different recommendations concerning standard usage in this area. Earlier normative handbooks tried to restrict врач пришла, preferred by a clear majority of informants, to colloquial speech. Švedova (1970: 555) already says that in such cases 'there is no strict rule for the choice of gender'. With хорошая бухгалтер, известная скульптор, the situation is different: the overwhelming majority of informants prefer the more traditional form with the masculine attributive adjective and so did, until recently, normative handbooks. Different attitudes towards уважаемая товарищ Иванова 'dear comrade Ivanova' have provoked a polemic involving Panfilov (1965), condemning this variant, and Janko-Trinickaja (1967), defending it. Švedova (1970: 489) allows this use of the feminine adjective in 'colloquial and relaxed speech' (непринужденная речь), and does not refer to it as non-standard.

The latest Academy Grammar (*Русская грамматика* 1980: ii. 57) goes further, declaring the semantic agreement, along with the formal agreement, in the adjective or adjectival pronoun standard (нормально), though admitting that forms such as новая секретарь 'new secretary', сама директор 'the director herself' are more common in the spoken language and in the press. Since semantic agreement in the modifying adjective or pronoun is a marked case (cf. the percentages below), those sentences where the noun is modified by an adjective or pronoun in the feminine require semantic agreement in the predicate as well, e.g. Наша врач пришла 'Our (fem.) doctor came', Дело рассматривала районная судья 'The case was presided over by the district (fem.) judge' (*Русская грамматика* 1980: ii. 57, 245), but not *Наша врач пришел, *Дело рассматривал районная судья. Likewise, if the person is named by her proper name, the semantic agreement becomes obligatory (*Русская грамматика* 1980: ii. 245), cf. in the example above: премьер-министр Индира Ганди рассказала . . .

---

[20] In general, the use of feminine forms seems to be characteristic of Voznesenskij's style, cf. also: Агрессорка,—добавлю, скифка . . . 'Aggressoress, I will add, Scythianess . . .' (quoted in Zemskaja (1992: 151)); врач случайная 'the doctor who happened to be there' (quoted in *Русская грамматика* (1980: ii. 57)).

This approach is essentially similar to the one applied to common gender nouns (see Chapter 3, p. 111–12): the nouns судья, врач are treated as grammatically feminine when referring to a woman, and consistency might require that the modifier and the predicate have feminine forms (see also Iomdin 1990: 110–11). Of course, in case of the formal agreement in the modifying adjective or pronoun, the predicate can have either formal or semantic agreement, e.g. Наш врач пришел (of a woman) and Наш врач пришла. (See also Zemskaja (1983: 110) for the discussion of these constructions in spoken Russian.)

In addition to the decisions on grammar, the choice between the semantic and grammatical agreement in cases such as врач пришел/пришла is related to sociolinguistic factors. One problem to which some of the RJaSO informants addressed themselves was whether women were being upgraded or downgraded by the various alternatives. The answers they and others have suggested are sometimes diametrically opposed. Thus the writer V. Bokov suggested that the form врач пришла is an attempt to honour women grammatically (Mučnik 1971: 231). Timofeev (1963: 227–30) says that the existence of separate feminine forms for nouns indicates the equality of women, and that wherever possible the special feminine noun suffixes should be used. A. V. Mirtov, in a remark from a dissertation quoted by Janko-Trinickaja (1966*b*: 194), says that the use of the same form for both men and women indicates the absence of discrimination between the sexes. Those concerned with this problem in English have tended, since the 1960s, towards the latter view (cf. their rejection of such forms as *poetess*, *authoress*, or *priestess* in reference to female priests in the Church of England, and the promotion of sex-neutral names such as *chairperson*), though it should be borne in mind that formal gender distinction, often paralleling sex distinction, is a much more important and integral feature of Russian than of English, and that there is no simple correlation between societies that practise discrimination against women and languages that have grammatical gender.

Related to this issue is the question whether the sex of the informant is relevant for the choice between semantic and grammatical agreement. While no information on this question is given in the RJaSO survey, the statistics collected by Wood and quoted in Corbett (1983: 38) suggest that there is a marked difference between sexes in the choice of the predicate agreement. In Wood's study, 50 per cent of male and 85.7 per cent of female speakers accepted the variant директор вошла в комнату; for наконец врач пришла, the ratio was 43.2 per cent to

82.1 per cent. (The difference between the sexes was much less tangible in the choice of semantic agreement in the adjective: 12.8 per cent of male and 14.3 per cent of female speakers.)

The surveys done by the RJaSO team and by Wood also suggest that the variation between semantic and grammatical agreement may be affected by the particular word determining agreement: such nouns as управдом and директор showed slightly higher percentages of semantic agreement than the noun врач. This differentiation may be inversely related to the numerical composition of particular professions and occupations. By the time of the RJaSO survey, medicine had become a predominantly female occupation; this was particularly true of general practice, which was implied in the sentence врач пришел/пришла (к больному): in the Soviet Union, general practitioners visited patients in their homes. The numerical representation of women as directors or managers was much less significant. Accordingly, the choice of the semantic agreement could help to emphasize the pragmatically unusual situation; in the case of the medical profession, this would simply be redundant.

Overall, in the conflict between derivational and syntactic means of referring to women exercising various professions and occupations, the twentieth century has seen a marked increase in the use of syntactic means relative to derivational means, although the results of this process have not always been entirely harmonious. Perhaps because of the existing variation, there has been a certain rearguard action in favour of resuscitating derivation, partly as a manifestation of linguistic purism and partly as language play. Thus the writer Natal´ja Il´ina, when replying to the RJaSO questionnaire, said that she rejects outright the forms врач пришла and хорошая бухгалтер, and would herself use врачиха and бухгалтерша (Mučnik 1971: 239). The latter is classed as colloquial by most dictionaries, while the former is non-standard. Such rearguard actions in favour of the feminine derivational suffixes are directly contrary to the prevailing tendency in the language, and seem unlikely to have any long-term effect.

7   Modes of Address and Speech Etiquette

Pronouns

Second-person pronouns

Russian, like nearly all other European languages, has a system of address entailing a choice between pronouns (including other parts of speech agreeing with them), depending on social factors. In Russian the pronominal system involves a choice between ты (hereafter abbreviated as T) and вы (abbreviated as V). The abbreviations T and V are also used here to refer to grammatical forms implying the potential existence of the pronoun itself; for example, понимаешь and понял, поняла are T, while понимаете and поняли are V. The social relationships corresponding to the patterns of choice between T and V are many and various, but the choice is basically indicative of social distance, i.e. its presence or absence to a greater or lesser degree.

Since V is grammatically obligatory in addressing groups of more than one person, the choice between T and V is restricted to situations in which only one person is addressed. The system is therefore fully operative only in relationships between two interlocutors.

Brown and Gilman (1972) compare choices of the T/V type in a number of European languages (not including Russian), showing the operation of three dyadic types in the dimensions of power and solidarity. The dyads in question are the symmetrical V (in which V is given and received by both speakers), the asymmetrical relationship (in which one speaker gives T and the other gives V), and the symmetrical T (in which T is given and received). The operation of these dyads in nineteenth-century Russian literature has been described by Friedrich (1966a, 1972). Brown and Gilman also trace the history of this kind of address in European languages (without Russian), but since the rules for the choice between T and V when addressing one person are undoubtedly different in Russian from other European languages, it may be as well to begin with an account and explanation of their emergence in Russia.

An important contribution to the history of this question was made by Černyx (1948), in which he refers to A. P. Sumarokov's discussion of the problem in the eighteenth century. Sumarokov (1718–77) attributed the growth of the use of V in addressing one person to the influence of French and thought it a new phenomenon. Černyx (1948: 91–8) was able to show, however, that in fact it is found very much earlier. Isolated instances occur as early as the late fifteenth century in diplomatic correspondence; it had been mostly restricted to diplomatic correspondence until Peter the Great's time, when it became more popular, probably due to the influence of German and Dutch. Although by the eighteenth century there is ample evidence of the use of V, there is also evidence of confusion; for example, a letter from Fonvizin to Ja. I. Bulgakov dated 25 January 1778 begins with V and ends with T (Černyx 1948: 99). Clearly, by the nineteenth century there was considerable social differentiation in pronominal address (Friedrich 1972: 278). Among the peasants V was little known and used, whereas it was in wide use among the nobility, so wide in fact that some nobles hardly ever used T, even to subordinates or their spouse. At the other extreme, many peasants were totally ignorant of V and even addressed nobles with T. For example, in Puškin's *Капитанская дочка* (1836) we find such forms as Думал ли ты, ваше благородие, что . . . 'Did you (T) ever think, sir, that . . .' only in the speech of uneducated characters (Černyx, 1948: 95 n.). There were also, however, a number of people in positions of (probably moderate) power, who carefully distinguished T from V and attached great importance to the distinction; see, for instance, Čexov's stories *Ты и вы* (1886), where the social make-up of the characters is unclear, and the second half of *Толстый и тонкий* (1883). In the nineteenth century there were a number of official spheres where the distinction was institutionalized. It was laid down that witnesses in court should be addressed as V—a procedure which could lead to misunderstanding when the witness was totally unfamiliar with the system and interpreted V as plural. It was also laid down that prisoners were to be addressed as T, even if they were from the privileged classes (Černyx 1948: 103 n.).

The asymmetrical relationship reflected by the use of T to subordinates and V to those in power was institutionalized in the army and, by convention at least, in industry. And these were two areas where early revolutionaries made attempts to change the rules of pronominal address. One of the demands made by the Lena strikers in 1912 was that the management should address the workers not as T but as V. In the army the regulations before 1917 actually named the ranks (officers down to sub-ensign (подпрапорщик)) which were to be addressed V, and added: 'To all lower ranks not named in the above list T will be used' (Černyx 1948: 107).

The rules of address in the army were changed by the February Revolution: Decree (*Приказ*) No. 1 of 1 March 1917, issued by the Petrograd Soviet of Workers' and Soldiers' Deputies, included under its seventh point the following (quoted by Černyx (1948: 108); see also Corbett (1976: 12)):

Offensive treatment of soldiers of all military ranks and in particular addressing them with T is forbidden, and any infringement of this, as well as any mis-understandings between officers and soldiers, must be reported by the latter to their company committees.

A decree of the Provisional Government (No. 114) dated 5 March 1917 contained similar provisions. On the pronominal question it said: 'I command . . . (3) That in addressing all soldiers, both on and off duty, V will be used' (*Сборник указов . . . 1917*: 318). Subsequent regulations made under the Bolsheviks confirmed the new practice. The 1918 *Устав внутренней службы* stated: 'All military personnel when addressing each other, both on and off duty, use V' (*Устав. . . . 1918*: 10).

But it is not easy to change modes of address by decree, and T con-tinued in use despite all efforts, mainly because a large proportion of the new commanders in the Red Army came from the ranks and from that social level at which T was unmarked, but also because they used it to express solidarity rather than power.[1] This common practice even prompted Friedrich's assertion that 'the Red Army reintroduced ты, eventually extending it to all subordinates' (1972: 282). The recent *Устав внутренней службы* (approved in 1960) continued to insist on V: 'On questions of duty military personnel must address one another with V.' (*Общевоинские уставы . . . 1971*: 14–15.) But breaches of this rule have been and still are not uncommon. The actual usage attested in the Army is summarized by Nakhimovsky (1976: 88–9): the subordinate must address the superior as V but the superior can easily use V and T; the officers use T to address each other but call each other by name in the presence of a soldier, since this would be interpreted as admitting the soldier to the officers' circle. Nakhimovsky illustrates this system by a dialogue between a soldier and two officers, where the

[1] Another reason, suggested by Černyx (1948: 108), is that some of the Red Army commanders had been officers in the old army and could not rid themselves of old habits; however, this is very unlikely given that the number of such commanders was small.

senior officer addresses the soldier as V, then as T and gives him a permission to go to town with V. On other uses of T and V in the army, see Kantorovič (1966: 31, 41, 66).

Overall, the use of T and V in the army suggests that the dimensions of power (in dialogues between a superior and a subordinate) and solidarity (in dialogues between holders of similar rankings) play a particularly important role in speech etiquette; this is probably due to a highly structured setting where many actions are codified in terms of the daily routine and a large number of formulaic expressions are used. The interesting fact, however, is that the actual usage of T in the army is in direct defiance of the rules.

The academic environment is another setting where the use of V is required by etiquette; in the pre-Revolutionary period, the use of V was obligatory in conversations between professors and students as well as in student-to-student and professor-to-professor exchange. The obligatory use of V in academia is reflected in the existing term 'academic V'. However, V is losing ground in academia as well. The use of V between students is practically non-existent (Nakhimovsky, describing the academic situation of the 1960s–early 1970s, refers to students in the academic system as the T generation (1976: 92)), probably reflecting the fact that the speakers are fairly young and are coming from an environment where the use of T is predominant (secondary school, family). The use of V between professors is determined by age, relative rank, and degree of informal social contact. The mutual use of V by students and professors remains an important element of academic etiquette; however, in practice, professors often use T to students, either in the classroom setting or, more so, in dialogues with individual students. The use of T seems to be more frequent in institutions of higher learning outside Moscow and Leningrad; on a visit to Simferopol´ State University in December 1987, one of the authors of this book heard only one out of five humanities professors use V to their students.

The professional system is close to the academic in that the use of T or V is supposed to be mutual; asymmetrical use is permitted only when the age gap between the interlocutors is substantial (Nakhimovsky 1976: 92–3; Formanovskaja 1982*a*: 72–3).

Only in the armed forces, institutions of higher learning, and in structured organizations such as factories and other places of work are there codified rules governing the choice of pronoun. It is evidently not considered a linguistic matter and is therefore ignored by the Academy Grammars. It is nevertheless a matter of interest to Russians as part of the general question of correct social behaviour, and is consequently dealt with in books on etiquette. Among these is Aasamaa (1974),[2] which considers the asymmetric form of discourse acceptable between the young (giving V, receiving T) and old (giving T, receiving V), and suggests that a young man may ask his elders to call him T while he continues to address them as V (Aasamaa 1974: 39). Another book dealing with etiquette from a prescriptive standpoint (including forms of address) is Pažin (1969), which on some points disagrees with Aasamaa. Pažin strongly emphasizes the fact that the use of V is a sign of good manners and condemns the use of T expressing power. He makes concessions to its use in certain circumstances, however: 'In small businesses with old-established traditions, where there is a considerable difference in the age of the workers and the managers, address with T on the part of the latter is recognized, particularly if their authority is indisputable' (Pažin 1969: 21–2).

A third source of recommendations on pronominal usage is Xodakov (1972), which mentions a number of points not included by Aasamaa or Pažin. Most significant of these is the fact that there are also situational factors involved and that to ignore them may offend against etiquette. This may involve switching from symmetrical T in private to symmetrical V in public. This is supported by Kantorovič who mentions a case of switching from reciprocal T in private to asymmetric usage in public in order to bolster the authority of the receiver of V (1966: 40–2).

Xodakov (in agreement with Pažin) condemns the T of power used by people in authority and refers to what he calls 'a certain inflation of the word T' (Xodakov 1972: 39), by which he apparently means that T is used more often than etiquette would allow. The leader of the campaign against the asymmetric usage of power is the writer V. Ja. Kantorovič, mentioned above, who in literary journals and in numerous editions of his book *«Ты» и «вы» (Заметки писателя)*, first published in 1960, has again and again advocated its abandonment (Kantorovič 1966: *passim*).

In his study of nineteenth-century usage Friedrich enumerates ten components determining the choice between T and V, viz.:

(1) Topic of discourse
(2) Context of the speech event
(3) Age

---

[2] The fact that this book has been translated from Estonian raises doubts as to its value as a source on Russian etiquette. A number of changes have been introduced in the Russian version, however, especially in the section on forms of address.

(4) Generation
(5) Sex
(6) Kinship
(7) Dialect (i.e. regional or social varieties)
(8) Group membership
(9) Relative authority
(10) Emotional solidarity

(Friedrich 1972: 276–8)

Most, if not all, of these components are included in the books on etiquette mentioned, though they are of course not enumerated in Friedrich's manner. But while the components are the same, the twentieth-century system of pronominal address is different from that of the nineteenth century, just as twentieth-century society is different.

Before the Revolution asymmetric usage often occurred within the family; it was particularly common among the peasantry and merchants but not characteristic of the intelligentsia (Kantorovič 1966: 41). Parents, fathers especially, gave T and received V from even adult children; in some circles, a husband gave T and received V from his wife. (The same usage operated also between some other kinship degrees.) In a pre-Revolutionary guide to etiquette in correspondence the examples of letters to parents all use V, whereas those to sisters, brothers, and friends use T (Nikolaev and Petrov 1903: 415–66). During the Soviet period asymmetric usage in the family became increasingly rare and is now restricted to rural areas, mainly in southern Russia (Jachnow 1974: 351). Xodakov mentions its survival with nostalgic approval (1972: 35). Ervin-Tripp's (1969: 100; 1972: 227) assertion that this is the only respect in which the old pronominal address system has changed is mistaken, however, for the asymmetric usage in power relationships of all kinds has to a very large extent given way to reciprocal usage. The prevailing ethic condemned the use of T to subordinates as offending the spirit of Soviet society. In Soviet fiction, for example, the non-reciprocal T was portrayed as a sign of boorishness and ignorance (Kantorovič 1966: 29–32).[3] In the 1960s the question was widely aired in the press and, following public discussion, the workers in some factories succeeded in persuading the management to use V. Subsequent proposals for the inclusion in local work regulations (правила

---

[3] Among Kantorovič's evidence is a quotation from N. Pogodin's *Янтарное ожерелье* in which a character who is corrupt and hated uses the T of power to a subordinate. However, this can be taken not just as evidence of the condemnation but also of the survival of asymmetric T (as is done by Ervin-Tripp (1972: 227) and Corbett (1976: 4)).

внутреннего распорядка) of instructions for workers to be addressed with V (Kantorovič 1966: 38, 45) have now been generally implemented (e.g. see Kačalovskij 1975). A particular quarter from which non-reciprocal T may still be heard is the militia; but here too its use evidently contravenes instructions. A proposal that militiamen should be formally empowered to address citizens with T was not only rejected but condemned (*Известия*, 29 January 1963, quoted by Kostomarov 1965: 41 n.).

The use of V to new acquaintances regardless of rank and age had become widespread by the middle of the twentieth century; in this respect, the language of the twentieth century differed from that of the nineteenth century, where this use of V was the norm only for the upper classes (Ervin-Tripp 1969: 100). The major age-group which remained unaffected by this change were the young people. Starting with the 1960s, the use of V to new acquaintances has again started to diminish, primarily due to the broader definition of the group known as 'young people': as noted by Nakhimovsky (1976: 92), those who are 30–5 can often use T to each other and avoid patronymics (this phenomenon is noticed, with disapproval, by Kantorovič (1966: 98–101)). As noted to us by Professor Alla Akišina, the use of T is more widespread between younger male speakers, even on first acquaintance. This use of T may be interpreted as a sign of solidarity.

Traditionally, the use of T was required if the addressee was not human; this rule was observed in addressing objects or animals, cf. in Puškin's *Конь (Песни западных славян,* 1834):

> Что ты ржешь, мой конь ретивый . . .
> Why are you neighing, oh my spirited steed?

and also in addressing supernatural beings, viz. God and tsars, whose power was viewed as God-given. Addressing the tsar as T had become obsolete by the nineteenth century, largely due to the influence of French, where *Vous, Sire,* was a standard norm of address. Meanwhile, the use of T in addressing God has remained unchanged, and is probably one of the clearest cases where variation is impossible.

Use of first- and third-person plural in reference to one person

In pre-Revolutionary Russia the use of plural forms to express deference was not restricted to the second person. There was also a system of third-person reference in which either the pronoun они replaced он or она even though referring to one person (with plural agreement), or other parts of speech occurred in the plural, even though the subject was grammatically (and really) singular. This peculiarity of Russian was noted by Maurice Baring and mentioned in his account of experiences in Russia at the time of the Russo-Japanese War:

'I want to speak to his honour,' the soldier said; 'he is washing his face in the washing-room . . .'
'Why don't you go and knock at the door?' we asked.
'They are' (to speak of a person in the third person plural is respectful in Russian, and is always done by inferiors of their superiors)—'they are "drink taken" (*oni wypimshi*),' he replied . . . (Baring n.d.: 190)

It would appear that this usage was restricted to certain social groups, low in the scale of power, especially personal servants, minor officials, etc. The claim that it was 'always considered as not corresponding to the norms of the literary language and of good form (хороший тон)' (Šmelev 1961: 55–6) requires qualification. To support his point Šmelev quotes the following exchange from Dostoevskij's *Подросток* (part I, chapter 6):

—Я их месяца три знала,—прибавила Лиза.—Это ты про Васина говоришь *их*, Лиза? Надо сказать *его*, а не *их*. Извини, сестра, что я поправляю, но мне горько, что воспитанием твоим, кажется, совсем пренебрегли.

'I knew them for about three months,' added Liza.
'Are you saying "them" of Vasin, Liza? You should say "him" and not "them". Forgive me, sister, for correcting you, but it distresses me that your education appears to have been quite neglected.'

The objection to Liza's use of the plural here is not that it was regarded as incorrect absolutely, however, but only inappropriate to her social position. This plural usage in pre-Revolutionary Russian deserves further, detailed study; it raises the interesting question whether the rules for assessing forms as standard or non-standard can also handle social variation. Whatever the former status of the third-person plural of deference, however, it has become increasingly rare in the standard language of the Soviet period, and there can be no doubt that nowadays such sentences as Мария Ивановна работают учительницей (Derjagin 1968: 139) belong exclusively to non-standard varieties, except when used as deliberate archaisms for ironic, comic, or some other special effect. In the following exchange from Chapter 10 of Bulgakov's *Мастер и Маргарита* (written 1929–40) it is used by one of the assistants to the magician Voland (who is really the Devil in disguise) adding to the alien (non-Soviet) aura surrounding the latter (reinforced by the titles господин and мосье often used to address or refer to Voland):

—Артиста Воланда можно попросить?—сладко спросил Варенуха.
—Они заняты,—ответила трубка дребезжащим голосом, а кто спрашивает?

'May I speak to the actor Voland?' Varenuxa asked sweetly.
'They are busy,' answered the telephone receiver in a jarring voice, 'and who is asking?'

The survival of third-person plural as an unmarked polite form to the present day is noted by Isačenko (1960: 414), however, who in August 1956 in Saratov observed the sentence (referring to a third person): Пусть они тебе скажут, они-то должны знать! 'Let him tell you, he certainly should know this!' Isačenko says it is a polite form used to refer to a third person *present at the conversation*. This particular use of third-person plural, which might also be a provincial feature, can be explained by another fact of Russian speech etiquette: one may not refer to a third person present at the time of the conversation by a third-person singular pronoun (see also below). However, according to Jazovickij (1969: 38–9), они is also used (in fact, particularly used) of respected persons *in their absence*. From a normative point of view, of course, it is condemned. Jazovickij favours the use of он or она to refer to the respected person in their absence and forename + patronymic in their presence. (See also Kantorovič (1966: 66).)

The use of the first-person plural, until the Revolution, was confined to the royal 'we' (e.g. Мы, Николай Второй . . . 'We Nicholas the Second') and, less rigidly, to the academic style (*pluralis auctoris*). While the use of the 'power' мы was abandoned, at least in writing, мы has become increasingly popular in academic and official style during the twentieth century. Though there are no explicit normative rules of academic style and academic etiquette, the academic я is rigorously avoided. The academic мы seems to combine the functions of *pluralis auctoris* and *pluralis modestiae*; it is used in alternation with impersonal passive, impersonal third-person plural, and constructions with inanimate subjects and objects. For example, on one page of an article discussing the norm in works of fiction (T. G. Vinokur 1974: 269), the author uses the academic мы in two cases (in one of these, the actual pronoun is omitted: сравним . . . 'let us compare . . .'); the passive

construction is used once, and the rest are various impersonal constructions. (See also Kostomarov (1994: 53) on the persistence of *pluralis
modestiae* in mass media and scholarly publications.)

An element in polite speech and address which is well known from
nineteenth-century literature is the particle -c (known as слово-ер(с)
from the old names of the letters c and -ъ) which was formerly added to
utterances, producing such combinations as Да-с, прошу-с. It was
restricted to towns and to the colloquial usage of speakers of the
standard language. Closely linked to V address, it emphasized social
distance. Although already in decline in the second half of the nineteenth
century, it survived into the twentieth and disappeared in the wave of
change following 1917 (Černyx 1949). It is retained, however, in some
discourse particles and interjections, e.g. ну-с 'well' (Corbett 1976: 12).

Names

Use of forenames, surnames, patronymics

Every Russian has three names, viz. forename (имя), patronymic
(отчество) and surname (фамилия). Various combinations of these
three units are used in address, the list of determinants being the same as
for the choice of pronoun (T or V). Names are inevitably used in conjunction with pronouns and thus various combinations correspond to
various points on the scales of power and solidarity. Names and titles,
together with pronouns, operate in a complex system of address which
still awaits description. Names and titles differ from T and V, however,
since they operate not only in a system of address but also in a system
of third- and first-person (self-naming) reference. The realization in
certain situations of types of first-, second-, and third-person reference
by names and titles among Russian intellectuals aged 30–60 at the
present day has been described in Nikolaeva (1972).

It is useful to divide forenames into (1) those which have a short form
(сокращенное имя) and (2) those which do not. (This is a separate
question from that of diminutives (уменьшительные имена), which
will be dealt with later separately.) The following is a list of some of the
common forenames belonging to Type 1, showing both full and short
forms:

Full form полное имя	Short form сокращенное имя
Александр	Саша, Шура, Саня, Алик
Александра	Саша, Шура, Саня, Аля
Алексей	Алеша, Алик
Борис	Боря
Валентин	Валя
Валентина	Валя
Виктор	Витя
Владимир	Володя, Вова
Евгений	Женя
Евгения	Женя
Екатерина	Катя
Иван	Ваня
Мария, Марья	Маша, Маруся, Маня
Николай	Коля
Петр	Петя
Татьяна	Таня
Юрий, Георгий	Юра

The number of names belonging to the other type is smaller. Examples of Type 2 are: Вера, Денис, Зоя, Игорь, Марина, Нина, Олег, Осип, Потап, Роза, Федот, Юлий. Many recently borrowed foreign names and acronym or anagram names (see Chapter 5) belong to this type, e.g. Азарий; Нинель.

In certain relationships and situations the appropriate mode of address is by forename alone, co-occurring with either T or V. If the forename in question belongs to Type 2, then the full (and only) form will be used; there is no other possibility. In the case of Type 1, however, there is a choice. In stylistically neutral address only the short form is appropriate, as the full form has an expressive function which varies according to the determinants of the situation and relationship between interlocutors. Type 2 lacks this function.

In a different set of relationships and circumstances, the appropriate mode of address is by forename and patronymic together (usually, but not always, co-occurring with V). In this case the full form of Type 1 is used (corresponding to the only form of Type 2). The total possible range of combinations of forename, patronymic, and surname is as follows:[4]

[4] See also Nakhimovsky (1976: 115–16).

(1) Full forename alone (Type 1), e.g. Владимир
(2) Full forename alone (Type 2), e.g. Роза
(3) Short forename alone (Type 1), e.g. Володя
(4) Full forename (Type 1 or 2) + patronymic, e.g. Татьяна Петровна
(5) Full forename (Type 1 or 2) + surname, e.g. Татьяна Иванова
(6) Full forename (Type 1 or 2) + patronymic + surname, e.g. Татьяна Петровна Иванова.
(7) Short forename (Type 1) + surname, e.g. Таня Иванова
(8) Patronymic alone, e.g. Петровна
(9) Surname alone, e.g. Иванова
(10) Diminutive or nickname alone.

Combinations other than the above (such as *Таня Петровна, *Владимирович Петров) are ungrammatical, at least in standard varieties. All the combinations given may occur as modes of address, though some are much rarer than others in this function.

In official documents the order is often surname + full forename + patronymic, e.g. Петров Владимир Андреевич, and rarely this order may also occur in speech, in which case it expresses an official attitude or possibly disapproval (Nikolaeva 1972: 138–40); the alternative order is full forename + patronymic + surname (Владимир Андреевич Петров), often with the forename and patronymic represented in writing by the initials (В. А. Петров). In the absence of proper accounts of the social and functional determination of Russian address by name and title both before and after the Revolution, only tentative assessments of change in the system can be made. Most obvious are the changes in the functions of combinations 1 and 8 above.

One of the newest developments in modern Russian is the diminishing use of patronymics in the official mention of an individual, for example, Владимир Петров or В. Петров. The trend to avoid patronymics started in the 1960s and soon became apparent in the press. Some examples (quoted in Kalakuckaja 1984: 149, 150, 145):

В редакционной почте этих лет нас просят рассказать о В. Лановом. (*Советский экран*, 1973, No. 4)

Our correspondents are asking us to tell them about V. Lanovoj.

Интервьюировала женщин Д. Рудая. (*Литературная газета*, 1981, No. 10)

The women were interviewed by D. Rudaja.

Идея «Окон» принадлежит блестящему мастеру рисунка М. Черемныху. (*Вечерняя Москва*, 22 January 1973)

The idea of 'Windows' belongs to the brilliant master of drawing M. Čeremnyx.

The absence of the patronymic seems to convey a sense of familiarity with the bearer of the name and is also a reflection of a shorter social distance between the referent and the user of the name (Formanovskaja 1982*a*: 119–22). Accordingly, continued use of the patronymic can be taken as an expression of particular respect and/or high social prestige. Though no normative rules on the avoidance of patronymics have ever been officially published, the names that continued to be used with the patronymics were the names of high officials, especially the Communist Party and government leaders. For example, on p. 1 of *Правда* of 18 April 1985, Mixail Gorbačev is referred to as М. С. Горбачев and Михаил Сергеевич Горбачев, while the people he meets are named by the forename only:

Во время знакомства с районом Михаила Сергеевича пригласила в гости . . . семья Никишиных—строитель Тамара и работник Главмосавтотранса Вячеслав.

During his tour of the district, Mixail Sergeevič was invited to the house of the Nikišins—Tamara, a construction worker, and Vjačeslav, an employee of the Moscow Transportation Agency.

The absence of a patronymic can also indicate a younger person; for example, in an article in *Правда* of 24 March 1985 (p. 2), describing vocational training, the names of older workers and directors invariably include the patronymic (Анатолий Леонидович Волозин, Николай Александрович Акулинко, директор объединения Иван Афанасьевич Ефанов), while younger workers are named by forename and surname only (Леонид Андреев, Владимир Громыко, З. Мохорева). This confirms that the use of patronymics is consistent with the V address and shows power and social distance; the absence of patronymics, on the contrary, is a sign of social equalizing. Since social equalizing is particularly relevant in the presentation of such events as sports or arts, the absence of patronymics is characteristic of the respective publications (the magazine *Советский экран*, quoted above; the newspapers *Советский спорт*, *Футбол-Хоккей*).

Despite the fact that this omission of the patronymic in official style is relatively new, it is not a novel development altogether: references to

popular figures (but not to government or party officials) by the forename and surname were also common in the press in the late
1920s–early 1930s. For example, the pioneers of the shock-worker
movement were known by their forenames and surnames only, e.g.
Мария Виноградова, Алексей Стаханов.

It is important not to lose sight of the fact that the threefold system of
forename, patronymic, and surname was not always in operation in
Russia. There are records of nobles with forename, patronymic, and surname dating from the fifteenth century onwards, but the word фамилия
and official interest in recording surnames date only from Peter the
Great's time (Unbegaun 1972: 11–19, 22–5; Superanskaja and Suslova
1981: 15–16).

Although nineteenth-century literature provides examples of patronymics and surnames in use among peasants, the claim that before the
beginning of the twentieth century they were only exceptionally used in
the everyday speech of the common people (Superanskaja 1969: 65–6;
Superanskaja and Suslova 1981: 22) is, on the whole, probably sound.
Even to the present day there are regions of Russia where anthropo-
nymical systems differing from the official one survive, though the
latter is of course used for official purposes everywhere (Superanskaja
1969: 64–7; Simina 1969; Čumakova 1970).

Unlike the Russian language itself, Russian modes of address have
not been standardized, except in so far as the threefold system of personal names has been canonized by the state administration and certain
handbooks on etiquette recommend certain usage. (To this we might add
those cases where a particular usage has been institutionalized, as in the
army, the courts, schools, etc.) Nor has there been a high degree of
normalization: even at the present time norms of address vary, both
regionally and from one social group to another. Even among speakers
of the standard language there are variations. The main territorial
distinction is between the towns and the countryside. The main social
distinction is between workers and intellectuals. It is therefore not
possible to distinguish unconditionally between standard and non-
standard address forms. Nevertheless, the system of reference by names
and titles in use among middle-aged intellectuals (Nikolaeva 1972),
even though not to be treated as standard, might well at least be taken as
a model for foreigners learning Russian.

The use of the patronymic alone is nowadays mainly restricted to the
countryside, and is said to be the appropriate form when both respect
and familiarity are present in the relationship (Bolla *et al.* 1970: 272–3).

It is particularly suitable for addressing old people (Kantorovič 1966: 121; 1974: 49). Among the nineteenth-century functions of the patronymic alone was one as a form of address between spouses.[5] This is now almost obsolete.

Spellings of the kind Иваныч found in nineteenth-century sources indicate that the normal allegro pronunciation of patronymics known to present-day Russian was already in existence then.[6] Syncope now produces realizations of the type Иванч, with the result that the type Никитич, Ильич (with the ending for masculine a-stems) is no longer automatically felt to be distinct from other patronymics (the type Иванович). This leads to hyper-correct spellings, such as Никитович, which, however, are still regarded as incorrect (Ickovič 1961).

In the nineteenth century, in addition to the present-day type ending in -ович (fem. -овна), patronymics in -ов(а), -ин(а), were still in use. Many surnames, such as Иванов, Еремин, are by origin patronymics of the short type. In the country systems other than the official threefold one have long been established, and in a twofold system it is often not possible to identify the second element in official terms, since patronymics and surnames are often identical. The following extract from a work of literature by a writer renowned for his knowledge of the Russian countryside demonstrates this problem:

На межрайонном совещании председателей колхозов и директоров совхозов Николай Алексеевич Аксенов, председатель колхоза «Пламя коммунизма»,—Аксеныч, как его попросту называли,—выдал такую огневую речь, что сам потом удивился. (V. Šukšin, *Правда*, in *Сельские жители*, Moscow, 1963: 176)

At the inter-district conference of collective-farm chairmen and state-farm managers Nikolaj Alekseevič Aksenov, chairman of the 'Flame of Communism' collective farm—Aksenyč, as he was simply called—made such a fiery speech, that afterwards he was surprised himself.

Thus, the use of the patronymic alone (along with the address in V) is characteristic of the countryside and presupposes a friendly or respectful attitude. It is also associated with the character type of a wise old man (Nakhimovsky 1976: 95). It was probably the respectful element of the patronymic usage and its character type connotations that brought about the practice, in the 1920s, of using patronymics alone to refer to popular political figures (Seliščev 1928: 81). The most famous example

---

[5] Attested, for example, in Puškin's *Дубровский* (1833).

[6] Cf. the example quoted from Čexov in Chapter 8, below (p. 305).

is Lenin's patronymic Ильич, by which he was both addressed and referred to, originally by the peasants (Bolla *et al.* 1970: 273)[7] and later by all sections of the population. The relevance of character connotations of a wise old man is confirmed by the fact that another common way of referring to Lenin, especially in the later decades of the Soviet society, used to be дедушка Ленин 'grandfather Lenin'. Seliščev's other example, Калиныч, is derived from the surname Калинин (itself by form and origin a patronymic).

Address by patronymic alone (and by pseudo-patronymics like Аксеныч) is much rarer in the towns; in particular, it is not used by intellectuals, who regard it as characteristic of the speech of peasants. The kind of exchange in which it is thought to be appropriate may be seen from two cartoons in *Krokodil*. In one the conversation is between a woman, who is apparently a shop assistant helping herself illegally to some of the stock, and a man, who appears to be a manager or supervisor:

—Ты почему так много выносишь?
—Так я же, Петрович, вчера не брала! (*Крокодил,* 1974, 2: 11)

'Why are you taking home so much?'
'Well, you see, Petrovič, I didn't take any yesterday.'

In the other, two watchmen are keeping guard over various items of imported equipment, and one says to the other:

Слышь, Петрович, говорят, скоро нам и зонтики импортные выдадут . . . (*Крокодил,* 1973, 31: 10)

'Have you heard, Petrovič, it's said that soon we shall be issued with imported umbrellas too . . .'

Of course, address in the country differs from urban address in many respects. Even without social and regional variation, the realizations of an otherwise uniform system would clearly vary functionally owing to the variation between urban and rural situations and relationships. In the intimacy of a small village the social distance corresponding to the use of V or forename + patronymic is rarer than in a town. It may be absent altogether. Investigation of the modes of address in the village of

---

[7] Examples of rural influence on urban speech are very rare; it is quite possible that the use of Ильич was originated from above, in order to create the image of a wise but friendly political leader. Even if the original use by the rural population did occur, it was definitely promoted, in a purposeful manner, by official propaganda. In the 1960s the use of such expressions as родной Ильич 'dear Il´ič' (along with the ideologically similar дедушка Ленин) became virtually obligatory in children's literature.

Akčim, Perm *oblast'*, for example, produced a very small number of instances of forename + patronymic, almost all of which were used in addressing newcomers or visitors. Address by patronymic alone is also very rare here, but appears to have a separate function, albeit very restricted. The most common form of address by name in Akčim is the long or short form of the forename (Gruzberg 1974: 51–4). In the village of Osipovka, Gor'kij *oblast'*, where a Central Russian dialect is spoken, address is realized almost exclusively in forms of the forename. Patronymics do not occur at all (Čumakova 1970).

The system for the use of forename alone has changed in one significant respect since the nineteenth century: the respective functions of the full and short forms of Type 1 are different from what they were. Nowadays the short form is stylistically neutral, while the full form is expressive.[8] In the nineteenth century the converse held: the long form was neutral and the short form expressive. Exactly when and how this change came about is a matter that has yet to be investigated, but it is well attested, especially by the usage portrayed in narrative fiction. For example, in Čexov's *Дама с собачкой* (1899) Dimitrij Gurov is addressed by his wife as follows:—Тебе, Димитрий, совсем не идет роль фата 'The role of a fop doesn't suit you at all, Dimitrij.' Gurov himself says to his beloved mistress: Но поймите, Анна, поймите . . . 'But understand, Anna, understand . . .'. In neither case is there reason to think any expressive meaning was intended by the author.

A significant observation on the use of a short form is made by the author in Čexov's *Дом с мезонином* (1896), where one of the heroines is introduced as follows:[9]

Когда она уехала, Петр Петрович стал рассказывать. Эта девушка, по его словам, была из хорошей семьи, и звали ее Лидией Волчанино-вой . . .

When she left, Petr Petrovič began his story. This girl, he said, was from a good family, and her name was Lidija Volčaninova . . .

Soon afterwards the author's words continue:

Лидия, или как ее звали дома, Лида, говорила больше с Белокуровым, чем со мной.

Lidija, or Lida as she was called at home, spoke more with Belokurov than with me.

[8] However, the precise stylistic distinction between long and short forms is not identical in all cases.

[9] Note also the use of the predicative instrumental with the verb звать 'be called', no longer possible in twentieth-century language.

The significant point is that Čexov felt an explanation necessary. Лида was then a marked form appropriate to domestic use. Nowadays (assuming address by forename alone) she would be called Лида everywhere, not only at home.

In present-day usage full forms (Type 1) function in several different ways, expressing either a positive or a negative attitude to the person addressed. The expressive information they convey depends on the situation and on who the interlocutors are. As Superanskaja (1969: 127–8) points out, the appropriate address form in a given set of circumstances depends on a number of determinants including age, social position, the subject of discourse, the situation, etc., and it is therefore not possible to divide particular forms into marked and unmarked. Nevertheless, as in the case of T/V, it is possible in the presence of a known set of determinants to say which forms of other parts of the address system are neutral and which are marked. In the case of the full forms of Type 1 forenames, however, there is no set of determinants in whose presence their use would be neutral. We therefore find ourselves unable to agree with Superanskaja's statement (1969: 134): 'For Russians the short form (сокращенное имя) is not the real forename. The real forename is recorded in a person's passport, and by that name he is addressed on official occasions.' In official situations it is most unlikely that anyone but a child would be addressed by his forename alone, and the full forename alone used to a child expresses a particular attitude on the part of the speaker. What is perhaps meant (but not stated) here is that on official occasions the full forename together with patronymic is used.

A position similar to Superanskaja's is taken in Bondaletov and Danilina (1970), where it is claimed that neither long nor short forms are neutral, but that each is connected with specific situations. Although certain situations are cited, there is no example of the use of the full form alone. In an earlier article Danilina (1969) argued that the short forms could be either affectionate or neutral, but that in most situations they were affectionate and occupied a special intermediate position. She here (1969: 159) stated bluntly that the full forms were stylistically neutral, but gave no relevant examples. It is doubtful whether any are possible.

The forms and functions of forenames, as of names and elements of address generally, have yet to be described adequately. Particularly needed is a scheme for distinguishing between full, short, and diminutive forms with a means of assessing the emotional information they convey. Superanskaja (1969: 132) puts forward a tentative framework as follows. Note that the full form is significantly absent from this scheme.

(1) The short forename (without 'emotionally loaded' suffixes), e.g. Юра, Таня
(2) Forms with suffixes of 'subjective assessment':
  (*a*) Caressing (ласкательное), e.g. Юрочка, Танюша
  (*b*) Diminutive (уменьшительное), e.g. Юрик, Танечка
  (*c*) Familiar/vulgar (фамильярное/вульгарное, грубое), e.g. Юрка, Танька
  (*d*) Teasing (поддразнивающее), e.g. Юрище, Танище (extremely rare)
  (*e*) Scornful (пренебрежительное), e.g. Юрашка, Таняшка
  (*f*) Pejorative (уничижительное), e.g. Юришка, Танюшка
  (*g*) Contemptuous (презрительное), e.g. Юрчище, etc.

Further suffixes, and further shades of emotion, are possible, e.g. Юраха, Танюха. However, of these forms, some are hardly ever used. The frequently used ones are (*a*)–(*c*), and it is often hard to draw a line between the caressing and the diminutive 'assessment'; sometimes, even the so-called 'familiar' form can be used as a diminutive in some speech situations (Formanovskaja 1982*a*: 118).

The use of the surname alone is generally rare in standard Russian; the surname is supposed to be accompanied by a title (see below). Let us mention, however, one area where the use of surnames alone is clearly marked, viz. the use of surnames to younger children. As early as pre-school, children are addressed by their surname alone if they misbehave or if the teacher is giving an order (e.g. Петров, сядь! 'Sit down, Petrov'). Nakhimovsky (1976: n. 5) cites the short story *Комаров* by Jurij Nagibin which is built around the use of the surname alone address to a 4-year-old boy. This usage continues into elementary and secondary school and is assumed by children themselves as a sign of negative attitude and an indicator of interpersonal relationships (Nakhimovsky 1976: 84–6).

Name-giving

In pre-Revolutionary Russia everyone had an officially noted religion. (Nationality, on the other hand, was not officially recorded.) All Orthodox children had to be christened and their names had to be chosen from the Orthodox Church's list (known as the *svjatcy*) containing the names of saints (Superanskaja 1970: 184). Other names were not permitted, but in any case only a fraction of the 2,000 or so names in the list were ever used. It was the custom to choose the name of one of the saints whose festival fell on the eighth day after the birth or on one of the first eight days of the child's life. This was not compulsory, at least in theory, but in practice the child was often given a name by the priest regardless of, or even contrary to, the wishes of the parents. The custom was in fact very closely observed, especially in the countryside, as has been shown by an analysis of the names given in an area spread over part of the Tambov and Penza *gubernii* in 1884. Here, for example, 91 per cent of all Tat´janas were born in January and 92 per cent of all Agrippinas in June (Nikonov 1974: 144).

The Church maintained records of those it had christened, but birth certificates were issued not by the Church but by secular authorities. The Church recorded the form of the name given in the Church calendar, but the secular authorities recorded secular forms, including even local forms. The result was inconsistency (Superanskaja 1970). This system came to an end when the Church was deprived of its power following the October Revolution. The duty of recording names was taken over by the загс (отдел записи актов гражданского состояния) and the Church's list ceased to have any legal significance. The end of restrictions had spectacular results. A mass of new names came into use in the 1920s, some of which were to acquire permanent popularity, but most of which were to disappear before long. The number of new names coming into use at this time was large, but the number of children being given them was fairly small, and in the country it was very small. A survey of girls' names given to babies born in 1930 in Kostroma and Penza has produced the following figures:

	Number of names			% of new names	
	Total	Old	New	% of all names	% of children
Kostroma	139	41	98	70	29
Penza	88	41	47	53	12

Figures for rural areas in the same part of Russia in the same year show greater conservatism. In the Čuxloma *rajon* of Kostroma *oblast´*, for example, less than one in six of the names given were new and only one baby girl in a hundred was given a new name (Nikonov 1974: 66–7).

The new names were of various kinds. In the first place there were foreign names such as Ада, Альберт, Альбина, Артур, Жанна, Роберт, Эдуард, Эмма, etc., which had been known from literature before the Revolution. Secondly, there were Old Russian names which had not been included in the Church's list; e.g. Лада, Рогнеда, Роксана, Руслан, Руслана, Рюрик, Святослав, Славомир. Here we may mention Светлана, which originated in Žukovskij's ballad of that name (1812) and is attested in neither the Church calendar nor Old Russian sources. It became very popular in the Soviet period. A third source was provided by words which previously had some other function as appellatives; e.g. Авангард, Альянс, Баррикада, Герой, Идея, Лира, Трактор, Электрификация (see also Chapter 5, p. 221). There were also former surnames: Веллингтон, Жорес, Марат, Маркс, Энгельс. Finally, there were new forenames derived from existing elements, including several stump-compounds. Among those which have survived is Майя, but even this is rare nowadays. Others, which are now never, or hardly ever, given to children were mentioned in Chapter 5 (p. 206).

The principal reason for giving names different from those in the Church calendar was to break with the past. Another reason was the rejection of the Church and its rules. It has been pointed out also that some of the strangest names may have arisen from sheer ignorance (Nikonov 1974: 69–70). Even such oddities as Винегрет 'vegetable salad', Эмбрион 'embryo', and Комментария 'commentary' have been noted, and it is easy to see a parallel with the kind of misunderstanding which led, for example, to substitution of элементы for алементы and of дистанция for инстанция (see p. 195 above). These names were simply fine-sounding exotic words to their users, who may not have known their meaning.

Yet another type of innovation was that of naming children with short forms, i.e. of recording names such as Ася (from Анна or Анастасия), Ира (from Ирина), Оля (from Ольга), Петя (from Петр), Слава (from Владислав, Станислав, Ярослав) on birth certificates. In the first twenty years or so of the Soviet period such cases, like other abnormalities, were at least as likely to be the result of low literacy as of deliberate intent.[10] These forms subsequently caused difficulties when the necessity arose of deriving patronymics from them (Superanskaja 1969: 134). At least one of such names, Ася, is now used as a name in its own right.

The sudden appearance of large numbers of new names and the

---

[10] This also explains many unusual spellings, such as Ерина (for Ирина), Владимер (for Владимир), Андилина (for Ангелина), Лианора (for Элеонора) (Nikonov 1974: 68, 255).

growth of the list of names being given to new-born children was an exceptional, temporary, and mainly urban phenomenon. A survey of the names given to babies in the towns of Kursk, Kaluga, Kostroma, Vladimir, Tambov, Penza, and Ul′janovsk, and in the surrounding country areas, shows that the list of names shrank considerably between 1930 and 1961. In the towns it was more than halved (Nikonov 1974: 76).

Before the Revolution the social distribution of forenames along class lines was relatively well established. Certain names were common among workers and peasants, others among the nobility and intelligentsia. Some names were even virtually taboo in one class or the other. Nikonov claims, for example, that 'it is impossible to imagine at the beginning of the present century either a Countess Matrena or Fekla, or a peasant Tamara' (1974: 15). There were, of course, changes in fashion, but usually, as a name became rarer among the lower class, so it became more common in the upper class, and vice versa. It is significant that this should be so despite the constraints of the Church calendar. The peasantry, no doubt, even when not actually coerced by priests, were more likely to follow the calendar, while the upper class was more likely to disregard custom (when they saw fit) and exercise choice, though they too were restricted to the names in the *svjatcy*.

The social dynamics of change in giving names is demonstrated by the example of Мария, which at the beginning of the nineteenth century was extremely popular among the nobility. It was also gaining popularity among the peasants, however, and from 1860 onwards, having become well known as a typical peasant's name, it declined rapidly among the nobility (Nikonov 1974: 15–16). The name was so frequent that it even developed the connotation 'typical Russian girl', which, according to some authors, is still perceived in the contemporary language (Superanskaja 1978: 32).

The social differentiation of forenames went further than a simple division into nobility and peasantry: there were also typical merchants' names (Савва, Фома, Гордей) and priests' names (Никон, Мисаил, Варлаам) (Bondaletov 1970: 18–19), though, in the priests' case, the forename given at birth could be changed by the student in the seminary. Typical peasants' names in the decade preceding the October Revolution were: Авдотья, Анна, Василий, Екатерина, Иван, Мария. At that time Александр(а) and Николай were typical of the nobility (Nikonov 1974: 16); for example, the last Russian Empress, née

Alix Hesse-Darmstadt, assumed the name Александра when she adopted Orthodoxy to marry Nicholas II.

Changes in the relative popularity of forenames following the Revolution mainly affected the old names given in the *svjatcy*, for none of the new exotic names permitted by the abolition of Church control were anywhere near the top of the popularity scale. By 1930 Анна, Василий, Екатерина, Иван, Мария were, in the towns at least, being rarely given to new-born children, having been replaced as the most popular names by Валентина, Владимир, Галина, Нина, Тамара, Юрий. Developments in the countryside followed the same pattern but more slowly.

By 1961 further changes in fashion had occurred; the names being most frequently given were Александр, Андрей, Владимир, Галина, Елена, Игорь, Ирина, Марина, Наталья, Ольга, Светлана, Сергей, Татьяна, Юрий. The countryside continued, more or less, to follow, but lagging behind the towns, while the towns themselves were (and are) led by Moscow. Many peasant names in common use before the Revolution had by 1961, or even earlier, fallen into obscurity: names such as Агафья, Аксен, Анисья, Архип, Афанасий, Матрена, Прасковья, Феврония, Фекла (Barannikova *et al.* 1970: 178–9). The increasing interest in religion in the late 1970s and especially in the 1980s (accompanied by a growing number of baptisms, on which no statistics are yet available) led to a revival of some names that were associated with Russian tradition and Russian Orthodoxy: Даниил, Гавриил, Марфа; the names of popular saints Алексей, Николай, and Георгий again became fashionable.

Of the post-1917 innovations Светлана has enjoyed the greatest success, but in 1961 Алла, Валерий, Виктория, Эдуард were still being given to a fair number of children (Nikonov 1974: 79). New popular figures had a certain effect on the popularity of names: for example, after the launch of the first and second manned spacecraft in 1961 and 1962 (with Jurij Gagarin on board the former and German Titov in the latter), the names Юрий and Герман enjoyed considerable success for the next several years.

The details of the popularity of names given here (quoted for the most part from Ščetinin 1968 and Nikonov 1974) are not based on surveys of the whole USSR or even the whole Russian Republic, but it is unlikely that a project of such dimensions would produce significantly different results from the surveys of representative samples already made. One conclusion common to them all is that the overall number of forenames in use is decreasing, and decreased particularly rapidly in the Soviet period. Study of the names given to new-born children in the Rostov *oblast'* (the results of which are probably not untypical) shows that the number of masculine names in active use (i.e. being given to over 0.6 per cent of new-born babies) fell from 310 in the seventeenth century to 165 in the first decade of the twentieth century. In the Soviet period, however, the number fell spectacularly to 49 in the first half of the 1960s. The number of female names in use at that time was only 21 (Ščetinin 1970: 249). One of the reasons for such a decline is the decrease in the number of children within a family: traditional families had several children, while the tendency in the twentieth century, especially in urban areas, was towards a single-child family. In a single-child family, the name given to this child no longer has to distinguish this child from the other siblings; this factor, along with the fashion in giving forenames, apparently played a significant role in reducing the name inventory.

In terms of the kind mentioned above, the question of social distinction of names along class lines no longer arises: there is no nobility and no merchant class. On priests' names we have no precise information, but Алексий, Сергий (not Сергей), Никон, Пимен are common names of modern Russian bishops and patriarchs. There are still differences between town and country, and within the town, between the intelligentsia and working class, but they are less marked than they used to be and can often be interpreted as the results of the time-lag in fashion. There is also a certain amount of regional variation, though this too has decreased since the Revolution and is still decreasing. The question of social variation on other lines has also been researched, and the results, while they do not justify the claim that 'the children of fitters, managers, manual labourers, and professors have the same names' (Nikonov 1974: 80), show that standard of education and profession are much less clearly reflected in choice of names than they used to be (Barannikova *et al.* 1970: 178–80) and in some districts are not reflected at all (Belyk 1970: 23). The influence of the Church calendar can still be seen in some rural areas: a count made in several *rajony* of the Brjansk *oblast'* reveals that the annual popularity peaks for certain names were as clear in 1966 as they had been in 1926 (Kondratenko 1970; Nikonov 1974: 145). On the other hand, a similar count in Sverdlovsk—probably typical of towns—shows total obliteration of traditional patterns (Korotkova 1970).

Legal requirements

After the Revolution the law restricting the choice of forename to those in the *svjatcy* was abolished, but the Soviet Union had its own laws dealing with names. The position was that parents registering their child's birth at the office of registrar (загс) had the right to give him or her any name they like, though the officials may draw their attention to the undesirability of odd names. The only circumstances in which the officials might have refused a name (according to a spokesman for the Ministry of Justice) were if it 'offended human dignity or is not compatible with Soviet morality' (Belyk N.A. «Юридическая служба «Известий». Имя, отчество, фамилия». *Известия*, 17 May 1974). If the parents were married the child's patronymic had to be derived from the father's forename, but an unmarried mother was allowed to choose any patronymic. The surname was the same as that of the parents, unless they had different surnames, in which case they made a choice between the two. In this, as in other matters, the officials were allowed to make a decision when the parents could not agree. If the mother was unmarried, the child was given her surname, unless the father and mother made a joint application or there was a paternity order in existence.

On marriage both partners jointly chose between three possibilities:

(1) Both surnames stay the same as before marriage.

(2) The wife takes her husband's surname.

(3) The husband takes his wife's surname.

In the early decades of the Soviet Union, hyphenated forms made up of both husband's and wife's surnames were often used; for example, a well-known Russian linguist N. S. Čemodanov had a double surname Čemodanov-Šor in the 1930s (later simplified to just Čemodanov). After the War, the practice of hyphenated surnames was abandoned in the Russian Republic but was allowed in the Azerbaidjan, Belorussian, Georgian, Moldavian, Tadjik, and Ukrainian Republics. However, since hyphenated surnames can have other origins (Superanskaja and Suslova 1981: 126–9), e.g. Bonč-Bruevič (of Belorussian origin), Petrov-Vodkin, Voroncova-Daškova, these were retained by their bearers.

It is perhaps worth noting in passing that before 1917 surnames too, owing to the different conditions governing their evolution in various sections of the population, were differentiated along class lines (Superanskaja 1973: 235; Nikonov 1974: 216; Avanesov 1975: 151; Kalakuckaja 1984: 16–39). The high degree of social mobility and the adoption of surnames by the non-Russian population in the Soviet Union must surely have confused former patterns.

Titles

Tsarist Russia preserved to the end its elaborate system of address by title, based on Peter the Great's Table of Ranks (Табель о рангах). Holders of ranks in the Table were addressed as follows:

Rank	Form of Address
1st and 2nd Classes	Ваше высокопревосходительство
3rd and 4th Classes	Ваше превосходительство
5th Class	Ваше высокородие
6th, 7th, and 8th Classes	Ваше высокоблагородие
8th to 14th Classes	Ваше благородие

In addition, the royal couple were addressed as Ваши (императорские) величества, other members of the royal family as Ваше (императорское) высочество, and princes and counts as Ваше сиятельство or Ваша светлость. Among equals in rank князь and граф were also used in address. Merchants were Ваше степенство (a form without official recognition), bishops Ваше преосвященство, and monks Ваше преподобие or Ваше высокопреподобие. The names of holders of ranks and members of the nobility were prefixed by their titles: e.g. князь Волконский, коллежский ассессор Ковалев, etc. (Nikolaev and Petrov 1903: 188, 407, 415–66). These titles were strictly adhered to, especially in correspondence, where the use of V in addressing a single person was signalled by the capital В (the practice still inviolable in CSR).

To the names of other members of privileged social strata the titles господин and госпожа were prefixed; the use of these names was a sign of respect. While it may not be easy to define exactly who might reasonably expect to be called господин or госпожа, it is at least obvious that before the Revolution the vast majority of the population was not, and did not expect to be, addressed and referred to in this way. It was thus, in social terms, far from being the equivalent of Mr, Mrs, and Miss, or similar titles in other European languages (Kantorovič 1966: 113). Those to whose names господин and госпожа were prefixed could be addressed as милостивый государь and милостивая государыня, or сударь and сударыня, or мосье, мадам, and мадемуазель, or барин, барыня, and барышня, or Ваша милость, the choice hinging mainly on the relative or absolute social status of the interlocutors, but partly on situational factors.

The bulk of the system just described officially ceased to operate with the publication of the Bolshevik decree abolishing civil ranks (Декрет об уничтожении сословий и гражданских чинов) (*Систематический сборник* . . .1919: 13). The titles господин and госпожа with their related forms of address were not affected by this decree, but being alien to the working class and, especially, to the peasants, they soon fell out of use (Suprun 1969: 42; Trofimenko 1973: 15). Сударь and сударыня also disappeared.

The address form товарищ originated long before 1917, but its use at the beginning of the century was mainly restricted to student and political groups (Seliščev 1928: 193).[11] In the plural, however, its sphere of use was wider, as we can see from the address Ко всем рабочим России от депутатов-рабочих Государственной Думы 'To all workers of Russia from working-class deputies of the State Parliament' published in the newspaper *Народный вестник* for 19 May 1906, which contains sentences such as the following: Итак, товарищи, между государственной думой и самодержавным правительством возникло столкновение . . . 'So, comrades, the State Parliament and the Tsarist autocratic government have confronted each other . . .'. Although it is used here to address *all* workers, the fact remains that the addressees are a finite social group. Since 1906 the functions of товарищи were extended to address almost any audience (with certain well-known exceptions, such as convicted and unconvicted prisoners, and foreigners from capitalist countries). In the Soviet Union, it became the most common form of plural address.

In the first post-Revolutionary period товарищ (both plural and singular) retained its exclusivity. It is characteristic that in *Известия* dated 27 October 1917 the statement Ко всем рабочим Петрограда 'To all workers of Petrograd' began Товарищи! whereas that addressed to the population at large (К населению Петрограда) began Граждане!

Гражданин, calque of the title *citoyen/citoyenne* 'citizen' introduced in the French Revolution as a general form of address expressing equality, was given legal status both by the decree abolishing civil ranks

---

[11] When the Bolsheviks gained power, certain students expressed opposition by abandoning товарищ and adopting коллега (Jakobson 1921: 19). The occasional use of the latter word was retained, though without formal recognition, in academia.

(see above) and by the decree О приобретении прав российского гражданства 'On gaining the rights of Russian citizenship' of 1918 (Uluxanov 1968: 177; Schubert 1984: 109 ff.).

According to Jakobson (1921: 19), товарищ had, even by 1920, to a large extent lost its socialist character and was becoming similar in function to Czech *pane*, except in the countryside where it was still so new that peasants would address delegates from Moscow as господин товарищ. It is likely, though, that the notion of ideological solidarity and loyalty to the Soviet regime, associated with товарищ, was revived in the 1930s, during the Stalin purges: it is at this time that when addressing his investigator as товарищ, an unconvicted prisoner or any other person under 'class suspicion' would be told Тамбовский волк тебе (Вам) товарищ 'I am no comrade of yours (lit. your comrade is a Tambov wolf)' (Nakhimovsky 1976: 98). This is suggested by the assertion that the neutral form of address to any citizen until the 1930s was гражданин/гражданка, and that only from the late 1930s did товарищ tend to replace it as a general form applicable to almost any Soviet citizen (Suprun 1969: 42–3): the society had become more homogeneous and the appearance of ideological loyalty was a *sine qua non* of anyone who remained free. At the same time the use of гражданин became a signal 'of the limitations of a citizen's rights or of real or imagined accusations' (Nakhimovsky 1976: 98).

In the post-Stalin period, товарищ became even more common, and гражданин became rarer, tending to be restricted to official or even unfriendly address (Uluxanov 1968: 177). In the 1960–1980s, гражданин was commonly used by the militia to members of the public, but the fact that even in this official usage it conveyed expressive information may be deduced from the following statement made by a senior militiaman when questioned on the need for its use: 'We often say товарищ. And the less it is necessary to replace the friendly товарищ with the official гражданин the easier for us' (*Литературная газета*, 12 May 1964, quoted by Kostomarov 1965: 40 n.).[12]

In the armed forces the use of titles and the corresponding address forms was abolished by *Приказ* No. 1 of the Petrograd Soviet, and this

---

[12] Meanwhile, the word гражданин continued to be used, without any negative connotations, in the meaning 'citizen (of a country)' and in fact became very frequently used in the 1970s with the introduction of the notion единая историческая общность советский народ 'the Soviet nation as a united historically motivated community' (introduced in 1972, at the 50th anniversary of the formation of the USSR) and гражданин Советского Союза 'citizen of the Soviet Union'.

was confirmed by an order of the Provisional Government on 5 March 1917 (*Сборник указов* . . . 1917: 318; Černyx 1948: 107–8). The new rules of address using господин генерал, господин полковник, господин унтер-офицер, etc., were in force for only a few months, for after October, in the new Workers' and Peasants' Red Army ranks were abolished (see also p. 251). The notion of superior and subordinate remained, however, and in exchanges between superior and subordinate the form товарищ + name of appointment was instituted; e.g. товарищ красноармеец, товарищ командир роты, товарищ командир полка, товарищ врач, etc. (*Устав* . . . 1918: 13–14). Since the word товарищ implied class solidarity, the oxymoron character of such combinations was probably negligible. Even with the subsequent re-introduction of ranks the system of address with товарищ has remained in operation to the present day; e.g. товарищ рядовой, товарищ сержант, товарищ ефрейтор, товарищ старшина, товарищ генерал, etc. The forms Рядовой Петров, Сержант Кольцов, etc. are used by superiors addressing subordinates (*Общевоинские уставы* . . . 1971: 12–15).

Even before the Revolution товарищ could be prefixed to nouns denoting jobs and also to surnames, though these uses were then common mostly in political circles. They now occur more widely. The combinations товарищ + forename alone (whether in address or reference) and товарищ + a professional noun (in reference), which occurred both before and after the Revolution for a time, are now obsolete. The following press extracts demonstrate these now archaic combinations:

Смерть вырвала из наших рядов товарища Веру, стойкого борца за дело социализма . . . (*Известия*, 2 November 1917)

Death has torn from our ranks Comrade Vera, a staunch fighter for the cause of Socialism . . .

На общем собрании товар. солдаты кричали: «Да здравствует Троцкий!» «Да здравствует Ленин!» (*Известия*, 4 November 1917)

At the general meeting the comrade soldiers cried: "Long live Trockij! Long live Lenin!"

As late as 5 November 1917 we find a letter to the editor of *Известия* from a regimental committee addressing him as господин редактор, but well before this it is clear that in certain circles господин in both address and reference has acquired an ironic, contemptuous component:

Верноподданые г-на Ленина обязуются верить ему на слово. (*Дело народа*,[13] 18 October 1917)
The loyal subjects of Mr Lenin pledge themselves to take him at his word.

The Bolsheviks in particular applied господин to their enemies[14] and they continued to do so: in the Soviet press of the 1970s and early 1980s, the critics of the Soviet regime, including dissidents, were called господа, e.g. господин Сахаров applied to the prominent dissident academician Saxarov prior to and during his exile in Gor´kij in 1980–85. Nevertheless, together with certain other pre-Revolutionary titles, господин (as well as the plural дамы и господа 'ladies and gentlemen') has continued to have a neutral function in addressing foreigners from capitalist countries. It is especially common in diplomatic usage, where titles such as Ваше величество, Ваше высочество, and Ваше превосходительство also occur. In diplomatic exchanges even Soviet leaders could be given the titles господин and Ваше превосходительство.

Unlike барин and барыня, which were identified with the old regime and quickly dropped, барышня survived for a time in both address and reference to young women, especially in certain professions (Seliščev 1928: 156; Karcevskij 1923: 14; Obermann 1969: 173–4). It was in use until the end of the 1920s, and still current in the 1960s (Obermann 1969: 198), but only as a form of reference, not of address. In the 1960s–1980s мадам might still occasionally be heard, especially from older people (Suprun 1969: 42; Trofimenko 1973: 15). It is also used as an ironic or disapproving form of address.

In the 1960s the desemantization of the word товарищ became particularly apparent in that it could no longer be appropriately used without the following surname, ranking, or occupational name. This brought about the problem of how to address strangers; this has led to proposals for the revival of сударь and сударыня (Solouxin 1964). This proposal was never taken seriously and the problem so far has remained unsolved. It certainly has not been solved by the introduction of молодой человек, мужчина, дедушка, to address men of different age, and девушка, женщина, бабушка, гражданочка to address women (Formanovskaja 1982*b*: 26–8). Of these forms of address, девушка has become particularly popular in colloquial usage; the fact that it is used to address saleswomen, waitresses, etc. regardless of their age is indicative

---

[13] Organ of the Socialist-Revolutionary Party. Its readers were addressed as товарищи.
[14] For examples of Lenin's use of this word, see Mizin (1975).

of its desemantization. However, this usage is rejected by normative grammar (cf. the recommendations in Formanovskaja 1982*b*: 43–4).

Since the use of the titles товарищ, гражданин is a relatively recent phenomenon, we can trace the gradual changes undergone by these words in the language of the twentieth century. Товарищ starts out as the title expressing solidarity and is so used in the pre-Revolutionary and early post-Revolutionary years. At this same period, the use of гражданин as a neutral title is necessitated. The complete intolerance to political dissent in the 1920s–1930s affects товарищ in that it begins to be used as a marker of ideological loyalty; hence the use of this title in addressing superiors in structured settings, e.g. товарищ начальник 'comrade supervisor' and V (Nakhimovsky 1976: 97) (see also p. 277 on the use of товарищ in the army). The loss by the word гражданин of its neutral status is a corollary to this change. The desemantization of товарищ is characteristic of the 1950s–1970s; by the late 1980s, the growing disillusionment with Soviet history stigmatizes this word (Formanovskaja 1989). Going beyond the period described in this book, the Russian language of the post-Soviet period has been trying to abandon the use of товарищ and to replace it with the older titles discussed at the beginning of this section. However, the revival of those titles has brought back the confusion in their use, even greater given that the society has dramatically changed. It remains to be seen what titles will emerge as neutral in this situation.

Pre-Revolutionary address also included the pseudo-kinship terms батюшка 'father' (diminutive), отец мой 'my father', матушка 'mother' (diminutive), мать моя 'my mother'. Apart from батюшка and матушка in a restricted use to address priests and their wives, they have all become increasingly rare in the last half-century (Formanovskaja 1982*b*: 42–3). The use in address of the ritual kinship terms крестный 'godfather', крестная 'godmother', кум and кума, which survived into the early part of this century, is now a thing of the past. A recent change in the use of true kinship terms is the decline in the use of дядя and тетя by nephews and nieces to address uncles and aunts, as in Спасибо, тетя 'Thank you, aunt', Скажи, дядя 'Tell me, uncle'. These kinship terms are now normally accompanied by names, as Спасибо, тетя Таня, Скажи, дядя Ваня. Meanwhile, the terms дядя and тетя alone (as well as more colloquial дяденька and тетенька) are used by children to adult strangers (Formanovskaja 1982*a*: 66; 1982*b*: 31, 45). (For further discussion of changes in kinship terms, see Friedrich 1966*b*.)

The strongly power-marked form of address человек and the conde-scending любезный, both used mainly to servants, disappeared totally and quickly after the October Revolution.

Other Aspects of Speech Etiquette

In addition to address forms, the norms of certain other typical sequences in specific settings have changed during this century. The commonest formulas expressing thanks, for example, are nowadays спасибо, большое спасибо. Благодарствуй(те), though it survived the Revolution, is now obsolete. The French borrowing мерси was standardly used until the 1930s and has since been retained in colloquial speech, where it is often used humorously. Certain other sequences of thanks are now used mainly by the older generation: покорно (or покорнейше) благодарю, я вам очень (крайне, глубоко, чрезвы-чайно) признателен (-льна), примите мою благодарность (при-знательность) (Akišina and Formanovskaja 1973: 76; 1978: 163). The formula благодарю (вас) was commonly used until recently (it is cited as a common one in Akišina and Formanovskaja (1978: 162)) but has also been on the decline since the 1970s, when спасибо has become predominant. Likewise, in replying to an expression of thanks, the formulas пожалуйста 'you are welcome' and не за что are replacing не стоит балгодарности and всегда к вашим услугам, which have now become formal and slightly archaic (Akišina and Formanovskaja 1978: 165).

In contemporary Russian apology is usually expressed by извини(те) or прости(те). Also widely used (and widely objected to) is из-виняюсь—a form commonly believed to have originated during the First World War, though really it is much older (Mazon 1920: 54; Karcevskij 1923: 17, 42; Azov 1923; Krysin and Skvorcov 1965). This form, originally described as 'very vulgar' (Karcevskij 1923: 42), has by now become simply colloquial; it is still not entirely acceptable as standard and is not given, for example, in Akišina and Formanovskaja (1973). Along with мосье, мадам, мерси, etc., the French form пардон (once in use in privileged circles) (Volkonskij 1913: 207) has become totally defunct; its occasional use in colloquial speech is con-sidered very vulgar. The same is true of слушаюсь, literally 'I obey', which was used before the Revolution by servants, waiters, etc. The pre-Revolutionary виноват(a) is now archaic, but may be heard from old people (Akišina and Formanovskaja 1978: 110). It was also used as a standard form of apology in the armed forces (Akišina and Formanovskaja 1970: 121).

As the telephone was introduced, several formulas appeared used as the first utterance in answering a call. The earliest ones, used at the beginning of the century, were у аппарата (or proper name + у аппарата); (proper name or name of institution) + слушает (e.g. приемная слушает); (я) слушаю; с вами говорят (разговаривают); говорите. Of these, only (я) слушаю and proper name + слушает have remained in active use. The phrase у аппарата was first replaced by на проводе and later, by the 1950s, by у телефона (e.g. Иванов у телефона). Other commonly used formulas in answering the telephone call are алло and да (, я слушаю) (Akišina and Akišina 1990: 9, 13, 14).

Other typical formulas which have fallen out of use or at least become rare and restricted to older speakers are:

Invitation: покорнейше прошу/прошу покорно (+ infinitive); пожалуй(те) + infinitive; милости прошу (милости просим, remarkably, is still current but only as a welcoming remark to a visitor); изволь(те); изволь(те) + infinitive.

Enquiry about a possible request: чем могу служить?; чем могу быть (вам) полезен (-зна)?; чем обязан(а)? The phrase чего изволите?, formerly used by servants and waiters and described by Ovsjannikov (1933: 313) as 'a lackey's phrase, indicating obsequiousness and grovelling', is now defunct.

Request: сделайте милость; сделайте (мне) одолжение; не откажите в любезности; не сочтите за труд; не окажете ли (вы) (мне) любезность are typically used in markedly formal contexts (Akišina and Formanovskaja 1973: 56; 1978: 70). The more resilient formula будьте добры, characterized as 'polite' by Akišina and Formanovskaja (1978: 69), has been on the decline since the 1970s, being gradually replaced by the universal пожалуйста.

Introduction: рекомендую(сь); прошу любить и жаловать; разрешите (вам) представить(ся).

Leave-taking: разрешите откланяться, позвольте откланяться, and честь имею are used by the older generation only (Akišina and Formanovskaja 1973: 40), though the latter has reappeared, probably as a conscious archaism, in educated urban speech of the 1970s–1980s (personal communication by Vladimir Belikov). The current formulas include до свидания, до встречи, всего доброго (little used by younger people); the word пока is discussed below.

Greeting: доброго здоровья is used by older people and sounds archaic (Akišina and Formanovskaja 1978: 27).

It is easier to identify archaisms than innovations, since innovation, to a large extent, has meant the functional extension of formulas which existed before the Revolution. It seems likely, in fact, that the number of elements in the etiquette structures before 1917 was greater than it is today. Choice between the elements, like that between address forms, depended on social factors, some of which have now disappeared. The tendency throughout the century has been towards the elimination of synonymous expressions; this resulted in the emergence of спасибо as the principal expression of thanks, здравствуйте as the main greeting, до свидания as the main leave-taking formula. Though one may be tempted to explain such simplification of speech etiquette by specific social factors (as it is done in Fessenko 1955: 198–209), it is striking that other languages have undergone similar simplification in the twentieth century: for example, the English *Would you please* or *Farewell* are becoming increasingly rare. Thus, the increasing flow of information and the faster tempo of everyday life are likely to have their toll on speech formulas. Among the obviously new formulas, however, we may mention привет (greeting) and пока (leave-taking). The latter, though known before the Revolution, has only subsequently become widely accepted and used (Jakobson 1921: 27; Azov 1923; Seliščev 1928: 74).

Finally, it should not be forgotten that the Russian speech etiquette and address systems were changing before 1917, albeit slowly. Kantorovič recalls, for example, that even before the Revolution it had become usual to address domestic servants with V, though T was then still the normal mode of address to a yard-keeper (дворник), a cabman (извозчик), or a peasant at a market (1966: 67). The Revolution accelerated the existing trend, however, and by the middle of the century Russian had reached a stage where the etiquette demanded the use of V to every adult stranger (the recent developments in addressing strangers, however, reflect the new encroachment of T upon V).

8 Orthography and Punctuation

Orthographical Reforms

The aspects of language change we have described so far in this book are only to a limited extent subject to the control of language planners. So far as pronunciation, stress, morphology, syntax, and vocabulary are concerned, language planning is largely a matter of assessing the changes that have already occurred and of deciding to what extent the codified standard should be adjusted to keep up to date. It is really a question of resolving conflict between standard and non-standard. Orthographical change is a different thing entirely, however, for orthographical change occurs exclusively through planning.

Orthography is also unlike the aspects of language dealt with so far in that it is concerned essentially with (*a*) the question of correctness, and (*b*) writing. Change in phonology, morphology, syntax, and vocabulary, on the other hand, takes place in all languages, whether they have writing and standardized forms or not. Nevertheless, when we are dealing with a standardized written language, such as Russian, and particularly with questions of change and standardization, the problems of orthography are similar to those of change in the levels of language proper. The standard/non-standard dialectic affects orthography as much as it affects them, for while there is no such thing as non-standard orthography, non-standard spelling clearly occurs as the mistakes made by those (particularly schoolchildren) who have not yet mastered the rules. If the rules are often broken this may mean that they are more difficult to learn than they really need to be and that there may be a case to be made out (as in the case of mistakes in pronunciation, grammar, or vocabulary) for changing the rules. The desire to eliminate non-standard (i.e. incorrect) spelling is usually the motive behind spelling reform, and pressure towards reform often comes from those who are most aware of the problems encountered in learning to spell, i.e. from schoolteachers, particularly those working with younger children. This has certainly been the case in Russia in the twentieth century.

Teachers of one kind or another were behind the pressure for reform which began to build up in the nineteenth century (Šapiro 1951: 191) and eventually resulted in the spelling reform of 1917–18. No doubt their primary objective was to make things easier for their pupils, but before long the question of reform became linked with the broader question of reducing illiteracy.

Despite Peter the Great's important reform of 1708–10 introducing the 'civil alphabet' (гражданский шрифт), spelling remained chaotic throughout the eighteenth and most of the nineteenth century. The main step towards standardization before 1917 was the publication in St Petersburg in 1885 of the first edition of Ja. K. Grot's manual *Русское правописание*, which, though it gained acceptance in schools, had no official authority, and was not universally recognized. It was, however, the nearest thing there was to an official orthographic code.

By the beginning of the twentieth century there were a number of organizations working for reform, prominent among which was the section of Russian language teachers of the Pedagogical Society at Moscow University (Šapiro 1951: 191; Černyšev 1947: 170). The section's special committee dealing with this question included among its members the subsequently famous linguistic scholar F. F. Fortunatov.

Even when it is obvious that a spelling system is inefficient and there is general agreement that change is necessary, it is often difficult even for experts to decide exactly what form change should take. There are few languages for which a purely phonemic system (i.e. one in which each symbol corresponds to a single phoneme) is suitable. It is always quite likely, as in the case of Russian, that certain phonological and morphophonemic issues will be in conflict, and that the most efficient system will therefore be a compromise, a morphonological system. If Russian spelling were to follow the phonological principle alone, it would produce a host of new difficulties by raising morphological doubts in the minds of its users. For example, the preposition в in Russian constitutes one morpheme, but it has two realizations as [v] or [f], depending on whether the sound immediately following is voiced or not, e.g. в доме ['vdomʲı] 'in the house', but в саду [fsʌ'du] 'in the garden'. Now if we were to follow the phonological principle exclusively we should have to write в before voiced sounds and ф before unvoiced sounds. We should have two symbols for one morpheme, and users of Russian, when writing, would have the problem of choosing between them. Generally, an efficient spelling system is one in which the sound system is represented as closely as possible in writing without upsetting the graphic representation of the grammatical system.

The inefficiency of the pre-1917 orthography was largely due to a superfluity of symbols. There were three cases of simple duplicates (phonologically speaking), viz. ѣ and е, и and i, ѳ and ф. The choice between the members of any of these pairs had no phonetic significance, and the occasions on which the ѣ/е and и/i choices were meaningful on other levels (e.g. в поле (accusative) 'into the field': в полѣ (prepositional) 'in the field'; мир 'peace': мiр 'world')[1] were so rare as to be negligible. The hard sign ъ, which was written at the end of every word ending in a hard consonant (except palatals, where the choice between ъ and ь was determined morphologically), e.g. столъ, лѣсъ, was also superfluous, since its mere absence could also indicate hardness.

Many of the opponents of change were in positions of power. They included the Minister of Internal Affairs D. S. Sipjagin who, at the same time as the Pedagogical Society was making proposals for the abolition of ѣ and ъ, intended actually to prohibit the printing of books in an orthography omitting these letters (Černyšev 1947: 170). Although no such prohibition ever came into force (partly thanks, no doubt, to the objections voiced by Academicians A. A. Šaxmatov and A. I. Sobolevskij in the name of the Academy of Sciences), the Society's application for the formation of a special commission to examine the question of spelling reform was rejected by the Ministry of National Education in February 1903 (Šapiro 1951: 191). The Academy, however, continued to show an interest in the matter and decided to set up a Commission on the Question of Russian Orthography. The Commission, which consisted of representatives of the Academy, schoolteachers, journalists, and writers, met on 12 April 1904 and agreed unanimously that simplification of the orthography was desirable (Černyšev 1947: 174–5). They then went on to discuss the desirability of abolishing certain letters and, having put the fate of each such letter individually to the vote, decided by large majorities in favour of the abolition of ѳ, ъ, и or i, and ѣ.[2] The Commission then set up a subcommission under the chairmanship of Fortunatov to work out questions of simplification not connected with the exclusion of letters. The first meeting of the subcommission took place the following day and in May that year the *Предварительное сообщение Орфографической подкомиссии* (*Preliminary Communication of the Orthographic*

---

[1] Мiръ 'world', rather than миръ 'peace', appeared in the title of L. Tolstoj's famous novel, though he was probably making use of the homonymy of the two words as well as their semantic affinity (Bočarov 1985).

[2] The voting figures are given in Černyšev (1947: 182).

Subcommission) was published in St Petersburg. The subcommission had obviously wasted no time; but meanwhile the subject of reform had begun to be aired in the press. The campaign against reform was led by the newspaper *Новое время* (Černyšev 1947: *passim*), and after publication of the Preliminary Communication the debate became somewhat heated. Not only were there a large number of people of power and influence who were opposed to change of any kind in the orthography, but there was also a large body of opinion in favour of only very restricted reform. This was the position of many members of the Academy, including the distinguished Slavist Vatroslav Jagić. The fact that the opposition had several prominent writers in their ranks, including Lev Tolstoj, undoubtedly strengthened their morale (Černyšev 1947: 217–18; Il´inskaja 1966: 87–8). V. I. Černyšev, who was himself a member of the original Commission and closely connected with the work of the subcommission, estimated that the only really devoted and active supporters of reform at that time were Šaxmatov and Fortunatov (Černyšev 1947: 227–8).

And so the movement for reform temporarily lost momentum, especially after the work of the subcommission was interrupted by the political upheaval of 1905–6 (Šapiro 1951: 193). The one section of Russian society in which considerable numbers never lost sight of the need for simplification of the orthography was the teaching profession. In 1907 a group of members of the State Parliament (Duma) who were also teachers wrote asking the Academy of Sciences not to postpone for too long its work on the spelling question and expressing the view that the complexity of the existing orthography was 'a considerable obstacle to the spread of literacy among the popular masses'. But their request had no effect (Černyšev 1947: 230).

The subcommission resumed its work in December 1910, and its proposals were published in May 1912 in St Petersburg as *Постановления Орфографической подкомиссии* (*Resolutions of the Orthographic Subcommission*). They took for granted the proposals made in 1904 to abolish ѳ, ъ, ѣ, and either и or i, and included the following further recommendations:

(1) The letter i to be abolished.

(2) The hard sign to be retained in the body of words after prefixes, e.g. подъезд, объем.

(3) The hard sign to be abolished at the end of words after the absolutely hard consonants ж and ш, e.g. рож (genitive plural of рожа 'ugly mug') but cf. рожь 'rye'.

(4) The hard sign to be abolished at the end of words after the absolutely soft consonants ч and щ, e.g. плач 'weeping' (cf. плачь, imperative of плакать 'to weep, cry').

(5) To retain the spelling -ться for infinitives of reflexive verbs (despite the fact that the -т is hard).

(6) To consider 'desirable but not obligatory' the use of ё.[3]

(7) The letter о to be written consistently after ж, ш, ц, ч, щ in stressed syllables, e.g. чорный 'black'. (Since these consonants are not affected by the soft/hard distinction, the use of о in some words (e.g. шовъ 'seam') and e (ё) in others (e.g. шелъ 'went') was (and still is) of no phonetic significance.)

(8) The prefixes воз-, из-, низ-, раз-, без-, чрез-, and через- to be written with с before all voiceless consonants, e.g. бесполезно (not безполезно 'useless'). (The existing rule affected only воз-, из-, низ-, раз-, which were written with з before voiced consonants and с before voiceless consonants except с itself; без-, чрез-, and через- were always written with з. Grot, though confirming this practice in his rules, considered it would have been better to write the -з- forms in all cases.[4])

(9) The masculine and neuter genitive singular endings to be written -ого, -его (replacing -аго, -яго). (It was decided to retain the existing spelling of masculine nominative and accusative singular adjectives, e.g. добрый 'good', синий 'blue', rather than write -ой, -ей, consistently for all adjectives regardless of stress.)

(10) To write -ые, -ие, consistently in the nominative and accusative plural of all adjectives and participles (replacing -ыя, -ія in the neuter and feminine).

(11) To write и (not ѣ) in они and одни in all plural genders and cases.

(12) To write ее (её) (not ея) as the genitive of она. (Up to now ее (её) had been written only in the accusative.)

(13) To simplify the rules for the division of words at the end of a line.

These proposals received no official recognition, and it was not until the beginning of 1917 that the question of reform was once again brought to the fore by the All-Russian Congress of Teachers of Russian

---

[3] This letter was relatively new to the Russian alphabet: it was first introduced in 1797, by Nikolaj Karamzin, as a replacement for *io* (*Русский язык. Энциклопедия.* 1979: 20).

[4] See Vinogradov (1965: 231).

in Secondary Schools (Всероссийский съезд преподавателей русского языка средней школы), which met in Moscow from 27 December 1916 to 4 January 1917 with 2,090 members present. The Congress sent an official letter to the Academy of Sciences (dated 10 February 1917), stating that 'for everyone who actually works in a school or is at least closely connected with one, there is not the slightest doubt that orthographic reform cannot be put off any longer . . .' (Černyšev 1947: 235).

It might well be thought that in the context of the events of February 1917 spelling reform did not stand very high in the scale of priorities. That the teachers thought otherwise may be seen from their letter, in which they declared: 'The members of the Congress are convinced that the difficult circumstances of the time we are living through not only cannot constitute an obstacle to the realization of reform, but on the contrary demand a drastic elimination of everything that up to now has prevented the broad development of popular education' (Černyšev 1947: 235).

On 27 February 1917 the monarchy fell. The letter from the Teachers' Congress was considered by the Academy at its General Meeting held on 29 March. Meanwhile the Provisional Government had been formed. The Academy reacted to the letter in the by now time-honoured way of appointing yet another commission to examine the question, but this time things proceeded rapidly. The new commission summoned a larger Assembly for Considering Simplification of the Orthography. Sixty-three people were invited to attend the meeting of the Assembly on 11 May, but only 30 of them were actually present. Šaxmatov, as chairman,[5] told the Assembly that the commission was proposing the acceptance of a considerably modified reform, including the retention even of ѣ and i. His own views were much more radical, and he was doubtless delighted to discover that the Assembly had no intention of accepting modified reform and to see it proceed to pass a set of resolutions which largely coincided with the proposals made by Fortunatov's subcommission in May 1912. The proposals of the Assembly of 11 May 1917 were as follows:

(1) Replacement of ѣ by e.

(2) Replacement of ѳ by ф.

(3) Exclusion of ъ at the end of words and of both parts of compounds such as контр-адмирал 'rear admiral', but its retention in the body of words as the separative sign.

---

[5] His co-reformer, Fortunatov, had died in 1914.

(4) Replacement of i by и.

(5) Acknowledgement of ё as 'desirable but not obligatory'.

(6) Replacement of з by с in the prefixes без-, вз-, воз-, из-, низ-, раз-, роз-, чрез-, and через-, when immediately followed by voiceless consonants, including с itself, but retention of з elsewhere.

(7) Replacement of -аго, -яго by -ого, -его in genitive singular of adjectives, participles, and pronouns.

(8) Replacement of -ыя, -ія by -ые, -ие in nominative and accusative plural of neuter and feminine adjectives, participles, and pronouns.

(9) Replacement of онѣ by они in the nominative plural of the feminine personal pronoun.

(10) Replacement of однѣ, однѣхъ, однѣмъ, однѣми by одни, одних, одним, одними, respectively.

(11) Replacement of ея by ее (её) in the genitive singular of она.

(12) Simplification of rules governing division of words at the end of a line.

(13) Acceptance of either spelling for words of the type встороне/ в стороне, сверху/с верху.

The only new points in these proposals were:

(1) Exclusion of the hard sign in the body of compound words like контр-адмирал.

(2) Retention of existing spellings with e or o after ж, ш, ч, щ, ц.

(3) Retention of the soft sign, in all positions.

(4) Acceptance of either spelling of words like сверху/с верху.

(5) Addition of роз- and вз- to prefixes written with с before voiceless consonants.

Šaxmatov asked the Academy to communicate these proposals to the Ministry of Popular Education, which had already expressed its willingness to adopt them for use in schools (Černyšev 1947: 240–1), but the Academy, with supreme lack of concern, postponed consideration of the question until autumn. Deputy Minister O. P. Gerasimov, who had himself been a member of the Assembly, was not prepared to wait for the Academy and simply asked Šaxmatov to forward precise details of the proposals. He then had the Ministry issue a circular, dated 17 May 1917 and addressed to the trustees of school areas, giving details of the reformed orthography and directing that the heads of schools take immediate measures to put the reform into effect from the beginning of the new school year. On 22 June the Ministry confirmed the circular and gave further instructions.

The Minister of Education immediately came under attack in the press. Among his opponents was a group of civil servants in his own ministry, who claimed that there were more important educational issues than spelling reform. The Minister, A. A. Manujlov, was supported by Professor (later Academician) P. N. Sakulin, who had taken a prominent part in the discussion in the Assembly on 11 May. In an article published in *Русские ведомости* Sakulin recalled that the reactionary ministers of education of the past would never have supported this reform, 'just as they did not support anything which tended towards the well-being of the masses' (Černyšev 1947: 243–5). By August Manujlov was Minister of Education no longer, and, as the proposed reform had been associated with him personally, rumours sprang up that it was not to be implemented after all. The Ministry denied this, but the proposals continued to be attacked in the press and their success was still not really assured when, on 25 October, the Provisional Government was overthrown and Soviet power established.

Up to now only the Ministry of Education had accepted the reform and ordered its implementation in schools. The Provisional Government had made no decision as to its implementation anywhere else. This ambiguous situation was cleared up by the Bolsheviks. On 23 December 1917 the People's Commissariat of Education issued a decree signed by A. V. Lunačarskij that 'all state and government institutions and schools without exception should carry out the transition to the new orthography without delay', and that 'from 1 January 1918 all government and state publications, both periodical (newspapers, magazines) and non-periodical (books, scientific works, collections, etc.)' should be printed in the new orthography. In schools the reform was to be introduced gradually, beginning from the youngest classes. There was to be no compulsory re-education of those who had already learned the old rules. For those at school already only violations of rules common to both old and new systems were to be considered mistakes.[6]

The rules in Lunačarskij's decree were no different from those put forward by the Assembly of 11 May, except that now вз- was omitted from the rule regarding the spelling of prefixes, but a new decree of the Soviet of People's Commissars, issued on 10 October 1918, made two minor changes: there was no mention of ё or of allowing compound adverbs to be written as one word or two. (Strangely enough, вз- was now reintroduced.) What these two points had in common was their ambiguous nature: the decision to remove them was probably due to

---

[6] The full text of the decree is given by Černyšev (1947: 247–8).

the belief that it would be better if all the rules were categorical and admitted no facultative variants.

The terms of the Decree of 10 October 1918 were thus as follows (Černyšev 1947: 248–9):

(1) The letter ѣ to be replaced by e.

(2) The letter ѳ to be replaced by ф.

(3) To abolish ъ at the end of words and the components of compound words, but to retain it within the body of words as the separative sign.

(4) The letter i to be replaced by и.

(5) To write без-, вз-, воз-, из-, низ-, раз-, роз-, чрез-, через-, with з before voiced consonants and с before voiceless consonants including с.

(6) To write -ого, -его (for -аго, -яго) in the genitive singular of masculine and neuter adjectives.

(7) To write -ые, -ие (for -ыя, -ия) in the nominative and accusative plural of feminine and neuter adjectives.

(8) To write они (for онѣ) in the nominative plural of the feminine personal pronoun.

(9) To write одни, одних, одними (for однѣ, однѣх, однѣми) in the feminine plural.

(10) To write ее in the genitive singular (for ея).

(11) In dividing words to observe only the following rules: a consonant (whether alone or in a group of consonants) immediately before a vowel should not be separated from the vowel, nor should a group of consonants at the beginning of a word be separated from a following vowel. The letter й before a consonant should not be separated from a preceding vowel.

Though not included in the Decree, the reform also abolished the names of the letters of the alphabet which had been in use since the Old Russian period; before the Revolution, letter names had been taught in everyday schools and Sunday schools. As a result, a number of set expressions that included names of letters became obsolete or unclear to Russian speakers. For example, the name of the letter ѣ was ять, and the expression на ять was used in the meaning 'well, well done'; in the second edition of the *MAS* (1981–4), this expression is identified as *prostorečno*. The changes in the alphabet included the final abandonment of ѵ (ижица), previously the last letter of the alphabet (though the trend not to use this letter had started earlier, see below). Accordingly, the expression от аза до ижицы 'from beginning to end, from A to Z' became less clear, and the competing от а до я eventually appeared.

The expression прописать ижицу 'to administer (corporal) punishment' became entirely obsolete. The adverb покоем 'U-shaped', based on the name of the letter п (покой), became semantically opaque; it can still be found in this meaning in literary texts of the first half of the twentieth century, e.g. in the description of Bulgakov's house in *Мастер и Маргарита* (Chapter 7 of the novel):

Степа Лиходеев . . . очнулся утром у себя в той самой квартире, . . . в большом шестиэтажном доме, покоем расположенном на Садовой улице.

Stepa Lixodeev . . . regained consciousness at his own place, in the same apartment in a large six-storey U-shaped house that was located in Sadovaja Street.

At present, the meaning of this adverb is unclear to many native readers and it is likely to be confused with that of спокойно 'calmly'.

The obsolete name of the letter н—наш—appears in Puškin's *Евгений Онегин* (1823), II. xxxiii:

И русский Н[аш] как И французский
Произносить умела в нос

And she could pronounce the Russian н in the French manner, nasalized.

Some other examples of words and expressions based on letter names are given in Vlasto (1986: 35–8).

As the old names of the letters of the alphabet fell out of use, the letters were given monosyllabic names, for example, бэ for б, ка for к, эр for р, etc. However, in some situations, for instance, in telecommunications, these short names could be easily confused with one another, and the need for longer, acoustically more salient names gradually became apparent. Though no language-planning policies seem to have been proposed for such situations, it has been common practice to use a popular forename as a name of the letter this forename begins with; for example, Анна or Андрей for а, Иван for и, Татьяна for т. If no popular forenames beginning with a respective letter can be found, a common noun or adjective is used, for example, цапля for ц, черный for ч, шапка for ш, щетка for щ, etc. When this practice started is hard to establish, since no mention of it is given in the literature; several people born in Moscow told one of the authors of this book that they heard the use of forenames as names of the letters of the alphabet as early as the 1920s.

Apart from a few minor adjustments, the orthography as amended by this Decree has remained in use from 1918 up to the present day.

Proposals for further reform have been made from time to time, however, and there is still a great deal of dissatisfaction with certain details of the existing system. Nevertheless, there can be no doubt that the reform of 1917–18 was of great social significance and opened up the way for the Soviet Government's campaign against ignorance and illiteracy. It is said that the language planner's hands are 'least tied when he can plan a language from the ground up, say in a wholly illiterate society' (Haugen 1966*b*: 16), but although the literacy rate was extremely low by European standards, Russia was by 1917 far from being wholly illiterate. Nevertheless, conditions for reform, if not ideal, were at least good, for the great majority of Russians were not going over to a new spelling system but learning to write for the first time. The fact that they were now able to learn the use of an orthography with relatively few inconsistencies was of great advantage to both learners and teachers. Among the minor benefits of the reform was the saving in print and paper: new editions of large literary works were found to be pages shorter than they had been before 1918.

Bearing in mind the general rule that the closer the fit between graphological and phonological systems the better, provided it is not so close as to affect the fit between graphology and morphology (cf. p. 284 above), we can see that the Russian spelling system was much improved after 1917. Grapheme and phoneme were certainly closer than they had been before, while the relationship between grapheme and morpheme had been seriously affected only in one case—Rule 5.[7] While this rule removed a phonological inconsistency, it might have been better, in the wider context of prefixes as a whole, to have allowed the morphological principle to prevail here. No concession to the phonological principle is made in the case of other prefixes (e.g. от- is never written од-, although before most voiced consonants it is so pronounced, as in отдать 'to give away' [ʌd'datʲ]), and the desirability of using forms with the letter з in all positions had been pointed out by Grot (cf. p. 287 above). On the other hand, the reform still left untouched certain inconsistencies in the relationship between sound and symbol, whose amendment would not have affected morphology, such as the use of г (pronounced [v]) in the genitive singular of adjectives and pronouns, in the word сегодня 'today', etc.

The Decree of 1918 (and for that matter the earlier proposals for reform too) only enumerated changes to be made. There was still no single code of orthographic rules. But by now it was at least clear that

[7] The morphological uses of ѣ (cf. p. 285) were of negligible advantage.

Grot's guide had been superseded. In fact, the new orthography was to remain uncodified until 1956.

The elliptical style of the 1918 Decree, especially the fact that it included no examples, suggests that it was intended to be read together with the Decree of December 1917 (and hence with the proposals of 11 May 1917 too). Rule 3, for example, deprived of the example контр-адмирал, does not make clear what is meant by the term 'compound words' (сложные слова). And Rule 9, though it was obviously intended to change the spelling of all plural cases, enigmatically omitted the dative. Now if these omissions are not simply mistakes (which, despite the fact that the Decree was drawn up in turbulent times, seems unlikely), they must mean that the additional information in the December decree was taken for granted. If this is so, one cannot but wonder whether the points concerning ё and the facultative division of compound adverbs were really meant to fall into abeyance. In practice, however, it was assumed that they were, and the other inconsistencies were ignored.

Another point which does not become clear from a reading of the various sets of proposals and decrees is the question of the letter v, called ижица. Some accounts of the reform tell us that it is thanks to the Soviet decrees that this letter disappeared (for example, V. V. Vinogradov 1965: 53). Yet neither of them mentions it. Nor do we find mention of it in any earlier proposals unless we go back as far as the commission which met in April 1904, when Fortunatov stated: 'this letter is nowadays usually not used, and even Grot . . . stated positively that ижица might be considered to have been removed from the Russian alphabet; so now there is no longer any need to put the question of removing this letter' (Černyšev 1947: 177). From 1904 onwards all those concerned with spelling reform appear to have assumed that the question of ижица had already been settled.

The 1918 Decree followed its predecessors in abolishing the hard sign except in its special function as the separative sign within the body of words. In this role it represents the phoneme /j/ immediately after a prefix ending in a consonant and before a vowel, e.g. съесть [sⁱjesⁱtⁱ] 'to eat'. It thus duplicated one of the functions of the soft sign, which, as separative sign, represents /j/ between any other consonant and a vowel, e.g. пью [pⁱju] 'I drink'. The proposals made by the Moscow Pedagogical Society in 1901 included the total abolition of ъ and the exclusive use of ь as separative sign. And there was a majority in favour of abolishing ъ (without qualification) in the Commission of 1904. The result of the eventual compromise decision to retain it after prefixes was that in texts written in the new orthography it had extremely low frequency—a fact which emphasized its anomalous status. The practice, which grew soon after 1918, of replacing it with the apostrophe (e.g. с'есть 'eat', под'езд 'entrance', and sometimes inverted as под'езд) may well have gained support from the belief that the letter ъ ought really to have been abolished altogether, and that to avoid its use was to follow the true spirit of the reform (Polivanov 1927: 185). (The choice of this particular symbol to replace the hard sign was not new. There had been experimental printing with the apostrophe in the nineteenth century.) But there was another, more concrete, reason for the introduction of the apostrophe in the 1920s. Certain printers hostile to the new government deliberately continued printing in the old orthography. The reaction of the Soviet authorities was to confiscate the types and matrices for the letters ъ, ѣ, ѳ, v, and i.[8] The fact that ъ still had a use (albeit vastly restricted) was either overlooked or ignored.

Towards the end of the 1920s, however, ъ began to be restored in printed publications, but meanwhile people had grown used to the apostrophe and some objected to the restoration of what they regarded as a pre-Revolutionary letter (Il'inskaja 1966: 92). The 1920s also saw the disappearance of the apostrophe and full stops used with acronyms (for examples, see p. 114 above) and the development of the present practice of writing them closed-up, e.g. MXAT, genitive MXATa 'Moscow Arts Theatre'.

Attempts to retain the old orthography in Russia were very short-lived indeed. During 1918, however, both systems were being used in print, and there were even a few cases of printers adopting only part of the new rules, i.e. dropping ъ, which was the easiest rule to follow, but otherwise retaining the old system.[9] Outside Russia, on the other hand, certain *émigré* groups have continued to use the old orthography intact even to the present day (see some examples in the Introduction above), and there are said to have been attempts to revive the old spelling in German-occupied Russian territory during the Second World War (Istrin 1988: 165–6).

But if attempts to retain the old orthography after 1917 were negligible, efforts to change spelling still further were more determined. In

---

[8] *Практика* . . . 1932: 66. The confiscation is said to have been carried out by a detachment of armed sailors who went round the Petrograd printers' shops (Il'inskaja 1966: 92; Suprun 1969: 15).

[9] Trockij's pamphlet *Международное положение и Красная Армия*, Moscow, 1918, for example, was printed in this way.

1929 a new Orthographic Commission was formed, and a new plan for orthographic reform was put forward the following year (Černyšev 1947: 250–1). Among the new proposals were:

(1) To replace ъ by ь as the only separative sign, e.g. сьезд 'congress'.

(2) To write ы (not и) consistently after ж, ш, ц, e.g. жырный 'fat'.

(3) To replace г by в in the genitive singular of adjectives, pronouns, and participles, e.g. доброво 'kind', ево 'his'.

(4) To write -ыи, -ии (not -ые, -ие) in the nominative and accusative plural of adjectives, e.g. добрыи 'kind', синии 'blue'.

(5) To write the present and perfective future endings of all stem-stressed verbs (including present participles) as: -ишь, -ит, -им, -ите, -ут (-щт), -ущий (-ющий), -имый, делаишь, любют, возют.[10]

These proposals had no effect in practice, but certain points they raised (some of which had been raised before) were to be considered again later. During the 1930s committees continued to work on minor adjustments, ironing out inconsistencies, and the preparation of a consolidated code of spelling rules, but there were no practical results. The work was interrupted by the Second World War and was not renewed in the last years of Stalin's rule: there were no meetings between 1940 and 1954 (Bukčina *et al.* 1969: 14). One of the notable orthographic phenomena of the late 1930s–1950s was the reinstatement of the letter ё, believed to have been initiated by Stalin himself because he was not always able to distinguish е and ё. No specific guide-lines on the use of ё were ever published, and this use receded again in the late 1950s–1960s. At present, ё is confined to children's literature and textbooks of Russian as a second language, i.e. editions whose readership is not expected readily to know the difference between е and ё.

The lack of a set of rules permitted the survival of certain inconsistencies. The use of double letters in loan-words, for example, varied a great deal (Panov 1965: 154–5). Eventually, in 1956, *Правила русской орфографии и пунктуации* (*Rules of Russian Orthography and Punctuation*) was published in Moscow, codifying the existing orthography and introducing a few minor adjustments in the interests of greater uniformity. It was the first complete set of spelling rules to be published since Grot's manual in 1885. The 1956 rules, which had the approval of the Academy of Sciences of the USSR and other official bodies, took into account the opinions expressed in a public discussion

---

[10] In 1930 the pronunciation reflected by любют, возют, etc. was still standard (see p. 28, above).

on spelling which had taken place in the columns of the main teachers' specialist publications in 1954. The year 1956 also saw the publication by the Academy of a comprehensive *Орфографический словарь русского языка* (*Orthographical Dictionary of the Russian Language*) composed in accordance with the Rules.

Among the new rules intended to counter inconsistency was one demanding that after prefixes (except меж- and сверх-) ending in a consonant the letter ы, not и, should be written, e.g. предыстория 'pre-history'. The problem arises from the fact that the final consonants of these prefixes remain hard even when used to form compounds whose root begins with the phoneme /i/. The и in a spelling such as предистория, therefore, is not consistent with the grapho-phonological rule that и (unlike ы) indicates that the consonant immediately preceding it is soft. The rule demanding the use of ы thus maintains the fit between sound and symbol at the expense of the morphological principle. Foreign prefixes контр-, пан-, суб-, транс-, etc. (e.g. субинспектор 'sub-inspector') and stump-compounds (e.g. Госиздат 'State Publishing House', from Государственное издательство) are specifically excluded from this rule. It has been pointed out that in practice the native prefixes двух-, трех-, and четырех- and certain foreign prefixes not mentioned in the 1956 Rules are also excluded (Es´kova 1964: 6). There has always been some uncertainty as to whether и or ы should be written in this position, and the more loan-words beginning with /i/ appeared and were used in compounds, the greater the problem became. In the 1930s there was utter inconsistency, for there was no rule in existence. By 1964, however, it was possible to state that, although spellings with и contrary to the 1956 rule were still occurring in print, those with ы were gaining ground. Against this, it has to be admitted that the new type was already gaining ground before 1956 and had been used sporadically even before 1917 (Es´kova 1964: 10–11).

The 1956 Rules brought a little more order to the problem of whether to write е or о after ж, ш, ч, щ, ц by abolishing alternations of the type чорт/черти 'devil(s)', жолудь/желудей 'acorn(s)' (henceforth черт, желудь) (*Правила* . . . 1956: 7–9). They also cleared up certain incon-sistencies in the use of the hyphen in compound adjectives and adverbs (*Правила* . . . 1956: 41–2, 47). Among the problems they have not been very successful in settling is the question of where to use э in foreign words (Bukčina 1974: 44–6). For example, the word диэта/диета 'diet' and its derivatives were commonly spelt with э in the 1940s and 1950s, though the variant with e was also found; from the 1960s onwards, the variant with e has become predominant. Ožegov (1972) does not even mention the variant with э.

The 1956 Rules also set the guide-lines in using capitalization, though these rules sometimes lacked consistency. For example, particles де, делла, дю, ла, ле, and some others are not capitalized in foreign names unless they are considered part of the name, which is sometimes signalled by the absence of space or by a hyphen (Rozental´ 1986a: 307), cf. да Винчи 'da Vinci' but Де Леон 'de Leon'. It is problematic, however, whether the particle is less part of the proper name in да Винчи or дель Сарто than it is in Дос Пассос or Дю(-)Белле. The 1956 Rules required capitalization of possessive adjectives in -ов, -ев, -ин, e.g. Сашины книги 'Saša's books'; however, as indicated by Šapiro (1961: 149), these adjectives often appear non-capitalized; though no statistical evidence is available, it seems that the absence of capitalization in such adjectives has been increasing in the 1960s–1980s.

The question of separating and hyphenating words in writing was also addressed by the 1956 Rules (*Правила* . . . 1956; Šapiro 1961: 114–43). In particular, the 1956 Rules introduced the hyphenated spelling of по-видимому 'probably', по-прежнему 'still', по-пустому 'in vain', which had previously been spelt without a hyphen. Again, the inconsistencies that were inherited from the earlier systems remained unresolved by the 1956 Rules: some adverbs with the prefix с-, etymologically related to the preposition с, were spelt as a single word (сбоку 'from the side', сроду 'originally'), while in adverbs с размаху 'briskly', с разбегу 'in running', с was treated as a preposition, therefore spelt as a separate word. The Rules explained this by introducing the distinction between adverbs (requiring one-word spelling) and expressions that were close in meaning to adverbs (spelt with a space); however, such a distinction seems to be arbitrary (Šapiro 1961: 135). The recent reference Bukčina and Kalakuckaja (1982) mostly follows the 1956 Rules, with relatively few changes.

The general question of reform was scarcely affected by the 1956 Rules, which were consolidatory rather than innovatory, and in 1962 a new Orthographic Commission was set up under the auspices of the Russian Language Institute of the Academy of Sciences of the USSR. Its proposals, which were published in 1964 both in the press and in a separate *Предложения по усовершенствованию русской орфографии* (*Proposals for the Improvement of Russian Orthography*), aroused widespread interest, and their appearance was followed by serious public discussion of them in the columns of certain newspapers and journals, as well as on radio and television. They were, of course, only proposals, and the Commission's objective in publishing them was merely to test public opinion. Nevertheless, there was a certain amount of confusion at the time which resulted in a few cases of schoolteachers taking steps to put the proposals into practice (Bukčina *et al.* 1969: 5).

Letters numbering over 10,000, expressing opinions on the proposals, were received by newspapers and journals and by the Russian Language Institute direct. They were subsequently all passed to the Institute, where they were studied and catalogued. Preliminary conclusions arising from this work were published in 1969 (Bukčina *et al.* 1969). The largest professional group among the authors of the letters was that of teachers, and the overwhelming majority of them were in favour of further reform and of the new proposals (Bukčina *et al.* 1969: 19–20). Writers also constituted a clearly defined professional group among those who wrote in, but in contrast to the teachers they were nearly all opposed to the proposals and, indeed, to reform of any kind. This picture of the distribution of support and opposition is a familiar one.

In the kind of public discussion which took place in 1964 writers are always likely to have influence out of all proportion to their numbers, for they are widely thought to be specialists in the linguistic field.[11] And so it was in this case. Among the prominent opponents of reform were the writers Vera Inber, Tixon Semuškin, Semen Kirsanov, and Leonid Leonov. The latter's outspoken opposition, in particular, had a great impact.

Not surprisingly, the writers' views on the relationship between sound and symbol show a fair degree of confusion. But letters from members of other professions show that the objections made by writers carried great weight with them, and the fact that the 1964 proposals remained proposals and nothing more was probably a result more of the opposition of the writers than of any other single cause.

The reformists at least learned that in any future attempts they might make it would be useful, if not essential, to have the support of writers of stature. By a decision of the Presidium of the Academy of Sciences of the USSR dated 5 February 1965 K. A. Fedin, L. M. Leonov, A. T. Tvardovskij, and M. V. Isakovskij became members of the Orthographic Commission (Bukčina *et al.* 1969: 23).

The 1964 proposals were as follows:

[11] Lest it be thought that all writers have always opposed orthographic reform, it is worth recalling that Čexov appears to have favoured it (Il´inskaja 1966: 88–9).

I. PROPOSED NEW RULES

(1) To use only ь as the separative sign, e.g. подьезд (for подъезд); to omit the separative sign altogether after сверх-, меж-, двух-, трех-, четырех-, пан-, транс-, контр-.

(2) To write и consistently after ц. The choice of и rather than ы was made in order to conform to the pattern established for the other consonants not forming part of hard/soft pairs, viz. ж, ш, ч, щ.

(3) After ж, ш, ч, щ, ц to write consistently о where the syllable is stressed, and е where it is not, e.g. жолтый (for желтый 'yellow'). But to write еще 'still, yet' with е (ё). Some foreign words would continue to be written with о in unstressed positions. It was pointed out that this simple rule (which had been tested experimentally in schools) would replace 14 rules in the 1956 Code.

(4) Not to write ь after ж, ш, ч, щ, e.g. доч (for дочь 'daughter'). This was not to affect the use of ь as the separative sign, e.g. instrumental singular ночью.

(5) To abolish а/о vowel-alternation in root syllables, e.g. возрост (for возраст 'age') because о appears in the same root when stressed, e.g. рост 'growth'. But плавец (for пловец 'swimmer') because плавать 'swim'. It was proposed to leave и/е alternations.

(6) To replace the two suffixes -инский, -енский with a single -инский, since -енский never bears the stress. To retain -енский only where considerations of word-formation make it desirable, e.g. Фрунзенский (derived from the proper name Фрунзе 'Frunze').

(7) To replace the two suffixes -иц, -ец with one, viz. -ец.

(8) To abolish double letters in certain foreign words, e.g. тенис (for теннис 'tennis'), and to produce a complete list (which would be fairly short) of words in which double letters might be retained.

(9) To write -нн- in participles with prefixes, e.g. написанный 'written', and -н- in those without, e.g. писаный 'id.'.

(10) To further simplify the rules for the use of the hyphen.

(11) To permit -ие (as well as -ии) in the prepositional singular of nouns with nominative singular in -ий and -ие, and in the dative and prepositional singular of nouns with nominative singular in -ия, e.g. о Василие (as well as о Василии 'about Vasilij'), на линие (as well as на линии 'on the line').

(12) To write у (not ю) consistently after ж and ш. Therefore жури (not жюри 'panel of judges'), брошура (not брошюра 'brochure'), etc.

(13) To write only o or e before the suffix -нька in diminutives, e.g. паенька (not паинька 'good child').

(14) To write достоен (for достоин 'worthy') and заец, заечий (for заяц 'hare', заячий 'id. (adjective)') to conform to the general derivation pattern exemplified in спокоен (спокойный 'peaceful'), европеец 'European' (genitive европейца).

(15) To write деревяный 'wooden', оловяный 'tin', стекляный 'glass' (instead of existing spellings with -нн-). These are the only three such adjectives and they have to be taught as exceptions to the existing rule in school orthography courses.

II. PROPOSED AMENDMENTS TO EXISTING RULES

(1) To permit either ы or и in compounds such as предысторический 'pre-historic'. The Commission stated that it found it impossible 'not to consider the wishes of specialists' (i.e. presumably specialists whose terminology is affected).

(2) Simplified rules were put forward on where to write words together, separately or with a hyphen, on the use of capitals, on the division of words, and on punctuation.

The Commission also published details of its deliberations on those rules from the 1956 code for which it proposed no change. These included:

(i) On ё the Commission stated: 'Despite the desirability of "obligatory ё" the experience of many years shows that in practice this letter does not catch on.'

(ii) The proposed replacement of -ьо- and -йо- in foreign words by ё, e.g. маёр for майор.

(iii) Spellings with э in foreign words.

(iv) The question of the prefixes ending in з: a possible revival of the pre-1917 practice was rejected.

Also rejected were proposals to go over to the Latin alphabet,[12] to replace и by i, and to change the shape of certain letters.

Although no actual changes have resulted from the 1964 proposals, the reactions they provoked from the public provided language planners with a store of useful information on beliefs, attitudes, and patterns of

---

[12] This proposal had also been made in 1919 and 1929–30 (Il´inskaja 1966: 93; Makarova 1969).

misunderstanding as to the relationship between sound and symbol. For example, the proposal to write и consistently after ц (viz. in the root of words цыган 'gypsy', цыпленок 'chicken' that had otherwise to be treated as exceptions, and in certain endings) aroused more opposition than any other (Bukčina *et al.* 1969: 58). The normal function of the graphemic opposition и/ы is to indicate the presence or absence of palatalization in the preceding consonant, but since the /ts/ phoneme does not form part of a palatalized/non-palatalized pair, the graphemic distinction has no phonetic meaning. The letters received show, however, that many of their authors believe that it *does* have phonetic meaning. A certain Ju. P. Tixonov of Kujbyšev even claimed, in a letter now with the Russian Language Institute, that цыган and циган were two different words with different meanings (Bukčina *et al.* 1969: 59). A less serious correspondent wrote: 'I don't want to eat огурци [cucumbers] and хлебци [crackers]. I want to eat огурцы and хлебцы. Believe me, they'll taste better that way' (Bukčina *et al.* 1969: 60). It is true that in the speech of the older generation of intellectuals a half-soft [ts] may be encountered in loan-words, and soft [tsʲ] does occur in some dialects, but the confusion in the minds of these correspondents clearly stems from the spelling alone.

Objections of another kind were made by those who believed that a change in the spelling would result in a change in pronunciation. Spelling pronunciations are not unknown to Russian, of course,[13] but the consistent use of и after ж and ш has had no influence whatever on the articulation of these consonants, and there is therefore no reason to think that it would affect ц (Bukčina *et al.* 1969: 61–2).

Objections to the proposal to abolish the soft sign after ж, ш, ч and щ also arise from the confusion of sound and symbol. Some correspondents claimed that they could distinguish between a hard and soft ж and a hard and soft ч, depending on whether or not the soft sign is written after them (Bukčina *et al.* 1969: 70–80). There is, of course, nothing in the sound system of Standard Russian to support this belief.

Throughout the period we have surveyed, most of the opposition to spelling reform has been based on prejudice and misunderstanding of the linguistic facts. The main supporters of reform have been linguists and schoolteachers, the former because they were aware of inconsistencies

---

[13] Even pre-Revolutionary ея and the adjectival ending -ыя had some influence on the pronunciation of educated Petersburgers (Polivanov 1927: 181; «Почта . . .» 1968: 105–6). Some examples of pronunciation changes which may be motivated by following the spelling were given in Chapter 1, above.

between the graphic and phonic systems, the latter because they were familiar with the day-to-day difficulties of pupils learning to read and write. The main opposition (as in other spheres) has come from writers, largely no doubt as a result of their attachment to what they regard as an important tradition of their craft. Some of the opposition stemmed from general conservatism. The political symbolism of both orthographic change and opposition to change may be seen in the continuing use of the old system in *émigré* groups and in attempts by the Germans to reintroduce it during the Second World War (cf. p. 295, above).

The Reform of 1917–18 was a decisive move in the campaign to abolish illiteracy. It removed many of the difficulties encountered in learning to read and write Russian by both native speakers and foreigners. Despite further minor amendments made in 1956 the system is still capable of being improved, as the 1964 proposals showed, though the inconsistencies as they stand are not serious.

The main difficulty in introducing spelling reform is persuading those who can already read and write to accept and use the new system. Nowadays, when virtually everyone who is capable of literacy is literate, this problem would be far greater than it was in the beginning of the century, simply because the number of people who need persuading is far greater. For this reason, sociological factors, including widespread myths and beliefs about the spelling system, must and are being taken into account by Russian language planners. For the issues are not purely linguistic, and if (as has been suggested) it is 'perhaps more difficult to hear and assess one's own speech accurately than to learn the existing orthographic rules' (Bukčina *et al.* 1969: 47), there may be good extra-linguistic reasons for retaining a system which linguistically is imperfect.

Punctuation

In the nineteenth century, no specific guide-lines existed for Russian punctuation. Apart from the most obvious use of a full stop and comma, there was much variation, determined partly by the influence of French (and later, German) punctuation rules and also by punctuation styles of individual writers. For example, Nikolaj Karamzin had a tendency to place a semi-colon between clauses linked by the conjunctions если . . . , то 'if . . . then', когда . . . , тогда 'when . . . then' (Šapiro 1955: 46; 1961: 169).

The major punctuation principles that have been in effect until the present time were first formulated by Grot in his *Спорные вопросы русского правописания* . . . , first published in 1873. The punctuation within a sentence was determined, in Grot's view, by the semantic relationships between the components of this sentence and by the syntactic structure of the sentence. Punctuation signs occurring at the end of the sentence (full stop, question mark, exclamation mark) were dependent on the length of the pause and the intonation of the utterance.

The role of punctuation signs other than full stop and comma was further analysed by Peškovskij in his articles «Роль выразительного чтения в обучении знакам препинания» (early 1920s), «Интонация и грамматика» (1928) (Peškovskij 1959: 19–32, 177–91) and by Ščerba (1935; 1983); both emphasized the role of punctuation in encoding the rhythmic components of texts and its stylistic nuances. Their approach, therefore, differed from Grot's in that they viewed punctuation as a tool of communicative perspective, rather than of syntax *per se*. In fact, however, it is impossible to separate the two, and Russian punctuation rules represent a compromise between the syntactic and the communicative structure of the text.

In his studies of punctuation, Ščerba distinguished between two punctuation types, the French and the German; the latter uses commas and dashes much more frequently, while in the former the semantic function of fewer punctuation signs is far greater. According to Ščerba, the Russian punctuation system is of the German type (Ščerba 1935: 366; Šapiro 1955: 326, 329; 1961: 46–8, 172–3).

Unlike the orthographic rules, the reform of 1917–18 did not affect punctuation, and the rules used in the 1920s–1940s were much the same as those outlined by Grot. However, in the 1930s, the need for punctuation reform was expressed by Bulaxovskij (1930), Šapiro (1930; 1955), and some others.[14] The 1956 Rules consolidated the changes that had been proposed earlier and played an important role in increasing uniformity in punctuation. The rules and their subsequent explanations distinguished between separative marks (отделяющие знаки), i.e. marks that separate two parts of a text, and parenthetic (or enclosing) marks (выделяющие знаки) that introduce additional, appositive elements of a text. The latter group includes paired marks, such as parentheses, quotation marks, paired commas, e.g. он, конечно, был прав 'he, of course, was right', and paired dashes, e.g. in Čukovskij's *Путаница* (1924):

[14] For a bibliography of Soviet works on Russian punctuation written between 1956 and 1976, see *Современная русская пунктуация* (1979: 254–9).

Но веселые зверята—
Поросята, медвежата—
Пуще прежнего шалят . . .

But the merry baby animals—
Piglets, bear cubs—
Are romping more than ever.

Despite this clear-cut functional distinction, confusion may still occur between the two functions of the same punctuation mark. For instance, in the following excerpt from *Правда*, the separative comma was erroneously interpreted as the left-hand component of a paired mark:

Только президент Рейган, а последнее время и вдогонку за ним другие представители Запада, много . . . говорят о «сверхвооруженности» СССР (*Правда*, 31 July 1983, quoted in Švarckopf 1988: 146–7)

Only President Reagan and, recently, other Western politicians who follow his lead have been insisting on the 'excessive' arms arsenal of the USSR.

If, indeed, the two commas introduced a parenthetical expression, the predicate of the main clause should have been used in the singular, agreeing with the singular subject Рейган.

One of the most controversial problems in modern Russian punctuation is the separation of direct speech and reported speech from the introductory phrase (the so-called authorial speech, Russian авторская речь or авторские ремарки). For example, Šapiro (1961: 187–8) notes the tendency to use the question mark, not a full stop, in sentences where the introductory phrase precedes a question, e.g.:

Петр Михалыч слушал Власича и в недоумении спрашивал себя: чем этот человек мог так понравиться Зине? (Čexov, *Соседи*, quoted in Šapiro 1961: 188)

Petr Mixalyč was listening to Vlasič and was asking himself in bewilderment: how could such a person have won Zina's affection?

The same sentence could also be punctuated differently, with a comma separating the introductory phrase and the question, and a full stop at the end.

This tendency is related to another trend, viz. to place the punctuation sign pertaining to direct speech after the postposed authorial speech. Such dislocation of the actual punctuation mark was already attested in nineteenth-century literature, but it has been steadily increasing in the twentieth century. Švarckopf (1988: 153–9) gives a large number of examples illustrating the use of the question mark, exclamation mark, ellipsis, or combinations of these instead of the full stop indicating authorial speech. For example:

Там не так сказано, —обрадовалась его ошибке Таня, он так редко ошибался! (Baškirova, *Рай в шалаше, или Татьянин день*, quoted in Švarckopf 1988: 154)

This is not the way it is phrased there—Tanja rejoiced at his mistake, it was so unusual for him to make a mistake.

Often the mark following the introductory phrase repeats the mark used in the direct speech, e.g.:

Вы собираетесь жениться, дорогой, милейший Александр Алексеевич . . . —Кутайсов выдержал паузу, многозначительную . . . (Glumov, *На рубеже века*, quoted in Švarckopf 1988: 155)

'You are planning to get married, my dear Aleksandr Alekseevič . . .'—Kutajsov held a pause, a meaningful one.

Another common problem is the variation between capital and small initial letters in the direct speech following author's remarks. Though the 1956 Rules did not specifically indicate that this second part of direct speech should be capitalized, the example from Gor´kij illustrating this usage has the capital letter (Švarckopf 1988: 172), and the capitalization seems obligatory if the second part of direct speech is represented by a new sentence.[15] Cf.:

В проулок убежал, говоришь?—вдруг и очень громко спросил Вараксин.—А вот я в проулке стоял. (Gor´kij, *Жизнь Клима Самгина*, quoted in Šapiro 1961: 227)

'So you are saying that he ran into the alley?' asked Varaksin suddenly and very loudly. 'And I myself was standing in the alley.'

However, this implicit rule is commonly violated, under the influence of nineteenth-century literature and literature in other languages: violations are particularly common in translations from foreign languages (Švarckopf 1988: 172–8).

Another area of variation concerns the use of the comma before a verbal adverb. If a verbal adverb is accompanied by several dependent words (thus forming an adverbial clause), the use of the comma is obligatory and does not seem to create any problems in everyday use.

---

[15] The 1956 Rules, in general, seem to have paid less attention to the codification of punctuation, and a number of normative descriptions soon followed clarifying these rules, e.g. Šapiro (1961: 156–229); Bylinskij and Rozental´ (1961); *Современная русская пунктуация* (1979); Ivanova (1982); Valgina (1983); Rozental´ (1984).

However, the use of the comma to separate an isolated verbal adverb or a verbal adverb with a short dependent word becomes problematic, cf.:

С неделю он прожил чего-то ожидая . . . (Gor´kij, *Жизнь Матвея Кожемякина*, quoted in Šapiro 1961: 217)

He spent about a week hoping for something to happen . . .

According to the rules, the verbal adverb is marked off by commas if it conveys secondary, background information and is not if it constitutes the communicative focus of a sentence (Šapiro 1961: 217). However, this criterion is relatively vague and leaves room for variation. The overall tendency in the twentieth century has been not to mark off such verbal adverbs, e.g. Он вышел хлопнув дверью 'He slammed the door and left'.

The rules generally require that elliptical sentence constituents, in particular copulas, should be replaced by a dash; for example, hoardings in the 1960s–1980s often carried the following advertisement: Хорошая профессия—водитель автобуса 'Bus-driver is a good occupation'. However, there are a number of exceptions to this rule (Šapiro 1955: 86–9; 1961: 205–7), and the low informational value of this type of dash often allows it to be omitted (Švarckopf 1988: 144). The variation in the use of the elliptical dash is also due to the fact that the dash has become increasingly important in signalling salient, fore-grounded information or focus of contrast. It is in this latter function that the dash is placed between the pronominal subject and the predicate or predicative phrase (Šapiro 1961: 206–7), e.g. in Axmatova's *Многим* (1922):

> Я—голос ваш, жар вашего дыханья,
> Я—отраженье вашего лица.
>
> I *am* your voice, the warmth of your breath,
> I *am* the reflection of your faces.

Paired dashes are also becoming increasingly popular in parenthetical function (Švarckopf 1988: 53–7, 100–19), cf. the example from Čukovskij's poem above.

Conclusion

ONE of the intellectual predecessors of this book, Ward (1965), concludes with a summary of tendencies observed in the Russian language throughout the first five decades of the Soviet period. Ward also makes some predictions about the fate of Russian in the later periods as well as its more long-term prospects. The goals of this brief conclusion are threefold: firstly, we will examine Ward's predictions to see which of them have been borne out and which have not; secondly, we will summarize the main tendencies of the language as discussed throughout this book; and thirdly, we will briefly comment on the latest period in the development of Russian, the period whose beginning roughly coincides with the end of the Soviet regime. In presenting our conclusions below, we will not be able to separate the first and second goals, and they will be treated as intertwined.

Ward's predictions regarding phonology included the continuing loss of hard [s] in the pronunciation of the reflexive particle, the elimination of the soft [ʃʲʃʲ] in favour of [ʃʲtʃʲ], a further decrease in palatalization assimilation, the persistence of *ikan´e*, and the loss of the special pronunciation of the pretonic жа, ша, ца (Ward 1965: 267). Only the first two predictions have been borne out, as we have shown in Chapter 1, though the loss of palatalization assimilation has been gradual, does not occur at the same rate in all consonantal clusters, and does not affect some clusters at all (see Chapter 1, p. 43). Concerning *ikan´e*, there are some indications, though very uncertain at this point, that *ikan´e* is less strong in the standard language as spoken by younger people, which might eventually lead to its decline. *Ikan´e* is certainly a phenomenon indicative of the reduction of a number of phonological variants, but despite the general tendency to reduce the number of phonological oppositions and to eliminate weak, less functional elements, the overall change in the phonological system cannot be uniformly described in terms of reduction. For example, though pretonic жа, ша, ца generally lose their special pronunciation, the [iᵉ]/[iᵉ] pronunciation remains alive and well in some words (see Chapter 1, p. 51). As a result, there are now more variants in the pronunciation of pretonic a than there were in OM. This suggests that a variety of factors affect change in pronunciation and stress, and often the effect of a certain factor, for example, semantics, may be counterbalanced by the effect of another factor. The adaptation of pronunciation to spelling has probably been the clearest single factor that has affected changes in pronunciation throughout this century.

Ward's prediction regarding the stress system consisted of an attestation and acknowledgement of change as such: while he foresaw the loss of 'anomalies', i.e. less frequent stress patterns (for example, in the nominal system, these are stress patterns E' and F', according to Zaliznjak (1967: 180–91, 226)), he also predicted the rise of new 'anomalies'. Stress change is induced by formal paradigm levelling, where mobile stress is to be avoided, and is motivated by semantic analogy to other words. Next, there are also the so-called *pragmatic factors*: words that are less frequent or that denote less familiar concepts tend to retain more conservative stress patterns, while common words denoting familiar concepts can develop innovatory stress. The familiarity of concepts is certainly a very fluid characteristic, and pragmatic factors play a crucial role in the diversity of stress changes in the language.

The prediction concerning the elimination of what Ward calls special case forms (Ward 1965: 268) is certainly sustained, as the number of words that have two distinct forms in the genitive and prepositional cases is gradually diminishing. Further, even as some forms of the partitive (second) genitive and second locative are retained, these forms are lexicalized, as we have shown in Chapter 3 above (p. 125–7). Another tendency in the reduction of these case forms consists of the elimination of case variation under negation, where the genitive of negation is receding under the advent of the nominative of subject and accusative of direct object. The increasing number of non-declined elements, for example, in compound numerals, in hyphenated compound nouns, in place-names and last names is another instance of ongoing change in twentieth-century Russian (see Ward 1965: 268–9). The use of short-form adjectives is ever decreasing, and more and more such adjectives become restricted to lexicalized or semi-lexicalized expressions (Ward 1965: 269; Gustavsson 1976; Timberlake 1993: 862).

However, some of Ward's predictions have remained pure theoretical points: contrary to his expectations, there has been no increase in the number of stump-compounds of any kind, and there has been little change in the system of aspect—which, however, was not antici-pated by Ward to change any time soon—despite the general claim that the imperfective has been gaining ground and taking over from the perfective in the twentieth century, more so in the spoken language (Forsyth 1970: 3–16, 78–81, 347–50; Zemskaja 1983: 119–26).

Overall, the most obvious changes in the grammar and syntax of present-day Russian include the increase in analyticity, shown in numerous instances throughout this book (see Chapters 3 and 4 in particular), and analogical changes in nominal and verbal government. There seems to be a tendency towards the rise of semantic agreement, especially if the controller of agreement follows the element agreeing with it (see Chapters 4 and 6).

Despite the claims that the ideological system has played a crucial role in the 'vulgarization' and 'bureaucratization' of Russian in the twentieth century, the spread of Russian as the first and primary language of hundreds of millions of people, promoted by mass media and compulsory schooling, has been a more influential factor in its development. (Meanwhile, most of the prescriptive grammars are still based on the literary language of the nineteenth and early twentieth centuries, rather than the standard language of the later period.) The gap between this exclusive language and the educated spoken language, which can also aspire to the status of standard, has increased greatly in the course of the twentieth century. As the nature of mass media has changed and spoken language has become accessible to a larger audience—through radio, cinema, television—the language itself has surrendered to faster change and more variation: it was no longer possible to ignore those 'less-than-standard' varieties that the earlier standard could afford to ignore. As a result, a language community is emerging where there is a greater number of individual varieties, each with its idiosyncrasies; the essential grammar that holds these individual varieties together has shrunk, as some redundant variants have been eliminated. However, owing to the idiosyncrasies of individual varieties, new variation will inevitably arise, although the nature of this variation is, at this point, very hard to predict.

One of the recent articles discussing the changes in present-day Russian is entitled «Дано ли нам предугадать?...» 'Is it given to us to predict?' (Gorbačevič 1990). Without attempting to foretell the future of Russian, we would like, however, to comment on some very recent phenomena which, by our deliberate choice, have remained beyond the scope of this book, viz. the changes in Russian in the late 1980s and early 1990s. The unanimous sentiment among Russian linguists and teachers of Russian is that post-Soviet Russian is changing at an unprecedented rate, and it is not infrequent for the essence of this change to be frowned upon. Below, we would like to offer some of our thoughts on the state of Russian at present, with the important reservation that ongoing change is usually harder to observe than a completed process. Our observations are based on the speech of young Muscovites born after 1970, on the speech of television announcers on central channels of Russian television in 1990–4, and on the Russian press of the early 1990s.

We believe that some of the changes that seem to be occurring so rapidly now actually reflect earlier changes that have accumulated in the language but have been impeded by normative grammars and handbooks. Examples of such change include further loss of the genitive of negation, further loss of the partitive (except in diminutives such as чайку), and increasing analyticity in the declension of numerals, compound or hyphenated nouns, geographical names (Kostomarov 1994: 201–4);[1] all these processes have been discussed in this book. The analytical tendencies have been more apparent in the spoken language (Zemskaja 1983: 95–101), and, as the standard language is becoming more open to spoken language influence, analyticity in the standard can be expected to increase more rapidly.

Other features do seem actually to represent more recent change. In pronunciation, as long as we are dealing with Moscow speech, strong or emphatic *akan´e* is very apparent. While *akan´e* in the standard language requires a/o to be pronounced as [ʌ] in the first pretonic syllable and to be reduced to the central vowel [ə] in the preceding syllables, modern Moscow pronunciation makes no such distinction, reducing all pretonic a/o to the back half-open [ʌ]. Thus, while the standard pronunciation of молоко and говорить is [məlʌˈko] and [gəvʌˈrʲitʲ], modern Moscow speakers, in careful speech, pronounce [mʌlʌˈko] and [gʌvʌˈrʲitʲ], with both pretonic vowels reduced to a back sound. Whether this feature will spread outside Moscow and stabilize as standard it is too early to tell. In allegro speech of the younger generation, another tendency is apparent, viz. to reduce both pre- and posttonic vowels to zero; as a result, rapid speech is increasingly perceived to consist of consonant clusters. In intonation, Kostomarov (1994: 207) indicates the increase of the so-called accidental rise, usually on the final word(s) of an utterance, for example на этом мы *заканчиваем*

---

[1] The increasing number of non-declined geographical names and other proper names is certainly related to the growing number of foreign names mentioned by Russian mass media; thus, most of the examples of non-declension cited by Kostomarov involve transliterated English names.

(accidental rise). While Kostomarov attributes this to the influence of American English, the spread of accidental rise may be due to a more general restructuring of Russian intonation contours, discussed in Chapter 2 above with regard to nexal contours.

In word-formation, a new suffix, which happens to be an English borrowing, is becoming very frequent: -инг (from -ing) (Moraru 1993: 53; Kostomarov 1994: 192). Though the ending -нк is not typical for Russian, numerous borrowings from English retain the suffix -инг in Russian and have become declinable, which is a sign of adaptation, cf. договор селинга 'selling contract' (Kostomarov 1994: 91). It still remains to be seen whether -инг will undergo the same assimilation as -изм, which in the second half of the twentieth century began occurring with Russian stems (see Chapter 5, p. 214).

In the case system, another case has been falling out of grace, following the genitive—the instrumental case. Except for the predicative function (работать кем-л. 'work as . . .', являться чем-л. 'be . . .') and certain set expressions, the prepositionless instrumental is receding, giving way to preposition-governed obliques, for example, вязать спицами against a more frequent вязать на спицах 'to knit with knitting-needles', or любоваться природой 'admire the nature' against любоваться на природу (Mrazek 1964; Muravenko 1990). In government, analogy with more common words similar in meaning has been playing an active role. For example, while the word автономный 'autonomous' cannot take its own object, it has been appearing with an object introduced by the preposition от, probably by analogy with such adjectives as свободный от + genitive 'free of smth.' or освобожденный от 'liberated from smth.' (Kostomarov 1994: 195). Another example of similar change involves the verb заметить 'note': though it should take the object in the accusative case, instances of заметить о plus prepositional are found, due to the influence of сказать о 'tell about'. (See also above, Chapter 4.)

A number of verbs which are supposed to take an object are commonly found in absolute use, i.e. without an object, for example, нарушать 'violate' used without an object in the meaning 'not follow the rules and regulations' (for other examples, see Kostomarov 1994: 194–5). Some verbs that require the reflexive себя begin to occur without this pronoun, for example представить 'imitate' used in lieu of представить себе 'imagine' (Kostomarov 1994: 194–5).

For reasons which are not entirely clear, there seems to be a tendency to use *singularia tantum* in the plural; thus, Kostomarov (1994: 189–90) cites the following example: предпринимательские риски '(lit.) entrepreneurial risks', взаимные озабоченности 'mutual concerns'.[2] In some instances, the use of the plural form reflects the fact that a respective word has developed a new, less abstract meaning, for example, бизнес, which originally meant 'business, endeavour' but has now acquired a more specific meaning 'enterprise, factory'.

One of the more striking syntactic features is the spread of postposed adjectives, for example, гарантии безопасности всеобщей 'guarantees of global safety' (from a television broadcast of ITAR TASS, 16 June, 1993), человека рядового все равно обманут 'an ordinary person will still be deceived' (television broadcast *Новости*, 3 January 1992). This is a relatively new feature; in the standard language the postposition of an adjective usually has the function of emphasis, and in the spoken language this postposition occurs, after a pause, as an afterthought (Zemskaja 1973: 241–64; 1981: 191–227; 1987: 138–45, 150, 162–74). The origin of postposed adjectives in more formal speech has probably been influenced both by emphatic constructions and the spoken language, but they now occur in formal spoken language without the expected pause. It is unlikely that the appearance of postposed adjectives would change the order of adjective and noun altogether: preposed adjectives are likely to remain more frequent than postposed ones, but some word order variation may eventually arise in the standard.

In speech etiquette, the most apparent change concerns the decreasing use of the patronymics: the age-group that goes by forename and surname only is increasing, by now including all those under 40 (see also Kostomarov 1994: 8). The shrinking use of patronymics is particularly supported by the press and television, where more and more political figures—who seem to be the last to relinquish patronymics (see p. 261 above)—are referred to by their forename and/or surname. If, indeed, patronymics fall out of use in standard Russian, they will serve as an example of a short-lived language feature, having appeared only in the eighteenth century (Unbegaun 1972: 11, 12, 15).

Ongoing change in present-day Russian is most evident in the lexicon, where two tendencies are worthy of note. First, as a reaction to recent socio-political change, the language is being purged of words associated with the Soviet period and ideology. Aside from the sweeping renaming campaign which resulted in the restoration of pre-Revolutionary place-names and the replacement of ideologically

---

[2] Several other examples cited by Kostomarov actually involve words that can have the plural.

marked names by more neutral ones, Russian has been trying to rid itself of common nouns, too. For example, товарищ has been replaced by господин, госпожа, which, however, have not been universally accepted as standard titles; the word отдел has been replaced by nineteenth- and early twentieth-century департамент; the 'Sovietized' word родина has been replaced by отечество '(literally) fatherland', and the name of the Russian Parliament, established in 1994, is (Государственная) Дума, following the name of the parliament (Дума) that existed in 1906–17. (See Kostomarov (1994: 118–24) for some other restored historicisms.) However, this trend is relatively minor compared to the tendency to calque or borrow words from English. Some of the obvious calques include the TV announcers' будьте с нами 'stay with us' (see also Kostomarov 1994: 37). The number of borrowings may seem threatening: Russian has been virtually flooded by English loan-words; some of them, such as инвестиции (also инвестмент) or эксклюзивный, seem pointless in view of the Russian (капитало)вложения or исключительный, специальный (depending on the context). Though this fact has been lamented most,[3] this seems to be a temporary phenomenon—just as many words recorded by Seliščev (1928) are no longer remembered by the majority of native speakers, so will the fascination of these English words recede, giving way to a more stable lexicon. But this would be a chapter in a book still to be written.

---

[3] For example, by participants of the conference *Русский язык и современность. Проблемы и перспективы развития русского языка* (Moscow, May 1991), who, nevertheless, concluded that the general state of Russian had remained healthy and presented optimistic prospects (Kostomarov 1994: 221–9).

Bibliography

References in Cyrillic are given in the order appropriate for the romanized transcription. A number following the name of a journal without a comma indicates the volume; a number separated by a comma indicates the issue in a given year. For the list of abbreviations see p. viii.

AASAMAA, I. 1974. *Как себя вести.* 4th edn. Tallinn: Valgus. (Trans. from Estonian, 1970, Tallinn).

AGEENKO, F. L., and ZARVA, M. V. 1984. *Словарь ударений для работников радио и телевидения.* 5th edn. Moscow: Russkij jazyk.

AKIŠINA, A. A., and AKIŠINA, T. E. 1990. *Этикет русского телефонного разговора.* Moscow: Russkij jazyk.

——and FORMANOVSKAJA, N. I. 1970. *Русский речевой этикет.* 1st edn. Moscow: Russkij jazyk.

—— 1973. *Речевой этикет (в таблицах и упражнениях).* Moscow: Russkij jazyk.

—— 1978. *Русский речевой этикет.* 2nd edn. Moscow: Russkij jazyk.

ALEKSEEV, D. I. 1961. «Склонение буквенных аббревиатур». In *Вопросы теории и методики изучения русского языка,* 62–82. Kuibyšev.

—— 1963. «Графические сокращения и слова-аббревиатуры». In Ožegov and Panov 1963, 145–60.

ALTAJSKAJA, V. F. 1960. «Переходные явления в лексике русского языка послеоктябрьского периода». *RJaš,* 5: 14–20.

ANDREEV, N. D. 1963. «Об одном эксперименте в области русской орфоэпии». *VKR,* 4: 49–52.

APRESJAN, Ju. D. 1974. *Лексическая семантика. Синонимические средства языка.* Moscow: Nauka.

ASTAF′EVA, N. I. 1974. *Предлоги в русском языке и особенности их употребления.* Minsk: Vyšèjšaja škola.

AVANESOV, R. I. 1947a. «Работа над русским произношением в школе». *RJaš,* 3: 1–22.

—— 1947b. «Вопросы образования русского языка в его говорах». *Вестник Московского государственного университета,* 9.

—— 1956. *Фонетика современного русского литературного языка.* Moscow: Izd. MGU.

—— 1961. «О нормах русского литературного произношения». *RJaš,* 6: 7–12.

—— 1975. «Ива́нов или Ивано́в». *RR,* 5: 151–2.

——1984. *Русское литературное произношение*. 6th edn. Moscow: Prosveščenie (earlier edns.: 1st (1950), 2nd (1954), 3rd (1958), 4th (1967), 5th (1972)).

——and BROMLEJ, S. V. 1986– , eds. *Диалектологический атлас русского языка: центр Европейской части СССР* (3 fasc.). Moscow: Nauka.

——and GORŠKOV, A. I. 1985, eds. *Диалектография русского языка*. Moscow: Nauka.

——and MORAXOVSKAJA, O. N. 1987, eds. *Русские диалекты: лингвогеографический аспект*. Moscow: Nauka.

——and ORLOVA, V. G. 1965, eds. *Русская диалектология*. 2nd edn. Moscow: Nauka.

——and OŽEGOV, S. I. 1959. *Русское литературное произношение и ударение. Словарь-справочник*. Moscow: Gos. izd. inostrannyx i nacional´nyx slovarej.

AZOV, V. 1923. «Открытое письмо Академии наук, Наркому Просвещения Луначарскому, Акцентру, Губполитпросвету, Сорабису, Управлению Актеатров, месткомам частных театров и всем грамотным людям». *Жизнь искусства* 43: 8.

BALAXONOVA, L. I. 1967. «Расческа, гребень, гребенка». *RR*, 6: 92–3.

BALDWIN, J. R. 1979. *A Formal Analysis of the Intonation of Modern Colloquial Russian. (Forum phoneticum, 18)*. Hamburg: Helmut Buske.

BARANNIKOV, A. P. 1919. «Из наблюдений над развитием русского языка в последние годы войны». *Ученые записки Самарского университета*, fasc. 2, 64–84.

BARANNIKOVA, L. I., DANILOVA, Z. A., and ČERNEVA, N. P. 1970. «Факторы, определяющие выбор личных имен». In Nikonov 1970, 177–82.

BARANOV, A. N., and Kazakevič, E. G. 1991. *Парламентские дебаты: традиции и новации*. Moscow: Znanie.

BARING, M., n.d. *What I Saw in Russia*. London: T. Nelson.

BARINOVA, G. A. 1966. «О произношении [ж́'] и [ш́']». In Vysotskij *et al.* 1966, 25–54.

BARINOVA, G. A., IL´INA, N. E., and KUZ´MINA, S. M. 1971. «О том, как проверялся вопросник по произношению». In Vysotskij *et al.* 1971, 315–42.

——and PANOV, M. V. 1971. «О том, как кодировался фонетический вопросник». In Vysotskij *et al.* 1971, 302–14.

BARNHART, R. K., STEINMETZ, S., and BARNHART, C. L. 1990. *Third Barnhart dictionary of New English*. New York: H. H. Wilson.

BELODED, I. K. 1964. «Теоретические проблемы изучения украинской литературной речи». *Известия Академии наук СССР. Отделение литературы и языка* 23: 473–80.

BELYK, N. A. 1970. «Некоторые правовые и социологические вопросы антропонимики». In Nikonov 1970, 9–23.

BEZDĚK, J., FORMAN M., KOPECKIJ L. V., and KOUT, J. 1974. *Пособие по лексикологии русского литературного языка*. Prague: Státní pedagogické nakladatelství.

BOBRAN, M. 1974. «Czasownikowa pojedyncza bezprzyimkowa wariacyjna rekcija silna w języku polskim i rosyjskim». *Slavia Orientalis* 23: 443–50.

BOČAROV, S. G. 1985. ««Мир» в «Войне и мире»». In Bočarov, S. G. *О художественных мирах*, 229–48. Moscow: Sovetskij pisatel´.

BOGATYREV, K. K. 1985. «Об одном проявлении прагматического фактора в современном русском языке (ударение глаголов на -ировать)». *Russian Linguistics* 9: 165–72.

BOGUSLAVSKIJ, I. M. 1985. *Исследования по синтаксической семантике. Сферы действия логических слов*. Moscow: Nauka.

BOJARKINA, V. D. 1983. «О некоторых особенностях новой глагольной лексики». In Kotelova 1983, 93–102.

BOLLA, K., PÁLL, E., and PAPP, F. 1970. *Курс современного русккого литературного языка*. Budapest: Akadémiai kiadó.

BONDALETOV, V. D. 1970. «Ономастика и социолингвистика». In Nikonov and Superanskaja 1970, 17–23.

——and DANILINA, E. F. 1970. «Средства выражения эмоционально-экспрессивных оттенков в русских личных именах». In Nikonov and Superanskaja 1970, 194–200.

BONDARKO, L. V. 1973. Review of Vysotskij *et al.* 1971. *VJa*, 2: 135–9.

——and VERBICKAJA, L. A. 1973. «О фонетических характеристиках заударных флексий в современном русском языке». *VJa*, 1: 37–49.

BORISOVA-LUKAŠANEC, E. G. 1983. «О лексике современного молодежного жаргона (англоязычные заимствования в студенческом сленге 60–70-х гг.)». In Skvorcov and Švarckopf 1983, 104–20.

BORKOVSKIJ, V. I. 1978, ed. *Историческая грамматика русского языка. Синтаксис. Простое предложение*. Moscow: Nauka.

——and KUZNECOV, P. S. 1965. *Историческая грамматика русского языка*. 2nd edn. Moscow: Nauka.

BORRAS, F. M., and CHRISTIAN, R. F. 1984. *Russian Syntax: Aspects of Modern Russian Syntax and Vocabulary*. 2nd edn. Oxford: Clarendon Press.

BORUNOVA, S. N. 1966. «Сочетания [ш'ч'] и [ш̄'] на границах морфем». In Vysotskij *et al.* 1966, 55–71.

——VORONCOVA, V. L., and Es´KOVA, N. A. 1983. *Орфоэпический словарь русского литературного языка*. Moscow: Russkij jazyk.

BRAGINA, A. A. 1973. *Неологизмы в русском языке*. Moscow: Prosveščenie.

BRATUS, B. V. 1972. *Russian Intonation*. Oxford: Pergamon Press.

BRIGHT, W. 1966, ed. *Sociolinguistics. Proceedings of the UCLA Sociolinguistics Conference 1964*. The Hague: Mouton.

BROIDO, V. 1987. *Lenin and the Mensheviks: The Persecution of Socialists under Bolshevism*. Aldershot (Hants): Gower & M. T. Smith.

BROMLEJ, S. B. 1973. «Противопоставленность I и II спряжений в русских говорах и в литературном языке». In Ju. S. Azarx *et al.*, eds. *Исследования по русской диалектологии*, 155–75. Moscow: Nauka.

BROWN, R., and GILMAN, A. 1972. 'The Pronouns of Power and Solidarity'. In P. P. Giglioli, ed. *Language and Social Context*, 252–82. Harmondsworth: Penguin (reprinted from T. Sebeok. 1960, ed. *Style in Language*, 253–76. Cambridge, Mass.: Technology Press of MIT).

BRYZGUNOVA, E. A. 1977. *Звуки и интонация русской речи*. Moscow: Russkij jazyk.

BUKČINA, B. Z. 1970. «Строп-стропа». *RR*, 1: 120.

—— 1974. ««Правила русской орфографии и пунктуации» (1956 г.) и орфографическая практика». *Известия Академии наук СССР. Серия литературы и языка* 33: 44–52.

—— and KALAKUCKAJA, L. P. 1974. *Сложные слова*. Moscow: Nauka.

—— 1982. *Слитно или раздельно? Опыт словаря-справочника*. Moscow: Russkij jazyk.

—— and ČEL´COVA, L. K. 1969. *Письма об орфографии*. Moscow: Nauka.

BUKRINSKAJA, I. A. 1983. «Ударенное окончание -и в предложном падеже существительных второго типа склонения в русских диалектах». In R. I. Avanesov, ed. *Русские народные говоры. Лингвогеографические исследования*, 89–93. Moscow: Nauka.

BULAXOVSKIJ, L. A. 1930. «К реформе русской пунктуации». *Русский язык в советской школе*, 3.

—— 1952. *Курс русского литературного языка*. 5th edn. vol. i. Kiev: Radjan´ska škola.

—— 1954. *Русский литературный язык первой половины XIX в.* 2nd edn. Moscow: Gosučpedgiz.

BUNIN, I. A. 1982. *Окаянные дни*. London: Zarja.

BUNING, J. E. J., and van SCHOONEVELD, C. H. 1960. *The Sentence Intonation of Contemporary Standard Russian as a Linguistic Structure*. The Hague: Mouton.

BUTORIN, D. I. 1964. «Употребление в распределительном значении количественных числительных с предлогом *по*». *VKR*, 5: 144–9.

—— 1966. «Об особых случаях употребления винительного падежа прямого объекта в современном русском литературном языке». In Kačevskaja and Gorbačevič 1966, 125–36.

—— 1969. «Компонент и компонента». *RR*, 5: 121.

BYLINSKIJ, K. I., and ROZENTAL´, D. È. 1961. *Трудные случаи пунктуации*. Moscow: Iskusstvo.

CEPLITIS, L. K. 1974. *Анализ речевой интонации*. Riga: Zinatne.

ČEREMISINA, N. V. 1989. *Русская интонация: поэзия, проза, разговорная речь*. Moscow: Russkij jazyk.

ČERKASOVA, E. T. 1967. *Переход полнозначных слов в предлоги*. Moscow:

Nauka.

ČERNUXINA, I. Ja. 1976. *Связь самостоятельных предложений в письменной речи*. In Zolotova 1976, 261–71.

ČERNYŠEV, V. I. 1914–15. *Правильность и чистота русской речи*. 2nd edn. St Petersburg: M. Merkušev.

—— 1915. *Законы и правила русского произношения*. 3rd edn. Petrograd: Imperatorskaja Akademija nauk. (Repr. in Černyšev 1970.)

—— 1970. *Избранные труды*. (5 vols.). vol. i. Moscow: Prosveščenie.

—— 1947. «Ф. Ф.Фортунатов и А. А. Шахматов—реформаторы русского правописания». In S. P. Obnorskij, ed. *А. А. Шахматов 1864–1920. Сборник статей и материалов*, 167–252. Moscow-Leningrad: Izd. AN SSSR.

ČERNYX, P. Ja. 1929. i. *Современные течения в лингвистике*. ii. *Русский язык и революция*. Irkutsk: Vostočnosibirskoe kraevoe izd.

—— 1948. «Заметки об употреблении местоимения *вы* вместо *ты* в качестве формы вежливости в русском литературном языке XVIII–XIX веков». *Ученые записки Московского государственного университета*. (*Труды кафедры русского языка*.), fasc. 137, part 2, 89–108.

—— 1949. «К истории форм вежливости в русском языке. О частице *с*». *Доклады и сообщения филологического факультета Московского государственного университета*, fasc. 8, 58–65.

Численность, размещение, возрастная структура, уровень образования, национальный состав, языки и источники средств существования населения СССР по данным Всесоюзной переписи населения 1970 года. 1971. Moscow: Statistika.

COMRIE, B., and STONE, G. 1978. *The Russian Language since the Revolution*. Oxford: Clarendon Press.

COOPER, R. L. 1989. *Language Planning and Social Change*. Cambridge: Cambridge University Press.

CORBETT, G. G. 1976. 'Address in Russian'. *Journal of Russian Studies* 31: 3–15.

—— 1983. *Hierarchies, Targets and Controllers: Agreement Patterns in Slavic*. London: Croom Helm.

—— 1991. *Gender*. Cambridge: Cambridge University Press.

CORTEN, I. H. 1993. *Vocabulary of Soviet Society and Culture: A Selected Guide to Russian Words, Idioms, and Expressions of the Post-Stalin Era, 1953–1991*. Durham, N. C. : Duke University Press.

ČUDAKOVA, M. O. 1972. *Мастерство Юрия Олеши*. Moscow: Nauka.

ČUKOVSKIJ, K. I. 1963. *Живой как жизнь. О русском языке*. 2nd edn. Moscow: Molodaja gvardija.

ČUMAKOVA, Ju. P. 1970. «К вопросу о формах личного имени в русской диалектной речи». In Nikonov and Superanskaja 1970, 200–5.

DAL´, V. I. 1980–82. *Толковый словарь живого великорусского языка*. 2nd edn. St Petersburg: M. Vol´f. (repr.: Moscow: Russkij jazyk, 1989–91).

DANILINA, E. F. 1969. «Категория ласкательности в личных именах и вопрос о так называемых «сокращенных» формах имен в русском языке». In Nikonov and Superanskaja 1969, 145–61.

DEMENT´EV, A. A. 1954. «О женских соответствиях к мужским в наименованиях действующих лиц». *RJaŠ*, 6: 13–14.

DENISON, N. 1968. 'Sauris: A Trilingual Community in Diatypic Perspective'. *Man* (NS) 3(4): 578–92.

DERJAGIN, V. Ja. 1968. «Уважаемый товарищ!» *RR*, 5: 139–40.

DRAGE, C. L. 1967a. 'Changes in the Regressive Palatalization of Consonants in Russian since 1870'. *Zeitschrift für Phonetik, Sprachwissenschaft und Kommunikationsforschung* 20: 181–206.

——1967b. 'Factors in the Regressive Palatalization of Consonants in Russian'. *Zeitschrift für Phonetik, Sprachwissenschaft und Kommunikationsforschung* 20: 119–42.

——1968. 'Some Data on Modern Moscow Pronunciation'. *Slavonic and East European Review* 46: 353–82.

DULEWICZOWA, I. 1981. *Transkrypcja i transliteracja wyrazów rosyjskich*. Warsaw: Państwowe Wydawn. Nauk.

——1983. *Wokatywna forma rzeczowników w języku polskim i rosyjskim.* (*Polonica*, 9.) Warsaw.

DURNOVO, N. N. 1971. «О склонении в современном великорусском литературном языке». *VJa*, 4: 90–103.

DURNOVO, N. N., SOKOLOV N. N., and UŠAKOV, D. N. 1914. *Диалектологическая карта русского языка в Европе*. Petrograd: Imperatorskaja Akademija nauk. (reproduced as supplement to Avanesov and Orlova 1965).

——and UŠAKOV, D. N. 1927. «Опыт фонетической транскрипции русского литературного произношения». *Slavia* 6, 2.

ECKERT, P. 1991, ed. *New Ways of Analyzing Sound Change*. San Diego: Academic Press.

ERVIN-TRIPP, S. M. 1969. 'Sociolinguistics'. In L. Berkowitz, ed. *Advances in Experimental Social Psychology*. iv. 93–107. New York: Academic Press.

——1972. 'On Sociolinguistic Rules: Alternation and Co-occurrence'. In J. J. Gumperz and D. Hymes, eds. *Directions in Sociolinguistics*, 213–50. New York: Holt, Rinehart, & Winston. (shorter version of Ervin-Tripp 1969).

ES´KOVA, N. A. 1964. «Графическая передача фонемы «и» в начале морфемы, не являющейся флексией или суффиксом, после твердой согласной предшествующей морфемы». In V. V. Vinogradov *et al.*, eds. *О современной русской орфографии*, 5–17. Moscow: Nauka.

——1967. «О недостаточности действующего правила употребления так называемой буквы ё». *VKR*, 8: 73–84.

FAKTOROVIČ, T. L. 1966. «Вратарь». *Этимологические исследования по русскому языку*, fasc. 5, 145–7.

FASMER (Vasmer), M. 1986–7. *Этимологический словарь русского языка.* Moscow: Progress.

FESSENKO (Fesenko), A. and T. 1955. *Русский язык при Советах.* New York: Rausen Bros.

FILIN, F. P. 1973. «О структуре современного русского литературного языка». *VJa*, 2: 3–12.

——1981, ed. *Лексика русского литературного языка XIX–начала XX века.* Leningrad: Nauka.

FLIER, M. S. 1990. 'Sonorant Cluster Variation in Russian'. *Wiener slawistischer Almanach* 25/6: 127–43.

FORMANOVSKAJA, N. I. 1978. *Стилистика сложного предложения.* Moscow: Russkij jazyk.

——1982a. *Русский речевой этикет: лингвистический и методический аспекты.* Moscow: Russkij jazyk.

——1982b. *Употребление русского речевого этикета.* Moscow: Russkij jazyk.

——1989. *Речевой этикет и культура общения.* Moscow: Russkij jazyk.

FORSYTH, J. 1970. *A Grammar of Aspect: Usage and Meaning in the Russian Verb.* Cambridge: Cambridge University Press.

FRIEDRICH, P. 1966a. 'Structural Implications of Russian Pronominal Usage'. In Bright 1966, 214–59.

——1966b. 'The Linguistic Reflex of Social Change: From Tsarist to Soviet Russian Kinship'. In S. Lieberson, ed. *Explorations in Sociolinguistics*, 31–57. Bloomington, Ind.: Indiana University Press.

——1972. 'Social Context and Semantic Feature: The Russian Pronominal Usage'. In J. J. Gumperz and D. Hymes, eds. *Directions in Sociolinguistics*, 270–300. New York: Holt, Rinehart, & Winston (shorter version of Friedrich 1966a).

GAK, V. G. 1976. «Номинализация сказуемого и устранение субъекта». In Zolotova 1976, 85–103.

GANIEV, Ž. V. 1966. «О произношении сочетаний «стк», «здк», «ндк»». In Vysotskij *et al.* 1966, 85–95.

GENKINA, È. B. 1954. *Переход Советского государства к новой экономической политике.* Moscow: Izd. političeskoj literatury.

GLOVINSKAJA, M. JA. 1966. «В защиту одного приема фонетического обследования». In Vysotskij *et al.* 1966, 163–72.

——1971. «Об одной фонологической подсистеме в современном русском литературном языке». In Vysotskij *et al.* 1971, 54–96.

——1975. «О зависимости морфемной членимости слова от степени его синтагматической фразеологизации». In *Развитие современного русского языка. 1972: Словообразование. Членимость слова*, 112–56.

Moscow: Nauka.

——Il´ina, N. E., Kuz´mina, S. M., and Panov, M. V. 1971. «О грамматических факторах развития фонетической системы современного русского языка». In Vysotskij *et al.* 1971, 20–32.

Golubeva-Monatkina, N. I. 1994. «Русская змиграция о русском языке». *Russkaja slovesnost´*, 3: 73–7.

Gorbačevič, K. S. 1966. «Премирова́ть или преми́ровать». *VKR*, 7: 211–13.

——1971. *Изменение норм русского литературного языка*. Leningrad: Nauka.

——1972. «Вариативность ударения в предложных сочетаниях (Энклитика и проклитика)». *RJaŠ*, 6: 51–7.

——1973, ed. *Трудности словоупотребления и варианты норм русского литературного языка*. Leningrad: Nauka.

——1974. «Вариантность ударения в формах инфинитива». *RJaŠ*, 5: 9–13.

——1978. *Вариантность слова и языковая норма*. Leningrad: Nauka.

——1990. «Дано ли нам предугадать?.. (О будущем русского языка)». *Russistik* 2/2: 70–80.

Gornfel´d, A. G. 1922. *Новые словечки и старые слова*. Peterburg: Kolos.

Городское просторечие. Проблемы изучения. 1984. Moscow: Nauka.

Gorškov, A. I. 1969. *История русского литературного языка*. Moscow: Nauka.

Granovskaja, L. M. 1983. «Некоторые особенности развития словарного состава русского языка в 20-е годы XX в. и проблема нормы». In Skvorcov and Švarckopf 1983, 47–70.

Graudina, L. K. 1964*a*. «О нулевой форме родительного множественного у существительных мужского рода». In Mučnik and Panov 1964, 181–209.

——1964*b*. «Развитие нулевой формы родительного множественного у существительных—единиц измерения». In Mučnik and Panov 1964, 210–21.

——1966. «Опыт количественной оценки нормы (форма род. ед. чая-чаю)». *VKR*, 7: 75–88.

——1980. *Вопросы нормализации русского языка*. Moscow: Nauka.

——Ickovič, V. A., and Katlinskaja, L. P. 1976. *Грамматическая правильность русской речи. (Опыт частотно-стилистического словаря вариантов)*. Moscow: Nauka.

Grigor´ev, V. P. 1961. «О нормализаторской деятельности и языковом «пятачке»». *VKR*, 3: 3–20.

Grot, Ja. K. 1873. *Спорные вопросы русского правописания от Петра Великого доныне*. St Petersburg: Imperatorskaja Akademija nauk.

——1885. *Русское правописание*. 3rd edn. St Petersburg: Imperatorskaja

Akademija nauk.

—— 1891–5, ed. *Словарь русского языка под ред. Я.К. Грота (А–Д)*. St Petersburg: Imperatorskaja Akademija nauk.

—— 1899. *Труды Я.К. Грота. II. Филологические разыскания*. St Petersburg: Imperatorskaja Akademija nauk.

GRUZBERG, L. A. 1974. «Лексика обращений в народно-разговорной речи». In A. A. Bel´skij *et al.*, eds. *Живое слово в русской речи Прикамья*, fasc. 4, 50–61. Perm´.

GUSTAVSSON, S. 1976. *Predicative adjectives with the copula BYT´ in Modern Russian*. (*Acta Universitatis Stockholmiensis*, 10.) Stockholm: Almqvist and Wiksell.

GVOZDEV, A. N. 1958. *Современный русский литературный язык*. Part I. Moscow: Gosučpedgiz.

HALLE, M. 1959. *The Sound Pattern of Russian*. The Hague: Mouton.

HAUGEN, E. 1959. 'Planning for a Standard Language in Modern Norway'. *Anthropological Linguistics* 1/3: 8–21.

—— 1966a. 'Linguistics and Language Planning'. In Bright 1966, 50–71.

—— 1966b. *Language Conflict and Language Planning: The Case of Modern Norwegian*. Cambridge, Mass.: Harvard University Press.

—— 1969. 'Language Planning, Theory and Practice'. In A. Graur, ed. *Actes du Xe Congrès International des Linguistes*. vol. i, 701–11. Bucarest: Éds. de l'Académie de la République Socialiste de Roumanie.

ICKOVIČ, V. A. 1961. «Никитич или Никитович». *VKR*, 3: 229–32.

—— 1968. *Языковая норма*. Moscow: Prosveščenie.

—— 1971. «Современные аббревиатуры». *RR*, 2: 74–9.

—— 1972. «Новые тенденции в образовании аббревиатур. (О путях включения аббревиатур в систему языка)». In V. P. Danilenko, ed. *Терминология и норма*, 88–101. Moscow: Nauka.

—— 1974. «Очерки синтаксической нормы 1–3». In Zolotova 1974a, 43–106.

—— 1982. *Очерки синтаксической нормы*. Moscow: Nauka.

IL´INA, N. E. 1980. *Морфонология глагола в современном русском языке*. Moscow: Nauka.

IL´INSKAJA, I. S. 1966, ed. *Орфография и русский язык*. Moscow: Nauka.

—— and SIDOROV, V. N. 1955. «О сценическом произношении в московских театрах. (По материалам сезона 1951/52 г.)». *VKR*, 1: 143–71.

IOMDIN, L. L. 1990. *Автоматическая обработка текста на естественном языке: Модель согласования*. Moscow: Nauka.

—— 1991. «Словарная статья предлога ПО». *Семиотика и информатика* 32: 94–120.

ISAČENKO, A. V. 1954, 1960. *Грамматический строй русского языка в сопоставлении с словацким*. Part I (1954), II (1960). Bratislava: Izd.

Slovackoj Akademii nauk.

Istrin, V. A. 1988. *1100 лет славянской азбуки*. 2nd edn. Moscow: Nauka.

Istrina, E. S. 1948. *Нормы русского языка и культура речи*. Moscow-Leningrad: Izd. AN SSSR.

Ivančikova, E. A. 1966. «О развитии синтаксиса русского языка в советскую эпоху». In Pospelov and Ivančikova 1966, 3–22.

Ivanova, T. A. 1967. «Именительный множественного на *-á* (*родá, тенорá, госпиталя́*) в современном русском языке». In Meščerskij *et al.* 1967, 55–78.

Ivanova, V. F. 1982. *История и принципы русской пунктуации*. Leningrad: Nauka.

Ivanova-Luk'janova, G. N. 1971. «Ленинградское [ш'ч']». In Vysotskij *et al.* 1971, 249.

Jachnow, H. (1973/)1974. 'Zur sozialen Implikazion des Gebrauches von Anredepronomen (mit besonderer Berücksichtigung des Russischen)'. *Zeitschrift für slawische Philologie* 37: 343–55.

——1980. *Zur Erklärung und Modelierung diachroner Wortbildungprozesse (anhand russischer substantivischer Neologismen)*. München: O. Sagner.

Jakobson, R. 1921. *Vliv revoluce na ruský jazyk*. Prague: n.p.

Jakovlev, K. I. 1976. *Как мы портим русский язык (об иностранных словах в нашем языке)*. Moscow: Molodaja gvardija.

Janko-Trinickaja, N. A. 1964*a*. «Проблема номер один. (Числительное в роли несогласованного определения)». In Mučnik and Panov 1964, 303–10.

——1964*b*. «Процессы включения в лексике и словообразовании». In Mučnik and Panov 1964, 18–35.

——1966*a*. «Кратный именительный в функции определния». In Poseplov and Ivančikova 1966, 174–85.

——1966*b*. «Наименование лиц женского пола существительными женского и мужского рода». In Zemskaja and Šmelev 1966, 167–210.

——1967. «И *уважаемый*... и *уважаемая*... (По поводу заметки А. К. Панфилова)». *VKR*, 8: 240–4.

Jazovickij, E. V. 1969. *Говорите правильно. Эстетика речи*. Leningrad: Prosveščenie.

Jelitte, H. 1990. *Die russischen Nomina abstracta des 20. Jahrhunderts. Teil I: Der lexikalische Bestand der ersten Hälfte des 20. Jahrhunderts*. (*Beiträge zur Slawistik*, 13). Frankfurt am Main: Lang.

Jiráček (Iraček), I. 1969. «Ударение существительных с суффиксом *-аж* в современном русском литературном языке». *Русский язык за рубежом*, 2: 92–4.

——1971. *Интернациональные суффиксы существительных в современном русском языке: структурно-сопоставительное исследование*. (*Spisy Univerzity J. E. Purkyně v Brně, Filozofická fakulta*, 168.) Brno.

JONES, D., and WARD, D. 1969. *The Phonetics of Russian*. Cambridge: Cambridge University Press.

JUGOV, A. K. 1975. *Думы о русском слове*. Moscow: Sovremennik.

KAČALOVSKIJ, E. 1975. «Кодекс петровцев». *Литературная газета*, No. 24, 11 June 1975, 10–11.

KAČEVSKAJA, G. A., and GORBAČEVIČ, K. S. 1966, eds. *Нормы современного русского литературного словоупотребления*. Leningrad: Nauka.

KALAKUCKAJA, L. P. 1966. «Колготки». *VKR*, 7: 166.

—— 1970. «О склонении имен собственных (морфологический тип на -*а* неударное)». In Kostomarov and Skvorcov 1970, 218–42.

—— 1984. *Склонение фамилий и личных имен в русском литературном языке*. Moscow: Nauka.

KALENČUK, M. L. 1993. «Орфоэпическая система современного русского литературного языка». Авотреферат докт. дисс. Moscow: Pedagogičeskij gosudarstvennyj universitet.

KALININ, A. V. 1971. *Лексика русского языка*. 2nd edn. Moscow: Izd. MGU.

KANTOROVIČ, V. JA. 1966. *«Ты» и «Вы». (Заметки писателя)*. Moscow: Politizdat.

—— 1974. *«Ты» и «Вы». Вчера, сегодня, в условиях научно-технической революции*. Moscow: Politizdat.

KARCEVSKIJ, S. I. 1923. *Язык, война и революция*. Berlin: Russkoe universal'noe izd.

KASVIN, G. A. 1949. «Основы настоящего времени глаголов 2-го спряжения». In *Материалы и исследования по русской диалектологии*. vol. iii. 47–56. Moscow-Leningrad: Izd. AN SSSR.

KIPARSKY, V. 1979. *Russian Historical Grammar*. Ann Arbor: Ardis. (Trans. from: Kiparsky, V. 1963. *Russische historische Grammatik*. Bd. 1. Die Entwicklung des Lautsystems. Heidelberg: C. Winter.)

KIRKWOOD, M. 1989, ed. *Language Planning in the Soviet Union*. London: Macmillan.

KLINSKAJA, L. I. 1957. «К вопросу обогащения словарного состава языка». *RJaŠ*, 3: 22–7.

KOGOTKOVA, T. S. 1970. «Литературный язык и диалекты». In Kostomarov and Skvorcov 1970, 104–52.

KOLESOV, V. V. 1967. «Развитие словесного ударения в современном русском произношении». In Meščerskij *et al.* 1967, 96–118.

—— 1991. *Язык города*. Moscow: Vysšaja škola.

KOLOMIJEC´, V. T. 1973. Розвиток лексики слов'янських мов у післявоєнний період. Kiev: Naukova dumka.

KOMTÈ, M. 1990. «Употребления местоимения «мы» в современном русском языке». *Russistik* 2/1: 18–25.

KONDRATENKO, G. I. 1970. «Наблюдение за употреблением личных имен в Брянской области». In Nikonov 1970, 115–17.

KONDURUŠKIN, S. S. 1917. *Толковый словарь (пособие при чтении газет).* Petrograd: Znanie.

KOROTKOVA, T. A. 1970. «Динамика личных имен свердловчан». In Nikonov 1970, 110–15.

KOSTOMAROV, V. G. 1959*a*. «Откуда слово *стиляга?*» *VKR*, 2: 168–75.

—— 1959*b*. «Словесные сорняки». *Литература и жизнь.* 16 Dec. 1959, 2.

—— 1965. «Культура языка в свете языковой политики». In T. A. Degtereva, ed. *Язык и стиль,* 3–55. Moscow: Mysl´.

—— 1971. *Русский язык на газетной полосе: некоторые особенности языка современной газетной публицистики.* Moscow: Izd. MGU.

—— 1994. *Языковой вкус эпохи. Из наблюдений над речевой практикой масс-медиа.* Moscow: Pedagogika-Press.

—— and LEONT´EV, A. A. 1966. «Некоторые теоретические вопросы культуры речи». *VJa,* 5: 3–15.

—— and SKVORCOV, L. I. 1970, eds. *Актуальные проблемы культуры речи.* Moscow: Nauka.

KOŠUTIĆ, R. (Кошутић, Р.) 1919. *Граматика руског језика.* № 1. *Гласови.* Petersburg: n.p.

KOTELOVA, N. Z. 1983, ed. *Новые слова и словари новых слов.* Leningrad: Nauka.

—— 1984, ed. *Новые слова и значения. Словарь-справочник по материалам прессы и литературы 70-х годов.* Moscow: Russkij jazyk.

—— 1987. «Процессы неологизации в современном русском языке последних десятилетий». *Linguistische Arbeiten* 63: 64–72.

—— and SOROKIN, JU. S. 1971, eds. *Новые слова и значения. Словарь-справочник.* Moscow: Sovetskaja Ènciklopedija.

KOŽIN, A. N. 1961. «Русский язык в дни Великой Отечественной войны». *Ученые записки Московского областного педагогического института,* vol. 102, fasc. 7, 630–48.

KOZINSKIJ, I. Š. 1983. *О категории «подлежащее» в русском языке. (Ин-т русского языка АН СССР. Проблемная группа по экспериментальной и прикладной лингвистике.* Предв. публикации, 156.) Moscow.

KREINDLER, I. 1982. *The Changing Status of Russian in the Soviet Union.* Berlin: Mouton.

—— 1985. 'The Non-Russian Languages and the Challenge of Russian'. In I. Kreindler, ed. *Sociolinguistic Perspectives on Soviet National Languages: Their Past, Present, and Future,* 345–67. Berlin: Mouton.

—— 1989. 'Soviet Language Planning since 1953'. In Kirkwood 1989, 46–63.

KŘÍŽKOVA, H. (Kržižkova, E.) 1968. «Предикативная функция прилагательных и существительных и структура предложения». *Československá Rusistika* 13: 210–19.

KRJUČKOVA, T. B. 1976. «Язык и идеология (к вопросу об отражении идеологии в языке)». Автореферат канд. дисс. Moscow: Institut jazykoznanija AN SSSR.

KRYSIN, L. P. 1964. «О словах *хлебороб* и *хлопкороб*». *RJaŠ,* 2: 24–7.

—— 1965*a*. «Иноязычная лексика в русской литературной речи 20-х годов». In Zemskaja and Šmelev 1965, 117–34.

—— 1965*b*. «К определению терминов «заимствование» и «заимствованное слово»». In E. A. Zemskaja and D. N. Šmelev, eds., *Развитие лексики современного русского языка.* 104–116. Moscow: Nauka.

—— 1968. *Иноязычные слова в современном русском языке.* Moscow: Nauka.

—— 1973. «К социальным различиям в использовании языковых вариантов». *VJa,* 3: 37–49.

—— 1974, ed. *Русский язык по данным массового обследования.* Moscow: Nauka.

—— 1989. *Социолингвистические аспекты изучения современного русского языка.* Moscow: Nauka.

—— and SKVORCOV, L. I. 1965. *Правильность русской речи. Словарь-справочник.* 2nd edn. Moscow: Nauka.

KUDRJAVSKIJ, D. L. 1912. *Введение в языкознание.* Jur´ev (Derpt): K. Mattisen.

KULINIČ, I. A. 1990. «Неографические источники изучения семантических инноваций: 70–80-е годы XX века». *RJK,* 21: 17–25.

KUZ´MINA, S. M. 1963. ««Борис Годунов» на сцене Центрального детского театра». *VKR,* 4: 144–53.

—— 1966. «О фонетике заударных флексий». In Vysotskij *et al.* 1966, 5–24.

KUZNECOVA, L. N. 1963. «Орфоэпические заметки о Центральном детском театре». *VKR,* 4: 138–44.

KUZNECOVA, O. D. 1970. «Балка и овраг». *RR,* 1: 117–18.

—— 1971. Задира, забияка. *RR,* 5: 96–8.

—— 1985. *Актуальные процессы в говорах русского языка.* Leningrad: Nauka.

LABOV, W. 1966. *The Social Stratification of English in New York City.* Washington: Center for Applied Linguistics.

LAKOFF, R. 1973. 'Language and Woman's Place'. *Language in Society* 2: 45–80.

LAPTEVA, O. A. 1968. «Внутристилевая эволюция современной русской научной прозы». In Vinokur and Šmelev 1968, 125–85.

—— 1976. *Русский разговорный синтаксис.* Moscow: Nauka.

LEHFELDT, W. 1985. Review of Borunova *et al.* (1983). *Russian Linguistics* 9: 72–80.

LEWIS, E. G. 1972. *Multilingualism in the Soviet Union.* The Hague: Mouton.

—— 1974. 'Linguistics and Second Language Pedagogy'. In T. Sebeok, ed. *Current Trends in Linguistics. 12. Linguistics and Adjacent Arts and*

Sciences, 2131–84. The Hague: Mouton.

LIEBOWITZ, R. D. 1986. 'Education and Literacy Data in Russian and Soviet Censuses'. In R. S. Clem, ed. *Research Guide to Russian and Soviet Censuses*, 155–70. Ithaca, NY: Cornell University Press.

LJUSTROVA, Z. N., and SKVORCOV, L. I. 1972. *Беседы о русском языке и культуре речи*. Moscow: Znanie.

LOPATIN, V. V. 1973. *Рождение слова*. Moscow: Nauka.

MAKAROVA, R. V. 1969. «Нужна ли латинизация?» *RR*, 4: 123–4.

MANAENKOVA, A. F. 1989. *Словарь русских говоров Белоруссии*. Minsk: Universitetskoe izd.

MAZON, A. 1920. *Lexique de la guerre et de la révolution en Russie (1914–1918)*. Paris: E. Champion.

MEL´ČUK, I. A. 1985. *Поверхностный синтаксис русских числовых выражений*. (*Wiener slawistischer Almanach*, 16.) Wien.

MEROMSKIJ, A. 1930. *Язык селькора*. Moscow: Federacija.

MEŠČERSKIJ, N. A. 1967a. *Развитие русского языка в советский период*. *Leningrad*: Izd. LGU.

——1967b. «О некоторых закономерностях развития русского литературного языка в советский период». In Meščerskij *et al.* 1967, 5–30.

——KOROTAEVA, È. I., GRUZDEVA, S. I., and MOISEEV, A. I. 1967, eds. *Развитие русского языка после Великой Октябрьской социалистической революции*. Leningrad: Izd. LGU.

MILEJKOVSKAJA, G., PETEL´ČIČ, R., and TIMOŠUK, M. 1988. *Материалы для словаря русского языка 70 и начала 80 годов XX века, не зарегистрированные в нормативных словарях*. i. Warsaw: Wyd. Uniw. Warszawskiego.

——1990. *Материалы для словаря русского языка 70 и начала 80 годов XX века, не зарегистрированные в нормативных словарях*. ii. Warsaw: Wydawn. Uniw. Warszawskiego.

MILJUTIN, V. 1918. «Как произошло название «народный комиссар»». *Известия*, 6 Nov. 1918, 3.

MILLS, M. H. 1990, ed. *Topics in Colloquial Russian*. New York: Peter Lang.

MIRTOV, A. V. 1941. *Лексические заимствования в русском языке в Средней Азии*. Taškent-Samarkand: n. p.

——1953. «Из наблюдений над русским языком в эпоху Великой Отечественной войны». *VJa*, 4: 99–108.

MIS´KEVIČ, G. I. 1967. «Комсомолия, пионерия». *RR*, 4: 6–8.

MIXNEVIČ, A. E. 1985, ed. *Русский язык в Белоруссии*. Minsk: Nauka i texnika.

MIZIN, O. A. 1975. «Обращения в произведениях В. И. Ленина». *RR*, 2: 29–35.

MORARU, M. 1993. «Слова английского происхождения в русском и румынском языках». *Filologie rusă* 1, 3: 50–9.

MOSKOVICH, W. 1989. 'Planned Language Change in Russian since 1917'. In Kirkwood 1989, 85–99.

MRAZEK, R. 1964. *Синтаксис русского творительного*. Prague: Státní pedagogické nakladatelství.

MUČNIK, I. P. 1961. «Двувидовые глаголы в русском языке». *VKR*, 3: 93–115.

—— 1963*a*, ed. *Развитие современного русского языка*. Moscow: Nauka.

—— 1963*b*. «Категория рода и ее развитие в современном русском языке». In Mučnik 1963*a*, 39–82.

—— 1964. «Неизменяемые существительные, их место в системе склонения и тенденции развития в современном русском литературном языке». In Mučnik and Panov 1964, 148–80.

—— 1971. *Грамматические категории глагола и имени в современном русском литературном языке*. Moscow: Nauka.

—— and PANOV, M. V. 1964, eds. *Развитие грамматики и лексики современного русского языка*. Moscow: Nauka.

MULLEN, J. 1967. *Agreement of the Verb-Predicate with a Collective Subject*. Cambridge: Cambridge University Press.

MÜLLER, O. W. 1971. *Intelligencija. Untersuchungen zur Geschichte eines politischen Schlagwortes*. Frankfurt: Athenäum.

MURAVENKO, E. V. 1990. «Виды орудийного значения и способы их выражения в современном русском языке». Автореферат канд. дисс. Moscow: Moscow State University.

MUSTAJOKI, A. 1985. *Падеж дополнения в русских отрицательных предложениях*. 1: *Изыскания новых методов в изучении старой проблемы*. (*Slavica Helsingiensia*, 2.) Helsinki.

—— 1990. «Унифицируются ли числовые подпарадигмы ударения русских существительных на -á?» *Wiener slawistischer Almanach* 25/26: 311–26.

—— and HEINO, H. 1991. *Case Selection for the Direct Object in Russian Negative Clause*. (*Slavica Helsingiensia*, 9.) Helsinki.

NAKHIMOVSKY, A. D. 1976. 'Social Distribution of Forms of Address in Contemporary Russian'. *International Review of Slavic Linguistics* 1: 79–118.

Население СССР за 70 лет. 1988. Moscow: Nauka.

NATANSON, È. A. 1966. «Термины профессионально-просторечного словообразования и их классификация». In *Проблемы лингвистического анализа*, 174–85. Moscow: Nauka.

NICHOLS, J. 1981. *Predicate Nominals: A Partial Surface Syntax of Russian*. (*University of California Publications in Linguistics*, 97.) Berkeley and Los Angeles: University of California Press.

—— 1988. 'Nominalization and Assertion in Scientific Russian Prose'. In J. Haiman and S. Thompson, eds. *Clause Combining in Grammar and*

Discourse, 399–427. Amsterdam: John Benjamins.

NICHOLSON, J. G. 1968. *Russian Normative Stress*. Montreal: McGill University Press.

NIKITINA, S. E. 1982. «Устная народная культура как лингвистический объект». *Известия АН СССР. Серия литературы и языка* 41: 420–9.

NIKOLAEV and PETROV (no initials given). 1903. *Светский хороший тон и умение жить и вести себя дома, в семье и обществе*, ed. O. P. Svetlov, 2nd edn. Moscow.

NIKOLAEVA, T. M. 1972. «К вопросу о назывании и самоназывании в русском речевом общении». In E. M. Vereščagin and V. G. Kostomarov, eds. *Страноведение и преподавание русского языка иностранцам*, 134–50. Moscow: Russkij jazyk.

—— 1977. *Фразовая интонация славянских языков*. Moscow: Nauka.

NIKONOV, V. A. 1965. *Введение в топонимику*. Moscow: Nauka.

—— 1970, ed. *Личные имена в прошлом, настоящем, будущем. Проблемы антропонимики*. Moscow: Nauka.

—— 1974, ed. *Имя и общество*. Moscow: Nauka.

—— and SUPERANSKAJA, A. V. 1969, eds. *Ономастика*. Moscow: Nauka.

—— 1970, eds. *Антропонимика*. Moscow: Nauka.

OBERMANN, M. 1969. *Beiträge zur Entwicklung der russischen Sprache seit 1917*. Meisenheim am Glan: A. Hain.

Общевоинские уставы вооруженных сил СССР. 1971. Moscow: Voenizdat.

ODÉ, C. 1989. *Russian Intonation: A Perceptual Description*. Amsterdam: Rodopi.

OGIENKO, I. I. 1914. *Русское литературное ударение. Правила и словарь русского ударения*. Kiev.

«Ответы на вопросник по норме». 1965. *VKR*, 6: 211–17.

OVSJANNIKOV, V. V. 1933. *Литературная речь*. Moscow: n.p.

OŽEGOV, S. I. 1947. «Существительные на -аж в русском языке». *Доклады и сообщения филологического факультета МГУ*, 3: 31–43 (shorter version in Ožegov 1974).

—— 1951. «Основные черты развития русского языка в Советскую эпоху». *Известия АН СССР. Отделение литературы и языка* 10: 22–37 (shorter version in Ožegov 1974).

—— 1953. «К вопросу об изменениях словарного состава русского языка в советскую эпоху». *VJa*, 2: 71–81.

—— 1955. «Очередные вопросы культуры речи». *VKR*, 1: 5–33.

—— 1972. *Словарь русского языка*, ed. N. Ju. Švedova, 9th rev. edn. Moscow: Russkij jazyk. (1st edn. (1949), 2nd rev. edn. (1952), 4th rev. edn. (1960)).

—— 1974. *Лексикология. Лексикография. Культура речи*. Moscow: Vysšaja škola.

—— and PANOV, M. V. 1963, eds. *Развитие современного русского языка*. Moscow: Izd. AN SSSR.

PANFILOV, A. K. 1965. «*Уважаемый* товарищ или *уважаемая* товарищ?» *VKR*, 6: 189–95.

PANOV, M. V. 1963. «О стилях произношения (в связи с общими проблемами стилистики)». In Mučnik 1963*a*, 5–38.

——1964. *И все-таки она хорошая!* Moscow: Nauka.

——1967. *Русская фонетика.* Moscow: Prosveščenie.

——1968, ed. *Русский язык и советское общество.* 4 vols. Moscow: Nauka.

——1971*a*. «О том, как кодировался вопросник по произношению». In Vysotskij *et al.* 1971, 294–301.

——1971*b*. «О членимости слова на морфемы». In *Памяти академика В. В. Виноградова*, 133–45. Moscow: Izd. MGU.

——1990. *История русского литературного произношения XVIII–XX вв.* Moscow: Nauka.

PAPERNYJ, V. 1985. *Культура «Два».* Ann Arbor: Ardis.

PARIKOVA, N. B. 1966. «О южнорусском варианте литературной речи». In Vysotskij *et al.* 1966, 125–35.

PATTON, F. R. 1990. 'Soviet Research on Substandard Speech'. In Mills 1990, 143–56.

PAUS, C. 1995. 'Social and Pragmatic Conditioning in the Decline of the Russian Partitive Case'. *Russian Linguistics* 18: 249–66.

PAVLIK, J. 1977. *Интонация повествовательного предложения в русском языке.* vol. i. *Предполагаемое членение предложений.* Odense: Odense University Press.

PAVLOVSKAJA, L. K. 1967. «Сложносокращенные слова». *RR*, 6: 16–19.

PAŽIN, V. N. 1969. *Как себя вести.* Leningrad: Lenizdat.

PEN´KOVSKIJ, A. B. 1967. «О некоторых закономерностях усвоения орфоэпических норм (*г* смычное и фрикативное)». *VKR*, 8: 61–72.

PESETSKY, D. 1982. 'Paths and Categories'. Unpublished doctoral dissertation, MIT, Cambridge, Mass.

PEŠKOVSKIJ, A. M. 1956. *Русский синтаксис в научном освещении.* 7th edn. Moscow: Prosveščenie.

——1959. *Избранные труды.* Moscow: Gosučpedgiz.

PIROGOVA, N. K. 1967. «О нормах и колебаниях в ударении (на материале глагола)». *Научные доклады высшей школы. Филологические науки,* 3: 14–22.

«Почта «Русской речи»». 1968. *RR*, 1: 104–20.

POKROVSKIJ, M. M. 1959. *Избранные работы по языкознанию.* Moscow: Izd. AN SSSR.

POLIVANOV, E. D. 1927. «К десятилетию орфографической реформы». *Родной язык в школе.* bk. 5, 180–9.

——1931. *За марксистское языкознание.* Moscow: Federacija.

——1974. *Selected Works. Articles on General Linguistics.* The Hague: Mouton.

Popov, A. S. 1964. «Именительный темы и другие сегментированные конструкции в современном русском языке». In Mučnik and Panov 1964, 256–74.

—— 1966. «Изменения в употреблении номинативных предложений». In Pospelov and Ivančikova 1966, 74–94.

Popova, Z. D. 1974. «Просторечное употребление падежных форм и литературная норма». In Zolotova 1974*a*, 176–86.

Pospelov, N. S., and Ivančikova, E. A. 1966, eds. *Развитие синтаксиса современного русского языка*. Moscow: Nauka.

Практика газетной корректуры. 1932. Leningrad: n. p.

Правила русской орфографии. 1956. Moscow: Gosučpedgiz.

Prokopovič, N. N. 1966. «О процессах структурного преобразования словосочетаний в современном русском языке». In Pospelov and Ivančikova 1966, 127–46.

——Deribas, L. A., and Prokopovič, E. N. 1981. *Именное и глагольное управление в современном русском языке*. Moscow: Russkij jazyk.

Protčenko, I. F. 1961. «Формы глагола и прилагательного в сочетании с названиями лиц женского пола». *VKR*, 3: 116–26.

—— 1964. «О родовой соотносительности названий лиц (из наблюдений над лексикой советской эпохи)». In Mučnik and Panov 1964, 106–37.

—— 1973. «Проблемы развития лексики и словообразования русского языка в советскую эпоху. (Социолингвистический аспект)». Автореферат докт. дисс. Moscow: Institut russkogo jazyka AN SSSR.

—— 1975. *Лексика и словообразование русского языка советской эпохи. (Социолингвистический аспект)*. Moscow: Nauka.

—— 1985. *Лексика и словообразование русского языка советской эпохи. (Социолингвистический аспект)*. 2nd edn. Moscow: Nauka.

Rappaport, G. 1984. *Grammatical Function and Syntactic Structure: The Adverbial Participle of Russian*. Columbus, Oh.: Slavica.

Raspopov, I. P. 1961. *Актуальное членение предложения*. Ufa: Gos. baškirskoe knižnoe izd.

Ray, R. S. 1963. *Language Standardization. Studies in Prescriptive Linguistics*. The Hague: Mouton.

Red′kin, V. A. 1966. «К дублетности ударения в русском языке». *VKR*, 7: 95–105.

Reformatskij, A. A. 1966. «[ɣusʼ]». *VKR*, 7: 119–21.

Rodionov, N. 1950. «Об одном неудачном словаре». *Культура и жизнь*, No. 16, 11 June 1950, 4.

Rœed, R. 1966. *Zwei Studien über den prädikativen Instrumental im Russischen*. Oslo: Universitetsforlaget.

Rogožnikova, R. P. 1966. «Активизация в современном русском языке подчинительных конструкций с союзами *раз* и *поскольку*». In Pospelov and Ivančikova 1966, 61–73.

ROJZENZON, L. I. 1966. «Заметки по русской лексикографии». *Этимологические исследования по русскому языку*, fasc. 5, 104–20.

——and AGAFONOVA, N. 1972. «К методике составления этимологического словаря русского языка». *Этимологические исследования по русскому языку*, fasc. 7, 175–9.

ROTHSTEIN, R. A. 1973. 'Sex, Gender, and the October Revolution'. In S. R. Anderson and P. Kiparsky, eds. *A Festschrift for Morris Halle*, 460–6. New York: Holt, Rinehart, and Winston.

ROŽANSKIJ, F. I. 1992. *Слэнг хиппи: материалы к словарю*. St Petersburg: Evropejskij Dom.

ROZENTAL´, D. È. 1964. *Культура речи*. 3rd edn. Moscow: Izd. MGU.

——1971. *Справочник по правописанию и литературной правке для работников печати*. 2nd edn. Moscow: Kniga.

——1984. *Справочник по пунктуации*. Moscow: Kniga.

——1986*a*. *Прописная или строчная? Опыт словаря-справочника*. Moscow: Russkij jazyk.

——1986*b*. *Управление в русском языке. Словарь-справочник*. Moscow: Kniga.

——and TELENKOVA, M. A. 1972. *Practical Stylistics of Russian*. Moscow: Progress.

RUDÈ, R. 1990. «О понятии причины и причинных отношениях». *Russistik* 2/1: 66–79.

Русская грамматика, vols. i–ii. 1980. Moscow: Nauka.

Русский язык в национальных республиках Советского Союза. Moscow: Nauka, 1980.

Русский язык. Энциклопедия. 1979. Moscow: Sovetskaja Ènciklopedija.

RYBNIKOVA, M. 1925. *Книга о языке*. 2nd edn. Moscow: Federacija.

RŽEVSKIJ, L. 1951. *Язык и тоталитаризм*. (L. Rshewsky. *Sprache und Totalitarismus*.) Munich: n.p.

ŠAFIR, JA. M. 1924. *Газета и деревня*. 2nd edn. Moscow: Federacija.

——1927. *Вопросы газетной культуры*. Moscow: OGIZ.

ŠANSKIJ, N. M. 1963–82. *Этимологический словарь русского языка*. Moscow: Izd. MGU.

ŠAPIRO, A. B. 1930. «О реформе русской пунктуации». *Русский язык в советской школе*, 3.

——1951. *Русское правописание*. Moscow: Izd. AN SSSR.

——1952. «Ударение в кратких прилагательных». *Доклады и сообщения Института языкознания*, I: 90–103.

——1955. *Основы русской пунктуации*. Moscow: Izd. AN SSSR.

——1961. *Русское правописание*. 2nd edn. Moscow: Izd. AN SSSR.

Сборник указов и постановлений временного правительства, fasc. 1, 27 февраля–5 мая 1917 г. 1917. Petrograd.

ŠČERBA, L. V. 1925. «Культура языка». *Журналист*, 2: 5–7.

ŠČERBA, L. V. 1935. «Пунктуация». In *Литературная энциклопедия*, vol. ix, 366–70. Moscow: OGIZ (reprinted in Ščerba 1973).

——1973. *Языковая система и речевая деятельность*. Leningrad: Nauka.

——1983. *Теория русского письма*. Leningrad: Nauka.

ŠČETININ, L. M. 1968. *Имена и названия*. Rostov-na-Donu: Izd. Rostovskogo universiteta.

——1970. «Историческая динамика употребления русских личных имен на территории бывшей Области войска донского и Ростовской области за 1612–1925 годы». In Nikonov and Superanskaja 1970, 248–52.

SCHALLERT, J. A. 1990. 'Intonation Beyond the Utterance: A Distributional Analysis of Rising and Falling Contours'. In Mills 1990, 51–65.

SCHUBERT, K. 1984. 'Modernes russisches Anredeverhalten'. In W. Winter, ed. *Anredeverhalten*, 73–114. Tübingen: Narr.

SELIŠČEV, A. M. 1928. *Язык революционной эпохи. Из наблюдений над русским языком последних лет (1917–1926)*. 2nd edn. Moscow: Rabotnik prosveščenija.

——1939. «О языке современной деревни». *Труды Московского института истории, философии и литературы*, vol. 5: 66–123.

SERIOT, P. 1985. *Analyse du discours politique sovietique*. Paris: Institut des études slaves.

SHAPIRO, M. 1968. *Russian Phonetic Variants and Phonostylistics*. (*University of California Publications in Linguistics*, 49.) Berkeley and Los Angeles: University of California Press.

——1985. 'Russian Masculine Plural Forms in -á'. *Russian Linguistics* 9: 173–9.

SIMINA, G. JA. 1969. «Фамилия и прозвище». In Nikonov and Superanskaja 1969, 27–34.

ŠIPOVA, E. N. 1976. *Словарь тюркизмов в русском языке*. Alma-Ata: Nauka.

ŠIRJAEV, E. N. 1986. *Бессоюзное сложное предложение в современном русском языке*. Moscow: Nauka.

SIROTININA, O. B. 1974. *Современная разговорная речь и ее особенности*. Moscow: Nauka.

Систематический сборник узаконений и распоряжений Рабочего и Крестьянского Правительства. 1919. Moscow.

SJÖBERG, A. 1964. *Synonymous Use of Synthetical and Analytical Rection in Old Church Slavonic Verbs*. Stockholm: Almqvist & Wiksell.

ŠKLOVSKIJ, V. B. 1925. «Ваши пожелания нашей художественной литературе?..» *Журналист*, 5: 29–31.

SKOBLIKOVA, E. S. 1959. «Форма сказуемого при подлежащем, выраженном количественным сочетанием». *VKR*, 2: 91–116.

SKREBNEV, JU. M. 1987. «Исследование русской разговорной речи». *VJa*, 1: 144–55.

SKVORCOV, L. I. 1972. «Профессиональные языки, жаргоны и культура речи». *RR*, 1: 48–59.

SKVORCOV, L. I. and ŠVARCKOPF, B. S. 1983, eds. *Литературная норма в лексике и фразеологии.* Moscow: Nauka.

Словарь Академии Российской по азбучному порядку расположенный. 1806–22. (7 vols.). St Petersburg: Imperatorskaja Akademija nauk (*SAR*). (repr.: Odense: Odense University Press, 1970–2).

Словарь церковно-славянского и русского языка. 1847. St Petersburg: Imperatorskaja Akademija nauk (*SCRJa*).

«Словарь произношений и ударений», 1971–2. *RR*, 1971, 4: 151–3, 5: 140–1, 6: 111–12; 1972, 1: 145–6, 2: 147–8, 3: 149–50, 4: 147–8, 5: 147–8, 6: 109–10 (SPU).

Словарь русского языка. 1895–1927. St Petersburg: Imper. Akademija nauk— Leningrad: Akademija nauk. (reprinted: London: Flegon Press, 1982.)

Словарь русского языка, ed. A. P. Evgen´eva (4 vols.). Moscow: Russkij jazyk, 1981–4 (*MAS*).

Словарь русского языка XI–XVII вв. Moscow: Nauka, 1975– .

Словарь современного русского литературного языка (АН СССР, Ин-т рус.яз.). 17 vols. Moscow: Izd. AN SSSR-Nauka, 1948–65 (*SSRLJa* 1948–65).

Словарь современного русского литературного языка (АН СССР, Ин-т рус.яз.). 20 vols. Moscow: Russkij jazyk, 1991– (*SSRLJa* 1991–).

ŠMELEV, D. N. 1961. «Стилистическое употребление форм лица в современном русском языке». *VKR*, 3: 38–59.

——1964. «О семантических изменениях в современном русском языке». In Mučnik and Panov 1964, 4–17.

——1977. *Русский язык в его функциональных разновидностях.* Moscow: Nauka.

——and ZEMSKAJA, E. A. 1988, eds. *Разновидности городской устной речи.* Moscow: Nauka.

ŠMELEVA, I. N. 1966. «Стилистические сдвиги в лексике современного русского языка». In Kačevskaja and Gorbačevič 1966, 24–42.

ŠMELEVA, T. V. 1992. «Повседневная речь как лингвистический объект». In Ju. N. Karaulov, ed. *Функционирование языка: лексика и грамматика*, 5–15. Moscow: Nauka.

SOLGANIK, G. JA. 1973. *Синтаксическая стилистика. (Сложное синтаксическое целое).* Moscow: Nauka.

SOLOUXIN, V. 1964. «Давайте поищем слово». *Неделя*, No. 4, 19–25 Jan. 1964: 23.

ŠOR, R. O. 1926. *Язык и общество.* Moscow: Federacija.

——1929. «О неологизмах революционной эпохи». *Русский язык в советской школе*, 1: 50–6.

Современная русская пунктуация. 1979. Moscow: Nauka.

«Современное сценическое произношение», 1967. *RR*, 1: 37–46.

ŠPIL´REJN, I. N., REJTYNBARD, D. I., and NETSKIJ, G. O. 1928. *Язык крас-ноармейца. Опыт исследования словаря красноармейца Московского гарнизона.* Moscow-Leningrad: Gos. izdatel´stvo.

STEPANOV, N. 1975. *Велимир Хлебников. Жизнь и творчество.* Moscow: Sovetskij pisatel´.

STONE, G. 1973. 'Language Planning and the Russian Standard Language'. *Transactions of the Philological Society, 1972* (1973): 165–83.

STROM, M. A. 1988. 'Innovation in Past Tense Mobile Stress in Contemporary Standard Russian'. Unpublished doctoral dissertation, University of California, Los Angeles.

SULERŽICKIE, M. and D. 1967. «Морская терминология и редакторская практика», letter to the editor. *RR*, 2: 65–9.

SUPERANSKAJA, A. V. 1959. «О произношении современной студенческой молодежи». *VKR*, 2: 157–62.

—— 1962. *Заимствование слов и практическая транскрипция.* (Институт языкознания АН СССР. Сектор структурной и прикладной лингвистики. Превдарительные публикации.) Moscow.

—— 1965a. «Род заимствованных существительных в современном русском языке». *VKR*, 6: 44–58.

—— 1965b. «Склонение собственных имен в современном русском языке». In A. A. Reformatskij, ed. *Орфография собственных имен,* 117–46. Moscow: Nauka.

—— 1968. *Ударение в заимствованных словах в современном русском языке.* Moscow: Nauka.

—— 1969. *Структура имени собственного. Фонология и морфология.* Moscow: Nauka.

—— 1970. «Личные имена в официальном и неофициальном употреблении». In Nikonov and Superanskaja 1970, 180–8.

—— 1973. *Общая теория имени собственного.* Moscow: Nauka.

—— 1978. «Апеллятив—онома». In id., ed. *Имя нарицательное и собственное,* 5–33. Moscow: Nauka.

—— and SUSLOVA, A. V. 1981. *Современные русские фамилии.* Moscow: Nauka.

SUPRUN, A. E. 1957. «К употреблению родительного и именительного падежей множественного числа прилагательного в сочетаниях с числительными *два, три, четыре* в современном русском языке». *Ученые записки Киргизского государственного педагогического института,* fasc. 3.

—— 1963. «Среднеазиатская лексика в русском языке». *Этимологические исследования по русскому языку,* fasc. 4, 145–59.

—— 1969. *Русский язык советской эпохи.* Leningrad: Prosveščenie.

SUVOROV, V. 1990. *Icebreaker.* London: Hamish Hamilton.

ŠVARCKOPF, B. S. 1985. «О концепции культуры речи в широком смысле в статьях В. В. Виноградова 1950–1960-х годов». In *История русского литературного языка и стилистика*, 18–24. Kalinin: Kalininskij gosudarstvennyj universitet.

——1988. *Современная русская пунктуация. Система и ее функционирование*. Moscow: Nauka.

ŠVEC, A. V. 1971. *Разговорные конструкции в языке газет*. Kiev: Izd. Kievskogo universiteta.

ŠVEDOVA, N. JU. 1966. *Активные процессы в современном русском синтаксисе*. Moscow: Nauka.

——1970, ed. *Грамматика современного русского литературного языка*. Moscow: Nauka.

SVETOZAROVA, N. D. 1982. *Интонационная система русского языка*. Leningrad: Izd. LGU.

TEKUČËV, A. V. 1974. *Преподавание русского языка в диалектных условиях*. Moscow: Pedagogika.

THELIN, N. B. 1971. *On Stress Assignment and Vowel Reduction in Contemporary Standard Russian*. (*Studia Slavica Upsaliensis*, 9.) Uppsala.

TIMBERLAKE, A. 1974. *The Nominative Object in Slavic, Baltic, and West Finnic*. Munich: O. Sagner.

——1993. 'Russian'. In B. Comrie and G. Corbett, eds. *The Slavonic Languages*, 827–86. London: Routledge.

TIMOFEEV, B. 1963. *Правильно ли мы говорим? Заметки писателя*. 2nd edn. Leningrad: Lenizdat.

TOBOLOVA, M. P. 1974. «Ударение в стихах». *RR*, 5: 42–7.

TROFIMENKO, V. P. 1973. «Формулы речевого этикета в разговорной речи. (На материале произведений А. П. Чехова)». Автореферат канд. дисс. Rostov-on-Don: Rostov University.

TRUBETZKOY (Trubeckoj), N. S. 1934. *Das morphologische System der russischen Sprache*. Travaux du Cercle Linguistique de Prague, v. 2, Prague. (Russian translation: Trubeckoj, N. S. 1987. «Морфонологическая система русского языка». In Trubeckoj N. S. *Избранные труды по филологии*. Moscow: Progress.)

——1958. *Grundzüge der Phonologie*. 3rd edn. Göttingen: Vandenhoeck & Ruprecht. (Russian translation: Trubeckoj, N. S. 1960. *Основы фонологии*. Moscow: Izd. inostrannoj literatury.)

UEDA, M. 1992. *The Interaction between Clause-Level Parameters and Context in Russian Morphosyntax: Genitive of Negation and Predicate Adjectives*. Munich: O. Sagner.

ULUXANOV, I. S. 1968. «История слов *горожанин—гражданин. Этимологические исследования по русскому языку*», fasc. 6, 166–78.

——1972. *О языке древней Руси*. Moscow: Nauka.

UNBEGAUN, B. O. 1972. *Russian Surnames*. Oxford: Oxford University Press.

Уровень образования, национальный состав, возрастная структура и размещение населения СССР по республикам, краям и областям по данным Всесоюзной переписи населения 1959 года. 1960. Moscow: Gosizdat.

Уровень образования населения СССР: по данным Всесоюзной переписи населения 1989 г. 1990. Moscow: Prosveščenie.

Ušakov, D. N. 1935–40. *Толковый словарь русского языка.* (4 vols.). Moscow: Sovetskaja ènciklopedija—Gos. izd. inostrannyx i nacional´nyx slovarej.

—— 1968. «Московское произношение». *RR*, 2: 43–9.

Ušakov, N. N. 1957. «Морфологические недочеты в окончаниях имен существительных и их предупреждение». *RJaŠ*, 5: 73–80.

Устав внутренней службы рабоче-крестьянской армии. 1918, n.p.

Uxanov, G. P. 1966. «Типы предложений разговорной речи, соотносительные со сложными синтаксическими единствами (предложения с препозитивной придаточной частью)». In Pospelov and Ivančikova 1966: 23–52.

Valgina, N. S. 1983. *Трудные вопросы пунктуации.* Moscow: Russkij jazyk.

Veksler, A. G. 1968. *Москва в Москве.* Moscow: Moskovskij rabočij.

Verbickaja, L. A. 1990. «Основные черты современной русской произносительной нормы». *Russistik* 2/1: 8–17.

Vinogradov, S. I. 1983. «О социальном аспекте лексической нормы (общественная оценка аббревиации и аббревиатур в 20-х-начале 30-х годов)». In Skvorcov and Švarckopf 1983, 70–88.

Vinogradov, V. V. 1938. *Очерки по истории русского литературного языка XVII–XIX вв.* 2nd edn. Moscow: Gosučpedgiz. (repr.: Vinogradov, V. V. 1982. *Очерки по истории русского литературного языка XVII–XIX веков.* 3rd edn. Moscow: Vysšaja škola.)

—— 1947. *Русский язык. Грамматическое учение о слове.* Moscow: Učpedgiz.

—— 1980 (1922). «О задачах стилистики. Наблюдения над стилем жития протопопа Аввакума». In id. *Избранные труды. О языке художественной прозы,* 3–41. Moscow: Nauka.

—— 1965, ed. *Обзор предложений по усовершенствованию русской орфографии.* Leningrad: Nauka.

—— Istrina, E. S., and Barxudarov, S. G. 1960, eds. *Грамматика русского языка,* rev. edn., 2 vols. in 3 bks. Moscow: Izd. AN SSSR.

—— and Švedova, N. Ju. 1964, eds. *Очерки по исторической грамматике русского литературного языка XIX в.* (5 vols.). Moscow: Nauka.

Vinogradova, V. N. 1984. *Стилистический аспект русского словообразования.* Moscow: Nauka.

Vinokur, G. O. 1929. *Культура языка.* 2nd edn. Moscow: Federacija.

Vinokur, T. G. 1974. «К вопросу о норме в художественной речи». In Zolotova 1974a, 267–82.

—— 1984. «Стилевой состав высказывания в отношении к говорящему и слушающему». In *Русский язык. Функционирование грамматических категорий: текст и контекст*, 135–54. Moscow: Nauka.

—— and ŠMELEV, D. N. 1968, eds. *Развитие функциональных стилей современного русского языка*. Moscow: Nauka.

VLASTO, A. P. 1986. *A Linguistic History of Russia to the End of the Eighteenth Century*. Oxford: Clarendon Press.

VOLKONSKIJ, S. 1913. *Выразительное слово. Опыт исследования и руководства в области механики, психологии, философии и эстетики речи в жизни и на сцене*. Petersburg.

VOLKOV, S. S., and SEN'KO, E. V. 1983. «Неологизмы и внутренние стимулы языкового развития». In Kotelova 1983, 43–57.

VOMPERSKIJ, V. P. 1964. «Склоняется ли слово *эхо*?» *VKR*, 5: 178–82.

VORONCOVA, V. L. 1959. «О нормах ударения в глаголах на -*ить* в современном русском литературном языке». *VKR*, 2: 117–56.

—— 1967. «Ударения в глаголах на -*ировать*». *Русский язык за рубежом*, 2: 82–5.

—— 1979. *Русское литературное ударение XVIII–XX веков: формы словоизменения*. Moscow: Nauka.

VROON, R. 1983. *Velimir Xlebnikov's Shorter Poems: A Key to the Coinages*. Ann Arbor: University of Michigan Press.

Всесоюзная перепись населения—всенародное дело. 1969. Moscow: Statistika.

VYSOTSKIJ, S. S., PANOV, M. V., REFORMATSKIJ, A. A., and SIDOROV, V. N. 1971, eds. *Развитие фонетики современного русского литературного языка. Фонологические подсистемы*. Moscow: Nauka.

—— and SIDOROV, V. N. 1966, eds. *Развитие фонетики современного русского литературного языка*. Moscow: Nauka.

WADE, T. 1992. *A Comprehensive Russian Grammar*. Oxford: Blackwell.

WARD, D. 1965. *The Russian Language Today: System and Anomaly*. London: Hutchinson University Library.

WORTH, D. 1983. 'Conditions on *á*-plural Formation in Russian'. *Wiener slawistischer Almanach* 11: 257–62.

XODAKOV, M. S. 1972. *Как не надо себя вести*. Moscow: Moskovskij rabočij.

YOKOYAMA, O. 1980. 'The History of Gerund Subject Deletion in Russian'. In C. Chvany and R. Brecht, eds. *Morphosyntax in Slavic*, 260–72. Columbus, Oh.: Slavica.

ZABOLOCKIJ, N. 1990 (1956). «История моего заключения». In *Серебряный век. Мемуары*, 659–71. Moscow: Izvestija.

ZALIZNJAK, A. A. 1967. *Русское именное словоизменение*. Moscow: Nauka.

—— 1977. «Закономерности акцентуации русских односложных существительных мужского рода». *Публикации отделения структурной и прикладной лингвистики МГУ* 8: 71–119.

—— 1980. *Грамматический словарь русского языка.* 2nd edn. Moscow: Russkij jazyk.

—— 1985. *От праславянской акцентуации к общерусской.* Moscow: Nauka.

ZARICKIJ, N. S. 1990. «Понятие историзма в отечественном языкознании и историческая лексикография». *RJK*, 21: 3–9.

ZEMCOV, I. 1985. *Советский политический язык.* London: Overseas Publications.

ZEMSKAJA, E. A. 1973, ed. *Русская разговорная речь.* Moscow: Nauka.

—— 1981, ed. *Русская разговорная речь. Общие вопросы. Словообразование. Синтаксис.* Moscow: Nauka.

—— 1983, ed. *Русская разговорная речь. Фонетика. Морфология. Лексика. Жест.* Moscow: Nauka.

—— 1987. *Русская разговорная речь: лингвистический анализ и проблемы обучения.* Moscow: Prosveščenie.

—— 1989. «Активный и пассивный аспект в изучении разговорного языка». *Russistik* 1/1: 7–17.

—— 1992. *Словообразование как деятельность.* Moscow: Nauka.

—— and KAPANADZE, L. A. 1978, eds. *Русская разговорная речь. Тексты.* Moscow: Nauka.

—— KITAJGORODSKAJA, M. V., and ROZANOVA, N. N. 1990. «Особенности мужской и женской речи». In *Язык. Система и подсистема,* 224–42. Moscow: Nauka.

—— and ŠIRJAEV, E. N. 1988. «Русская разговорная речь: итоги и перспективы исследования». In Ju. N. Karaulov, ed. *Язык: система и ее функционирование,* 121–52. Moscow: Nauka.

—— and ŠMELEV, D. N. 1965, eds. *Развитие лексики современного русского языка.* Moscow: Nauka.

—— 1966, eds. *Развитие словообразования современного русского языка.* Moscow: Nauka.

ZINDER, L. R. 1960. *Общая фонетика.* Leningrad: Izd. LGU.

ZOLOTOVA, G. A. 1964. «Развитие некоторых типов именных двусоставных предложений в современном русском языке». In Mučnik and Panov 1964, 275–302.

—— 1973. *Очерк функционального синтаксиса русского языка.* Moscow: Nauka.

—— 1982. *Коммуникативные аспекты русского синтаксиса.* Moscow: Nauka.

—— 1974*a*, ed. *Синтаксис и норма.* Moscow: Nauka.

—— 1974*b*. «О характере нормы в синтаксисе». In Zolotova 1974*a*, 145–75.

—— 1976, ed. *Синтаксис и стилистика.* Moscow: Nauka.

—— 1979, ed. *Синтаксис текста.* Moscow: Nauka.

Subject Index

Index of Proper Names

Index of Russian Words

Given the nature of this book, several entries in this index relate to items that are unacceptable or marginal in Contemporary Standard Russian.

DATE DUE

MAY 3 1 1997	
MAY 2 1 1998	MAR 1 1 2001